San Francisco, 1865-1932

University of California Press
Berkeley • Los Angeles • London

San Francisco, 1865-1932

Politics, Power, and Urban Development

William Issel and Robert W. Cherny

University of California Press
Berkeley and Los Angeles, California

University of California Press, Ltd.
London, England

Library of Congress Cataloging in Publication Data

Issel, William.
  San Francisco, 1865–1932.

  Bibliography: p.
  Includes index.
  1. San Francisco (Calif.)—Politics and government.
2. San Francisco (Calif.)—Economic conditions.
I. Cherny, Robert W.   II. Title.
F869.S357I86   1986   979.4′61   84-16328
ISBN 0-520-05263-3

Printed in the United States of America
1 2 3 4 5 6 7 8 9

For Sarah and Rebecca
and David, Darryl, Meri, and Zoe

Contents

POSTSCRIPT: FROM THE POLITICS OF POLARITY
TO THE POLITICS OF HYPERPLURALISM / 213

Maps

Tables

Preface

The past few decades have seen a number of fine monographs and dissertations on particular aspects or individuals in the history of San Francisco. Photographic histories and essays and treatments of the city's architecture have abounded. There have been, however, few efforts at historical synthesis of long-term patterns in the city's development. This book, we hope, builds upon the work done by those who have researched particular aspects of the city's history, extends it with additional research at many points, and puts it into a long-term perspective. Our objective has been to explore the nature of power, patterns of politics, and the process of urban development over the two-thirds of a century when San Francisco reigned as the premier city of the West. We have hoped in the process to make some contribution to current discussions of the nature of power in American cities.

We began to develop this project more than five years ago and have accumulated many debts of gratitude over the intervening period. Much of our research has been conducted at four institutions, and they deserve special thanks: the libraries of the University of California, Berkeley, especially the Bancroft and Doe libraries; the library and archives of the California Historical Society; the San Francisco Public Library, especially the San Francisco History Room; and the Leonard Library at San Francisco State University. Special thanks must go to the staff of the Bancroft Library, to Waverly Lowell, Judy Sheldon, and Joy Berry at the California Historical Society, to Gladys Hansen and her staff at the San Francisco History Room, and to our friends and colleagues at the Leonard Library. Other important research took place at more specialized archives, and important assistance came from John Donofrio and Teresa Hickey of the Bank of America Archives; Harold Anderson and Robert Chandler of the Wells Fargo Bank Archives; Susan Richards and Marilyn Fullmer of the Hibernia Bank; the staff of the Federal Archives and Record Center, San Bruno; and the staff of the San Francisco Registrar of Voters. During the spring of 1982, Robert Cherny pursued his research while teaching at the University of Nebraska, Lincoln, and owes thanks to the staff of both the Love Library at the university and the Nebraska State Historical Society. Charles Fracchia and Michael Kazin provided copies of their own unpublished work, and Coldwell Banker Company sent a copy of a limited edition company history.

Barbara Barton, Charles Lévy, Lynn Long, and Carl Silvio served at various times as research assistants, helping in locating political data. Thanks must go to them and also to the students in our proseminars and seminars and in the course we developed in 1981, "The History of San Francisco." There are those who insist that one never really understands a subject until one has taught it; the teaching of the history of San Francisco has provided invaluable opportunities to develop and refine ideas.

David A. Williams provided helpful comments on our original prospectus. David Selvin read an early draft of Chapter 4 and gave a long and helpful critique of it. Zenobia Grusky read Chapters 1 and 2 and made useful editorial suggestions. Jules Tygiel read an early draft of the entire manuscript and made many contributions to both style and substance. Michael Kazin, Arthur Mejia, and Moses Rischin read later drafts and made helpful comments. Alain Hénon of the University of California Press contributed initial encouragement and helped in securing a financial advance. Thanks are also due to Mary Renaud and Estelle Jelinek of the University of California Press for the painstaking thoroughness with which they edited our manuscript. San Francisco State University provided assistance in the form of two Faculty Development Grants and both sabbatical leaves and partial leaves without pay for both of us. Aljona Andrejeff typed an early draft of Chapter 3, and Margaret Cullinane did the final draft of the entire manuscript. Both were most helpful in spotting problems of consistency and form. The maps and the diagram in the appendix were prepared by Adrienne Morgan.

The editors of *Labor History* have given permission to adapt William Issel's article "Class and Ethnic Conflict in San Francisco Political History: The Reform Charter of 1898" as part of Chapter 7. Jack Taylor of Boyd and Fraser Publishing Company has given permission to use parts of our *San Francisco: Presidio, Port, and Pacific Metropolis*; most of them appear in Chapter 1. Parts of Chapter 5 first appeared in *San Francisco Arts Policy*, a background paper prepared by the Urban Center, San Francisco State University, for the Art Commission of the City and County of San Francisco.

Special thanks are due to our families and friends who have put up not only with our long hours at the typewriter or tucked away in the library but also with obscure anecdotes and stories.

We began this project by working through and agreeing upon detailed outlines. Initial responsibility for drafting the introduction and Chapters 1, 2, 5, and 7 fell to Issel; Cherny drafted Chapters 3, 4, 6, 8, and 9. We read and reread each other's work at every step along the way, contributing changes in both style and substance. The process has, at times, been synergistic; the end result is one for which we both bear full responsibility, both for its contributions and for any errors that may have escaped our attention.

Introduction

This book explores the relationships among politics, power, and urban development in San Francisco during the period 1865 to 1932, a period marked by great upheavals in the character of life in the United States. Whether described as an era of industrialization, a period of transformation, or a time when Americans searched for order, set about on a quest for community, or experienced the end of American innocence, these sixty-seven years brought forth the modern period of U.S. history.[1] Many of the institutions of municipal government that typify today's cities came into existence during this period. Because San Francisco presided over the Pacific Coast as its preeminent city in 1865 and stood as a thriving national metropolis sixty-seven years later, its particular history is significant in its own right. But the study of power, politics, and urban development in San Francisco can also shed light on the larger question of the role of politics in the urban development process.

For almost two decades, social scientists have been developing both a body of information and a set of explanations regarding patterns of urban political power in the United States. Although much has been accomplished in documenting the particular characteristics of specific cities, we still lack a reliable account of the ways in which the politics and power relations of cities have affected the nature and the process of urban development. Attempts by geographers and economists to explain this process promise to overcome the limitations of case studies, but the level of abstraction in these attempts has meant that they gloss over the unique features of individual cities. Political scientists and sociologists have contributed an analytically precise vocabulary to the topic of urban power structures, and they have developed an impressive array of research techniques to identify powerful groups and individuals and to study decisions by which these interests are expressed. Their perspective brings a gritty realism to the study of urban politics, but it also minimizes the ways in which historical patterns differ from those of the post–World War II era. These social scientists have yet to agree on a general outline of the ways political life and power relationships shape the historical development of cities. Considerable differences of opinion exist over the very definition of such crucial terms as *power* and *urban development*. If historians differ on these key questions, their disagreements mirror the lack of consensus among political scientists, economists, geographers, and sociologists, whose theoretical and methodological studies have served as models for historical research.[2]

The debates among social scientists have slowly settled into a three-sided contest among pluralists, elite theorists, and Marxists. Pluralists, drawing on the tradition represented by Robert Dahl's study of New Haven, Connecticut, define power as the ability of actors to achieve some or all of their goals, even when opposed, and portray power as fragmented among a variety of competing groups, no one of which is clearly dominant in a majority of decision-making areas in the local community. The pluralists deny that economic and political power inevitably inhere in the same individuals; they focus instead on both access to resources and choices about the use of resources. They tend to reject the notion that a national ruling class includes those who make crucial decisions about public policy at the local government level. Pluralists argue that a flourishing competition among groups of many kinds ensures equitable representation in the mosaic of occupational, ethnic, and other pressure groups who mobilize themselves to participate in urban policy making. Urban development, in the pluralist reading, emerges from policy forged at the hearth of interest group conflict, bargaining, and accommodation.[3]

The elite theorists' alternative to the pluralist point of view, representing a tradition of scholarship beginning with Floyd Hunter's analysis of Atlanta, Georgia, finds that urban development policy results from decisions by a well-defined group of representatives of powerful economic institutions. Contrary to the pluralists' emphasis on governmental officeholders as playing the central role in orchestrating urban development, those who advocate elite analysis see private economic interests as the key architects of the built environment. Political institutions, though important, play a role entirely secondary to the activities and initiatives of business leaders, according to elite theorists. Whereas pluralists reassure us that democracy of a kind perseveres in the interplay of group competition, elite theorists deny the existence of democracy except as a satisfying symbol with which elites lure the people into relatively quiet acceptance of the widespread inequalities of income, wealth, and opportunities that characterize American society. At the city level, as well as nationwide, political officeholders—both elected and appointed—do the bidding of a cohesive upper economic class.[4]

Elements of the elite interpretation of the relationship between power and urban development appear in the Marxist approach, but Marxist scholars place their argument firmly upon a foundation of class analysis. From a Marxist point of view, urban development results from decisions made by a ruling class that controls the major income-producing property of the nation and ordinarily controls, as well, a working class whose labor provides the profits that sustain American capitalism. Classes, in the Marxist concept, are categories of people bound to one another by inseparable relations associated with property and its ownership. From a Marxist point of view, as William Domhoff points out: "If there is an upper class it must be a ruling class, because staying 'upper' is what 'ruling' is all about."[5] Because Marxism has frequently been confused with economic determinism by scholars in the United States and criticized for being simplistic, Marxist students of urban development have taken pains to point out the ways their theories can direct attention to complexity. Nonetheless, much of the Marxist literature on the relationship between power and urban development suggests a static quality that amounts to little more than an announcement to pluralists and elitists that the argument about who governs and who benefits can be resolved by adopting different theoretical assumptions. A case in point comes from David Gordon who baldly states:

> The process of capital accumulation has been the most important factor structuring the growth of cities; city growth has not flowed from hidden exogenous forces but has been shaped by the logic of the underlying economic system. . . . the transitions *between* stages of urban development have been predominantly influenced by problems of *class control in production,* problems erupting at the very center of the accumulation process.[6]

All three of these contrasting theoretical approaches proceed according to a deductive method of research in which hypotheses derived from the theoretical assumptions are tested against evidence drawn from specific cases of urban development. The rich diversity and the protean complexity of specific historical cities, though accorded a nod from practitioners of each of the approaches, tend to be treated as poor relations. Prominence is given to evidence, often of a statistical nature, that is directly useful in the carefully constructed statements of relationships that can be deduced from the theories.[7]

Social scientists, particularly Marxists, have tended to err in the direction of imposing formulas on the history of urban development according to their particular theoretical orientations. Historians have usually paid attention to the irreducible features of particular cases of urban development and power at the expense of constructing generalizations about common elements in the history of urban development in the United States. While most historians who have written about the distribution of power in American communities have followed either the pluralist or the elitist approach, their conclusions tend to be heavily influenced by the particular character of groups in the cities they have studied. David Hammack has recently summarized the literature and finds six versions of the two interpretations that power derives from wealth (elite theory) or from political organization (pluralism). The "dominant historical view," according to Hammack, is that urban political democracy has increased since the nineteenth century as more and more groups have come to participate in community decision making.[8] Samuel Hays, arguing that most of the groups who participate represent upper-class members of the community rather than a cross section of the population, takes issue with the dominant viewpoint. Hays, citing the gradual centralization of authority since the 1870s and the rising power of business groups and professional classes, claims that the distribution of power in local communities has become more and more one-sided as lower-income groups have withdrawn from or have been forced out of active political participation. Edward Pessen, Michael Katz, and James Weinstein agree that inequality played a central role in the structure of community politics at the local level during the nineteenth and early twentieth centuries, and they attribute the control exercised by a wealthy elite to both the structural features of American capitalism and the conscious manipulation of governing institutions by class-conscious business leaders. This version of community power analysis, a position that Hammack calls "stratificationist," comes closest to the Marxist analysis developed by David Gordon.[9]

The practice of dividing a community into a small cohesive group of well-to-do elite members who are the true rulers (whether or not they hold political office) and the majority who are political ciphers has an impressive pedigree in American historical writing. Historians such as Arthur Schlesinger and Blake McKelvey, who found that a "patrician elite" controlled urban development, and those such as Frederick Jaher, who discovered a displacement of a preindustrial commercial elite by a capitalist ruling clique, agreed that power in American communities was concentrated in the hands of an elite of economic and social notables.[10]

Several historians have taken issue with the omnipotent political role that both stratificationist and patrician elite writers seem to have granted to the economically dominant groups in local communities. Herbert Gutman, John Buenker, and Richard Wade have presented evidence that supports their contention that working-class and ethnic groups have sometimes successfully challenged the authority of their employers and dominant wealthy members of society. Community power, in this version, has sometimes been dispersed among a variety of groups depending on the history of political relationships in a particular community. Political parties and elections, working-class institutions and strikes, and the alliances and coalitions that develop in relation to them have created a dispersion of power that other interpretations ignore or downplay.[11] Urban development, according to this viewpoint, cannot be understood apart from the dynamic process of politics that emerged within particular communities.

In this book, we examine control over urban development in San Francisco, seeking to determine whether control was dispersed among many groups from all levels of society or concentrated in the hands of a small ruling elite drawn from the wealthy. In exploring the nature of power, one question will concern the nature of participation in San Francisco political life and whether it became more broadly based or less so over the sixty-seven-year period. We will concern ourselves with what Domhoff has called "social power," the domination of one group by another, by investigating the distribution of goods, services, and opportunities during the period as one way to determine who benefits from the social system.[12] We will pursue the question of who directs or governs important institutions in order to identify the network of individuals central to political, economic, social, and cultural activities. One important aspect of this question is the extent of overlapping memberships in various community institutions. A final question concerns decision making in San Francisco. Here our concern is with the pluralists' question of who wins in important community decisions. Throughout the book, our central theme will be the politics and the struggles over power that created twentieth-century San Francisco.

Power during this period in San Francisco appeared to political activists as a prized commodity whose public nature in no way precluded its being used for private ends. The point, grasped by working class and business class alike, was to make public policy a vehicle for the realization of a desirable future for all San Franciscans. The private visions of the future that danced in the heads of workers and capitalists, Catholics and Protestants, native-born and immigrant, diverged remarkably little in the years between 1865 and 1932. While worker protest sparked political movements for greater equality, political participation modified militance and spread the values of the well-to-do among the poor and the aspiring working class. This fact of cultural history, often seized upon as the nucleus of American "exceptionalism," was crucial to the pattern of class and ethnic politics that affected the distribution of power in San Francisco.

Despite some important exceptions due to the tradition of labor radicalism, the politics of urban development in San Francisco proceeded according to an ideology of privatism, prosperity, and progress. Although inequalities appeared and reappeared within the city's society with predictable regularity, few accepted class, ethnicity, or gender as a handicap to getting ahead. Melioration of the wretched lot of poor San Franciscans went hand in hand with structural reform of municipal government to benefit capitalist entrepreneurs. Hopeful families of blue-collar wage earners hoarded savings in order to purchase houses and become part of respectable city society. Having settled into developing neighborhoods, they built strong working-class communities centered on parish churches and public and parochial schools. Often grooming their sons for a skilled trade or public employment and their daughters for good marriages or lives of devotion in schools or convents, the heavily Catholic working-class population of mainly Irish stock also voted for responsible municipal government and for the efficient administration of tax collection and revenue expenditure. Like the local business elite, both blue-collar and white-collar homeowners regarded San Francisco's premier role in the economic development of the Bay Area and the Pacific Basin as a source of civic pride and personal prosperity.

The San Francisco creed of privatism, prosperity, and progress by no means precluded sharp words, and sometimes intense conflict, between the haves and the have-nots. Class conflict, in kaleidescopic mixture with ethnic loyalty and racial bigotry, filled streets with determined marchers, polling places with hopeful voters, and jails with dejected idealists. Several episodes highlighted fleeting periods when loyalty to fellow workers submerged the more typical individualistic competition that kept class consciousness mostly within the covers of left-wing pamphlets or on the lips of members of small radical sects. Class-conscious political activity proved more consistently successful among the representatives of San Francisco capital. From the boardrooms of large corporations to the lounges of prestigious clubs, from the mayor's chambers to the Chamber of Commerce, a sense of community among businessmen gradually became a formal ideology of domination. The business community never assumed the shape of a monolith; differences based on particular interests kept alive a circulation of ideas among the leaders of the city's commercial and industrial activities. Dominance coexisted with what became necessary compromises with, and a limited set of leadership roles for, the "aristocrats" of the labor movement who led the skilled craft unions, especially in the building trades. But these compromises had to be forced on the city's business leaders. Compromise mainly affected municipal administration and hence proved liable to influence and persuasion. Compromise almost never generated challenges to the consensus that favored public support for urban development that would enhance private capital. San Franciscans demonstrated an abiding faith in the creed that prosperity would trickle down automatically from the rich all the way to the deserving poor.

San Francisco's political history demonstrates the need to consider the getting and exercising of power in relation to political microclimates based on shifting combinations of personality, social groups, coalitions, and issues. Chapters 2–5 describe the patterns of economy and society as they evolved in San Francisco during the period. Those aspects of power that can be considered structural (institutional) and systemic (class and ethnicity) will be analyzed in these chapters. This section seeks to answer the questions of who benefits from the social system and who directs or governs important institutions. Chapters 6–8 concern the political development of San Francisco and take up the situational (decision-making) aspects of power. This section will document the answers to the question of who wins on important decisions in the community.

Chapter 1

Commercial Village to Coast Metropolis

On June 4, 1874, a group of pioneers who had sailed around Cape Horn to California on the *Panama* celebrated a twenty-fifth reunion. After a sumptuous banquet in the Club Room of the Grand Hotel, the forty-niners listened to ex-senator William McKendree Gwin describe the contributions made by his generation to the building of San Francisco.

> When we landed here, the permanent population of San Francisco did not exceed one thousand; now it is over two hundred thousand. The ground beneath us was a shapeless mound of sandy desert. Diagonally across from where we are sitting is a strip of ground, covered with almost worthless buildings, that sold the other day, as an investment, for $300,000. The 100-vara lot, of which that strip was a small portion, cost, at the date of our arrival, $16, just the fee for issuing the alcalde's title.[1]

A half-century earlier, when only a Spanish imperial outpost stood on the future site of San Francisco, an English traveler had lambasted the very connection between profit and city growth that infused Gwin and his audience with pride. "GAIN! GAIN! GAIN! is the beginning, the middle and the end, the *alpha* and *omega* of the founders of American towns," declared Morris Birkbeck. His disgust grew as he traveled through the country, but few Americans shared his critical attitude toward the business of city development. John Reps has pointed out: "Louder—much louder—rose the huckster voices of the land boomers, the townsite promoters, and the wholesalers and retailers of frontier land."[2] Reps's observation applies to San Francisco as much as to frontier cities in other parts of the nation. Whether on the edge of the Pacific, the banks of the Mississippi, the rim of Lake Michigan, or the shores of the Ohio, America's mid-nineteenth century cities took shape as commercial ventures. San Francisco's urban pioneers, like those whose mercantile and financial activities shaped St. Louis, Chicago, and Pittsburgh, eagerly turned natural resources into profitable social commodities. In the process, they transformed sites they regarded as wilderness wasteland into urban places they proudly described as civilized settlements.

BEFORE THE GOLD

The site upon which San Francisco was to develop struck eighteenth-century representatives of imperial Spain as a likely place from which to protect their claim to northern California. They chose the site because of its location at the entrance to one of the world's largest harbors. Up to fourteen miles wide and sixty miles long, the bay covered, in all, four hundred square miles. Father Font, a member of the Spanish expedition of 1775, described the bay as "a marvel of nature . . . the harbor of harbors." Font was convinced that "if it could be settled like Europe there would not be anything more beautiful in all the world."[3] Hubert Howe Bancroft, writing with the benefit of hindsight in 1888, discounted the adverse effects of forty-three hills on a forty-eight-square-mile site, along with the disagreeable wind, fog, and sandy soil, to say that the San Francisco peninsula seemed "topographically marked for greatness." The imperatives of imperial policy, not the determining features of topography, placed the Spanish presidio and mission at the entrance to the bay instead of in a more salubrious spot.[4]

Spanish control of the Bay Area, an outgrowth of the imperial policy of "defensive expansion" designed to counter Russian ambitions in the area, lasted until 1822. The San Francisco settlement, never intended to become a city, seemed rudimentary and backward in the eyes of imperial rivals who made periodic visits. English Captain George Vancouver, during his journey around the world, stopped in San Francisco Bay in November of 1792 and found "not an object to indicate the most remote connection with any European, or any other civilized nation." Russian Lieutenant Nikolai Alexandrovich Khvostov, during an 1806 visit, attributed the Spanish avoidance of "industries" to cultural sources when he described the residents as religious fanatics. But the remarks attributed by Count Nikolai Petrovich Rezanov to Governor José Joaquin de Arillaga, that "everybody at present recognizes the possibilities of trade but us, who pay with our own purses for our negligence," suggest that imperial policy played a crucial role in the maintenance of practices inimical to commercial capitalism. Adelbert Von Chamisso recorded in his diary during the visit of the *Rurik* in 1816 that the Spanish had "not a single boat in this glorious water basin" and added that one of the Russians had to repair the halyards on the flagpole because no one at the presidio could climb the pole. By then, imperial policy and local custom seem to have reinforced each other to the point where cultural values central to "the business revolution" taking place in the United States, a continent away, would have seemed alien indeed.[5]

Historian Thomas Cochran has used the term *business revolution* to refer to an interrelated set of changes in the American business system during the first decades of the nineteenth century. Modifying the long-standing emphasis on technology and natural resources as the prime movers of economic growth, Cochran draws on recent research in urban historical geography to suggest that "upward change in the rate of economic growth depends more on a society that under certain conditions fosters improvements in the business structure for better utilizing land, labor, capital, and entrepreneurship than it does on the particular local resources." Stressing the importance of society and culture, Cochran adds that "neither available resources nor technology can by themselves cause change and growth; they require a social system that produces the knowledge and roles necessary to make use of the latent factors."[6]

Well before California became a state in 1850 and long before San Francisco became chief entrepôt for the gold rush, American merchants from New England and the Northeast began to pull Spanish and Mexican California into the orbit of the business system of the youthful United States. Governor Arillaga recognized the potential of "the Bostonians" when he described to Count Rezanov in 1806 "their determined demands" for trade with Spanish ports, which "finally overcame the resistance of the same ministers who, a few years before, would not and did not consent." "As I have personally witnessed in our waters the enterprise of the citizens of this republic, I am not surprised at their success. They flourish in the pursuit of trade, being fully aware of its possibilities."[7]

The propensity for the pursuit of trade that so impressed Governor Arillaga was a feature of what might be called the business culture of the northeastern United States. The traditions and the environment of the region had contributed to the making of a culture that placed high premiums on "innovations in craftsmanship and business policy." Practical, utilitarian, problem-solving techniques took precedence over the guiding hand of inherited customs. A culture favorable to rapid economic development, along with "a well-developed artisan background in the proper industries, freedom for entrepreneurial action, and a high degree of governmental security against interference" contributed to "long-run forces" that were "not dependent on market conditions at any given time."[8]

The restless seeking after domestic and foreign trade on the part of the merchant capitalists of this culture created demands that enlarged the scope of operations. This led to greater specialization of business practices and to a greater division of labor. Merchants drew on the power of government to promote, rather than to regulate, their activities. Such state assistance, when combined with higher profits, allowed for investment of the large amounts of capital necessary to improve transportation and speed up the transmission of business information. This increased flow of capital stimulated further specialization and greater efficiency in finance: brokers established stock exchanges, dealers in commercial paper emerged, specialized law firms started operations, and investment bankers went into business. Businesses began to operate more economically, decisions could be made on the basis of better information, and the leading commercial centers generated new businesses of all types.[9]

The development of this kind of city-centered business system, already underway when Governor Arillaga made his observations about "the Bostonians" in 1806, was becoming a distinguishing feature of American economic life by the time Mexico secured its independence from Spain in 1821. The California ports at Monterey and San Francisco had grown accustomed to the presence of Yankee and English sea-going merchants, who exchanged finished goods for the lumber, tallow, hides, and pelts provided by the Californians.

The valuable pelts of sea otters attracted over one hundred ships out of Boston, New York, and Philadelphia during the last thirty years of Spanish control over California. By the beginning of the 1820s, Boston firms such as Bryant, Sturgis, and Company, which had made considerable profit in the sea otter trade, had established regular connections between Boston, California, Hawaii, and China. When the Mexican government authorized trade in hides and tallow at California ports in 1822, Bryant, Sturgis, and Company seized the opportunity to tap a new supply of raw material for the growing shoe and harness industry in New England. Alfred Robinson, who first saw California in 1829, was a commercial agent for Bryant, Sturgis, and Company, as well as other firms; one historian estimates that Robinson alone shipped half a million hides to New England ports.[10]

Yankees like Robinson, though active up and down the coast in pursuit of cargo, amounted to only a handful of Americans in a society of *Californios*. Yet their activities in the villages that served as centers for the hide trade made the names of San Diego, Los Angeles, Santa Barbara, Monterey, Santa Cruz, and Yerba Buena well known in Boston merchant houses during the 1830s. "Knowledge follows hard on the wings of commerce," writes Norman Graebner, "especially when trade is profitable."[11] During the peak of the hide trade in the mid-1830s, American merchants could sell their manufactured goods for prices that averaged 300 percent above the Boston cost. The lure of such profits attracted competition. In the 1830s, six to eight ships vied for the California market, but by 1842 sixteen ships were on the scene. By 1846, three of the largest companies had deserted the trade. Henry Price's complaints to his California agent (and later San Francisco merchant leader) William Howard typified Boston's disillusionment: "I am getting sick," Price wrote in 1846, "of a business that I once realy [sic] loved, and it is my misfortune to have the brunt of the whole thing heaped upon me by the Stockholders." The hide trade "was once a profitable business but It now looks like a disasterous [sic] business. . . . If we had all of us Invested our money in unimproved Real Estate in this City for the last three or four years It would have been a most profitable business instead of imbarking [sic] in the California business."[12]

The demise of the hide trade did not imply a decline in the enthusiasm about California ports that the previous decade's profits had stimulated among American merchants. Yerba Buena, the tiny commercial village established by Englishman William A. Richardson in 1835, sparked American interest even more than some of the other ports by reason of its location at the entrance to San Francisco Bay. Richardson demonstrated the entrepreneurial instincts that distinguished the growing number of American and European settlers in California from the *Californios*. Whether English like Richardson, native-born like Jacob Leese, West Indian of African background like William A. Leidesdorff, or Irish-American like Jasper O'Farrell, the pioneers of commercial Yerba Buena in the 1830s and 1840s brought a fundamentally different view of the world to the territory they shared with families carrying names like Vallejo, Martinez, De Sola, and Sanchez. The plantation economy, caste society, and culture of gracious hospitality of the *Californios* stood in marked contrast to the market-oriented practices and the savings-and-investment mentality of the pioneers. Even when the immigrants married into families of local gentry and became adopted citizens of the Mexican republic, as did Richardson, Leese, and Alfred Robinson, they continued to pursue their Anglo-American cultural values of capital accumulation.

Although the Mexican government followed an official policy of controlled economic activities, historians have described how its practical day-to-day operations amounted to a virtual laissez-faire paradise for enterprising capitalists. An *ayuntamiento* (town council) appointed by the provincial governor for Yerba Buena stopped meeting for lack of business. When the *alcalde* (mayor), who had little to do, rejected Jacob Leese's application for a land grant beside the cove, Leese obtained it from the governor at Monterey. Richardson, far from being hindered by the Mexican government's official policy of control over the economy, became captain of the port and maintained a thriving contraband trade in Sausalito across the bay. The informality and personal character of this period allowed such latitude for individual enterprise and is perhaps best symbolized by the town fathers' practice of keeping the pueblo's official map and street plan, smudged and barely legible from frequent erasures, behind the bar of a saloon.[13]

Travelers to California (Richard Henry Dana in 1836, John Wilkes in 1841) found nothing impressive about the village of Yerba Buena, but they invariably used superlatives to describe San Francisco Bay. Dana's popular *Two Years Before the Mast* (1840) contributed to the large body of information about the Bay Area that was carried east by the growing volume of transportation between California and the Northeast during the late 1830s and 1840s. Wrote Dana:

> If California ever becomes a prosperous country, this bay will be the centre of its prosperity. The abundance of wood and water; the extreme fertility of its shores; the excellence of its climate, which is as near to being perfect as any in the world; and its facilities for navigation, affording the best anchoring grounds in the whole western coast of America—all fit it for a place of great importance.[14]

Convinced by advisers that the United States needed the bay for the benefit of American whalers, Andrew Jackson had instructed his minister to Mexico to purchase both the Bay Area and the surrounding territory as early as 1835. International rivalry over the bay began in earnest when the Hudson's Bay Company opened its branch in Yerba Buena in 1841. South Carolina's John Calhoun, writing in 1844, pushed for American acquisition of San Francisco Bay and predicted that a city built on its shores would become "the New York of the Pacific Coast, but more supreme, as it would have no such rivals as Boston, Philadelphia, and Baltimore." Massachusetts Senator Daniel Webster spoke on behalf of New England constituents when he argued in March of 1845 that "the port of San Francisco would be twenty times as valuable to us as all Texas."[15] The master of the ship *Tasso*, which had plied the California trade from 1841 to 1843, described the situation as he saw it in 1845:

> There is some considerable capital that will be expended in filling up the country round San Francisco with Americans and that I *know* and eventually you will have another revolution like 1836. With this exception, instead of setting the Mexican ensign it will either be an American one or a new one and American Agents and American capital will be at the bottom of it. You have no idea what feeling there is here with regard to California and Oregon which bye and bye is only used as a blind for the settlement of San Francisco. The egg is already laid not a thousand miles from Yerba Buena and in New York the chickens will be picked.[16]

By June 1846 relations between the United States and Mexico moved from mutual suspicion to war. U.S. troops occupied Yerba Buena and Sonoma, the Bear Flag Revolt having prepared the way for U.S. control over California. President James Polk and his secretary of war had already commissioned the New York Volunteer Regiment and assigned it a twofold mission: to pacify California's Mexican population and to colonize the area. On July 9, Captain John B. Montgomery officially took possession of Yerba Buena in the name of the United States, and on August 26 he appointed Washington A. Bartlett, one of his officers, as the first American mayor. Alfred Robinson's *Life in California*, published the same year, predicted great changes for "the noble, the spacious bay of San Francisco" if the United States would annex the territory. Thousands of ships, new towns beside the bay, river steamers, factories, and sawmills, he argued, would follow the release of creative enterprise that American control would foster. "The whole country would be changed, and instead of one's being deemed wealthy by possessing such extensive tracts as are now held by the farming class, he would be rich with one quarter part. Every thing would improve; population would increase; consumption would be greater, and industry would follow."[17]

American settlers followed the flag to California in modest numbers in 1846 and 1847. The majority of Yerba Buena's population were white males born in the United States, but the city also housed visible minorities of English, Irish, Germans, Scots, Spanish-speaking *Californios*, Indians, New Zealanders, and South Americans. Two hundred Mormons, unwelcome in many parts of the country, arrived in August 1846 under the leadership of Sam Brannan. By March 1848, the population had increased to just over eight hundred.

The leading merchants and lawyers of Yerba Buena immediately put their stamp on California's major commercial settlement by changing both the basis for the port's future internal growth and its relations with other Bay Area towns. Few among the new arrivals, convinced as they were of the settlement's inevitable evolution toward Pacific greatness, had patience with the traditional Mexican policies of selling only one plot of land to each resident and of preserving the waterfront for government uses. At first, in late 1846, American authorities issued land grants according to the Mexican laws and refused to allow private development of the waterfront. But after some controversy, Mayor Bartlett authorized a new survey of the pueblo, which extended the borders of the town, established the street pattern of the future city, and became the basis for a flurry of land speculation in late 1847 and early 1848.[18]

Bartlett's successor, Edwin Bryant, transferred hundreds of acres of waterfront land to the town, thereby preparing the way for individual ownership. In the words of historian William Pickens: "The best tradition of American capitalism, the driving initiative of private ownership could now develop the waterfront."[19] Jasper O'Farrell's survey of the city's territory and the mayor's actions, which made land into a commodity subject to the market, stood as major portents of change in 1847. So too had Barlett's order in January 1847 to change the name of Yerba Buena to San Francisco. Predicated on the assumption that the town needed to associate itself with the bay in order to develop a premier role in Pacific trade, the name change blunted the campaign by the town fathers of Benicia to attract shipping to their port at the head of the bay and helped preserve the position already established by Yerba Buena's commercial leaders.[20]

PACIFIC COAST METROPOLIS

James Marshall's discovery of gold on January 24, 1848, triggered a vast migration of profound social and economic impact. Historian Carey McWilliams captured the essence in his *California: The Great Exception* (1949): "The lights went on all at once" in California. San Francisco became an immediate beneficiary. Arriving gold seekers needed a landing place from which they could make the trek to the gold fields, and San Francisco had the best-developed port in the Bay Area. Miners in the mother lode needed tools and provisions, and the wharves already in place in San Francisco offered merchants a port from which to transfer goods from clipper ships to river steamers for the up-river voyage to Sacramento. Younger sons of leading Boston families sought business opportunities in a place less clogged with competition than New England and flocked to the rudimentary houses of commerce going up on Montgomery Street. Levi Strauss, a Jewish immigrant from Germany living in New York, moved his merchant business to San Francisco and took his stock of dry goods with him. Other New Yorkers, including many Irish Catholic artisans, carried only a set of tools and a hope for instant wealth.

By the summer of 1849, Yerba Buena cove had become crowded with abandoned vessels. The village consisted of a helter-skelter assembly of canvas tents, wooden shacks, and warehouses, and the population, according to one observer, "numbering perhaps 5,000, is as heterogenous as their habitations. Such a meeting of languages and jargons and of tongues the world has seldom seen. It is a modern Babel." Bayard Taylor wrote that "of all the marvellous phases of the history of the Present, the growth of San Francisco is the one which will most tax the belief of the Future." He found the city "an actual metropolis . . . filled with an active and enterprising people and exhibiting every mark of permanent commercial prosperity."[21]

Like other American cities, San Francisco experienced a dizzying rate of population turnover between 1850 and 1870, especially among blue-collar workers. For restless members of the laboring class, "moving on" was something of a vocation. Only one in ten stayed in the city for three decades, and three out of four left within eight years of arriving. But if thousands left to try their luck elsewhere, many thousands took their places. By the beginning of the Civil War, San Francisco (then the fifteenth largest city in the nation) had a population of 50,000. By the time the war ended in 1865, the city's population had passed the 100,000 mark. By 1870, only nine cities in the nation outranked San Francisco, and of the country's fifty largest cities San Francisco was the only one west of St. Louis.[22]

Compared with the country as a whole, San Francisco, while not quite "a modern Babel," certainly contained a diverse population. Whereas only one in ten of the U.S. population in 1850 was born overseas, half of San Francisco's residents claimed foreign birthplaces. In 1860, the city's population of foreign-born remained about the same, putting it in third place among America's immigrant centers. The population also tended to have a distinctly urban and Northeastern–Middle Atlantic background. This was especially true for the city's merchants, half of whom hailed from either Massachusetts or New York.[23]

By 1860, visitors to San Francisco could find almost 3,000 Chinese and almost 2,000 Afro-Americans among the roughly 57,000 residents, but the most numerous faces on the streets were those of the immigrants from the British empire and Germany. By the end of the sixties, those born in Ireland, Germany, China, and Italy accounted for one of every three San Franciscans. San Francisco stood not only as one of the nation's leading immigrant centers but also as a particularly Irish—and Roman Catholic—city.[24]

Whether native-born American, Irish, or German, Catholic or Protestant, black, yellow, or white, San Francisco's heavily male population spent its working days on or near the wharves, warehouses, countinghouses, and workshops of the waterfront district. Women steadily increased their share of the population to about 40 percent by the mid-sixties; most spent their working days in their homes. The lives of both women and men were molded by the dramatic importance of the city as the freight handler of California and mercantile headquarters of the West. Although a thorough tour of the city on the eve of the Civil War would have turned up about two dozen farms of over one hundred acres each, where families cultivated vegetables and dairy products for local consumption, the lion's share of the city's economic livelihood did not come from either agriculture or industry. Instead, building on pre–gold rush beginnings, San Francisco's merchants, bankers, and real estate developers created during these years a preeminently trade-oriented urban center, complete with financial institutions and the industry necessary to serve the needs of a regional and local economy relatively isolated from the eastern United States.

San Francisco merchants expanded their trade so quickly in the four years after the discovery of gold that only three cities—New York, Boston, and New Orleans—could claim a larger share of the nation's foreign commerce. By the time General Pierre Beauregard fired on Fort Sumter in Charleston Harbor and opened the Civil War, San Francisco's harbor ranked number six in total freight handled. As California agriculture developed during the late fifties and sixties, goods for the coastal trade began to fill the holds of more ships than did goods for eastern ports, but trade with the Pacific islands and the Far East also grew. San Francisco merchants developed a near-monopoly of the Hawaiian and Philippine trade, created a respectable business with Japan, and shared the China trade with New York City.

San Francisco merchants eagerly sought public support for the promotion of the city's commercial success. The subsidy granted the Pacific Mail Steamship line in 1846 set an important precedent. The Chamber of Commerce, organized in 1849, actively pursued similar government aid. When the Tariff Act of 1861 reduced the duty-free warehousing privilege from three years to three months, the Chamber bristled at the potential injury to San Francisco's economy. "San Francisco, occupying a peculiar and commanding geographical position," the Chamber pointed out, "is engaged in opening upon the Pacific, a new and boundless field for American commerce. . . . Congress should, so far as the Constitution permits, make sure special provision for them as circumstances might demand." Because Victoria, British Columbia, operated as a free port, the Chamber feared that "with unwise restrictions upon the Commerce of San Francisco, Victoria may, by the aid of English capital," take over as "the grand distributing depot of the Pacific." San Francisco's Milton S. Latham, former congressman, collector of the port, and Democratic member of the Senate in 1861 (he was later to become manager of the London and San Francisco Bank), worked with the Chamber of Commerce on behalf of a warehouse bill designed to counter this danger to the city's trade.[25]

Compared with commerce, banking, and real estate, manufacturing played a minor role in the local economy. True, the city ranked number nine in the value of manufactured goods produced in 1860, with over two hundred manufacturing establishments, but 52 percent of all manufacturing was related to the refining of gold and other metals. Also, the value of the manufactured goods reflected the fact that wages in San Francisco were almost three times higher than in the Middle Atlantic region. The city showed no signs of a large industrial sector, and only 1.6 per thousand of the city's population worked in industry compared with 5 per thousand for the country as a whole.

San Francisco's economy developed according to a pattern of decidedly uneven prosperity. During the decade of the fifties, the local economy experienced four separate cycles of boom and bust, related more to a local oversupply of goods than to national economic patterns. The infant trade unions of the city tended to collapse during hard times, and during the prosperous years inflated wages and the high turnover of laborers kept opposition to employers at a minimum. Chamber of Commerce efforts to bring stability and efficiency into the market had only minimal success, and efforts to lure larger numbers of immigrants to the city in order to keep down labor costs proved only a bit more successful.[26]

The two decades after the discovery of gold witnessed the transformation of San Francisco from a staging area for the gold fields to a commercial city, which, except for its fogs, gusty winds, and sandy hills, possessed all the social characteristics of its eastern and midwestern counterparts. The city's share of single men living in hotels near their places of business declined, and the numbers of families, women, and children gradually increased. By 1865, residential neighborhoods could be clearly distinguished from the central business district. The city's working-class majority divided itself into a transient and unmarried group, who filled boardinghouses along the northern and southern waterfront, and a more permanent family sector. The general direction of working-class residential development, whether of bachelors or of families, was into the flat land south of Market Street. Merchants, who had lived intermixed with their employees in the early years, gradually sought respectability by segregating themselves by moving northwest of Market Street or by ensconcing themselves in exclusive South Park (modeled after similar enclaves in London) or by building imposing showplace houses on Rincon Hill.

Respectability turned out to be neither as easily achieved as the widely publicized success stories promised nor as elusive as it might have been in the West Country of Ireland, the small towns of Bavaria, or the mines and mills of Wales and England. White males born in the United States possessed a decided advantage in San Francisco, as they did throughout the country. Considerably less than half of the population, they filled three out of four of the high-status merchant positions. At the other extreme, Chinese residents lived under segregated conditions, which resulted in their being regarded as "the lowest order in the city." Between these extremes, San Franciscans sorted themselves into class, ethnic, and regional groupings that transcended occupational classifications and contributed to the creation of a complex social mosaic. The Irish immigrants and their children, though heavily dependent on laboring jobs, made slow but steady gains in white-collar positions and property ownership but lagged behind Germans and the native-born. The small Afro-American population, though not squeezed as a group into segregated quarters, almost always worked in the service sector of the economy. Germans, very numerous in middle- and lower-status merchant firms, improved their fortunes steadily. German Jews, estimated to be well over half the German population, frequently made "spectacular" improvements.[27]

As planked sidewalks and streetcars replaced muddy lanes and mounted adventurers, San Francisco's social structure assumed a shape similar to that of New York, Boston, Philadelphia, or Brooklyn. Fewer than 5 percent of the male labor force of the city owned between 75 and 80 percent of personal and real property in the fifties. Six of every ten very wealthy men came from the merchant class, and four of every five were born in the United States. (By contrast, half the city's population had been born overseas.) Despite the high rate of business failure due to the ups and downs of the economy and despite the tendency of large numbers of merchants to stay only a few years, a permanent core of settled wealthy Protestant merchants developed during the fifties and sixties. Catholic and Jewish merchants, though in smaller numbers, made their way into this group of wealthy businessmen, as did a few black merchants.[28]

The city's similarity to commercial ports elsewhere in the United States, clearly discernible in its social structure, extended even to "the appearance of the business community in San Francisco" as early as 1850. Bayard Taylor found that

> slouched felt hats gave way to narrow-brimmed black beavers; flannel shirts were laid aside, and white linen, though indifferently washed, appeared instead; dress and frock coats, of the fashion of the previous year in the Atlantic side, came forth from trunks and sea-chests; in short, a San Francisco merchant was almost as smooth and spruce in his outward appearance as a merchant anywhere else.[29]

Regardless of their dress, the few merchants in San Francisco's black population found themselves subject to the kinds of prejudice and discrimination that flourished everywhere during the pre–Civil War decade. Like Jews and the Irish, who suffered less discrimination on the Pacific Coast than on the Atlantic Coast, blacks fared somewhat better in San Francisco than in the South. According to *The Annals of San Francisco*, an early history: "The Chinese and the free negroes, of whom there was now a goodly sprinkling, were 'the hewers of wood and the drawers of water' of the place." In 1863, Charlotte L. Brown, a black woman, was put off one of the Omnibus Railroad Company's streetcars when a passenger reminded the conductor that "colored persons were not allowed to ride." While the case was settled in 1866, with the court awarding damages to Brown, the defense attorney claimed to be accurately describing community attitudes in his statement that "mulatto and negro persons were and have been regarded by the entire Public of the said City of San Francisco (with a few exceptions) . . . as unfit to be associates or fellow travellers." The attorney was Irish-born future U.S. Senator Eugene Casserly. "The Admission of such negro or mulatto persons to ride in this defendents [*sic*] cars as passengers," he wrote, "was and has been extremely disagreeable to said public." Casserly insisted that if the president of the company, Irish entrepreneur Peter Donahue, allowed blacks to ride, "it would greatly prejudice this defendant and its cars with said public and cause it very generally to cease using or travelling in the same."[30] Historian Douglas Henry Daniels concludes that "prejudice was mild compared to anti-Chinese sentiments or Negrophobia in the south, but it was still disturbing, partly because it was not as iron-clad as elsewhere."[31]

For black San Franciscans and the Chinese, as for the more privileged and less subordinated Jewish, Irish, German, and old-stock Protestant residents of the city, "associational life" offset the harsher aspects of nineteenth-century urban existence. Like their counterparts in other towns and cities across the nation, the settlers of the fifties and sixties expressed their attachment to national origin, cultural heritage, and social or economic status by means of voluntary organizations. San Franciscans, like the Americans observed by Tocqueville east of the Mississippi a generation earlier, had "not only commercial and manufacturing companies, in which all take part, but associations of a thousand other kinds, religious, moral, serious, futile, general or restricted, enormous or diminutive."[32]

Churches, fraternal lodges, benevolent societies, social clubs, literary circles, trade unions, and merchants' organizations sprang up in San Francisco. The black community communicated through its newspapers, the *Pacific Appeal* and the *Elevator;* convened four separate Colored California conventions between 1855 and 1865; and worshipped in a number of black churches.[33] Irish settlers celebrated the city's first St. Patrick's Day in 1851 and formed their Hibernian Society in February 1852. The first all-women's group in the Irish community was the St. Mary's Ladies Society founded in 1859 by the Sisters of Mercy. Irish military associations, such as the McMahon Grenadier Guard and the Montgomery Guard (1859), and charity groups such as the Irish-American Benevolent Society (1860), coexisted with political organizations such as the Fenians (founded between 1856 and 1859). Irish Catholic churches (St. Patrick's on Market Street was founded in 1851) grew in number with the population and moved uptown with it in the 1860s.[34] Protestant churches multiplied to the point where the former mayor of Salem, Massachusetts, could congratulate members of the Sons of New England in 1854 that they had "built up a city of which we may all justly be proud. Everywhere over its surface, in New England fashion, arise the spires of churches and schoolhouses."[35]

Jews from Poland and northern Germany established the congregation Sherith Israel in 1850, the same year that southern German Jews founded Emanu-El.[36] The French Benevolent Society (1851) established a hospital almost immediately, and the German General Benevolent Society (1854) had a hospital and nearly six hundred members in 1856. The Chinese built such a cohesive network of associations in their segregated community that William Ingraham Kip, the first Episcopal bishop in California, found that "it was more difficult to establish a mission among the Chinese in San Francisco than in China."[37]

POLITICS AND THE VIGILANCE COMMITTEES

Businessmen tended to dominate San Francisco's associational life just as they controlled most of the city's wealth. When volunteer fire companies emerged in response to the disastrous fires in the congested business district near the cove, merchants took leadership roles, and their names filled well over half the spaces on the membership lists. When churches and synagogues began to show themselves on the city skyline, merchants led the congregations, and when militia companies drilled and paraded in Portsmouth Square, merchants gave the orders. Members of the business community also presided over the city's political institutions as they gradually decided that they needed to guide the choice of candidates for political office, change the structure of municipal government, and alter the contents of public policy. This development was accompanied, however, by considerable, sometimes violent, controversy.[38]

The merchant reformers claimed to represent "the people" against a corrupt and inefficient one-party system dominated by politicians who put personal aggrandizement before public interest. Actually, San Francisco's record of efficiency stood up quite well when compared with other Amer-

ican cities of the time, and corruption and financial mismanagement flourished in the private sector as well as in the public. The merchants claimed
to uphold law and order against rampaging villains who respected neither
business property nor family propriety. In fact, the committees of vigilance
organized by the city's merchants in 1851 and 1856 to establish control over
municipal politics carried out reigns of terror that were flagrant violations
of state and local legal codes. Several interrelated issues supplied the background to this period of political turmoil: impatience with the results of
political party competition for local office; suspicion of Irish Catholic voters
and mistrust of one particular Irish Catholic political broker who played
the game to win and quickly established a successful record; desire to keep
the tax burden as low as possible, even at the risk of short-changing city
services; desire on the part of the merchants—and especially their wives—
to stamp the city political system with the seal of family-centered
respectability.[39]

During the gold rush boom of 1848 and 1849, visitors to San Francisco
could expect to find almost anything but Victorian family respectability.
The prospects of instant wealth that moved well-connected pre–gold rush
merchants like William Howard to recommend migration to his relatives in
Boston also lured hundreds of speculators from more obscure backgrounds. For Howard and other Protestant merchants used to exercising
daily command over the affairs of the commercial village, appointment to
the first city council and membership in the convention that drafted California's first constitution seemed a logical extension of personal influence.
Municipal government, from the standpoint of these men, ought to have
been synonymous with inexpensive city housekeeping by the successful
businessmen of the community.[40]

Similar convictions informed William Howard's brother, George, who
complained from Boston during the heated presidential campaign of 1844
that James Polk was "brought in by foreigners, mostly Irish who have been
naturalized and paid to vote for him." William Gay, another Boston corre-
spondent, warned Howard a month later that unless Congress made drastic
changes in the immigration laws, "we shall soon be ruled by the rabble and
the mob."

> Not a boy in our public schools of 14 years of age but is better acquainted
> with the institutions of our country, and know wherein their interests lie,
> than nine out of ten of these ignorant, bigoted Irish who control the elections
> in our States. The Irish are making great inroads . . . and I trust our people
> will get their eyes open before it is too late.[41]

The phobia against foreign influence expressed by George Howard and
William Gay existed wherever American commercial cities attracted Irish
immigrant workers during the late 1840s. But the anxieties felt by New
Englanders about the future of their Protestant culture did not lessen their
zeal for exporting it to San Francisco. William Henry Thomas and his group
traveled to San Francisco in 1849 with the advice of Edward Everett, president of Harvard College, ringing in their ears: Go with "the Bible in one
hand and your New England civilization in the other, and make your mark

on the people and the country." The Reverend Timothy Dwight Hunt wanted to go even further and "make California the Massachusetts of the Pacific." Twenty-two-year-old Robert B. Wallace, son of a Pennsylvania state government auditor, apparently took such admonitions seriously. He was impressed by the "splendid buildings equal to our eastern cities" that he found in San Francisco in 1852. He complained to his father, however, that "everything is to captivate the senses, but to me it is disgusting."[42]

David Broderick, a stonemason's son whose Roman Catholic father had been born in Ireland, defined the relationship among personal culture, political success, and public affairs in a different way from William Howard. Broderick's experience of leadership had come from the militaristic rough and tumble of New York City ward politics, and for Broderick the logical vehicle for achieving personal success and exercising public influence had been the Democratic party. Broderick's belief that the Democratic party ought to be considered the legitimate vehicle for the exercise of municipal government matched the belief of most of the large number of Irish Catholic voters. Their change of address had not changed their conviction that party politics offered the most efficient means of achieving desirable city policy and that the party most suited to Irish Catholic ends remained the party of Jefferson and Jackson.[43]

During 1849 and 1850, as Broderick and other professional politicians began to develop a party organization capable of turning out loyal voters and controlling officeholders, the leaders of the city's merchant community carried out the first of three experiments in extralegal government. Affronted by the way in which the Hounds, a group of mercenaries hired by businessmen to protect property and maintain order, had exceeded their charge and themselves become a public menace, a 230-man committee led and organized by the merchants arrested the Hounds. Dissatisfied with the record of the mayor, the committee appointed its own representatives ostensibly to help him judge the Hounds, thereby overriding the legally constituted authorities and establishing a precedent for the future.

The establishment of official city charters in 1850 and 1851 symbolized a movement away from frontier informality and toward institutionalized mechanisms of municipal administration. The April 1851 elections illustrated the extent to which some of the volatile issues of New York and Boston politics had successfully made the journey to San Francisco. The Broderick Democrats had by then established a viable vote-getting organization, whose methods sometimes bordered on fraud and skirted the edge of bribery. Their opponents had begun to fight back by insisting that the body politic stood in danger of ruin by "wild Irishmen." Issues of real estate development constituted the lifeblood of much day-to-day politics during this period, and tensions increased as those real estate speculators whose interests suffered because of decisions of Democratic party judges made charges against the corruption of the political system. These allegations about the legitimacy of the courts, combined with outrage over a robbery and the large number of thefts that accompanied a fire in May, moved merchants to establish a Committee of Vigilance in June 1851. The committee purposely excluded blue-collar workers, accused the predominantly

Irish immigrants from Australia known as "Sydney Ducks" of being particularly prone to criminal behavior, hanged four men, banished fourteen from the city, and turned fifteen over to city authorities. The committee, numbering some five hundred, stayed active until the autumn when it demonstrated its political side by nominating a slate of independent candidates for the September elections.[44]

Dramatic as it was, the 1851 committee turned out to be only a dress rehearsal for a more comprehensive vigilante episode led by William Coleman five years later. Between these two outbreaks of "frontier justice," the city's Democrats, although beset by challenges from the Whig and then the American (antiforeigner) parties, nonetheless continued to attract the majority of the votes from the city's working-class neighborhoods and its Irish Catholics. Critics correctly accused the Democrats of fraudulent election practices, but their complaints that David Broderick had made the city into his personal fiefdom and that he had terrorized opposition newspaper editors and voters into quiet subservience were, in the words of historian Roger Lotchin, "totally absurd." Absurd or not, such rhetoric about the tyranny over the popular masses by the Democratic few became the justification for what Robert Burchell has called "a very neat surgical operation on the body politic" by the 1856 Committee of Vigilance. Once again, as in 1851, a violent crime provided the spark that ignited the rush to extralegal judgment. This time it was the murder of a newspaper editor who had been especially lionized by politically savvy and socially active wives of San Francisco merchants and professional men. This time, however, vigilante activists generated an active opposition in the form of a Law and Order Committee with a heavily Irish membership, and permanent control over the city's political institutions became necessary for the vigilantes' own self-protection.[45]

Despite this opposition, the vigilantes managed to deport almost three dozen of the Democratic activists and to discredit their party under the guise of cleaning up the city. As before, the Committee of Vigilance fielded a slate of candidates, this time under the banner of a "People's party," for the fall elections. The reform slate was swept into office by a two-to-one majority with middle-class family neighborhoods providing a heavier vote for the new party than the districts near the waterfront. Only the downtown working-class First District remained loyal to the Democrats.

Once in office, the new government instituted a typical set of mid-century business reforms: fiscal policies designed to minimize the tax rate and maintain the city's reputation among merchants in the East and political policies designed to minimize participation in nominations and elections by unmarried, unpropertied, and heavily Irish Catholic members of the working class. Many of the Irish Democrats dropped out of politics after 1856, though many others continued to campaign for, and occasionally win, election to the Board of Supervisors. The prestige position of mayor went only to Protestant merchants until after the Civil War, and the legacy of the People's party dominated the San Francisco scene for nearly twenty years. By the time the Civil War began in 1861, the city had experienced nearly four years of government by the self-styled reformers of the People's party. Although they governed the city under the charter that had been partly written by the discredited Broderick Democrats in 1855, the vigilantes and their defenders wrote the history of the 1856 days according to the plot that made the merchants into heroic defenders of urban virtue. The Broderick Democrats appeared as rogues and "politicians," assigned to the lower reaches of the human species.[46]

Disagreements about the legitimacy of what participants continued to call "the revolution" of 1856 persisted nonetheless. William Tecumseh Sherman, a San Francisco banker at the time, had opposed the vigilantes and supported the Law and Order Committee. Years later, in a letter to lawyer John Doyle, Sherman repeated his doubts that "merchants are more to be trusted in the principles of justice than Coke, Blackstone, Kent, etc., etc."

> In 1856 at San Francisco Judge Norton was as good as any Judge today in St. Louis. The Grand Jury as fair and the petit Jury as reliable, yet it stands recorded in history that all were corrupt, and the community was compelled by a sense of self protection to take justice into its own keeping. They were successful, and "Success is Success."[47]

The political offshoot of the Committee of Vigilance, the People's or Taxpayers' party, maintained its hegemony during the Civil War years. San Francisco merchants shared in the business boom brought on by the Civil War, as did all of the city's population. By maintaining loyalty to both the Union and the gold standard and by banning greenbacks from the city, merchants could buy goods selling for $1.70 to $2.50 in paper money for a dollar's worth of gold. They invested the profits in the newly discovered Nevada silver mines or in California real estate. The city's merchants also profited from the sudden demand for California's agricultural goods, as production soared from $29,000 in 1859 to almost $3 million in 1861. The high cost of transportation and the new protective tariffs passed by the Republicans stimulated a more diversified manufacturing sector. Capital invested in industry increased ten times during the decade 1860–1870, the industrial work force increased almost twenty times, and the value of manufactured goods almost four times.[48]

By the time the nation took up the burden of Reconstruction in 1866, San Francisco stood poised on the brink of regional urban leadership and national prominence. The completion of the transcontinental telegraph in 1861, the passage of the Pacific Railway Act in 1862, the establishment of the Bank of California in 1864, and the opening of the San Francisco and San Jose Railroad in the same year provided visible evidence of the city's key position in the West and its growing importance in the nation.

Chapter 2

Business and Economic Development

For thirty years after the discovery of gold, San Francisco stood virtually unchallenged as the economic capital of the Pacific Slope. A recent historian of the urban West describes San Francisco during the 1880s as the "Rome of the Pacific Coast; all roads led to it." The U.S. Census Office called San Francisco "the commercial metropolis of the Pacific Coast." Its population growth made it the ninth largest city in the country by 1880 and put it in the eighth rank by 1900. (See Table 1.) San Francisco controlled local trade with Bay Area counties as well as coastal trade from Panama to Alaska. Twenty-one percent of the total population of California, Oregon, and Washington lived in San Francisco, the city's merchants handled 99 percent of the coast's imports and 83 percent of its exports, and San Francisco manufacturers produced 60 percent of the region's goods. Five railroad lines tied the city to its hinterland, and five ferry lines brought commuters from around the bay. The city's rapid development as an adjunct to the mining business of California and Nevada allowed it to achieve a dominance that made Oakland, San Jose, Stockton, and Sacramento "jewels in San Francisco's crown" by 1880. The city had more manufacturing establishments, more employees in workshops, greater capitalization, larger value of materials, and higher value of products than all the other twenty-four western cities combined.[1]

San Francisco also led the West as a center of finance. As early as 1868, ten insurance companies operated out of San Francisco headquarters, with about $6 million in capital; thirty-five firms from outside the state operated branches in the city. The Bank of California and the Pacific Bank operated under state charters by the end of the sixties, as did thirteen unincorporated banks, several savings banks, and seven savings and loan institutions. By 1887, the 148 banks in the rest of the state outnumbered San Francisco's

TABLE 1
San Francisco Population and Percentage of Increase, 1860–1930

Date	Population	Percentage of Increase
1860	56,802	89
1870	149,473	163
1880	233,959	57
1890	298,997	28
1900	342,782	15
1910	416,912	21
1920	506,676	21
1930	634,394	25

SOURCES: Table 3, "Population of Civil Divisions Less Than Counties," U.S. Census Office, Department of the Interior, *Ninth Census of the United States: 1870*, 3 vols. (Washington, D.C.: U.S. Government Printing Office, 1872), p. 91; Table 80, "Population: 1900, 1890, and 1880," U.S. Census Office, Department of the Interior, *Abstract of the Twelfth Census of the United States: 1900* (Washington, D.C.: U.S. Government Printing Office, 1904), p. 102; Table 10, "Composition and Characteristics of the Population, for Cities of 10,000 or More: 1920," U.S. Bureau of the Census, Department of Commerce, *Fourteenth Census of the United States: 1920*, 11 vols. (Washington, D.C.: U.S. Government Printing Office, 1922), 3:118; Table 23, "Population by Sex, Color, Age, etc., for Cities of 50,000 or More by Wards or Assembly Districts: 1930," U.S. Bureau of the Census, Department of Commerce, *Fifteenth Census of the United States: 1930*, 6 vols. (Washington, D.C.: U.S. Government Printing Office, 1932–1933), 3:287, pt. 1.

twenty-six banks, but the city had almost twice the assets ($144,368,813) of all other California counties combined ($79,786,557).[2]

San Francisco strengthened its premier position in the region as the decade of the 1880s progressed. The value of foreign imports increased from nearly $40 million in 1886 to over $51 million in 1889. Commerce with other states and territories, overland and sea-borne, came close to $70 million by the early 1890s, and the city ranked fourth in the value of imports and fifth in the value of exports. Only New York, Boston, and Philadelphia (and the latter by only a small margin) topped San Francisco in the value of imports. San Francisco's export trade fattened on the shipping of wheat and flour, prompting a writer in 1891 to boast that "like a second Egypt we help to feed the nations." By the nineties the city's exporters depended primarily on "the products of our own soil, mines, and industrial establishments, so that every increase in quantity and value means a corresponding increase in home industry."[3]

Manufacturing also contributed to San Francisco's economic growth between the 1860s and the 1880s. In the ten years after the gold rush, manufacturing in San Francisco had been "both directly and indirectly the hand maiden of commerce." By the 1880s, manufacturing had become as important to the city's economy as trade and commerce, with 41 percent of the growth of employment in the previous decade coming from the increase of manufacturing jobs as compared with only 35 percent from jobs in trade and transportation. The persistence of San Francisco's relative isolation from the country's leading manufacturing centers, combined with the gradual lowering of the costs of raw materials and labor, plus the accumulation of local capital, led to the eventual replacement of many imported manufactures by home industries between the 1860s and the 1880s. By then, San

Francisco had a "broadly based," diversified, manufacturing sector.[4] (See Table 2.)

In 1870, the census figures showed the city's value of manufactured goods to be just over $37 million, whereas in 1890 the total came to over $118 million, or about $300 per capita. The number of companies of every size doubled during the period, with greatest growth in very small and very large firms. New firms proliferated, and while over one hundred establishments employed between twenty-five and fifty workers, the typical workshop hired fewer than five hands as late as 1880. Foodstuffs, clothing, textiles, hardware, leather, and provisioning accounted for approximately half of manufacturing employment and about a third of the manufacturing output of the city. By 1890, the processing of foods earned $50 million, fabrication of metals $10 million, leather goods $10.5 million, textiles $13.5 million, lumber $14.5 million, with another $20 million contributed by all other manufacturing.[5]

Eight times out of ten, capital for the development of San Francisco manufacturing during this period came from the profits made by merchandisers or from savings deposited by wage earners. "Practically all of this capital," according to economic historian Robert Trusk, "was accumulated in California by men who were engaged directly or indirectly with the products they later manufactured." San Francisco steadily increased its share of California's manufacturing, suggesting an analogy with the "pattern of development characteristic of many underdeveloped countries today where economic growth is localized in spatially restricted zones."[6]

The boot and shoe industry, along with the cigar industry, amounted to about $10 million of the total value added by manufacture in 1890, but they, like "every other carried on in the city, [were] cast in the shade by the sugar refining industry." Something of a local success story, the sugar-refining business (estimated at $17 million in 1890) owed much of its success to the efforts of Claus Spreckels, who as president of the California Sugar Refinery brought a "renaissance" to the business. Spreckels established his first refinery in 1863 at the corner of Brannan and Eighth streets, and by 1884 his huge works in the Potrero District could be described as "the most complete concern of the kind in the world, and in size ranks with the great refineries of Brooklyn, New York, and St. Louis." One of the three giants that controlled the nation's sugar business in the nineties, Spreckels's prod-

TABLE 2

San Francisco's Share of California Manufacturing and Population

	Percentage of Manufacturing		
Year	Employment	Value Added	Percentage of Population
1860	25	40	15
1870	49	55	27
1880	65	69	24

SOURCE: Robert A. Elgie, "The Development of San Francisco Manufacturing, 1848–1880: An Analysis of Regional Locational Factors and Urban Spatial Structure," master's thesis, University of California, Berkeley, 1966, p. 49.

ucts dominated "the entire trade of the region." No other single manufacturing industry could match sugar refining in value of products, although
canned goods were valued at $4 million, beer generated $3.5 million, and
coffee and spices earned $1.5 million. Clothing manufacture ($4 million),
doors, sashes, and other lumber items ($3 million), and leather goods exclu-
sive of boots and shoes (over $3 million) headed the list.[7]

Except for the handful of industrial firms of the scale of Spreckels's
refinery, San Francisco's economic life in the 1880s was centered primarily
in the area bounded on the west by Larkin Street, on the southwest by
Seventh Street, and on the north and east by the waterfront. The bustle of
trade on the city streets reflected the city's major activities.

> Fruits, canned, dried and green, salmon and other articles of food figure
> largely. Wine to drink for the East, Mexico and Central America and the
> islands of the Pacific, contributes its share. Lumber to build houses in all parts
> of the world from Australia to Scotland, including our famous redwood. . . .
> Then come groceries and manufactured goods of every description to the
> islands of the Pacific Sea.[8]

The clamor of the commercial city was nowhere as marked as at the point
where waterfront activity joined with the busy traffic of merchandising and
wholesaling at the lower end of Market Street. Market Street's unusual 120-
foot width made it a dramatic swath that separated most of the financial and
commercial city on the north from the more industrial sectors to the south.

A traveler alighting from one of the ferries at the foot of Market Street
in the 1880s would have found surroundings familiar to residents of other
port cities, whether Boston, New York, Philadelphia, or Baltimore. For
example, the firm of Coffin and Hendy, already two decades old in the mid-
eighties, stood close by the water, selling ship chandlery and naval stores.
Next door another twenty-year-old business, the shipping agents Goodall,
Perkins, and Company, directed the Pacific Coast Steamship Company (which
they had originally organized and later sold to eastern capitalists of the
Villard syndicate). Goodall, Perkins, and Company launched the first steamers engaged in the whaling trade, and they owned large holdings of stock
in the Oceanic Steamship Company and the Arctic Oil Works. The company
also served as the agents of the Pacific Coast Railway Company and the
Oregon Railway and Navigation Company. Between them, these railroads
and the shipping lines handled much of the coastal trade between San Diego
and Alaska except for coal and lumber.[9]

A bit further down Market Street, the four-story, red-brick building of
Hawley Brothers Hardware Company announced its products (and suggested the importance of agriculture in California) with huge painted signs:
"Schuttler Farm and Spring Wagons, Portable Engines, Threshers, Buckeye
Mowers and Reapers, Headers, Gang Plows, Cultivators, Rices' Straw Burning Engines." The wagons, steam tractors, and harvesting machines parked
on the pavement outside made the firm's business clear to everyone who
passed by. Thirty years in business, this corporation handled a payroll of
$5,000 a month, declared annual sales from imports and manufactures of
close to $2 million, and tapped the entire region west of the Rockies, Mexico,
South and Central America, and Hawaii.[10]

In 1852, two years before Charles A. Hawley opened his hardware store in San Francisco, Collis P. Huntington and Mark Hopkins set up a similar business in Sacramento. In 1870, after they and Leland Stanford and Charles Crocker, the other members of the "Big Four," completed the Central Pacific's transcontinental railroad, Huntington and Hopkins opened a branch of their hardware business in San Francisco. During the 1880s, the firm's four-story building provided an imposing reminder of the wealth of its owners. In addition to hardware, the firm handled all sorts of iron and steel products; traded throughout the Pacific states, the territories, and Mexico; operated a branch on Broad Street in New York; and stood on such a firm foundation of capital that, in the words of one contemporary, "its credit in commercial circles is equivalent to cash."[11]

Manufacturers occupied the upper floors of four-story buildings further west on Market Street, lending this part of downtown San Francisco something of a New York flavor. Kraker and Israel established their workshop for the making of women's and children's clothing in the face of "almost overwhelming opposition" from eastern competitors in 1865, but in twenty years they had managed to displace imports to the point that one sympathizer claimed that "the entire Pacific Coast" was "under tribute" to them. S. and G. Gump (founded in San Francisco in 1860) employed fifty workers in the production of mirrors, mouldings, frames, hardwood mantles, and bric-a-brac furniture. A few blocks away on Stevenson Street, a similarly large building housed both the woolen import business of Stein, Simon, and Company and the wine vaults of J. Gundlach and Company, owners of the "Rhinefarm" vineyards near Sonoma and suppliers of California wines to the East.[12]

Some of the wine from the Gundlach cellars may have found its way to the dining rooms of the Grand Hotel or the Palace Hotel, establishments facing each other across New Montgomery at its junction with Market. Like the Baldwin Hotel further up Market at the corner of Powell, the Palace Hotel opened in the 1870s, offering guests their choice of 755 rooms. With its seven-story, red-brick facade visible for miles in most directions, the hotel had "myriads of bay windows," which served to "partly relieve the imposing exterior from the appearance of oppressive massiveness by which it would otherwise be characterized."[13]

The Hibernia Savings and Loan Society, the city's leading savings bank in 1880 with over $15 million in resources, stood only a few steps away. The bank's president and board of directors still consisted of the wealthy group of prominent Irish-Americans who had organized the bank in 1859. Myles D. Sweeney served as president, Robert J. Tobin acted as secretary, and real estate developer John Sullivan, as well as iron manufacturer and railroad entrepreneur Peter Donahue and French merchant Gustave Touchard, served on the board. By the 1880s, the Hibernia had already played an important part in the business and residential development of the city by financing both the acquisition and subdivision of property and the construction of downtown commercial structures and outlying family dwellings. San Francisco's large Irish population made up the largest single group of depositors and borrowers, but the bank did not deal with Hibernians exclusively. The immigrant French banker François L. A. Pioche financed his subdivisions in San Francisco's Mission, Potrero, and Visitacion Valley districts with loans from the Hibernia, and the bank subsequently made hundreds of loans for the construction of modest wooden rowhouses in these predominantly working-class neighborhoods. William Chapman Ralston built his Palace Hotel (on a site originally owned by Hibernia's first president John Sullivan) with Hibernia loans that totaled $1 million.[14]

The Nevada Bank, the city's leading bank in 1880 (capitalized at $10 million with over $20 million in resources), rested upon wealth from the Comstock that had been brought to San Francisco by its "Silver King" founders. Established in 1875 by James C. Flood and William S. O'Brien in the chaotic last days of William Ralston's tenure as president of the Bank of California, the Nevada Bank's solvency contributed to the city's financial stability in the latter part of the depression-wracked decade of the 1870s. John W. Mackay and James G. Fair, the other two "Silver Kings," also served as directors. The Nevada Bank, at Montgomery and Pine streets, was only a short walk from the California and Sansome Street location of the Bank of California.[15]

Like the Nevada Bank, the Bank of California brought profits from Nevada silver to San Francisco where it was transformed into capital for the development of commerce, industry, and the built environment. Before he died in 1875 at the age of forty-nine (probably from a stroke while swimming on the day he was forced out as the bank's president), Ralston used the bank's resources to initiate a dizzying array of developments in San Francisco and the Bay Area. "He wanted," wrote friend and associate Asbury Harpending forty years later,

> to see his State and city great, prosperous, progressive, conspicuous throughout the world for enterprise and big things. I think it was this imagination, this ambition, that kept hurrying him into one big undertaking after another, many of which were way ahead of time.

Ralston's San Francisco projects included a southern extension of Montgomery Street, the Mission Woolen Mills, the Cornell Watch Factory, the Kimball Carriage Factory, the West Coast Furniture Factory, a sugar refinery, a dry dock at Hunter's Point, and the Palace and the Grand hotels.[16] William Alvord headed the Bank of California in the eighties. An importer and wholesaler, Alvord had been one of the founders of the Risdon Iron Works and a former city mayor. Bank of California resources ($10 million), though only half those of the Nevada Bank in 1880, still stood at over twice those of its closest rival. Ten of the city's eighteen largest banks stood nearby on California Street, and all but two—the California Savings and Loan Society on Powell Street and the Savings and Loan Society at 619 Clay Street—were within a two-block radius of the Bank of California.[17]

Several blocks to the north, finance gave way to commerce. Some manufacturing could also be found here in the eighties. Eugene Thomas, for example, at 617 Sansome Street, operated an importing firm specializing in French wines, liquors, truffles, Vichy water, and other continental delicacies. Drake and Emerson, established in 1863, carried out their commission business in fruits and vegetables on Sansome between Washington and Merchant streets.[18]

J. W. Schaeffer and Company, a pioneer in cigar making on the West Coast and president of the Cigar Manufacturers Association, produced Green Seal, Bon Ton, Chromo, and Correro cigars at 231 and 323 Sacramento Street. H. Plagemann and Company, founded in 1862, produced the Las Operitas and Sublime brands nearby. Smokers who preferred cigars and tobacco from New York, Virginia, or Havana could visit Esberg, Bachman, and Company at the northeast corner of California and Battery streets. At Clay and Sansome streets, also close by Chinatown, Porter, Slessinger, and Company operated their boot and shoe factory and marketed their "Iron Clad" products throughout the region.[19]

Lower California Street housed the offices of one of the state's leading flour mills, Sperry and Company. The firm kept its city office at 22 California Street while the mills in Stockton ground out the thousand barrels a day that were then shipped via the San Joaquin River to San Francisco and then all over California as well as to China. Battery, Front, and Davis streets were crowded with other commission merchants and importers, whose warehouses covered large plots of land, as well as small manufacturers. Moody and Farish, for example, oldest wool commission merchants on the West Coast, represented the region's largest wool growers and had recently expanded into handling the lucrative trade in hops. Baker and Hamilton, at the intersection of Market, Davis, and Pine streets, occupied the entire lower part of a block, and its warehouse held agricultural implements and hardware that the firm sold throughout the Pacific region.[20]

Baker and Hamilton had begun near Sacramento in 1849. Levi Strauss opened in San Francisco in 1853. By the mid-1880s, Strauss's dry goods business occupied a four-story building and employed "a small army" of workers who maintained the company's connections with both large and small settlements throughout the West. Kahn Brothers and Company, located at 25 and 27 Battery, imported silks, velvets, cashmeres, and other fancy goods from Germany, France, and England. San Francisco retailers depended on Kahn Brothers for products direct from Belfast, Glasgow, St. Etienne, Roubaix, Lyons, and Paris.[21]

Smoke from factory chimneys and sounds from foundries filled the air in the streets leading away from Market Street on the south, distinguishing that district from the north side of Market. David Kerr manufactured carriages, wagons, and heavy trucks at his factory on Beale Street. Tatum and Bowen produced heavy sawmill machinery nearby.

The National Iron Works, at Main and Howard streets, employed one hundred men building stationary engines, ore crushers, and flour and sawmill equipment. Established in 1879, the firm had up-to-date equipment, which allowed it to compete successfully with more established companies. One of these, Aetna Iron Works at 217 Fremont Street, established in 1866, originally specialized in mining machinery but later diversified its products. W. F. Buswell, located at 108 Main Street, manufactured quartz and flour mills, elevators, and sidewalk hoists and had prospered since the founding of the company in 1858. Liebes Brothers and Company, on Fremont Street, employed five hundred workers in a factory situated on the upper floors of their building, and they sold their brands profitably in New York, New England, and the southern United States despite competition from the locals.[22]

In the Potrero District close to the southeastern shore of the city, the Union Iron Works and the Pacific Rolling Mills joined Spreckels's California Sugar Refinery to create a heavy industry sector. The Union Iron Works, begun in 1849 as a modest concern by Glasgow-born (of Irish parents) Peter Donahue, was headed by George W. Prescott in the late 1880s, with Irving M. Scott as general manager. Over 1,200 workers operated the mammoth plant that spread across fifteen acres and included a complete shipyard, a rolling mill, foundries, pattern shops, machine shops, and one of the largest hydraulic lift docks in the United States. The firm produced mining machinery, heavy agricultural implements, ships, and even locomotives. William Alvord headed the Pacific Rolling Mills, located nearby at Potrero Point, where eight hundred workers operated six trains of rollers, twenty-five furnaces, fifty-four boilers, fifteen engines, and eight steam hammers. The Pacific Rolling Mills turned out 30,000 tons of iron and 10,000 tons of steel annually. It had rolled the first steel rails made on the Pacific Coast (for the Mission Street Railroad) and supplied the tracks for the Market Street cable railroad system. Its engines also powered sea-going craft and ran machinery in the Comstock.[23]

The gradual extension of the living and working environment of San Francisco south and west into the Mission District and the Western Addition came with, and depended on, the construction of a network of transportation lines that rapidly connected the new areas with the central business district and the city to the suburbs. The Market Street Railroad dated back to 1857, and by the eighties numerous other lines flourished. The Hayes Valley line connected the growing Western Addition to the central business districts, and the Potrero and Bay View line allowed workers from south of San Francisco to commute to the industrial district in the Potrero, to adjacent Butchertown, as well as to the South of Market and waterfront areas. Both these lines belonged to the Market Street system. The Omnibus Railroad Company gave passengers access to the residential parts of the Mission District as far south as Twenty-sixth Street, as did the City Railroad Company. Both the Central and the Sutter Street lines eased the trip from downtown San Francisco beyond Russian Hill and the Western Addition to the edge of the city's built-up territory in the Pacific Heights and Presidio areas and helped make the areas along their routes desirable residential districts. Golden Gate Park could be reached by taking one of the cars of the Geary Street, Park, and Ocean Railroad, and for a five-cent fare riders could cross the business district on the North Beach and Mission line.[24]

The city's streetcar lines all radiated from either the ferry slips, the Southern Pacific Railroad's Townsend Street depot, the Pacific Mail Steamship Company's wharf, or the steamboat landing at the foot of Broadway Street. These termini of both water-borne and land transportation bustled with passengers and freight activity and served to remind both residents and visitors of the importance of what Alfred Chandler has called "the first modern business enterprise," the railroad. In San Francisco, "the railroad" meant the Southern Pacific. "By 1877," a University of California economist wrote in 1922, "the Central Pacific–Southern Pacific combination was in control of over 85 percent of all the railroads in California, including all the lines of importance around San Francisco Bay, except the San Francisco and North Pacific Railroad, and in the Sacramento and San Joaquin Valleys."[25]

When James O'Leary, editor of the city's *Journal of Commerce,* wrote his section on "money" for an 1891 book describing San Francisco's leading entrepreneurs, he headed the list of millionaires with the names of railroad magnates Leland Stanford and Charles Crocker. Stanford and Crocker, together with Collis Huntington and Mark Hopkins, began their careers and their fortunes outside San Francisco, then transferred their business headquarters and homes to the city. All four had been moderately successful Sacramento merchants when approached by Theodore Judah in 1860 for support of a transcontinental railroad. Rebuffed by more conservative San Franciscan investors, Judah hoped to tie the country together with steel rails. With the Civil War suggesting the need to connect California to the Union cause, Judah found success in the form of a congressional subsidy. Whereas Judah had pursued a vision of national unity, the Big Four were driven primarily by dreams of the commercial gains possible by means of a rail connection to the Mother Lode. Only later did they sense the potential bonanza of the transcontinental trade. The Big Four used the massive federal subsidy and a small initial investment of their own to eventually seize control of the transportation for virtually the entire Pacific Coast. In 1873 they moved their company headquarters to San Francisco, and Crocker, Hopkins, and Stanford moved to the city, where they built elaborate mansions atop Nob Hill.

Leland Stanford, most visible of the four, held the presidency of the railroad for twenty-eight years and also served briefer periods as governor and a U.S. senator. He and his wife Jane erected Stanford University as a memorial to their son, endowing it with the Stanford fortune. Huntington, reputedly "the brains of the group," moved to New York, coming west only twice each year and finally buying a modest (and rarely used) Nob Hill mansion in the 1890s. A cynical, tight-fisted, tenacious Yankee who acquired eastern railroad interests in addition to his western holdings, he maneuvered Stanford out of the presidency in 1890 and grabbed the office for himself.

The magnificence of the mansions of the Silver Kings and the Big Four and the massive character of their wealth and power caused the display of luxury by others to pale in comparison. George Hearst, for example, a brilliant self-taught mining geologist, reaped a fortune from the Comstock Lode in the 1860s and, in partnership with James Ben Ali Haggin, controlled a vast mining empire that included silver mining in Utah, gold in South Dakota, copper in Montana, and other interests in Idaho and Mexico. Hearst also owned land throughout California and in Texas, New Mexico, Arizona, and Mexico. As a gesture of support for the Democratic party, he bought the nearly bankrupt *San Francisco Examiner* in 1880 and underwrote its deficits for the next decade until his son, William Randolph Hearst, made it profitable. From 1886 until his death in 1890, George Hearst represented California in the U.S. Senate.

Hearst lived on Nob Hill, but Peter Donahue lived in a forty-room mansion in the city's older enclave for the rich on Rincon Hill, not far from the site of his iron foundry in Happy Valley. Donahue's multifaceted entrepreneurial activities made him a sizable fortune. Besides the Street Railroad, the San Francisco Gas Works, the San Jose Railroad, and the San Francisco and North Pacific Railroad, Donahue had also helped organize the Hibernia Bank and the State Investment Insurance Company.[26]

Donahue's numerous directorships made him a typical member of the top echelon of San Francisco's business community in the eighties. One of the founding members of the Southern Pacific Railroad Company in 1870, he was one of the three directors in addition to the Big Four. Lloyd Tevis was one of the others, and like Donahue, Tevis also had banking interests. Brother-in-law of Hearst's partner James Haggin, president of Wells Fargo Bank Company for many years, Tevis became one of California's largest landholders and had investments in the Risdon Iron Works, the Spring Valley Water Company, the California Street Railroad, San Francisco real estate, and gold and silver mines. Tevis's Taylor Street house, "one of the most capacious and elegant in San Francisco," was located two blocks from the mansion of George Hearst.[27]

William Alvord's business address at the Bank of California put him in close proximity to the office of Lloyd Tevis on Montgomery Street. Alvord lived on Harrison Street on Rincon Hill, not far from Peter Donahue's mansion. Alvord, like Milton Latham, who had also lived on Rincon Hill before moving to New York, combined business enterprise with political service. Alvord started out in the wholesale hardware business, then sold out in order to invest in and supervise the construction of the Risdon Iron Works. He served a term as mayor and found time from his banking business to sit four years as a police commissioner and ten years as a park commissioner.[28]

Like Lloyd Tevis, James Phelan had faith in the speculative possibilities of San Francisco real estate, and in 1881–1882, he spent half a million dollars to construct the Phelan Building on property he owned at the northwestern corner of Market, Dupont (now Grant), and O'Farrell streets. Phelan came with his parents and two brothers from Queens County, Ireland, in 1821; his father, a graduate of Dublin's Trinity College, hoped to find relief from Irish rural life in the commerce of New York City. Phelan had already developed successful commercial ventures in New York, Philadelphia, and several southern cities when he opened a wholesale liquor firm with his brother in gold rush San Francisco. The profits from wholesaling allowed him to branch out into wheat, trade, and banking, and he organized the lucrative First National Gold Bank of San Francisco in 1870. He lived near Mission Dolores on a three-and-a-half-acre site and spent summers in Santa Cruz.[29] Phelan, though a benefactor to Catholic activities and city charities, lived a largely private life by the eighties, while his son, James Duval Phelan, directed the banking firm.

Banker Horace Davis, president of the Savings and Loan Society, headed the Chamber of Commerce in 1883–1884, directed the Produce Exchange between 1866 and 1876, and successfully ran for two terms as a member of the House of Representatives. Davis, unlike Phelan, came from Puritan stock, with a father who had been governor as well as senator from Massachusetts. Davis graduated from Harvard before sailing around Cape Horn to California in 1853 and later commanding a ship for the Pacific Mail Steamship Company. He established the successful Golden Gate Flouring Mills in 1860. By the end of the 1880s, he was both the president of the University of California and a trustee of the new Stanford University.[30]

George C. Perkins, who lived in Oakland, regularly commuted to his office at Goodall, Perkins, and Company at 10 Market Street. The firm's shipping business still thrived during the 1880s, but Perkins occupied himself with the office of governor of California, as well as his presidency of the Merchants' Exchange, his trusteeships of the Academy of Sciences and the State Mining Bureau, and his directorship in the First National Bank of San Francisco and a half-dozen other corporations.[31] Both Perkins and his partner Charles Goodall started out in life as sailors before the mast. Goodall, a Methodist immigrant from England and a dedicated temperance advocate, served as president of the local YMCA. He also served a term in the state assembly and as a trustee of Stanford University. Goodall evidently preferred the city to the suburbs and lived in a substantial house in the Western Addition.[32]

Political office attracted men of lesser wealth than Stanford, Perkins, and Goodall. Henry M. Black, an Irish immigrant to San Francisco by way of Boston, manufactured prize-winning carriages and served on the city school board as well as in the state legislature. Edward Pond, a native New Yorker whose wholesale liquor business allowed him to live comfortably at a respectable California Street address, served as director of the San Francisco Savings Union and the Sun Insurance Company, as well as a city supervisor and mayor.[33]

Other businessmen devoted attention to social organizations and provided both the capital and the loyalty that made them pivotal institutions in the city's life. Kalman Haas and William Steinhart, German Jewish immigrants, were typical. The grocery business of Haas Brothers was well established by the eighties, and Kalman Haas belonged to the Chamber of Commerce and the Board of Trade and played a leading role in a number of Jewish charities. Steinhart was director of the Pioneer Woolen Mills and the Gold and Stock Telegraphy Company, a charter member and trustee of the Hebrew Orphan Asylum, and the founder and first president of the B'nai B'rith organization (1856).[34]

Steinhart and Haas, like Horace Davis, James Phelan, William Alvord, Peter Donahue, and Charles Crocker, were among the most prominent businessmen in San Francisco from the 1860s to the 1880s. Journalist Henry George may well have had them in mind in 1868 when he wrote that "the great city that is to be will have its Astors, Vanderbilts, Stewards and Spragues, and he who looks a few years ahead may even now read their names as he passes along Montgomery, California, or Front streets." George proved correct in his guess that men with "established businesses" would "become richer for it and find increased opportunities; those who have only their own labor will become poorer, and find it harder to get ahead."[35] As Peter Decker has written in a recent study: "Occupational advancements were limited to the white-collar sector," and movement "from the blue-collar world into either the white-collar occupations or the elite ranks declined significantly after the 1850s." Decker's analysis of the "second generation" of the business community (1870–1880) also makes the point that by the 1880s, stockbrokers, bankers, real-estate speculators, company executives, importers, and manufacturers, along with attorneys and physicians, accounted for nearly two-thirds of the total group of economic leaders.[36]

This business elite, well established by the end of the eighties, continued to shape the direction of the city's economic life during the half-century after 1890. In this respect, San Francisco presents a striking illustration of Thomas Cochran and William Miller's observation that it is "impossible to exaggerate the role of business in developing great cities in America."[37] Charles Lindblom's words apply as much to San Francisco as to eastern and midwestern cities. In San Francisco as elsewhere, "a large category of major decisions" would be "turned over to businessmen, both small and larger." Business leaders would "become a kind of public official and exercise what, on a broad view of their role, are public functions." Businessmen played a "privileged role in government," their influence "unmatched by any leadership group other than government officials themselves."[38] Herbert Hoover, writing some twenty years after leaving the White House, used similar language when he described his friend Milton H. Esberg as one of San Francisco's business leaders whose role in urban development "represented a phenomena [sic] unique to American life. The greatest good fortune of American villages, towns, and cities," wrote the former president, "is a citizen outside its government who gives that leadership which makes for cooperation in the spiritual and physical progress of the city."[39]

Precise definitions of business leadership elude historians because, as Burton Folsom has written, "no one has yet figured out a foolproof way to measure someone's economic influence." One standard that provides useful information is membership on the boards of directors of incorporated companies. If a person who holds at least three directorships in San Francisco firms (two if he was a company officer) is considered an "economic leader," some two hundred men qualify for the title during the 1890–1930 period.[40] Several dozen of this number, the officers and directors of the city's largest companies, comprised the nucleus of San Francisco business leadership. At the center of this network of individuals stood James Duval Phelan and William Henry Crocker, both born in 1861. Upon his father's death in 1888, young Crocker assumed responsibility for the Crocker railroad and banking interests. Phelan took primary control of family real estate and banking interests when his father died in 1892.

The younger Phelan lived until 1930, and "Will" Crocker died in 1937. Their stately funerals at St. Ignatius Church and Grace Cathedral attracted "the wealthy and prominent . . . in shining limousines" as well as "others who walked."[41] The honorary pallbearers—some three dozen friends of the deceased—comprised a quarter of the city's economic leaders, whose participation on boards of directors linked them with most of the rest of San Francisco's business leadership. Like Phelan and Crocker, these men were responsible for the direction of San Francisco's largest industries, banks, insurance companies, land development firms, shipping and transport companies, and utility companies. Whether Protestant, Jewish, or Catholic, the men who gathered to pay homage to Crocker and Phelan shared the conviction that profitable business and urban progress went hand in hand. As Leland Cutler, who represented the Chamber of Commerce at the Phelan funeral, put it years later:

> I suppose my participation in public affairs attracted business to my company and I was always on the lookout for it. I can't recall, however, of any civic work I did with the idea of getting business. I never gave it a thought. I like people, I wanted to help my city and believed in progress generally.[42]

Phelan's work as president of the Federation of Improvement Clubs of San Francisco, like his chairmanship of the Adornment Association (which aimed to create a "city beautiful"), demonstrated his belief in civic progress. As mayor (1897–1902) and U. S. senator (1915–1921), Phelan worked with the Merchants' Association and the Chamber of Commerce in support of policies to aid San Francisco development. He traveled to Europe in 1913 as an unofficial representative of the U.S. State Department to publicize the opening of the city's Panama Pacific International Exposition in 1914. Phelan's elective offices set him apart from most San Francisco business leaders, but his banking, insurance, and real estate interests kept him in the thick of the city's economic life. When silver magnate James Fair died, Phelan took his place as president of the Mutual Savings Bank. The First National Gold Bank had been organized in 1870 by the elder Phelan, who had then served as its president; after his father's death, Phelan served as a director for the First National. Phelan's friend, Rudolph Spreckels, son of "sugar king" Claus Spreckels, served on the board of the Mutual Savings Bank and as president of the First National. Phelan and Spreckels also shared responsibilities as chairman of the board and president, respectively, of the United Bank and Trust Company. Organized in 1923, the United Bank and Trust brought together the pioneer era Sacramento–San Joaquin Bank of Sacramento (with branches in Stockton, Oakdale, and Modesto) with the Union National Bank of Fresno and the Merchants National Bank of San Francisco. Phelan remained chairman of the board until the United merged with the Bank of America of California. Both Phelan and Spreckels continued the development of their fathers' downtown property holdings. Phelan built offices on the choice corner bounded by Market, O'Farrell, and Stockton streets. Spreckels, president of City Investment Company, constructed an eighteen-story office building and the Strand Theater on the Market Street lots in the Claus Spreckels estate.[43]

One of the co-founders of the First National Gold Bank in 1870 along with the elder Phelan was James M. Moffitt (1827–1906). Moffitt's son,

James Kennedy, later served along with the younger Phelan on the boards of the First National and Mutual Savings. The elder Moffitt had also been a director of the Mutual Savings Bank, the First National, the Oakland Bank of Savings, and the Oakland Gas Light and Heat Company. He had helped to found Blake, Moffitt, and Company, which, after its incorporation in 1884 as Blake, Moffitt, and Towne, became the leading supplier of paper to the Pacific Coast region. The company had opened branch offices up and down the Pacific Coast and in the Sacramento and San Joaquin valleys by the time James Kennedy Moffitt assumed the presidency of the firm in 1927. Like Phelan, Moffitt also served as a University of California regent.[44]

Another Phelan associate as director and president (1923–1925) of the First National Bank was John A. Hooper (1838–1925). Besides his thirty-year service as a director of the bank, Hooper presided over a half-dozen California lumber companies ranging from Port Costa in the north to San Pedro in the south. Hooper's lumber found its way into both San Francisco and Los Angeles buildings, and he also supplied much of the construction material for the boom town of Tombstone, Arizona, in 1882. Three of Hooper's four brothers joined him in the lumber business. One of them, Charles A. Hooper, helped to create Pittsburg, in Contra Costa County, by bringing heavy industry to the site in the form of the Columbia Steel Corporation (later a unit of U.S. Steel). His oldest daughter married Wigginton E. Creed (1877–1927), and Creed took over the presidency of Columbia Steel when his father-in-law died in 1916. A Fresno native, Creed financed his legal education at New York Law School by working as principal of the Fresno High School. After finishing his law degree, he worked in New York as secretary for pioneer California banker D. O. Mills. Like Phelan and Moffitt, Creed served as a University of California regent, but he put in a stint as president of the university as well as president of the Pacific Gas and Electric Company.[45]

Creed and Hooper socialized at the Pacific Union Club, as did another of Phelan's fellow directors of the First National Bank, Walter S. Martin. President of a real estate management firm, Martin Investment Company, as well as of the Eastern Oregon Land Company and member of the board of Pacific Telephone and Telegraph Company, Martin was a Georgetown University graduate who lived, like many of San Francisco's business leaders, in the suburbs. Hooper, like his neighbor financier Henry T. Scott (at whose home President McKinley stayed during his 1901 visit to San Francisco), lived in the city's Pacific Heights neighborhood. Creed, however, lived in Piedmont across the bay, and so did Moffitt, while Phelan lived at his estate in Saratoga. Martin and Phelan both belonged to the Burlingame Country Club.[46]

In addition to his real estate and banking interests, Phelan involved himself with the insurance business, and his fellow directors of the California Pacific Title Insurance Company (formed in 1886) included John S. Drum, Emanuel S. Heller, and Jesse W. Lilienthal, Jr. Drum lived in Hillsborough, belonged to the Burlingame Country Club and the Pacific Union Club, and like Phelan was a Democrat and a Catholic. Drum devoted himself to a San Francisco law practice, then served for twenty years as a bank president, retiring from the American Trust Company in 1929. He also had interests in public utilities, serving as director of Pacific Gas and Electric and the East Bay Water Company, was a director of Columbia Steel, and sat with Martin on the board of the Eastern Oregon Land Company. In 1917, Secretary of the Treasury William Gibbs McAdoo appointed Drum head of war savings programs in California, and President Woodrow Wilson named him to one of the War Finance Corporation's committees in 1918. He also served a term as president of the American Bankers Association (1920–1921).[47]

During the first half of the 1920s, one of San Francisco's most prominent Jewish attorneys, Emanuel Heller, served on the board of the California Pacific Title Insurance company with Phelan. During the 1920s and 1930s, so did the son of Jewish attorney and financier Jesse Lilienthal. Heller put in some thirty years as the attorney for the San Francisco Stock and Bond Exchange. One of the most influential Democratic party activists in California, he was a director of the Union Trust Company, later vice-president of the Wells Fargo Bank and Union Trust Company, president of the Bankers Investment Company, and director of the Market Street Railway and the Spring Valley Water Company. His father-in-law, Isaias W. Hellman (1843–1906) had preceded him as president of Bankers Investment Company, had also been a founder and president of the Farmers and Merchants Bank of Los Angeles, and had moved to San Francisco where he reorganized the Nevada Bank and eventually took over the presidency of the Wells Fargo Nevada National Bank. Lilienthal's six directorships easily qualified him as a member of San Francisco's economic leadership group, but his father had also occupied a prestigious position within the city's business elite before his death in 1919. Besides his presidency of the United Railroads and his position as vice-president of the Anglo-California Trust Company, the elder Lilienthal had served on the boards of no less than eighteen corporations. His cousin, Ernest Reuben Lilienthal, served as president of one of these companies, and by World War I he had made it the largest wholesale liquor firm in the West. Ernest's son-in-law, Milton Esberg, the son of a pioneer cigar manufacturer, was one of the city's nationally prominent businessmen, as was his brother Alfred I. Esberg. The elder Jesse Lilienthal's brother, Philip N., had been one of the founders of the Anglo-California Bank in 1873 and a director of the Union Iron Works.[48] When Philip Lilienthal died in an automobile accident in 1908, he had already become one of California's leading bankers. His memberships in the Union League and the Bohemian Club, like his directorships in the San Francisco Free Library and the Philharmonic Society, gave him many opportunities for informal social contacts with Protestant business leaders such as William H. Crocker.

William H. Crocker, perhaps the most important single figure in the city's business elite during the early twentieth century, had begun his banking career in 1883. Rabbi Max Lilienthal had turned to his friends the Seligmans, New York bankers, for help in placing his sons Jesse and Philip in business, but Charles Crocker organized a new firm for his son William. The Crocker-Woolworth Bank was incorporated in September 1886, just a month before William married Ethel W. Sperry, thereby uniting two of

California's wealthiest and most successful business families. When Charles Crocker died in 1888, William organized and became president of the Crocker Estate Company to manage his father's interests in the Central and Southern Pacific railroads and his real estate investments in San Francisco, Sacramento, and Merced. The following year, he began construction of the Crocker Building at Market and Post streets in the heart of downtown San Francisco. The Crocker Bank moved into the building in 1892, and in mid-1893 Crocker became bank president when R. C. Woolworth died.[49] Crocker's reputation rested on his conviction that a natural harmony existed between corporate growth and community progress. John Drum, president of the American Trust Company, testified:

> No man ever loved San Francisco more than Will Crocker did, and no other one man ever did so much to develop and better it. No one today knows how many worthy business enterprises were launched or "put on their feet" by his financial assistance, but I can tell you the number is legion.[50]

In 1897, Crocker and his brother-in-law, Polish Prince André Poniatowski, put California's first hydroelectric plant into operation when they built the Blue Lakes Powerhouse on the Mokelumne River near Jackson. In 1902, they opened a larger plant, to serve the Crocker-Poniatowski gold mines, as well as parts of the cities of Oakland, San Jose, and San Francisco. They organized the Consolidated Light and Power Company, a distribution firm that absorbed smaller companies in San Mateo, Redwood City, and Palo Alto, and they bought the United Gas and Electric Company, thereby developing the means to serve a market that extended from San Bruno to San Jose. After buying out the prince, who returned with his family to Paris, Crocker sold his utility interests in March 1904 to the group that established the Pacific Gas and Electric Company in October 1905. Crocker also provided capital to start the first cement-producing company on the Pacific Coast. Incorporated in 1905 as the Santa Cruz Portland Cement Company, the firm owned one thousand acres of land and a cement plant in Santa Cruz County, and by the mid-1930s it produced ten thousand barrels per day and owned extensive docking facilities in Portland, Oregon, and in Stockton, Long Beach, and Oakland harbors. George T. Cameron, protégé of William H. Crocker at the Crocker Bank and later president of the Chronicle Publishing Company, became president of the Santa Cruz Portland Cement Company in 1908. In 1906 Crocker arranged for a loan to establish the profitable Goldfield Consolidated Mines in Nevada. The mines produced over $100 million, paid high dividends, and replenished the Crocker Bank's gold deposits during the financial panic of 1907. During the next two years, Crocker began oil investments that led to the organizing of the Universal Oil Company in 1911. With headquarters in the Crocker Building in San Francisco, William Willard Crocker on the board, and Daniel J. Murphy (treasurer of Crocker Bank) as vice-president, the Universal Consolidated owned some 2,000 acres in Kern and Fresno counties, leased another 1,100 acres in Kern and Los Angeles counties, and produced over 1 million barrels per year during the mid-1920s.[51]

With eastern financier Bernard Baruch, William H. Crocker helped finance the Alaska Juneau mine, and he served as treasurer, director, and member of the executive committee of the Bunker Hill and Sullivan Mining and Concentrating Company for forty-six years. This firm mined and smelted silver, lead, and zinc in Kellogg, Idaho, and controlled other mines in Idaho, Washington, and the Yukon. Financial headquarters of the Bunker Hill Company moved to San Francisco shortly after Crocker expanded its capital and came into its management in 1891. Besides his mining activities, Crocker also headed the Crocker-Huffman Land and Water Company that developed agricultural property near Merced, farmed the land and raised livestock, opened the First National Bank of Merced to provide credit facilities for prospective buyers, and built a municipal water system for the city of Merced. In 1920, Crocker sold the irrigation system (470 miles of canals serving 50,000 acres) to the Merced Irrigation District.[52]

Crocker drew on his friendships with leading East Coast business leaders, such as Bernard Baruch, and his associations with fellow directors of corporations, such as the Equitable Trust Company of New York and the Metropolitan Life Insurance Company, when he personally secured millions of dollars worth of loans for the post-earthquake reconstruction of San Francisco in 1906. James Phelan also played a key role in planning and financing the reconstruction process. So did Henry Scott (president of the Mercantile Trust Company, chairman of the board of Pacific Telephone and Telegraph Company, and president of the Burlingame Land and Water Company), John D. McKee (president of the Mercantile National Bank, chairman of the board of the American Trust Company), C. O. G. Miller (president of the Pacific Lighting Corporation and of the Key System Transit Company), and J. B. Levison (president of the Fireman's Fund and three other insurance companies and director of the Alaska Commercial Company). Crocker, however, "stood out especially," according to William F. Humphrey, president of the Tidewater Oil Company for twenty-five years and long-time head of San Francisco Olympic Club. Years later Humphrey maintained that "it would be impossible to overemphasize the importance of the role [Crocker] played in the drama of San Francisco's restoration."

> Not only did he rally the business, financial and industrial leaders of the community—as no other man could—to begin the reconstruction before the ruins were cold, but he, more than any other one man, was responsible for obtaining the tremendous amount of money and credit which this stupendous task required.[53]

Crocker's biographer found a dozen other informants who corroborated Humphrey's testimony.

The disaster of 1906 provoked what Humphrey described as a "wonderful fraternalism" among the leaders of San Francisco business life. "Old rivalries were forgotten; old jealousies disappeared, and even bitter enmities of long standing were wiped out. Everyone was in the same boat, so we forgot all else and pulled as a team."[54] This spirit of business brotherhood found expression in the merger of the four largest business organizations into the Chamber of Commerce in 1911 and in both the Portola Festival of 1909 and the Panama Pacific International Exposition of 1915. The Chamber marked the reestablishment of downtown San Francisco as a business center; the latter two events demonstrated the renascence of the entire city.

Both celebrations received their inspiration and their direction from the few dozen business leaders who formed a social and business network around Phelan and Crocker. One of them, Charles C. Moore, became president of the exposition in 1911. He had previously demonstrated his executive abilities by convincing seven European governments to dispatch warships to San Francisco Bay to dramatize the Portola Festival. Head of his own engineering firm, director of the Anglo-California Trust Company and the Anglo and London Paris National Bank, Moore had served a term as president of the San Francisco Chamber of Commerce (1908–1909) and had been chairman of a citizens committee to eradicate bubonic plague in 1908. Although he belonged to the Union League, the Bohemian Club, and the Pacific Union Club, Moore seems not to have attended the luncheon at the Pacific Union Club in the fall of 1909 when William H. Crocker, Henry Scott, and several others revived retailer and real estate developer Reuben B. Hale's idea for a world's fair in San Francisco. Crocker, first as temporary chairman of the Ways and Means Committee and later as vice-chairman of the Finance Committee and chairman of the board of directors and the Building and Grounds Committee, saw the project through to completion and made an official opening speech on February 20, 1915.[55]

In 1916, Crocker became a member of the Republican Party National Committee, and like his friends Wallace M. Alexander (1869–1939) and Milton Esberg (1875–1939), who served on the national Republican Finance Committee, he played an active role in party politics. Pundits have referred to Crocker, Alexander, Esberg, and Archbishop Edward J. Hanna as "the four musketeers," or, adding Charles H. Kendrick, president of Schlage Lock Company, as "the big five" in San Francisco public life during the 1920s and 1930s.[56] Alexander, like Crocker a Yale graduate, was born in Maui, the son of missionary parents. President of Alexander and Baldwin, a sugar factoring company, Alexander held vice-presidencies in the California and Hawaiian Sugar Refining Company, Hawaiian Commercial and Sugar Company, Matson Navigation Company, and the Honolulu Consolidated Oil Company and served as director of Columbia Steel, the Savings Union Bank and Trust Company, Home Fire Insurance, Gladding McBean, and Pacific Gas and Electric. Alexander worked to develop trade with Japan by helping to found the Institute for Pacific Relations (1908), traveling to Japan with a San Francisco business commission (1920), and serving as the chairman of the Japanese Relations Commission of California. He supported such Pacific economic development throughout the 1920s as president and member of the board of directors of the San Francisco Chamber of Commerce.[57]

Wallace Alexander entered the sugar-producing, shipping, and refining business after graduating from Yale in 1892. Both his father and his mother's family (the Cooks, of Castle and Cook) had been pioneers in Hawaiian sugar plantations during the 1870s and 1880s. Milton Esberg went into his father's wholesale cigar business, Esberg, Bachman, and Company, after graduating from the University of California in 1896. By 1917, he had become vice-president in the General Cigar Company of New York, and during the 1920s and 1930s he served as a director of the Mercantile Trust

Company, Southern California Gas Corporation, Pacific Lighting Corporation, the Southern Pacific Golden Gate Ferries, and others. Like Congregationalist Alexander, who was a trustee, Esberg, who was Jewish, had connections with Stanford University as a member of its national board. Esberg joined both Alexander and Crocker as a member of the Bohemian Club, and when former President William H. Taft visited San Francisco in 1919, it was Esberg and Alexander who greeted him.[58]

When Milton Esberg married the daughter of Ernest Lilienthal in 1901, he established family connections with the president of the Pacific Coast's largest wholesale liquor firm. Esberg's father-in-law also headed the Sierra Iron Company and the Netherlands Farms Company, served as vice-president of the Union Sugar Company, the Alameda Sugar Company, the Alameda Farms Company, and as director of several real estate companies. Lilienthal had himself joined an established San Francisco German-Jewish pioneer merchant family when he married Hannah Isabelle Sloss in 1876. Her father, Louis Sloss, had been one of the original partners in the Alaska Commercial Company, along with Lewis Gerstle. The Sloss and the Gerstle families maintained very close ties and lived together as a kind of extended family, whether in San Francisco on Van Ness Avenue and Washington Street or in San Rafael in adjacent summer houses.[59]

The connections between the Sloss and the Gerstle families helped bring together Ernest Lilienthal and J. B. Levison. Levison (born in 1862) was marine secretary of the Fireman's Fund Insurance Company when he married Alice Gerstle in 1896. The couple lived at 1316 Van Ness Avenue between 1898 and 1901, in a house rented to them by Lilienthal. By the time of the Russo-Japanese War (1904–1905), Levison had moved up to the vice-presidency of Fireman's Fund. The Lilienthal Company had agreed to work as a purchasing agent for the Russian government, and its chartered ships were trying to slip past the Japanese blockade to deliver supplies to Vladivostok. Lilienthal asked Levison to provide the risk insurance on his cargoes, and Levison did so as an independent broker. It was, he later wrote, "a most exciting time for me, to say nothing of the fact that it was my first experience with war risk insurance." Levison eventually became president of Fireman's Fund Insurance, vice-president of the Gerstle Company, and director of the Alaska Commercial Company and was in charge of musical entertainment at the 1915 exposition.[60]

The Levison family lived next door to the Mortimer Fleishhacker family in the Pacific Heights District. Mortimer Fleishhacker became Levison's brother-in-law when he married Bella Gerstle (Alice's sister) in 1904. Mortimer and his brother Herbert were the sons of pioneer Sacramento and San Francisco merchant Aaron Fleishhacker (1820–1898). Mortimer was born in 1866 and Herbert in 1872. The Fleishhacker brothers managed their father's interest in the wholesale paper business before going on to make highly successful investments in electric power between 1896 and 1906, in Oregon as well as California. Herbert became manager of the London, Paris, and American Bank in 1907 and president of the Anglo and London Paris National Bank in 1911. Mortimer Fleishhacker, like his brother a director of more than a dozen diverse corporations, became president of the Anglo-California Trust Company in 1911 and chairman of the board of Anglo and London Paris National Bank in 1932. Mortimer Fleishhacker was a Republican and a University of California regent. Crocker's Finance Committee for the Panama Pacific International Exposition conducted all of its business through Herbert Fleishhacker's Anglo and London Paris National Bank.[61]

To San Francisco business leaders, the exposition constituted an architectural advertisement of the city's renascence after the 1906 catastrophe, as well as a dramatic symbol of its actual role in the California and Pacific Coast economy. "San Francisco," according to a Chamber of Commerce booklet published for the exposition, "bears the same relation to the Pacific Coast that New York does to the nation." "Booster" remarks of this kind typified the speeches and publications of Chamber of Commerce representatives, as well as the pronouncements of the city's mayors, during the thirty years after the earthquake and fire. At the same time, however, the leaders of the San Francisco business community gradually redefined their position in relation to the growing economic importance of Alameda and Contra Costa counties and in response to the rapid advancement of Los Angeles. Between 1900 and 1920, the Los Angeles population grew from 102,000 to 577,000 whereas San Francisco increased from 343,000 to 507,000. The assessed valuation of San Francisco increased from $413 million to $820 million while that of Los Angeles moved from $103 million to $1,276 million. The population growth of Los Angeles and its rising wealth have been called a "reversal of the old, long-established order of things." To some extent, however, this dramatic process of growth represented evidence of the successful policies of San Francisco corporations, for the city's economic leaders contributed both to the economic growth of Los Angeles and to the expansion of other parts of the state.[62]

After 1906, San Francisco's manufacturing establishments decreased in number and in value of product compared with pre-earthquake days. But the city could still lay claim to the title of "financial reservoir of the Pacific Coast." In 1911, San Francisco's bank clearings ($2,427,075) nearly equaled those of Los Angeles, Portland, Seattle, Tacoma, Oakland, and San Diego combined ($2,531,899). "In San Francisco," wrote the editor of the *Chamber of Commerce Journal,* "are made most of the great plans for state development." The city provided headquarters for corporations whose operations constituted "the industrial 'vital functions' of California." The growth of manufacturing in the East Bay, in the words of Contra Costa County entrepreneur H. C. Cutting,

> means as much to San Francisco as though it took place within her own city limits, for financially it is all one. We grow together. An immense development is going to take place here, and San Francisco will always be the main office, the money reservoir where these industries will be financed."[63]

The investments of John D. Spreckels in San Diego offer a vivid illustration of the ways San Francisco entrepreneurs contributed to economic growth outside the Bay Area. One of the sons of Claus Spreckels, John Spreckels first visited San Diego in 1887 and soon secured a franchise to build a wharf and coal bunkers to supply fuel to the Santa Fe Railroad and to local industry. When the real estate boom of the 1880s ended, Spreckels purchased a controlling interest in the Coronado Beach Company, as well as the water, railroad, and ferry companies associated with the development of Hotel Del Coronado and the island. Within five years, he and his brother Adolph had become the sole owners. During the 1890s and the first decade of the new century, Spreckels developed a water supply system for San Diego; bought the entire south side of downtown Broadway Street; built a series of office, hotel, and theater buildings; purchased the majority of the stock of the city's two banks and consolidated them; assumed control over two daily newspapers; and reorganized and expanded the city's streetcar system. Spreckels also bought controlling interest in a tire company, a wallboard factory, and a fertilizer plant, but his most heralded project turned out to be his leadership in building a transcontinental railway line to San Diego. In 1923, not quite four years after the first cars of the San Diego and Arizona Railway pulled into Union Station, Spreckels made a public reply to charges by local critics chagrined by the way the San Francisco businessman had made himself a power in San Diego's economic life. "I was a young man," he said,

> a young American business man, looking for opportunities. I was out to find a big opportunity to do big constructive work on a big scale—and in San Diego I thought I foresaw just such a chance. . . . It is insinuated that because I undertook those basic developments I have set myself up as a sort of special providence or "savior" of San Diego. Nonsense! I made those larger investments to protect the investments I had already made. I am a business man, not a Santa Claus—nor a damn fool. Any man who claims to invest millions for the fun of being looked up to as a little local tin god is either a lunatic or a liar. I, gentlemen, am neither. I simply used plain, ordinary business sense.[64]

The economic projects of John Spreckels in San Diego, like the civic work of his brother Adolph in San Francisco, attracted publicity partly because of the glamour and notoriety associated with the family name. Other, less celebrated, businessmen made similar investments, directed equally powerful corporations, and contributed to San Francisco's economic leadership in analogous ways. Even men who spoke most aggressively about what a 1921 Chamber of Commerce report called "the contest for Pacific Coast Supremacy"[65] between San Francisco and its urban rivals made their decisions about company policy on the basis of what Spreckels called "business sense." Hence, Colbert Coldwell could speak as president of the Chamber of Commerce in 1923 of the need for San Francisco to "capitalize its natural advantages and step up its voltage for the competitive tournament among world cities," while opening a Los Angeles office of his real estate firm Coldwell, Cornwall, and Banker in 1924 and an Oakland office in 1925. Three years later, the firm's Los Angeles profits had grown from $36,802 in 1927 to $90,316 in 1928, while the San Francisco office had registered a decline from $162,275 to $130,234. James Bacigalupi, president of the Bank of Italy, in 1925 urged readers of *San Francisco Business* to alter their perception of San Francisco's economic role, "to think in terms of a metropolitan area, rather than a distinct and isolated political subdivision." Bacigalupi's definition of metropolitanism matched the practice of both the Bank of Italy, then beginning its statewide expansion through branch banking, and Coldwell, Cornwall, and Banker, then beginning its expansion into southern California and the East Bay. According to Bacigalupi, San Francisco's metropolitan area stretched "from the sun-scorched Tehachapi Mountains to the snow-capped peak of Mt. Shasta; from the sentinel Sierras to . . . an awakening Orient."[66] It is tempting to regard such demands for a domestic "Open Door policy" as the rhetorical counterpart to San Francisco business expansion into new territory during the interwar years.[67]

Development of California's transportation network offers a case in point. San Francisco businessmen pushed railroad transportation into the interior and beyond the urban centers during the interwar years. The Ocean Shore Railroad Company connected San Francisco to Santa Cruz, and the Northern Electric Railway served Sacramento valley towns and operated streetcar lines in Chico, Marysville, Yuba City, and Sacramento. Rudolph Spreckels and Benjamin H. Dibblee, both descendants of San Francisco business pioneers and themselves leading figures in the 1920s, sat on the board of directors of the Petaluma and Santa Rosa Railroad. Herbert Fleishhacker served as president of the Central California Traction Company, even after control of the firm shifted in 1928 to the Southern Pacific, the Western Pacific, and the Santa Fe railroads. Originally started in 1905, the company's interurban electric railway carried passengers and freight from Sacramento to Stockton and owned parts of the Sacramento and Stockton waterfronts. San Francisco's role in valley transportation still included river transport connecting San Francisco, Sacramento, and Stockton. The Yosemite Valley Railroad Company, operating between Merced and Yosemite National Park, was a San Francisco company (William H. Crocker served on the board and John Drum was president in the mid-twenties), and so was the Western Pacific Railroad (organized in 1903 with headquarters in San Francisco). The Western Pacific connected Oakland and San Francisco to Salt Lake City and owned terminals in San Francisco (seventeen acres) and Oakland (one hundred acres, including half a mile on the Oakland inner harbor).[68]

The Southern Pacific Company, despite antitrust challenges, maintained its wide-ranging transportation holdings. Besides its national operations and statewide lines, the Southern Pacific controlled electric interurban railways between San Francisco and San Jose and electric trolley cars in San Jose, Santa Clara, and Fresno. By the mid-thirties, the Southern Pacific's Electric Railway Company owned over five hundred miles of track centered at Los Angeles and extending into Los Angeles, San Bernardino, Riverside, and Orange counties.[69]

What the Southern Pacific represented to railroad transportation, the Pacific Greyhound Corporation meant to bus transportation. From its Pine Street headquarters, it operated a bus service connecting the major cities of the West and Southwest. Branch lines served adjoining territory, and the company's 302 buses covered approximately 20 million miles each year by the mid-thirties. Another San Francisco company, Yellow and Checker Cab

Company (Consolidated) operated 260 cabs in Los Angeles in addition to its 315 San Francisco cabs. The Dumbarton Bridge, constructed specifically for motor vehicle traffic, opened in 1927, providing easier auto and truck connections between San Mateo County and southern Alameda County. Two of William H. Crocker's long-time associates, George Cameron and Daniel Murphy, served as directors, and officers met in the company's head-quarters in the Crocker Building.[70]

Agricultural development, like transportation, experienced rapid expansion during the interwar years, and San Francisco firms played a central role. Ernest Lilienthal and Mark L. Gerstle organized the Netherlands Farm Company in 1912 to reclaim some 25,000 acres of Yolo County land on the banks of the Sacramento River. Lilienthal had by that time begun his own hop-growing ranches in the Livermore valley, and he sold the crop on the London market through his Pleasanton Hop Company. Other San Franciscans organized similar corporations to reclaim, develop, and farm tens of thousands of acres in nine California counties. The famous ranch lands of Miller and Lux included over 270,000 acres in Merced, Madera, Fresno, Kern, and Kings counties in California, as well as holdings in Nevada and Oregon. San Francisco was headquarters for the firm, and its directors included the president of the Bank of California, Frank B. Anderson, and Marcus C. Sloss and Allen L. Chickering of Chickering, Thomas, and Gregory, a prestigious city law firm.[71]

Frank Anderson, along with Herbert Fleishhacker and other San Francisco financiers, reorganized the Natomas Company of California in 1914, and Anderson became its president. Two of Marcus Sloss's brothers joined Herbert Fleishhacker and John McKee as officers and members of the board of directors. Besides its 66,000 acres of agricultural land, the Natomas Company operated rock-crushing plants, gold dredgers, and a water company. Both Herbert and Mortimer Fleishhacker sat on the board of California Delta Farms, a San Francisco company with 38,000 acres in the San Joaquin River delta. Joseph DiGiorgio, who controlled some forty companies by 1920, organized the massive DiGiorgio Fruit Corporation in that year. With holdings in California, Georgia, Florida, Washington, and Idaho, the company put itself among the world's largest producers and marketing firms by the middle 1930s. From headquarters near the San Francisco Ferry Building, DiGiorgio operated its fruit production empire, as well as its winery in Delano, its lumber and box company in Klamath Falls, and its Baltimore Fruit Exchange. DiGiorgio also owned one-half of the stock in the New York Fruit Auction.[72]

San Franciscans also conducted large-scale Bay Area residential property development through firms such as the Lagunitas Development Company operating in Marin County and the Baywood Park Company's activities in San Mateo County. The Parr-Richmond Terminal Corporation of San Francisco owned ninety-one acres of waterfront and industrial property in Richmond, participated in a joint venture with the city of Richmond to develop terminal facilities, and operated that city's wharf and warehouses and its sugar-docking facilities. The Pacific Dock and Terminal Company bought and subdivided over seventy acres along the waterfront in Long Beach during that city's harbor improvement during the 1920s. San Franciscans also played an active part in the development of tourist and recreational sites during the interwar years, particularly on the Monterey Peninsula, where William H. and William W. Crocker, Herbert Fleishhacker, Kenneth R. Kingsbury, William Humphrey, and Henry Scott created the Del Monte Hotel and Del Monte Forest Lodge.[73]

San Francisco's role in the oil and hydroelectric industries of the 1920s and 1930s provided the city's business leaders with another avenue of participation in California's economic development during the interwar years. San Francisco entrepreneurs Joseph D. Grant and Wallace Alexander played leading roles in the activities of the General Petroleum Corporation, the Honolulu Oil Company, Associated Oil Company, and the Standard Oil Company of California. John Barneson, who was one of the directors of the 1915 exposition, headed the General Petroleum Corporation, organized in 1916 and acquired by Standard Oil of New York in 1928. Joseph Grant, who first met Barneson at a San Francisco club and became a fellow yachtsman at the San Francisco Yacht Club, became first vice-president and a member of the executive committee. He later described the company's scope of operations:

> The corporation held and developed acreage in practically all the principal oil fields of California. An immense refining plant had been established at Vernon, near Los Angeles, and a remarkable pipeline (owned by a subsidiary) extended from the Central Midway district across Tejon Pass and down to that company's refinery and to tidewater—a distance of 184 miles. Another pipeline led from Lebec to Mojave, where the company supplied oil for the fuel requirements of the Santa Fe Railway—a pioneer in the burning of oil in locomotives. . . .
>
> At Los Angeles Harbor a terminal was maintained by us which kept busy a fleet of fourteen tankers, with a carrying capacity of 1,000,000 barrels! Ships transported our oil to many countries—to Argentina, to Japan, and to far Cathay. . . . During the expansion of markets, the company entered intensively into the retail sale of its products. Our distributing system covered the Pacific Coast from Alaska to Lower California, nearly 2,000 independent dealers were selling "General" products.[74]

In 1925, the Associated Oil Company owned 42,190 acres in California, Texas, and Alaska, refineries at Avon and in Los Angeles, and pipelines from oil fields to port facilities, plus railway tank cars and sea-going tankers. Associated Oil showed net profits of over $14 million in 1924. Standard Oil of California earned a net profit of over $18 million ten years later during the Depression year of 1934. From his office in the Standard Oil Building at 225 Bush Street, company president Kenneth Kingsbury supervised the corporation's nearly 500,000 acres of oil-producing land in the United States, as well as over 1 million overseas acres held under contract. Standard's refineries and pipelines in the Bay Area and in southern California, like its sales and distributing subsidiaries, all took their direction from headquarters in San Francisco.[75]

Joseph Grant later explained how he happened to involve himself in hydroelectric power development in 1911.

Why? I had money to invest. A friend had told me of a dam site on the Upper Klamath River adapted to the production of power on an immense scale. I looked at that site. What I saw took my breath away: a vision splendid of tremendous possibilities. Perhaps I had a touch of mountain fever. Anyway, I persuaded some friends of mine to join me; we got control of the power site; we went joyously to work.

The new company, named the California-Oregon Power Company, eventually operated nine generating plants and supplied light and power to forty-four cities and towns in southern Oregon and northern California. Milton Esberg sat on the board of directors along with his neighbor John McKee, who became president of the firm. In 1926 Grant and the board sold "Copco" to the Standard Gas and Electric Company of Chicago.[76]

Grant was also a director, along with Charles Moore, president of the 1915 exposition, of the Coast Counties Gas and Electric Company, which sold electric power and natural gas in Santa Cruz, Santa Clara, Monterey, and San Benito counties. Ferdinand Reis, Jr., head of San Francisco's Pacific States Savings and Loan Company, also served as president of Midway Gas Company, operating a natural gas pipeline from Kern County gas fields to Los Angeles, and as a director of the Northern California Power Company. Northern California Power supplied electricity to Shasta, Tehama, Glenn, Butte, and Colusa counties, as well as water and natural gas to Redding, Willows, and Red Bluff.[77]

San Francisco bankers Benjamin Dibblee, Mortimer and Herbert Fleishhacker, Frank Anderson, William H. Crocker, and John McKee helped shape hydroelectric power development by their work as directors of California's most powerful utility corporations: Northwestern Electric Company (founded in 1911), Great Western Power Company (1906), Western Power Corporation (1915), and Pacific Gas and Electric Company (1905). By 1915, Pacific Gas and Electric's operations served over half the state's population, in two hundred communities, including eight of the eleven largest cities. During the mid-1920s, Wigginton Creed occupied the presidency, and Wallace Alexander and A. B. C. Dohrmann joined the board of directors. By 1935, Pacific Gas and Electric's territory encompassed 46 counties and 656 cities, including San Francisco, Oakland, Berkeley, Sacramento, Stockton, San Jose, Fresno, and Bakersfield.[78]

In 1908, C. O. G. Miller (born in San Francisco in 1865) organized the Pacific Lighting Corporation as a holding company to own the stock of the Los Angeles Gas and Electric Corporation. Educated at the University of California, Miller had taken over as treasurer of Pacific Lighting Company in 1886, and he assumed the presidency in 1898. By 1935, with Miller still at the helm, and Wallace Alexander, William W. Crocker, and Milton Esberg on the board of directors, the corporation had made itself the southern California utility giant. Its Los Angeles Gas and Electric Corporation supplied gas and electric power to Los Angeles and sixteen nearby communities. Pacific Lighting Corporation also owned all of the common stock of the Southern Counties Gas Company and over 99 percent of the common stock of the Southern California Gas Company.[79]

Control over communications throughout the Pacific Coast region likewise gravitated to San Francisco business leaders. By 1915, the Pacific Telephone and Telegraph Company (1906) had come under the direction of Henry Scott (chairman of the board). William H. Crocker, Walter Martin, and H. D. Pillsbury all served on the board of directors. When Scott stepped down as chairman, Pillsbury took his place, and by 1935 Allen Chickering and Charles K. McIntosh (who had succeeded Frank Anderson as president of the Bank of California) sat on the executive committee. Pacific Telephone's territory included California, Oregon, Washington, Nevada, and northern Idaho, and by 1935 the headquarters staff of this communications empire had moved into the company's new building on New Montgomery Street. A few doors away, the Telephone Investment Corporation conducted its monopoly over telephone service in the Philippine islands.[80]

The sugar industry continued to serve as an area for investment by San Francisco business leaders during the interwar years. John A. Buck and his son John A., Jr., and John McKee, as well as William Matson and John L. Koster, involved themselves as officers and directors of the Hutchinson and the Honolulu Plantation companies. Wallace Alexander and Frank Anderson were both directors of the Hawaiian Commercial and Sugar Company and the California and Hawaiian Sugar Refining Companies (its headquarters moved to Honolulu in 1926 after a reorganization). Mortimer Fleishhacker served as one of the two trustees for the Calamba Sugar Estate on Luzon in the Philippines, and Ernest Lilienthal, C. H. Crocker, and B. P. Lilienthal directed the Alameda Sugar Company, which manufactured beet sugar grown in Sutter County. They also had interests in Union Sugar Company's twelve thousand acres of beets and its factory in Santa Barbara County.[81]

By the mid-1920s, California produced nearly 30 percent of the canned goods and preserved foods of the United States. The California Fruit Canners' Association, organized in 1899, owned and operated thirty factories capable of an output of 5 million cases in 1915. The company changed its name to the California Packing Corporation the following year. By 1935 it had absorbed three other canneries, as well as the venerable Alaska Packers Association. Leonard E. Wood, former governor-general of the Philippines and friend and adviser to Republican presidents, had become president of the firm, and Frank Anderson served as a member of the Finance Committee. Seventy-six plants, including those in the Hawaiian and Philippine islands, thirteen canneries in Alaska, five California ranches, sea-going ships, a shipyard, and a terminal at Alameda all operated under the company's flag. The firm's brand names—particularly Del Monte and Sun-Kist—had become household words by the mid-thirties. Hunt Brothers Packing Company (formed in 1896) included Wallace Alexander on its board for a time. The corporation expanded from four to eight canneries during the twenty years between 1915 and 1935, and its operations expanded to include warehouses, cold-storage facilities, and canneries in the state of Washington.[82]

San Francisco also maintained its role in meat packing, viticulture and brewing, flour milling, salt manufacturing, and the supply of cold-storage facilities for perishable commodities. John Hooper's brother, C. J. Hooper, presided over the Western Meat Company, which by 1925 operated branches in San Francisco, Sacramento, Fresno, Oakland, San Jose, and Stockton. C. O. G. Miller served as first vice-president of the California Wine Association prior to Prohibition, and Mortimer Fleishhacker and H. D. Pillsbury served as directors during the dry years, helping to supervise the company's liquidation. By the mid-1930s, the Acme Brewing Company had revived its San Francisco brewery and started a Los Angeles plant. Banker Herbert Fleishhacker sat on the board of the Rainier Brewing Company in 1935; the company operated branches in Los Angeles, Portland, and Seattle in addition to its San Francisco plant at 1550 Bryant Street. Sperry Flour Company and Albers Brothers Milling Company owned between them twenty-six mills in California, Oregon, and Washington during the mid-1920s. The Golden State Company, successor to a dairy products firm organized in 1905, operated forty manufacturing and distribution plants in California by 1935. The Langendorf United Bakeries (1928) maintained locations in San Francisco, Berkeley, San Jose, Los Angeles, and Seattle by 1935. Leslie-California Salt Company controlled salt lands on San Francisco Bay and in San Bernardino County. The National Ice and Cold Storage Company of California (1912)˙ manufactured ice at forty-three California plants and operated fourteen cold-storage warehouses in eleven California cities.[83]

San Francisco's lumber companies flourished during the interwar years and expanded to keep pace with the increased demand. The Union Lumber Company (1891) owned 60,000 acres of redwood near Fort Bragg, as well as railroad and shipping facilities to transport its products. Two other firms owned over 68,000 acres in Siskiyou and Del Norte counties, besides the town site of Weed, sawmills, railroad equipment, and steamers. The Pacific Lumber Company (1905) held 42,000 acres of redwood in Humboldt County, two sawmills in Scotia, and an eastern sales agency. Other San Francisco companies owned extensive timber lands in Shasta, Mariposa, and Tuolumne counties in California and Coos, Douglas, and Curry counties in Oregon.[84]

Paper manufacturing comprised an important sector in San Francisco business; leadership in the industry's expansion during the early twentieth century came from a closely associated group of the city's leading Jewish businessmen. Louis Bloch had become president of the Crown Willamette Paper Company (1914) by 1925, and both Herbert and Mortimer Fleishhacker served on the board. The company owned plants in Washington, Oregon, and California. Isadore Zellerbach, son of a pioneer paper merchant and president of the Zellerbach Corporation, was a good friend of Herbert Fleishhacker. In 1928, the Zellerbach Corporation and Crown Willamette merged to become the Crown Zellerbach Corporation. Fleishhacker continued as a director, and Bloch became chairman of the board. The company dominated its industry in the West by the mid-thirties, with timber lands in the United States and Canada; paper and pulp mills in California, Oregon, British Columbia, and New York; wholesale divisions in California, Oregon, Washington, Nevada, and Utah; and sales offices in fifteen cities throughout the United States. J. D. Zellerbach served as president of the Fibreboard Products Corporation, manufacturer of boxes, cartons, wallboard, and other paper products, and J. D. and Isadore Zellerbach also served as officers and directors of the Olympic Forest Products Company, the Grays Harbor Pulp and Paper Company, and the Rainer Pulp and Paper Company.[85]

As California's population increased after World War I, San Francisco retailers expanded throughout the state. The Owl Drug Company quadrupled the number of its stores between 1915 and 1925 and expanded to California, Oregon, Washington, Colorado, and Utah, as well as Chicago, Milwaukee, and St. Paul. A. B. C. Dohrmann and Frederick W. Dohrmann, Jr., expanded the Dohrmann Commercial Company's (1904) crockery, glass, chinaware, and cutlery business (originally founded as the Nathan-Dohrmann Company in 1886) to Oakland, San Jose, Stockton, Fresno, Sacramento, Los Angeles, San Diego, and Portland. B. F. Schlesinger and Sons operated department stores in Oakland, Portland, and Tacoma, while the Hale Brothers owned five department stores in northern California. I. Magnin and Company's main store served downtown San Francisco shoppers, but the firm also built branches in wealthy areas throughout the state. Sherman, Clay, and Company's (1892) wholesale and retail music and radio stores served northern and southern California, Reno, Portland, Tacoma, Spokane, and Seattle. Foster and Kleiser Company, an outdoor advertising company with headquarters in San Francisco, maintained billboards in 550 cities and towns in California, Oregon, Washington, and Arizona.[86]

As San Francisco business leaders gained experience in conducting operations throughout the Bay Area, California, and the Pacific region, they gradually came to see the city as the headquarters of a regional economy whose health required attention to an "international viewpoint." By the early 1930s, worried by the onset of the Great Depression, the officers and directors of firms in San Francisco, Alameda, Contra Costa, and San Mateo counties put aside the rhetoric of competition that had flourished during pre–World War I years and the early twenties. In its place came a concept of metropolitan cooperation that provided a better match to the actual state of affairs and defined San Francisco as the "Hub City" for an integrated economic region. Now, following a decade of discussion and debate about various proposals for metropolitan cooperation (a particularly noteworthy attempt came with Frederick Dohrmann's Regional Plan Association), business leaders declared "the area to be one economic unit." The Chambers of Commerce of San Francisco, Oakland, and San Mateo spearheaded a drive "to foster the industrial development of the whole area as a recognized industrial and commercial unity." San Francisco would occupy a special position:

> Characteristic of any regional industrial development is a centering of executive headquarters of manufacturing corporations, banks, and financial houses, transportation companies, and privately operated public utilities in one city in the region. From that city—in our case San Francisco—radiate the wires of central executive management and direction and of financial supply that greatly help to bind the whole area together.[87]

By the beginning of the 1930s, when the San Francisco Chamber of Commerce published reports designed to lure investors away from Los Angeles, Portland, and Seattle, they dramatized the advantages of the Bay

Area rather than of San Francisco. San Francisco businessmen themselves led the way toward a decentralized industrial economy in the region. When Joseph Grant and other investors ("for the most part," he said, they were "descendants of California pioneers") organized the Columbia Steel Corporation in 1908, they chose a Contra Costa County site

> because of its strategic position on the deep waters of upper San Francisco Bay, because it is reached by transcontinental railroad lines—and because it was believed that labor conditions there would be less disturbed than in San Francisco.[88]

Caterpillar Tractor Company (1925) operated plants at San Leandro, Stockton, and Peoria, Illinois, and eventually moved its executive offices to Peoria as well. Western Pipe and Steel Company (1910) placed its manufacturing plants in Fresno, Taft, Vernon, South San Francisco, and Phoenix. The Great Western Electro-Chemical Company (Mark Gerstle, vice-president, and Mortimer Fleishhacker, chairman of the board) produced its chemicals at Pittsburg. Atholl McBean, active in the Chamber of Commerce as president and director, was president of Gladding, McBean, and Company (Wallace Alexander and William W. Crocker served on the board). Gladding, McBean, and Company manufactured terra-cotta, brick, tile, and other clay products at eleven California, Oregon, and Washington sites, none of them in San Francisco where its headquarters were located. (McBean served on numerous boards, including Crocker Bank, Standard Oil, Pacific Telephone, and Fireman's Fund.) General Paint Corporation had half a dozen plants from Tulsa to Seattle, including one in San Francisco. Consolidated Chemical Industries operated plants in Houston, Fort Worth, Baton Rouge, Boston, and Buenos Aires, besides its factory in San Francisco.[89]

By the end of the 1930s, Alameda and Contra Costa counties had outdistanced San Francisco in the value of their manufactured products ($596,749,000 to $313,253,000). Likewise, the value of trade to other San Francisco Bay ports ranked higher than that loaded and unloaded on the San Francisco docks. The tonnage and value of trade in San Francisco Bay ports, however, easily surpassed that of Los Angeles, and the Bay Area could maintain its claim to be the third leading American port after New York and Philadelphia. Measured in dollar terms, San Francisco's livelihood still depended heavily on its traditional role as a goods handler. In 1939 the city's manufacturers produced goods valued at $313,253,000, its retailers sold $383,554,000 worth of products, and its service sector took in receipts of $61,893,000. The sales of wholesale firms, however, amounted to $1,377,614,000.[90]

Despite its relative decline as a manufacturing center, San Francisco unquestionably deserved the title "Wall Street of the West," a term applied by the *San Francisco Call and Post* in 1926 when it devoted a special section to "The Magic City of Western Finance." The city's bank clearings of $7,913,846,281 put it in fifth place in the nation in 1937, following New York, Philadelphia, Chicago, and Boston. The Federal Reserve Bank of San Francisco was headquarters of the Twelfth Federal Reserve District, the Pacific Coast Stock Exchange operated on Pine Street, and the city was the insurance center of the West as well. In 1934, San Francisco had seventeen state banks with 171 branches compared with Los Angeles's sixteen state banks and 56 branches and Oakland's two state banks and 2 branches. San Francisco's state banks had 40 percent of California's total paid-up capital bank stock, 15 percent of bank surplus, and 51 percent of its undivided profits.[91]

San Francisco's position in the regional economy made it, like Los Angeles to the south and Seattle to the north, vulnerable to the vicissitudes of the Great Depression. However, the Depression did as much to dramatize the power of the San Francisco business elite as it did to demonstrate the shortcomings of the economic order. The several dozen top members of the San Francisco business community met the challenges posed by the Depression with the same combination of civic nationalism and noblesse oblige they had displayed in the aftermath of the 1906 earthquake and fire and in the organization of the Panama Pacific International Exposition. United by their friendships and social affiliations, often linked by family ties, and frequently the sons of pioneers, they also prided themselves on their contributions to San Francisco's economic development and the city's role in the economic progress of California. When some one thousand demonstrators marched under the banner of the Communist party to the city hall to protest against unemployment in the first week of March 1930, businessman-mayor James Rolph, Jr., upstaged their leaders and turned the protest parade into a rally for future progress. George Hearst, Richard Tobin, Marshall Hale, Alfred Esberg, Harold Zellerbach, and Mortimer Fleishhacker demonstrated their dedication to the future by serving on the advisory board of Mayor Rolph's Citizens' Committee to Stimulate Employment for San Franciscans.

The directors and officers of the San Francisco Community Chest likewise consisted of the leaders of the city's business institutions, with William H. Crocker serving as president and Wallace Alexander and Mortimer Fleishhacker as vice-presidents. In the early spring of 1932, with the nation in the grip of the worst depression in American history, a small group of business leaders demonstrated their trust in the city and their conviction that San Francisco would enhance its role as the hub of a thriving Bay Area economy: George T. Cameron, A. P. Giannini, Leland W. Cutler, Herbert Fleishhacker, and two lesser-known associates began their work as the Financial Advisory Committee of the San Francisco–Oakland Bay Bridge project.[92]

Chapter 3

Life and Work

> The Slot was an iron crack that ran along the center of Market Street, and from the Slot arose the burr of the ceaseless, endless cable that was hitched at will to the cars it dragged up and down. In truth, there were two Slots, but in the quick grammar of the West time was saved by calling them and much more that they stood for, "The Slot." North of the Slot were the theatres, hotels, and shopping district, the banks and the staid, respectable business houses. South of the Slot were the factories, slums, laundries, machineshops, boiler works, and the abodes of the working class.

So wrote Jack London a short time after the earthquake and fire storm that leveled both sides of the Slot. London added, rather unnecessarily, that "the Slot was the metaphor that expressed the class cleavage of Society."[1]

London's description etches a division sharper than it was in fact. Nonetheless, the neighborhoods of the city were indeed differentiated by both class and ethnicity. Throughout the latter half of the nineteenth century and the early twentieth century, the lives of many San Franciscans shaped themselves along the two dimensions of work and residence. The concepts of work, family, and neighborhood were closely related for large numbers of San Franciscans, and separation of these concepts for the purposes of analysis must be accompanied always by the realization that the complex whole involved patterns of interaction that made it more than just the sum of the parts.

WORK

The nature and location of work in San Francisco from the mid-1860s through the early 1930s show a high degree of consistency despite the 388 percent increase in the size of the work force and despite the virtually complete destruction of the built environment midway through the period in 1906. Table 3 summarizes major divisions of the work force over time and illustrates long-term patterns of change. During the six decades, the professional sector and the trade and transportation sector slowly increased their proportions of the work force, and both the manufacturing and the service sectors slowly decreased. These changes must be clearly understood as changes in *proportions*. The *number* of workers in all sectors increased, albeit more rapidly in some than in others.

In 1890, San Francisco ranked eighth in the nation in total size. Of the fifteen largest cities, only Washington had a larger proportion of its work force in the professional sector. Only two cities had a smaller proportion of their work forces in manufacturing—New Orleans and Washington. Each of the other twelve cities had more than 35 percent of its work force in manufacturing, ranging from 35.3 percent for Boston to 47 percent for Philadelphia. No other city had a more even balance than San Francisco among the three largest economic sectors of domestic and personal service, trade and transportation, and manufacturing and mechanical industries.[2]

San Francisco's position both as chief entrepôt for the Pacific Coast and as the center for a coasting trade extending from Panama to Alaska explains why trade and transportation held such a large proportion of the city's work force. Its position as financial and corporate capital of the West explains

TABLE 3

Major Divisions of the Work Force, 1870–1930

Year	Professional Services (%)	Domestic and Personal Services (%)	Trade and Transportation (%)	Manufacturing and Mechanical Industries (%)	Total Work Force
1870		40.6	25.7	32.2	68,352
1880		33.5	28.8	35.8	104,650
1890	5.7	30.6	28.2	33.2	147,269
1900	7.0	26.2	33.7	31.6	163,858
1910	6.2	21.0	39.2	31.8	223,713
1920	7.5	19.2	40.6	30.9	265,666
1930	8.3	18.3	45.2	27.1	333,573

SOURCES: Table 66, "Occupations: Fifty Cities," U.S. Census Office, Department of the Interior, *Compendium of the Ninth Census* (Washington, D.C., 1872), pp. 618–619; Table 36, "Persons in Selected Occupations in Fifty Principal Cities," U.S. Census Office, Department of the Interior, *Tenth Census of the United States: 1880*, 22 vols. (Washington, D.C., 1883), 1:902; Table 117, "Total Persons 10 Years of Age and over Engaged in Gainful Occupations and in Each Class of Occupations, Classified by Sex, for Cities Having 50,000 Inhabitants or More: 1890," U.S. Census Office, Department of the Interior, *Eleventh Census of the United States: 1890*, 15 vols. (Washington, D.C., 1892), vol. 1, pt. 2, pp. 628–629; Table 43, "Total Males and Females 10 Years of Age and over Engaged in Selected Groups of Occupations, Classified by General Nativity, Color, Conjugal Conditions, Months Unemployed, Age Periods, and Parentage, for Cities Having 50,000 Inhabitants or More: 1900," U.S. Census Office, Department of the Interior, *Twelfth Census of the United States: 1900*, 37 vols. (Washington, D.C., 1902–1904), 20:720–724; Table 3, "Total Persons 10 Years of Age and over Engaged in Each Specified Occupation, Classified by Sex, for Cities of 100,000 Inhabitants or More: 1910," U.S. Bureau of the Census, Department of Commerce and Labor, *Thirteenth Census of the United States: 1910*, 11 vols. (Washington, D.C., 1914), 4:200–201; Table 2, "Total Males and Females 10 Years of Age and over Engaged in Each Selected Occupation, Classified by Color or Race, Nativity, and Parentage, and Age Periods, for Cities of 100,000 Inhabitants or More: 1920," U.S. Bureau of the Census, Department of Commerce, *Fourteenth Census of the United States: 1920*, 11 vols. (Washington, D.C., 1922–1923), 4:1226–1230; Table 3, "Gainful Workers 10 Years Old and over, by General Divisions of Occupations," U.S. Bureau of the Census, Department of Commerce, *Fifteenth Census of the United States: 1930*, 6 vols. (Washington, D.C., 1932–1933), 4:173.

TABLE 4
Major Types of Manufacturing, 1900

Description	No. of Establishments	No. of Wage Earners	Value Added (in $ millions)	Capitalization (in $ millions)
Processing of agricultural products and preparation of food	433	6,174	10.1	17.1
Foundry, forge, machine shop, and sheet-metal products	179	4,660	5.7	7.6
Printing, publishing, bookbinding, and lithographing	250	2,765	2.7	3.5
Construction and wooden ship building	614	3,442	4.5	2.3
Factory-made clothing, shirts, and furnishings	181	4,631	3.1	2.2
Factory-made boots and shoes	23	855	0.7	1.2
Tobacco products	105	977	0.8	0.5
All others	2,217	18,218	25.3	45.5
All others as a percentage of the total	55.4	43.4	47.2	56.8

SOURCE: Table 8, "Manufactures in Cities by Specified Industries: 1900," U.S. Census Office, Department of the Interior, *Twelfth Census of the United States: 1900*, 37 vols. (Washington, D.C.: U.S. Government Printing Office, 1902–1904), vol. 8, pt. 2, pp. 52–57.

other unique features of the city's occupational structure. In 1890, San Francisco had more lawyers than cities half again its size and more proportionately than Boston or New York. In 1910, clerical jobs claimed one of every ten San Franciscans with an occupation. These patterns persisted throughout the 1920s. There was one banker or broker for every ninety-one employed males in 1930, and one-sixth of all employed San Franciscans filled clerical positions that year.[3]

San Francisco never became a major manufacturing center on the order of Pittsburgh or Detroit, either in terms of dominating the national production of one or more items or in terms of the manufacturing sector dominating the economy of the city. Nonetheless, from the 1860s to the 1930s, a substantial part of the work force engaged in manufacturing. Table 4 summarizes data for the largest components of the manufacturing sector in 1900.[4]

Just as the city's economy was diversified, so too were its people ethnically heterogeneous. Table 5 summarizes census data on race, nativity, and origin for 1870, 1900, and 1930. Throughout this period, those of foreign parentage constituted well over half the city's population, and at times more than 70 percent. The Irish arrived among the first during the gold rush and remained numerically dominant throughout the nineteenth century. Germans, including Protestants, Catholics, and Jews, stood next in numbers throughout the nineteenth and early twentieth centuries. Scandinavians

TABLE 5

Race, Nativity, and Origin of the Population of San Francisco, 1870, 1900, and 1930 (percentages)

Population	1870	1900	1930[a]
White, born in United States[b]	49.7	64.5	69.6
Parents born in United States[b]	19.9	24.4	37.1
Parents foreign-born[b]	29.8	40.1	32.5
White, foreign-born[b]	41.5	30.4	24.2
Chinese and Japanese	8.0	4.6	2.6
Black	0.9	0.5	0.6
Origin of whites of foreign stock[c]			
Ireland	35.1	27.5	16.5
Germany	18.5	22.9	15.4
England, Scotland, Wales, English			
Canada	12.8	10.1	16.0
Sweden, Norway, Denmark	2.4	5.9	8.5
Italy	2.2	6.2	16.1
All others	29.0	27.4	27.5

SOURCES: Table 5, "General Nativity and Foreign Parentage," U.S. Census Office, Department of the Interior, *Ninth Census of the United States: 1870*, 3 vols. (Washington, D.C., 1872), 1:304; Table 8, "Nativities of the Population of Principal Cities," ibid., pp. 386–391; Table 57, "Aggregate, White, and Colored Population, Distributed According to Native or Foreign Parentage, for Cities Having 25,000 Inhabitants or More: 1900," U.S. Census Office, Department of the Interior, *Twelfth Census of the United States: 1900*, 37 vols. (Washington, D.C., 1902–1904), vol. 1, pt. 1, p. 868; Table 59, "Total Persons Having Both Parents Born in Specified Countries, or of Mixed Foreign Parentage, for Cities Having 25,000 Inhabitants or More: 1900," ibid., pp. 876–877; Table 15, "Composition of the Population, for Cities of 10,000 or More: 1930," *Fifteenth Census of the United States: 1930*, 6 vols. (Washington, D.C., 1932–1933), vol. 3, pt. 1, p. 261; Table 17, "Indians, Chinese, and Japanese, 1910 to 1930, and Mexicans, 1930, for Counties and for Cities of 25,000 or More," ibid., p. 266; Table 19, "Native White of Foreign Parentage or Mixed Parentage, by Country of Birth of Parents, for Counties and for Cities of 10,000 or More: 1930," ibid., p. 272.

[a]The 1930 census also includes 1.2 percent Mexican (not identified as to nativity) and 1.8 percent unidentified.

[b]The 1870 data are projected from the total population, less Chinese, Japanese, and black.

[c]The 1870 data are based on all foreign-born; the 1900 and 1930 data are based on all whites of foreign parentage.

and Italians were comparative latecomers, arriving in significant numbers only late in the nineteenth century. Most San Franciscans were white, especially after the 1890s when the Chinese population of the city declined by about half.

Many occupations were ethnically distinctive. Table 6 summarizes data for 1900. Although some occupations were disproportionately of one group, none was totally restricted, and only a few stand out as having great disproportion. Ethnic patterns within occupations usually represent tendencies rather than majorities. Thus, the Irish were found in disproportionate numbers in the building trades (including 54 percent of plasterers, 44 percent of roofers, 43 percent of masons, and 33 percent of plumbers), the metal trades (40 percent of blacksmiths, 38 percent of iron and steel workers), various transportation-related jobs (including 36 percent of teamsters), and day laborers (43 percent). Thirty percent of all employed women were Irish, including 30 percent of female teachers, a third of all female merchants, 40 percent of all female laborers, 37 percent of female servants, and 37 percent of female laundry workers. Germans were more likely than the Irish to be merchants, shopkeepers, or artisans. Half the city's cabinet-makers were German, and Germans made up 40 to 50 percent of watch-

TABLE 6

Composition of the Work Force, by Occupational Categories and Parents' Place of Birth, 1900

Occupational Groups	United States	Great Britain	Germany	Ireland	Sweden, Norway, Denmark	Italy	China[a]	All Others
					Parents' Place of Birth			
Professions	36.3%	11.0%	14.1%	15.6%	1.9%	1.4%	2.6%	17.0%
Bankers and brokers	29.9	10.2	26.4	15.1	2.0	1.3	1.7	13.4
Agents, salespeople, clerks, accountants, bookkeepers, etc.	29.7	9.6	20.0	18.9	2.0	1.7	2.5	15.6
Messengers and errand runners	20.3	7.8	18.2	21.8	4.1	2.7	8.5	16.7
Merchants and dealers	13.1	5.9	31.2	12.1	1.7	1.2	20.6	14.2
Tradespeople (bakers, barbers, butchers, cabinetmakers, coopers, harnessmakers, etc.)	17.4	6.9	26.5	20.1	3.2	3.0	2.7	20.1
Boardinghouse, saloon, restaurant, livery stable operators and employees	17.2	6.2	24.1	27.6	3.9	3.3	0.8	17.0
Building trades	23.3	13.4	16.3	23.7	5.4	2.0	0.5	15.3
Metal trades	16.1	13.5	15.0	31.0	4.5	2.5	1.0	15.5
Miscellaneous blue collar (railway, draymen, etc.)	24.0	8.5	13.0	34.1	3.8	3.4	0.9	12.3
Sailors and boatmen	12.0	8.3	11.5	8.3	38.2	0.6	0.2	20.9
Fishermen, hucksters, bootblacks	5.6	3.1	8.0	8.4	4.3	40.3	13.7	16.6
Laborers	13.4	6.0	11.1	39.9	5.9	6.4	5.2	12.2
Servants, waiters, housekeepers, janitors	11.2	4.9	14.4	21.7	6.5	1.8	20.8	18.7
Garment and textile workers	14.2	4.8	7.9	22.3	1.9	3.8	30.6	14.7
Laundry workers	6.3	1.9	4.1	13.2	1.9	1.0	52.4	19.4
Cigarmakers	4.2	1.2	11.2	3.5	0.7	2.5	68.3	8.4
All employed workers	20.2	9.6	17.4	21.3	5.0	3.6	7.6	15.3

SOURCE: Table 43, "Total Males and Females 10 Years of Age and over Engaged in Selected Groups of Occupations, Classified by General Nativity, Color, Conjugal Condition, Months Unemployed, Age Periods, and Parentage, for Cities Having 50,000 Inhabitants or More: 1900," U.S. Census Office, Department of the Interior, *Twelfth Census of the United States: 1900*, 37 vols. (Washington, D.C.: U.S. Government Printing Office, 1902–1904), 20:720–724.

[a]Estimated by deducting the number of blacks from the total category "Colored."

makers and clockmakers and repairers, bakers, and butchers. Eighty percent of all workers in beer brewing were German. German women were far less prominent in the work force than were Irish women; only 15 percent of the female work force were German, and they were concentrated in mercantile and other white-collar occupations.[5]

NEIGHBORHOODS

San Francisco's residential areas differed from one another in ethnicity, sex, marital status, occupations, and income. Seven distinct neighborhoods may be discerned in San Francisco from the mid-1870s through World War I:

1. South of Market: an area with many single men, often young, often in jobs requiring few skills, often living in boardinghouses; but also including families, especially before 1906, usually tenants, with family heads typically in unskilled or semiskilled occupations
2. Mission District: an area of family units and home ownership, with family heads often skilled workers or small-scale entrepreneurs
3. Western Addition and nearby areas: unquestionably middle-class, often upper middle-class, based on family units and home ownership, with family heads often merchants or professionals
4. Nob Hill–Pacific Heights: distinctly upper-class
5. Chinatown: Chinese, with many single males, poorly paid, segregrated both residentially and occupationally, an area in many ways virtually autonomous
6. North Beach: predominantly Italian after about 1900, family-oriented but with many young single males; largely working-class, but with a significant number of Italian businessmen and professionals
7. Downtown: including waterfront workers, clerical workers, merchants, and professionals living in apartments and hotels; also a vice district

By the mid-1880s, and in some cases ten years earlier, the basic characteristics of each of these areas had become clear. Throughout the 1890s and early twentieth century, few changes occurred in these patterns; indeed, some neighborhoods became more homogeneous in the early twentieth century. After 1900, new neighborhoods developed in the Sunset and Richmond districts as families followed the streetcar lines into what had shortly before been sand dunes along either side of Golden Gate Park. Map 1 indicates the approximate boundaries of these major geographic areas.

South of Market. In 1900, nearly one San Franciscan in five lived South of Market, in the area between Market and Townsend, from the waterfront to Eleventh Street, the most densely populated part of the city except for Chinatown. Warehouses stood near the piers and along Townsend Street, interspersed with considerable manufacturing. Howard Street between Main and First was the center of a number of foundries and machine shops. Breweries, boot and shoe factories, furniture factories, paint and varnish plants, packing box makers, and the like lined the streets south of Market. The area closest to the waterfront contained the homes of many sailors and waterfront workers, as well as some workers in the factories and plants of

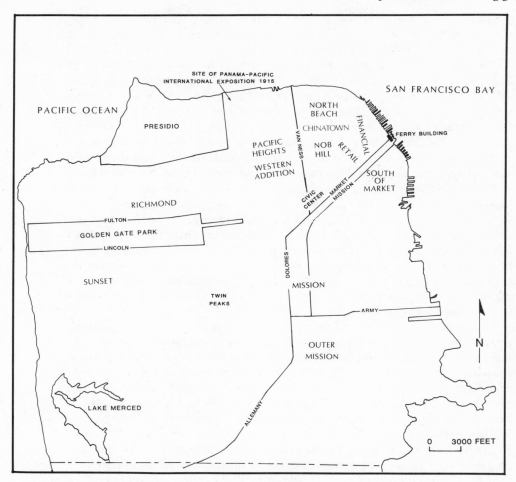

Map 1.   Major Residential Areas

the area. Along the waterfront, males made up almost 70 percent of the residents in 1900, and nearly 90 percent in 1910. Somewhat to the west were more women and families proportionately, but less so in 1910 than in 1900. Half the population was foreign-born with Irish, Scandinavians, and Germans most prominent. Citywide, the average dwelling held 6.4 people, but here the average stood at ten in 1900 and nineteen in 1910.[6]

San Francisco at the turn of the century had more boatmen and sailors than any other American city, more even than New York. In 1890, one working male in forty found employment as a seafarer, and by 1910 the proportion of sailors and deckhands among working males had increased to one in thirty-two. When other waterfront workers—longshoremen, warehousemen, and so forth—are added to the seafarers, the waterfront provided employment to one of every twenty employed males in 1910. This proportion had not changed as late as 1930.[7] Along the streets near the waterfront stood sailors' boardinghouses, saloons, restaurants, and places of amusement catering to young, single men.

Boardinghouses did more than just provide a place to sleep when in San Francisco. There sailors could buy provisions (often on credit), relax in the saloon, borrow money, and secure employment. Boardinghouse keepers served as middlemen between ships' captains and boarders; they were, in fact, virtually the only way to find a job on a ship. The Yakela family ran one such boardinghouse at 214 Steuart Street. John Yakela kept a saloon on the ground floor and lived in the building with his wife and three children. All but the youngest Yakela, twelve-year-old Edward, had been born in Finland. Seventy-three sailors made their home at 214 Steuart, although most of them, at any given time, were away from the city aboard ship. There were few "old salts" at Yakela's—only two were over forty-five, and the oldest was fifty-two. Two were younger than twenty-three. Eighty percent were between the ages of twenty-three and forty. More than half the boarders were Scandinavians (twenty-nine) or Finns (eleven). The other thirty-three came from a dozen different ethnic backgrounds, with Germans most numerous (ten), followed by English (five). Only three had both parents born in the United States.[8]

The prominence of Scandinavians at Yakela's boardinghouse is not surprising, for San Francisco's Scandinavians were concentrated overwhelmingly in seafaring. Throughout the late nineteenth century, over a third of those from Sweden, Norway, and Denmark found employment as boatmen or sailors. In 1900, those of Scandinavian parentage made up 5 percent of the city's total work force but 38 percent of the sailors and boatmen. Finns were not listed in the census, but they were so prevalent in the coasting lumber trade that steam schooners carrying lumber were called "Russian-Finn men-of-war." A survey by the Sailors' Union of the Pacific at the turn of the century showed its members to be 40 percent Scandinavian, 11 percent Finnish, 10 percent German, and only 9 percent American-born.[9]

Sailors were not the only single males living in boardinghouses South of Market. Migratory casual workers—hoboes and tramps—came to San Francisco, especially during the winter months or during periods of economic depression. Miners who worked in the Sierra, sailors employed in fishing off Alaska, agricultural workers from the interior valleys, and lumbermen from along the coast would come to the city with a "stake" when winter weather prevented work. This pattern seems to have intensified during the early twentieth century. The rebuilding after the destruction of 1906 included few of the houses and flats typical of streets like Natoma, Tehama, and Minna before 1906 and, instead, more institutions catering to single males. By 1910, the area was largely male, an area of cheap hotels and lodging houses, saloons, pawnshops, and missions. During December 1913, a survey was made of the "ten and fifteen cent lodging houses and the cheap hotels of the foreign quarter" (South of Market and parts of North Beach and Downtown). Forty thousand seasonal laborers were counted "lying up" in San Francisco, with a winter stake estimated to average thirty dollars. Within South of Market, seafarers and waterfront workers usually stayed east of

Third Street, seasonal workers such as loggers and miners between Third and Sixth, and clerks and low-paid white-collar workers west of Sixth.[10]

Before 1906, however, many families lived South of Market. Then, much of South of Market consisted of two- or three-story wooden rowhouses packed so tightly that their backs almost seemed to meet as well as their sides. Larger masonry buildings stood along Mission and along some of the other major thoroughfares, but on the narrow, residential alleys that ran east and west, parallel to the major thoroughfares, wooden residential buildings were the rule. The description of South of Market provided by kindergarten director Kate Douglas Wiggin for 1878 needs little amendment for the period before 1906:

> The scene is a long, busy street in San Francisco. Innumerable small shops lined it from north to south; horse [-drawn street] cars, always crowded with passengers, hurried to and fro; narrow streets intersected the broader one, these built up with small dwellings, most of them rather neglected by their owners. In the middle distance were other narrow streets and alleys where taller houses stood, and the windows, fire-escapes, and balconies of these added great variety to the landscape, as the families housed there kept most of their effects on the outside during the long dry season.
>
> Still farther away were the roofs, chimneys, and smokestacks of mammoth buildings—railway sheds, freight depots, power-houses, and the like—with finally a glimpse of the docks and wharves and shipping.[11]

Tehama Street, thirty-five feet wide, running parallel to and between Howard and Folsom streets, is one of these narrow residential streets. In 1900, 120 people lived on the south side of Tehama between Second and Third streets. Thirteen houses contained twenty-four households, twenty-two of them based on kinship. Forty-nine of the street's seventy adults lived with a relative. Seven families had a boarder not related by kinship or marriage, three families had two boarders, and one had six. Although not related by kinship, boarders typically came from the same ethnic group as the family with whom they lived. Only two households, of two people each, consisted of people not related by either kinship or marriage. Six families included only two or three members, seven had four, nine had five or more. Eighteen of the twenty-two families had both husband and wife present. Of the seventy adults, thirty-three had two Irish parents and another four had one Irish parent. Seven had German parents, five were Scandinavian, and the rest came from a dozen different ethnic backgrounds. Only one had both parents born in the United States.[12]

Thirty-eight of the forty-one adult males on Tehama Street had identifiable occupations, as did nine of the twenty-nine adult women. Eighteen of the men's occupations required little skill or training—day laborer, hod carrier, longshoreman, hackman, sailor, fisherman. Several were somewhat more skilled: a fire captain, sailmaker, plumber, tailor, iron moulder, stationary engineer, and boilermaker. Two were small businessmen—one a saloonkeeper and another a fruit peddler. The adult women included four who did laundry, two nurses, an actress, a house cleaner, and a landlady. Residence and kinship were often related to work. Timothy Gill and his wife Bridget had six boarders, one of whom tended bar in Gill's saloon. Two of Gill's other boarders were marine firemen. The Quinn brothers worked as warehousemen (one of them a foreman), perhaps at the same location. Three washerwomen lived in the same building. Clarence van Tassel lived with his brother's family, and both brothers worked in a factory making wooden boxes. Joseph Stromberg and John O'Hara, both teamsters, lived in adjoining buildings as did George Dreisbach and Samuel Levein, both tailors. Two nurses were mother and daughter.[13]

The area around the 100 block on Tehama was characteristic of South of Market more generally. At the end of the block, between Mission and Folsom on Third Street, stood seven restaurants, fourteen lodging houses, and thirty-two saloons. Kate Douglas Wiggin observed that "all the most desirable sites were occupied by saloons," and, she added, "it was practically impossible to quench the thirst of the neighborhood." Up Third Street and around the corner on Mission loomed St. Patrick's Church, largest parish west of the Mississippi. The Salvation Army had a spot on the same block, and Congregation Beth-Menahim Streisand was on the other side of Fourth Street, a bit south of Mission. Nearby blocks also included an Episcopal mission, a German Methodist church, a Methodist church, and a Presbyterian church. Other churches of major Protestant denominations and several other Jewish congregations were scattered through the South of Market region. Jefferson Primary School was down Tehama near First Street, St. Patrick's school was almost the same distance in the opposite direction, and there was a Hebrew school maintained by the Jewish Educational Society. The Grand Opera House stood on Mission near Third Street, and the Young Men's Institute, a Catholic organization, was on Fourth Street near Market. Irish-American Hall was down Howard, across Fourth Street. Federation Hall, across the street, was the meeting place for the Bakers' Union, the Laborers' and Hodcarriers' Union, and the United Brotherhood of Labor. Several printing trades unions met up Third Street, near Market. Although the area showed a high concentration of restaurants (a third of all in the city) and lodging houses (half of all in the city) as early as 1880, the area continued to include many working-class families, at least until the 1906 earthquake and fire, and to include family institutions such as schools and churches, and a range of ethnic institutions as well.[14]

Despite the number of families (before 1906) and social institutions, a pattern of deprivation comes through even in the bare data collected by the census taker in 1900. Joseph Lesaudro, a day laborer, his wife Josephine, their four children, and Josephine's sister and her husband were one of the five families living at 163 Tehama. The oldest Lesaudro girls, ages ten and twelve, were employed as hatmakers. A Polish widow and her three children rented the house next door; she worked as a housecleaner to keep her children in school and rented space to two lodgers, both also Polish, one of them a saloon cook and the other a baker's helper. Michael Ryan, a day laborer, rented half of 155 Tehama. His two boys, ages fourteen and thirteen, both worked, and the family had a boarder. Charles Robert, a French-born dishwasher, rented 149 Tehama with his wife and four children. The two older children, ages thirteen and sixteen, were both employed. Denise Bailey, 153 Tehama, was the sole homeowner on the block. She rented rooms to five families in addition to her own, took in two boarders with her own family, and her two oldest daughters, ages fifteen and eighteen, worked as cigarmakers. Two blocks north of the Lesaudros, Ryans, Roberts, and Baileys stood the Palace Hotel, the most luxurious hotel in the world at the time it opened, and across the street from it was another luxury hotel, the Grand. Only a few short blocks separated luxury and poverty, success and hardship. Guillermo Prieto, in 1877, was struck by the same contrast: "Behind the palaces run filthy alleys, or rather nasty dungheaps without sidewalks or illumination, whose loiterers smell of the gallows."[15]

Mission District. Very different patterns of life and work characterized the Mission District, the large area along Mission Street, beginning at about Twelfth Street where Mission curves to run north and south, and extending west from Mission to the base of Twin Peaks and east to the industrial areas along the bay. While the Mission contained many neighborhoods, the area as a whole had a number of unifying characteristics during the late nineteenth and early twentieth centuries.

The Mission was primarily an area of families. In 1900, more than 95 percent of the population in the few blocks along each side of Mission lived with family members or spouses, among the highest proportions in the entire city. Predominantly white, the population was about a quarter foreign-born and three-quarters or more of foreign parentage, with Irish and German the largest groups. The Mission was an area of single-family and two-family homes, its population density far below the citywide average and much lower than the densely packed South of Market. The street pattern of the area, however, was not much different from South of Market. The major thoroughfares that ran east and west through South of Market all curved at about Twelfth Street, to run north and south through the Mission District. By 1880, streetcars ran on these thoroughfares—Valencia, Mission, Howard (now South Van Ness), Folsom, Harrison, and, closer to the bay, Kentucky (now Third). Later, by 1902, there were also car lines on Bryant, Castro, and Guerrero, as well as a number of cross-town lines. Narrower residential streets ran between and parallel to these major thoroughfares, where one-, two-, or three-story wooden rowhouses housed one or two families. Businesses catering to the surrounding neighborhoods sprang up on the major thoroughfares, and large wooden churches were scattered at frequent intervals.[16]

Bartlett Street is a narrow residential street between Mission and Valencia. The 400 block on Bartlett, in 1900, had sixteen houses, which held seventeen households, divided almost equally between homeowners and renters. Of the forty-nine adults and twenty-eight children living on the block, only five of the adults were not family members—two of them were servants, three boarders. Six families consisted of two or three members, seven had four or five, and four had six or more. Thirteen of the sixteen families had both husband and wife present. Among the forty-nine adults, twelve had one or both parents born in Ireland, ten had one or both parents born in Scotland, seven had at least one English-born parent, five had parents born in Germany, and fifteen had both parents born in the United States.[17]

Nearly all the adult males on Bartlett Street had an occupation, but only three of the adult women worked for a paycheck. The largest number of the men held skilled blue-collar jobs, four in the metal trades, four in the building trades, one a printer, one a patternmaker. Two were supervisors, a foreman for the Southern Pacific Railway and a superintendent for the California Dry Dock Company. Only one, a boarder, worked as a day laborer, employed at a sheet-metal works. Eight held low-level white-collar jobs— four clerks, a collector, a customs inspector, a streetcar conductor, and a gateman for the Southern Pacific. Three were professionals—a lawyer, a physician, and a pharmacist. Two women were teachers, and the only other employed woman was a live-in servant for an elderly couple. Kinship and occupation were often closely related. All three men in the Jones family were ironworkers, one son as a machinist at Union Iron Works, the father and the other son as contractors, the only clearly identifiable entrepreneurs on the block. Two of the three Rutherford brothers also worked in the metal trades, one as a boilermaker, the other as a blacksmith. A carpenter's son was also in the building trades, albeit as a plumber. The son of the dry dock superintendent worked in a shipyard, perhaps the same one as his father. The printer's son was an apprentice printer. Two brothers were clerks.[18]

The area around the 400 block on Bartlett held a wide variety of social institutions. Bethany Congregational Church was on that block, and three blocks up Bartlett was a Baptist church. An Episcopal mission church was located a few blocks to the west on Fair Oaks Street. Four German-speaking churches—Calvinist, Lutheran, Methodist, and Catholic—were all nearby. Methodist, Presbyterian, and Unitarian churches were not far distant. In addition to St. Anthony's Catholic Church (German), there was also St. James, at Twenty-third and Guerrero. Haight Primary School was close by, on Mission between Twenty-fifth and Twenty-sixth. The block bounded by Bartlett and Valencia, Twenty-second and Twenty-third streets contained both Horace Mann Grammar School and Agassiz Intermediate Grammar School. There was also an evening school for adults at Horace Mann. St. Anthony's maintained a parish school, and the Academy of the Immaculate Conception was near St. James. Mission High School, at Eighteenth and Dolores, was the only public high school in the district, but most residents of the area could reach it by a streetcar ride and a walk. Masonic Hall, on Mission between Twenty-second and Twenty-third, was the meeting site not just for the Mission Masonic Lodge and the Order of Eastern Star, but also for the Knights of Pythias, Native Sons of the Golden West, Order of Chosen Friends, Woodmen of the World, and two varieties of Foresters. Odd Fellows and Workmen met at Fraternal Hall, three blocks up Mission from Masonic Hall. Another Workmen's lodge met on Twenty-fourth Street, two blocks east of Mission. The Mission *Turn Verein* (gymnastics club) had a hall on Eighteenth near Valencia where the San Francisco *Männerchor* (men's chorus) and, most likely, other German groups met. In comparison with Tehama

Street, the area around Bartlett Street had more churches, many more fraternal and social groups, and many fewer saloons. Only seven saloons and four restaurants were to be found in the area bounded by Mission and Valencia, Twenty-fourth and Army streets.[19]

The churches and lodges near Bartlett Street represent only a few of the social organizations and institutions to be found in the area. Every major Protestant denomination had put down roots in the Mission, usually in several locations—four Congregational churches, two Episcopal churches and two missions, three Evangelical churches (two German), three Lutheran churches (one Scandinavian, two German), six Methodist churches (one Swedish, one German), and five Presbyterian churches. In addition to St. Anthony's and St. James, there were four other Catholic parish churches in the area. The largest ethnic groups were Irish and German, with the Irish numerically dominant. B'nai David was the only synagogue in the Mission District, and its congregation was small. A survey in the late 1930s found only 8 percent of the city's Jewish population in the Mission.[20]

There was but one small city park in the Mission District until 1905 when a cemetery at Eighteenth and Dolores was converted into Dolores Park. However, many places of recreation and amusement served the area. Woodward's Gardens, an elaborate private amusement park extending from Mission to Valencia and between Thirteenth and Fourteenth streets, opened in 1866; it featured live and stuffed animals, an amphitheater and art museum, botanical displays, and statuary. It remained a popular place for twenty-five years. The first San Francisco appearance of the Ringling Brothers' Circus, in 1900, was in the Mission at Sixteenth and Folsom. Baseball was popular in the Mission District; the first organized game in the city was played in the Mission at Sixteenth and Harrison. A diamond was opened at Twenty-fifth and Folsom in 1868, and Recreation Park at Eighth and Harrison opened in 1897. Recreation Park, relocated to Fifteenth and Valencia in 1907, was home to the San Francisco Seals of the Pacific Coast League and, after 1926, to a second team, the San Francisco Missions. Both teams moved to Seals Stadium at Sixteenth and Bryant, also in the Mission, with the beginning of the 1931 baseball season. A race track opened in 1864 at Railroad Avenue between Twenty-fourth and Twenty-eighth streets (now Third Street, between Yosemite and Carroll).[21]

The Mission District as a whole had many characteristics not only of a family area but also of distinctly working-class or lower-middle-class families. An area with many religious or social institutions, it was home to many of the skilled workers employed in the manufacturing areas south of Market or along the bay, as well as home to some businessmen and professionals— those whose businesses were in the Mission, and others who had grown up there or who preferred the area for a variety of reasons. Some Mission District houses were clearly upper middle-class or even upper-class, home to successful merchants, ship captains, politicians, contractors, lawyers, or manufacturers. The dominant tone, however, was working-class. After the destruction of 1906 (which spared much of the Mission), the area became even more working-class and more Irish as families left South of Market

and followed Mission Street south. For the next thirty years or so, until
World War II, many Mission residents were consciously Irish, often consciously working class, and very conscious of being residents of "the Mish."

Western Addition. Although some upper-middle-class businessmen and professionals were to be found throughout the Mission District, these groups
appeared in larger proportions elsewhere in the city. Before 1906, and to
a great extent before World War II, the Western Addition was home to
much of San Francisco's upper middle class. The Western Addition formally
refers to the area opened for residential construction in 1855, west of the
survey previously in effect, extending from Larkin Street to Divisadero,
north of Market. The destruction in 1906 stopped at Van Ness, leaving the
rest of the Western Addition relatively unscathed by earthquake and fire.
Before 1906, Van Ness was a street of elaborate mansions, and Polk Street
(one block to the east) was an area of small shops and stores. Frank Norris
chose Polk Street for the location of the dental office and sleeping room of
the title character in his first novel, *McTeague.* After 1906, Polk and Van
Ness both became commercial thoroughfares. Fillmore Street, a shopping
thoroughfare running north and south through the center of the Western
Addition, briefly became a commercial center for the city after 1906, before
the downtown stores were rebuilt. As that happened, some of the houses
around Fillmore began to be subdivided into apartments, and the Western
Addition began to change from an upper-middle-class neighborhood of
homeowners. At about the same time, Japantown began to develop along
Buchanan between Geary and Pine. Following World War I, a black neighborhood developed nearby, west of Fillmore between Geary and Pine. Before
1906, however, the Western Addition remained largely upper-middle-class
and upper-class, home to businessmen and professionals. The houses were
similar to those elsewhere in San Francisco in the late nineteenth century—
two- and three-story rowhouses, with little or no yard in front. Reflecting
the higher income levels and social pretensions of most Western Addition
homeowners, many of their houses were both larger and architecturally
more elaborate than those of the Mission District. Harriet Lane Levy's
description of the 900 block on O'Farrell could have been repeated time
and again for much of the rest of the Western Addition:

> The houses on the north side of O'Farrell acquired variation by the swell of
> a bay window, or the color of a painted surface. All buildings gave out a fine
> assurance of permanence. . . . The planked street, held together by thirty
> penny spikes, resisted the iron shoes of the heavy dray horses. Houses, side-
> walks, street were of the best wood provided by the most reliable contractors,
> guaranteed perfect.[22]

In the heart of the Western Addition, about 95 percent of the population
lived in families in 1900, and—unlike most of the rest of the city—women
outnumbered men. About 30 percent of the people were foreign-born, and
three-quarters were of foreign parentage. Here were to be found the largest
concentrations of Germans in the city. Here too were significant numbers
of Asians, probably half of them in Japantown, the others throughout the
area as live-in servants.[23]

The 1700 block on Bush Street had many of these characteristics. There were twelve houses on that block and twelve families, one—and only one—per house. Two families, both headed by widows, each had two boarders or "guests." Ten families had a live-in servant, and one family had two. Nine families owned their homes, three rented. Families here, as in the Mission and South of Market, were large. Four consisted of three people, two had four or five, and six had six or more. Of the forty-one adults, not including servants, twenty-four had both parents born in Germany and Austria. Eight had one or both parents Irish, six had one or both parents born in England or Scotland, two were of French parentage, and two had both parents born in the United States. Among the twelve servants, four were Irish, two were Chinese, and only one was born in the United States. In only two families, both of them Irish, was the servant of the same ethnic background as the family.[24]

Many of the residents of the 1700 block on Bush were Jewish, as were many others in the Western Addition at the turn of the century. One block west down Bush was the Bush Street Temple, home of Congregation Ohabai Shalome, one of the most conservative in the city. On the 1700 block of Bush lived Jacob Nieto, rabbi of Congregation Sherith Israel, a more liberal temple. Sherith Israel had been located downtown at Post and Taylor streets from its early days in 1868 to 1905 when a temple was dedicated in the Western Addition at California and Webster streets. Other congregations also established temples in the Western Addition beginning in the 1890s, moving from Downtown or South of Market. The largest temple in San Francisco, Emanu-El, a reform congregation formed by Bavarians, remained downtown on Sutter Street until the 1920s. Other Jewish institutions were also to be found in the Western Addition. Mount Zion Hospital opened on Sutter near Scott in 1898, and in 1913 a new building was completed at Post and Scott. The Jewish Educational Society operated a Hebrew school in the Western Addition beginning in 1908. The Sinai Memorial Chapel (Chevra Kadisha) began in the South of Market area in 1901 but moved into the Western Addition in the next decade. In the late 1930s, 24 percent of the city's Jewish population lived in the Western Addition, another 32 percent lived directly to the west in the Richmond district, and 16 percent were directly north of the Western Addition in Pacific Heights and the Marina.[25]

The occupations of all residents of the 1700 block on Bush are clearly identifiable. Of the twenty-three adult males, the largest number were merchants: a father-and-son crockery business, a partner in a wholesale notions company, a partner in a clothing company (wholesale, manufacturing, importing), a retail cigar store owner, and a father-and-son cigar-importing business. Others on the block were employed by merchants. Leopold Baer's son Sam was a clerk at Sachs Brothers, selling gentlemen's furnishings; his other son Henry, sixteen years old, was a notions clerk, most likely in his father's business, Gerson and Baer. Arnold Pollak's son Berthold was a salesman for Zellerbach and Sons, paper merchants; his sixteen-year-old son Irving was a stationery clerk, perhaps for the same firm. Joseph Adelsdorfer's son Max was a manufacturer's agent, and Anna Herrold's son Hugo was a clerk for the Harbor Commission. Bella Clapp, boarder with Anna Herrold, was the bookkeeper for a firm of wholesale grocers, and the brother of Rabbi Nieto was a tea salesman. In all, eleven of the street's twenty adult males who were employed were in merchandising. Morning on the block must have seen a parade very like that recalled by Harriet Lane Levy from her childhood a few blocks away:

> At nine o'clock every morning the men of O'Farrell Street left their homes for their places of business downtown; dressed in brushed broadcloth and polished high hats, they departed soberly as to a funeral. The door of each house opened and let out the owner who took the steps firmly, and, arriving on the sidewalk, turned slowly eastward toward town. A man had not walked many yards before he was overtaken by a friend coming from the avenue. Together they walked with matched steps down the street.
>
> All the men were united by the place and circumstances of their birth. They had come to America from villages in Germany, and they had worked themselves up from small stores in the interior of California to businesses in San Francisco.[26]

In addition to the merchants and clerks on Bush Street, three adult males were at school, two of them brothers, both at dental school. The remaining adult males included a piano teacher, a lawyer, a mining investor, a rabbi, and the French consul; one, seventy-year-old Cornelius Driscoll, listed himself simply as "capitalist." *All* were in white-collar occupations. There were also two live-in Chinese cooks. In addition to Bella Clapp, the bookkeeper, twelve other women were employed: Kate Maroney's daughter and one of her boarders as school teachers, one as a live-in governess, and nine as live-in servants.

The Western Addition after 1906 became more Jewish in the same way the Mission District became more Irish. However, a wide variety of other groups could be found in the Western Addition, just as many groups other than Irish lived in the Mission. Virtually all Protestant denominations had communicants in the Western Addition—Baptist, Disciples of Christ, Congregational, Episcopal (four), Lutheran (one English, one German), Methodist (one English, one Japanese), Presbyterian (five), and Unitarian. There were also five Catholic churches, including St. Mary's Cathedral. A bit later a significant Russian community developed in the Western Addition, complete with church and school. Lowell High School was on Sutter between Gough and Octavia, Sacred Heart Academy was at Franklin and Ellis, and St. Paul's Lutheran conducted a German school at Eddy and Gough. There were also other public and Catholic primary schools scattered throughout the district. King Solomon's Masonic Lodge met on Fillmore, as did also the Workmen and Foresters. Other social institutions catering to Western Addition residents were located in the downtown area, among the offices of wholesale and retail merchants.[27]

Nob Hill–Pacific Heights. As one travels north on Fillmore Street through the Western Addition, the terrain begins to rise at about California Street. The higher one goes physically, the higher the income levels. Pacific Heights, an upper-class residential district, was technically a part of the Western

Addition, but it differed significantly from most of the area. Stretching westward between California and Union, from Van Ness to Presidio, Pacific Heights continued the patterns established atop Nob Hill in the 1870s, and Nob Hill–Pacific Heights may be considered as one major division of the city, an elite district perched on high ground, there to see and to be seen.

The heights to the north and west of the central business district had long attracted the city's commercial and financial elite. South Park, the elite neighborhood of the 1850s, in the heart of South of Market, soon was overwhelmed by the surrounding industrial area, especially after a massive effort reduced a high hill barring Second Street from continuing to Townsend. Thereupon, the city's elite migrated to the lower slopes of what was then called the California Street Hill, soon to become Nob Hill. With the development of the cable car, construction on Nob Hill was no longer limited to the lower slopes.[28]

In the 1870s, the top of the hill saw the construction of elaborate—some would say bizarre—mansions by some of the wealthiest and most powerful families in the West. Charles Crocker, one of the Big Four of the Southern Pacific Railroad, built his home where Grace Cathedral now stands. Ambrose Bierce, a journalist, said of this house: "There are uglier buildings in America than the Crocker home on Nob Hill, but they were built with public money for a public purpose; among the architectural triumphs of private fortune and personal taste it is peerless." Next to Crocker's house, across Taylor Street to the east, was the more modest (and some would say more tasteful) home of David Colton, chief counsel for the Southern Pacific; Colton's home was later purchased, but seldom used, by Collis Huntington, another of the Big Four. Next, across Yerba Buena Street to the east, was the town house of James Flood, one of the Silver Kings, masters of the Comstock Lode. Diagonally across the street on the corner of Mason and California was the home of another of the Big Four, Mark Hopkins, a house that Gertrude Atherton once said "looked as if several architects had been employed, and they had fought one another to a finish." Next to the Hopkins house was the home of Leland Stanford, the final member of the Big Four, president of the Southern Pacific until 1890.[29]

On the corner of Taylor and Sacramento streets, a block north of the Crocker house, was the residence of George Hearst, mining millionaire. Directly across the street from the Crockers were the Tobins, of the Hibernia Bank. A block south and west was Theresa Fair, divorced wife of James Fair, another of the Silver Kings. Others on the hill included William Coleman of Vigilance Committee fame; James Haggin, a partner of Hearst; and Haggin's brother-in-law and partner Lloyd Tevis. Crocker's house may well have been the most exuberant in its architectural pretentiousness, but the Flood mansion was the most ostentatious, constructed at a cost of $1.5 million, built of brownstone brought from Connecticut, surrounded by a $30,000 bronze fence requiring the full-time attention of one servant just to keep it polished. As the San Francisco Junior League put it in their survey of the city's architecture published in 1968: "The Nob Hill householders of the 1880's and 1890's were not the sole proprietors of the State of California—but they may well have represented the majority interest."[30]

Houses in the Pacific Heights area west of Nob Hill could not be seen so readily from afar, but their residents included millionaire merchants and manufacturers, mining and shipping magnates, and others of great wealth and power. There lived Michael H. de Young of the *San Francisco Chronicle;* William Bourn of the Spring Valley Water Company; William Whittier, partner in the largest paint company on the West Coast; and various descendants of Charles Crocker, James Flood, and Claus Spreckels. Well over a third of the families listed in *Our Society Blue Book,* a listing of "people of social standing and the highest respectability," were on or near Pacific Heights in 1902. After 1906, fewer new mansions were built in the city by the most wealthy, who typically maintained country homes down the peninsula in Belmont or Burlingame, or north in Marin County, or across the bay. Some of the Pacific Heights homes, in fact, served as town houses for families who lived outside the city, just as Flood built his Nob Hill mansion as a town house, complementing his Menlo Park country home. Scattered through Pacific Heights were entire blocks of more modest homes, similar to those of the Western Addition, built and occupied by upper-middle-class merchants like those of the Western Addition. The Pacific Heights area in the late nineteenth and early twentieth centuries had abundant civic amenities, boasting more parks than in all of the Mission District. Streetcar lines ran on nearly all the major east-west thoroughfares of the area, providing easy movement from home to the central business district.[31]

Chinatown. The intersection of California and Mason streets lies at the crest of Nob Hill, location of the Flood and Hopkins mansions and of the Fairmont Hotel (the foundation of which James Fair intended, until his death, as the base of the grandest Nob Hill house of them all). Three blocks down California Street toward the bay is Grant Avenue (Dupont Street until 1908), center of the densely populated Chinese quarter that in the late nineteenth century took in the blocks from California to Broadway, between Kearny and Stockton streets. To white San Franciscans, Chinatown seemed sometimes bizarre, sometimes revolting, but always exotic. It was a city within a city, with its own social and economic systems, virtually autonomous with its own forms of government exercised through clan and district associations and the Chinese Consolidated Benevolent Association, the "Six Companies." The physical appearance of Chinatown today, without the neon signs and some of the pseudo-Chinese architectural flourishes, is probably very close to what it was in the late nineteenth century.[32]

Architectural historian Randolph Delehanty notes: "When the district burned down completely in 1906 it was almost immediately rebuilt (most of it with salvaged bricks) to be much like the downtown Civil War city." Although the buildings looked much like those in the rest of the city, the banners, signs, and other aspects of Dupont Street made it distinctly Chinese. One visitor in the 1870s described the scene: "The Chinamen were clothed in plainly-cut blue tunics, had straw or cloth covering their heads, and shoes on their feet resembling slippers down at the heels. The shops were adorned with pendant flags bearing inscriptions in Chinese. The entire street was filled with these strangely decorated and strangely arranged shops." Arnold

Genthe, a German-born photographer who has left the largest collection of pictures of the area, described Chinatown at the turn of the century: "The painted balconies were hung with windbells and flowered lanterns. Brocades and embroideries, bronzes and porcelains, carvings of jade and ivory, of coral and rose crystal, decorated the shop-windows. The wall-spaces between were bright with scarlet bulletins and gilt signs inscribed in the picturesque Chinese characters." Buildings covered every part of each block. Narrow alleys, wide enough for several people abreast, but too narrow for vehicular traffic, ran every which way through the centers of blocks, connecting buildings in the center to the larger streets.[33]

Throughout its existence, Chinatown has been densely crowded. In the nineteenth and early twentieth centuries, men from the same village with the same name frequently shared a room:

> In 1913, all the cousins from the Liu family in my village had one big room so all the members could fit in it, and we slept in that room, cooked in that room, one room. Anybody who had a job had to sleep outside the room, because he could afford space and get a bed for himself. Anybody who couldn't find work slept in the beds in this room. At the end of the year, all the members would get together and figure out all the expenses.

At times in such rooms, beds were attached to the walls like shelves and used in shifts.[34]

In 1890, the Chinese population of San Francisco was 90 percent male. As late as 1920, the figure was 78 percent. This imbalance between the sexes helped to create a thriving vice traffic in Chinatown, just as a similar imbalance along the waterfront created a similar traffic there. In 1885, a special committee appointed by the Board of Supervisors contributed to prevailing anti-Chinese sentiments by locating 567 Chinese prostitutes, 104 houses of prostitution, 26 opium "resorts," and 109 "barricaded gambling dens," all within the six square blocks of Chinatown. During the 1920s, the San Francisco Police Department's Chinatown Squad made a determined effort, largely successful, to eradicate vice activities, although many gambling establishments survived.[35]

Three occupations accounted for 36 percent of all Chinese workers in 1870: laundry workers, 64 percent of whom were Chinese; textile mill operatives, 64 percent Chinese; and cigar and tobacco industry workers, 93 percent Chinese. Chinese were also disproportionately represented among boot- and shoemakers, tailors, fishermen, hucksters and peddlers, laborers (25 percent), and servants (18 percent). During the 1870s and early 1880s, many Chinese worked truck gardens in parts of the Western Addition, others fished on the bay, and still others were door-to-door peddlers, selling vegetables grown and fish caught by their countrymen. Truck farming and fishing later became Italian occupations, but the Chinese peddler was long a familiar sight, delighting children of the Mission District and the Western Addition with his visits.

> Chung Ling was fruit and fish man. He carried the combined stock, suspended in two huge wicker baskets balanced upon a long pole, across his shoulders. . . . The uncertainty of the contents of the baskets—today only

apples and cauliflower; tomorrow, cherries and corn; today, shiny silver smelts; tomorrow, red shrimps with beards and black-beaded eyes—made a delight of his coming.

Another memoir noted that "if there was a Chinese holiday, tucked with the vegetables [would be] little bags of Chinese candy and nuts, gifts to us children." In 1870, there were some 1,100 miners resident in San Francisco, 31 percent of whom were Chinese. Since the city had no mining operations, most of these were probably unemployed miners who had left the Sierra for the city, possibly driven from the mineral areas.[36]

Asians, most of whom were Chinese, constituted 7 percent of the city's work force in 1900. Laundry workers were still predominantly Asian (52 percent), as were cigarmakers (68 percent); garment workers were 31 percent Asian. However, Italians were replacing the Chinese as hucksters and peddlers. Italians made up 28 percent of that occupation and the Chinese only 15 percent. The same pattern appears in fishing, where the Chinese had outnumbered the Italians in 1870. By 1900, Italians accounted for 51 percent of fishermen, Chinese for only 13 percent. The proportion of Chinese among servants and waiters held stable, but the proportion of Chinese laborers declined markedly, from 25 percent in 1870 to 5 percent in 1900.[37]

Manufacturing industries with many Chinese workers showed lower wages than other manufacturing occupations. The average men's clothing worker earned $319 per year in 1900, and the average cigar worker made only $358, both well below the citywide average of $525. One factory owner in 1876 acknowledged that "to Chinamen, on an average we pay less. . . . If the Chinamen were taken from us, we should close up tomorrow." One woolen goods factory in 1880 employed both Chinese and white labor for some tasks. Carders prepared wool for spinning by brushing it to disentangle the fibers; a Chinese carder was paid $1.00 per day in 1880 (down from $1.08 for 1870–1879), but a white boy made $1.75 for the same work. Between 1870 and 1880, the wages of white carders fluctuated considerably, between $1.25 and $2.00, but the general trend was upward. The wage paid Chinese carders was stable until 1880 when it was cut by eight cents per day. Similarly, white weavers made $1.25 per day throughout the period 1870–1880, but Chinese weavers made only $1.08 from 1870 to 1879, and $1.00 in 1880. Chinese laborers earned $1.00 per day, and there were no white laborers. The only other employees paid only $1.00 per day were white women. White laborers in a furniture factory, by contrast, earned $2.00 per day, and in some years $2.50. In a boot and shoe factory employing white labor, the wages varied from $2.50 to $3.00 per day, but in a woolen mill, wages for Chinese workers varied from only $1.00 to $1.20 in 1880.[38]

Most Chinese worked in or near Chinatown. The 1885 supervisors' committee found 427 sites for cigar making, 599 for boot and shoe making, 974 for clothing manufacturing, 255 for underwear, and 71 other work rooms, with a total of 2,326 employees and 1,245 sewing machines. Such work rooms were to be found everywhere, from the third and fourth stories to "cellars which are certainly dark, and probably unhealthy" (the observation of an English visitor around 1870). Other Chinese worked outside

Chinatown—as fishermen, launderers (Chinese laundries existed through-out much of the city, places of both work and residence), and as servants in the Western Addition and on Nob Hill and Pacific Heights. Travel outside Chinatown, however, was potentially dangerous.

> I myself rarely left Chinatown, only when I had to buy American things downtown. The area around Union Square was a dangerous place for us, you see, especially at nighttime before the quake. Chinese were often attacked by thugs there and all of us had to have a police whistle with us at all times. . . . once we were inside Chinatown, the thugs didn't bother us.[39]

Chinatown was a segregated area, as thoroughly segregated as black dis-tricts of the South during the same time period. Chinese could not become citizens through naturalization, could not present testimony in court, could not marry a white person, could not live outside Chinatown except in laun-dries or as domestic servants, and had been driven from many occupations. There was a school in Chinatown, and Chinese children were not allowed to attend any other public school until the period just before World War I. Discrimination became especially intense during the last quarter of the nine-teenth century not only in San Francisco but also throughout the West. One immediate consequence was that Chinese from small towns throughout the West flocked to the relative safety of San Francisco's Chinatown. Another consequence was that many returned to China. Between 1890 and 1900, the Chinese population of San Francisco dropped by about half, and it continued to decline until 1920. Some remained in the Bay Area, as fish-ermen in small villages outside San Francisco, but the Chinese population of the entire state fell by at least a third during that decade.[40]

North Beach. In 1900, Dupont Street was the center of Chinatown from California to Broadway. Across Broadway, however, the language of Dupont Street was not Cantonese but Italian. North Beach—named for a beach long since vanished as the waterfront had been moved northward by land-fills—was the center of San Francisco's Italian community, a predominantly working-class community but one that also included businessmen and pro-fessionals. Initially the area at the base of Telegraph Hill had been known as the Latin Quarter and had included French, Italian, Mexican, Spanish, and Portuguese residents, living "in low houses, which they transformed by balconies into a semblance of Spain." Then, the Italians were to be found on the slopes of Telegraph Hill.

> Their shanties [formerly home to Irish waterfront workers] clung to the side of the hill or hung on the very edge of the precipice overlooking the bay, on the verge of which a wall kept their babies from falling. . . . It was more like Italy than anything in the Italian quarter of New York and Chicago.

Eventually the Italian settlement overflowed Telegraph Hill and inundated North Beach, making the area near Montgomery Avenue (renamed Colum-bus Avenue in 1910) and Broadway a "Little Italy," filled with Italian stores, shops, theaters, restaurants, churches, and social organizations.[41]

By 1910, 30 percent of all the residents of the area bounded on the south by Broadway and on the west by Jones had been born in Italy, and fewer than 20 percent of the adults' parents had been born in the United States. Two-thirds of the population was male, and population densities were well above the citywide average. By 1910, the area bounded by Jones and Broadway had an average of eight people per dwelling. In the early twentieth century, two other Italian neighborhoods developed, one in the Outer Mission District, near the southern boundary of the city and the truck farms of the peninsula, and a smaller one on Potrero Hill. These outlying Italian settlements, however, were more scattered and never developed into rivals of North Beach as the centers of Italian economic and cultural life.[42]

Although there were factories in North Beach, for example, the Ghirardelli chocolate factory and Domenico di Domenconini's Golden Grain macaroni factory, most Italians were not to be found in factory work. By 1900, four occupations had become distinctively Italian, accounting for nearly 22 percent of all Italian males in the work force: hucksters and peddlers, 28 percent of whom were Italian; agricultural laborers, 34 percent Italian; fishermen and oystermen, 51 percent; and bootblacks, 90 percent. Italians were largely unrepresented in white-collar occupations, among merchants and dealers (except as fruit and vegetable sellers), and in the construction and metal trades. Only among laborers did the proportion of Italians exceed their proportion of the total work force, and only 6 percent of the city's laborers were Italian.[43]

To a major extent, the economic life of North Beach was dominated by fishermen and truck farmers. Feluccas with orange-brown lateen sails plied the bay, and larger boats moved out through the Golden Gate to do deep-sea fishing. The Filbert Street wharf, known as Italy harbor, was the center of the fish trade until 1900 when Fisherman's Wharf was built on its present site near the foot of Columbus. There the boats unloaded the day's catch, and street peddlers (both Chinese and Italian) bargained with fishermen. By 1900 the fishermen were largely Sicilians, and the truck farmers and agricultural laborers were predominantly Ligurians. Commission merchants tended to be Genovese, and the street peddlers, for both fish and produce, were largely Lucchesi, from Tuscany. Truck farms were located throughout the Outer Mission District, beyond the areas built up in housing, and down the peninsula south of the city. Most farmers were either tenants or employees, but a few owned their own tracts. In the early twentieth century, increasingly, Italians began to dominate some aspects of food processing, notably pasta making, wine making (especially in areas to the north of San Francisco, but to some extent within the city), cheese making, and the canning of fruit, vegetables, and fish.[44]

The Bank of Italy was unquestionably the most successful of the North Beach enterprises. Founded in 1904 by Amadeo Peter Giannini, a successful produce merchant, the bank broke with precedent by catering not to the most successful entrepreneurs (several other Italian banks did that), but instead to the small businesses and working people of North Beach. When the earthquake struck in 1906, the bank was still so small that Giannini could load all the cash reserves ($80,000), records, and most of the office furniture onto two wagons and save them from the fire. Five days after the fire had burned itself out and while the great fireproof vaults of the major banks were still too hot to be opened, the Bank of Italy resumed business, financing reconstruction of North Beach and other parts of the city as well. In 1907, Giannini opened a branch in the Mission District, and mergers soon added branches in San Jose (1909), Los Angeles (1913), and elsewhere in the state. Giannini acquired banking interests in New York and Italy as well. By 1927, the Bank of Italy was the third largest bank in the nation, but only the largest of several Giannini-run banking chains. Two years later, most of the Giannini banks in California merged to become the Bank of America.[45]

Downtown. Bounded on the west by the Western Addition, on the south by South of Market, on the north by Nob Hill, Chinatown, and North Beach, and on the east by the bay is Downtown, an area that included the ware-house-wholesale district along the waterfront, the Financial District along Sansome and Montgomery between California and Market, a shopping district adjoining the Financial District on the west, a hotel district west and south of the shopping district, and a high-density residential district overlapping and west of the hotel district and, more generally, throughout Downtown. A vice district, the Barbary Coast, stretched along Pacific Street for a half-dozen blocks inland from the waterfront. Helen Hunt Jackson recorded her initial impression of Downtown:

> When I first stepped out of the door of the Occidental Hotel, on Montgomery Street, I looked up and down in disappointment.
> "Is this all?" I exclaimed. "It is New York—a little lower of story, narrower of street, and stiller, perhaps. Have I crossed the continent only to land in Lower Broadway on a dull day?"

Jackson soon discovered that there was more to San Francisco than a New York with smaller buildings and narrower streets, but her initial impression underlines the fact that Downtown in San Francisco was, in many ways, not greatly different from the downtown area of any of the dozen or so major cities of the day. The typology of urban development outlined by David Ward fits the San Francisco case as well as it does Boston.[46]

The area nearest the waterfront had characteristics similar to its counterpart South of Market—high population density, more than two-thirds male, half foreign-born, and only half of the population living in families. Further inland, between Mason and Van Ness, the population was quite different from that along the waterfront. Only three-quarters lived in a family (compared with 84 percent citywide and more than 95 percent in the Mission or Western Addition), but the population was almost evenly divided between men and women. The population density was the highest outside South of Market and Chinatown, not surprising for an apartment-house district. This area of the city had the highest proportion of people with both parents born in the United States; Germans took first place among foreign-stock groups. Many of these people were employed in the central business district as clerks, salespeople, professionals just beginning their practices, or business people who chose to live near their work. Hotel living was an old tradition in the city, one still followed by many in the late nineteenth and early twentieth centuries, including such prominent people as James Fair, who lived at his Lick House. Samuel Williams, in 1875, defined some social essentials:

> Living at a first-class hotel is a strong presumption of social availability, but living in a boarding-house, excepting two or three which society had indorsed as fashionable, is to incur grave suspicions that you are a mere nobody. But even in a boarding-house the lines may be drawn between those who have a single room and those who have a suite.[47]

□   □   □

This survey of patterns of life and work in the major neighborhoods of San Francisco has come full circle, back to Market Street, across which stood foundries and warehouses, factories and shipyards, boardinghouses and saloons. Of the major areas of the city, some were more ethnically homogeneous than others, and some showed greater homogeneity of occupation and income. Only the Chinese were segregated, prohibited from living outside Chinatown, barred from many occupations. Those Chinese willing to accept occupational segregation could live outside Chinatown as laundrymen or servants, and the Chinese in Chinatown were able to engage in occupations otherwise closed to them (the building trades, for example) so long as their employers or patrons were also Chinese. Next to the Chinese, the Italians were the most ethnically concentrated, both residentially and occupationally. Unlike the Chinese, however, there were no barriers to Italians who sought to move outside group patterns, and successful Italian businessmen could be found down the peninsula or, in the 1920s, in the new Marina District between Pacific Heights and the bay. The bulk of Irish Catholics may have lived South of Market or in the Mission, as skilled workers or laborers, but Irish Catholics were also the masters of Nob Hill palaces and Pacific Heights mansions, including the Floods and Fairs, the Tobins and Phelans, and others. Germans—Protestant, Catholic, and Jewish—were not just merchants and shopkeepers but also skilled workers and day laborers and were to be found South of Market, in the Mission and Western Addition, and on Pacific Heights.[48]

Nonetheless, there were clear patterns linking ethnicity, sex, marital status, occupation, and neighborhood. These patterns closely resemble models of labor-market segmentation developed over the past decade by some labor economists, who have divided the labor market into an upper primary tier, a lower primary tier, and a secondary market. The upper-tier primary market consists largely of white-collar professional and managerial positions, the lower-tier primary market largely of blue-collar occupations that pay reasonably well and have good working conditions, some chance of advancement to the level of foreman or supervisor, and—above all else—stability of employment. The secondary labor market is low paying, with poor working conditions, little chance of advancement, often harsh and arbitrary discipline, and—above all else—highly unstable employment conditions with frequent periods of unemployment. Michael Piore has linked these three segments of the labor market to three social class groups described in sociological studies: middle class (the upper-tier primary market), working class (lower-tier primary market), and lower class (secondary market).[49]

San Francisco at the turn of the century shows the characteristics of three such segment classes. The lowest level of the secondary segment, characterized by sweatshop conditions and low pay, was avoided by most workers except Irish women and Chinese men, who, because of their concentration in low-paying work with sweatshop conditions, were the most discriminated-against members of the work force. The secondary labor market also included day laborers, servants, and waiters and such blue-collar occupations as teamsters, sailors and boatmen, and longshoremen and warehousemen. These occupations were filled largely by Irish men, but with some specific occupations filled largely by Scandinavians or Italians, and with some jobs including significant proportions of Irish women, Chinese men, or blacks. Blacks were concentrated in the service sector and were excluded from a number of occupations.

The lower tier of the primary market (working class) included most of the metal trades and building trades, many shopkeepers and tradespeople, many small hotel and restaurant owners, saloonkeepers, and some merchants, especially those whose operations were small in scale. Samuel Walker, in 1875, told of a wealthy San Franciscan giving a party, forced to choose which of his many acquaintances he would invite: " 'We must draw the line somewhere, you know,' and he drew it bravely between wholesale and retail. The man who sold soap and candles by the box was decreed to be within the 'sacred pale' of society's most elect. The man who sold soap and candles by the pound was voted a social Philistine." The upper tier of the primary market included the remaining merchants—those who sold their soap and candles by the box—and other white-collar business occupations and the professions.[50]

While the lines dividing these three segments of the labor market become reasonably clear in historical perspective, they were not necessarily hard and fast barriers for most workers. Chinese, blacks, most women, some Italians, and, apparently, some Scandinavians were limited in various ways and to differing degrees, but the vast majority of the work force—the native stock, British, German, and Irish men—were not excluded from any level. The lines dividing Irish hackmen from Irish plumbers, German bartenders from German restaurateurs, Jewish clerks from Jewish merchants, were highly fluid. Some recent sociological studies suggest that one key difference between uncertainty of employment (secondary market) and stability (primary market) is in some part a state of mind or a stage of development of the individual. Such views note that many workers in the secondary labor market are youths, offspring of the working class and middle class. In San Francisco at the turn of the century, the occupations with the smallest proportions of married men—teamsters, bartenders, sailors, day laborers, servants, and the like—also had the largest proportions of workers between the ages of sixteen and twenty-four. This seems to support the notion that the decision to marry typically accompanied a decision to change occupations and to move into the lower tier of the primary market because of the need for stability of employment.

Some workers never moved from lower-class instability to working-class stability, for varied reasons. Lack of available jobs in the lower tier of the primary market might discourage marriage because of the difficulty of supporting a family on secondary market earnings. Conversely, a great disproportion between men and women might make marriage impossible for lack of a spouse and might cause some single males to remain permanently in the secondary market out of lack of incentive to seek primary market employment. Others might be barred from the primary market because of ethnic- or sex-based discrimination. Regardless of cause, one effect was that males in the secondary labor market, outside families, sometimes exhibited behavior patterns described as extended adolescence and were often seen by the larger community as "boys" (regardless of their age) because circumstances had prevented them from developing patterns of behavior defined as adult by the larger community. Piore suggests: "Their life tends to be characterized by an effort to escape routine through action and adventure."[51] In San Francisco, the four-to-three ratio between men and women seemed to dictate inevitably that a quarter of the city's men would remain unmarried and never become heads of families, a status that the dominant cultures of the city—Mission, Western Addition, elite, or North Beach—defined as marking the transition to adult status. The existence of South of Market, a large lower-class district catering to young single males, reinforced this tendency.

During the third of a century following the destruction of 1906, many of these patterns of residence, work, ethnicity, and family not only continued but also in some instances intensified. Numerous researchers—on neighborhoods, ethnic groups, or architectural history—all agree that after 1906 the South of Market became more the domain of single men, that the Mission became more Irish, that the Geary-Fillmore area of the Western Addition became more Jewish, and that North Beach became more Italian.[52]

During the first third of the twentieth century, several new residential areas developed, most of them extensions of patterns already well established by 1900. New elite districts—Presidio Heights, Sea Cliff, Forest Hill, St. Francis Wood—were extensions of the patterns established in the Nob Hill–Pacific Heights area. The Richmond District, west from the Western Addition between the northern edge of Golden Gate Park and the southern boundary of the Presidio, became home to middle-class families, many of them moving west from their previous homes. Temple Emanu-El moved there in 1926, squarely on the boundary between the western extension of Pacific Heights and the eastern edge of the Richmond. Eventually other congregations were established in the central Richmond as well. There, too, many Russians settled after World War I, and small onion-domed Russian Orthodox churches were scattered through the Richmond during the 1920s and 1930s. There the new Russian Orthodox Cathedral was built in the early 1960s. (It had previously been located at Fulton and Fillmore in the Western Addition.) If the Richmond was, in many ways, a westward extension of many of the social and cultural patterns of the Western Addition at the turn of the century, new areas in the Outer Mission—Portola, Excelsior, Miraloma, Ocean View, Ingleside—were extensions of the Mission District, inhabited by skilled workers and lower-middle-class entrepreneurs and professionals, Irish, Italian, and German Catholic. The largest of the new districts, the Sunset, taking in roughly the southwestern quarter of the city, was developed in the 1920s, 1930s, and 1940s, after the Twin Peaks and Sunset streetcar tunnels were completed in 1917 and 1928. The Inner Sunset, the area between Kirkham Street and Golden Gate Park, out to about Twelfth Avenue, was built up before World War I, and in the rest of the Sunset mass-constructed rowhouses were built in the 1920s, 1930s, and 1940s. The Sunset was heterogeneous, with many middle-class families of Irish descent mixed with those of western European descent. By 1940, several huge Spanish mission–style Catholic parish churches had risen above the surrounding two- and three-story rowhouses.[53]

Understanding these interrelated patterns of ethnicity, occupation, residence, and class is essential not only for an understanding of the politics of the city (Chapters 6 through 9) but also for an understanding of many of the patterns of labor relations in the city, a topic to be explored in the next chapter.

We have no labor troubles. . . .
We give the men what they want.
—S. H. KENT, president of the
San Francisco Building Exchange, 1905

Chapter 4

Unions and Employers

Lucile Eaves, an early sociologist, wrote in 1910 that there was "evidence of such early trade-union activity in San Francisco that one is tempted to believe that the craftsmen met each other on the way to California and agreed to unite." In the winter of 1849, San Francisco carpenters asked for a wage increase and struck when employers refused. Printers organized the first trade union a few months later, teamsters organized soon after, and both sailors and musicians went on strike before the year 1850 was out. These early organizations, like their counterparts in the cities of the East, lasted but a month, a year, sometimes a few years, with only a few surviving much longer. Local unions appeared, fell apart, then reappeared later in a different form. Activists created citywide central bodies, but they usually soon disappeared, to be replaced by some new group. After the 1880s, however, an increasing number of organizations survived the crises—depression, lost strikes, employer opposition—that had spelled death for earlier efforts.[1] The history of San Francisco's labor relations falls into three time periods: from the revival of unions in the 1880s up to 1901, from 1901 to 1919, and from 1919 to the mid-1930s.

UNION ACTIVITY IN THE 1880s AND 1890s

The first of these periods saw the emergence of many of the institutions and institutional patterns that would dominate later time periods, as earlier varieties of labor organization slowly evolved into different forms. The 1880s and early 1890s brought San Francisco and the rest of the nation both economic growth and a degree of prosperity. Throughout much of the 1880s, wheat and wool poured from the interior through San Francisco outward to the world. The city's population grew by more than a quarter, the number of manufacturing establishments increased by a third, capital invested in manufacturing more than doubled, and the number of workers employed went from 28,442 to 48,446. The expansionary economy of the 1880s and the first few years of the 1890s allowed employers to grant wage increases, and the average annual earnings of San Franciscans employed in manufacturing rose from $525 in 1880 to $639 in 1890, despite the generally deflationary tendency of the times.[2]

During the early 1880s unions revived, reorganized, or formed in many trades. The city's expanding economy provided an ideal setting for some of these unions to post early successes; employers, reluctant to lose any of their share of this growth, gave in to union efforts, thereby repeating the pattern of the 1850s and late 1860s when unions had formed and made gains during periods of prosperity and economic expansion. Very few unions had established national affiliations before the 1880s, but during that decade many San Francisco unions did so, giving themselves a more direct link to information about other cities and a source of assistance in times of crisis.[3]

Anti-Chinese agitation constituted a staple of city politics in the 1870s (see Chapter 6), and the revival of unions in the 1880s brought with it a transfer of anti-Chinese agitation to labor groups. White boot- and shoe-makers, cigarmakers, and clothing workers had long viewed Chinese labor as a threat to their wages and working conditions. They had tried to protect themselves by urging consumers to boycott Chinese-made goods and to buy only products with white-labor labels. Anti-Chinese boycotts made up much of the activities of the Trades Assembly, a central body formed in 1878. Generally inactive during its first three years, the Trades Assembly jolted into action when Frank Roney became its president in 1881. The assembly added new affiliates, opposed Chinese labor and the leasing of convict labor, questioned candidates for office, and lobbied for labor legislation in Sacramento. One success came in 1883 with the creation of a state Bureau of Labor Statistics.[4] By that time, however, the Trades Assembly had ceased to meet. Two new groups, the Knights of Labor and the International Workingman's Association, siphoned off energies of labor activists from the Trades Assembly, and Frank Roney—centrally important in many of the assembly's activities—shifted his attention to other arenas.

Knights of Labor District Assembly 53 for San Francisco and the Bay Area organized in 1882. A year later it counted fifteen local assemblies, including eight trade assemblies. Some unions previously in the Trades Assembly apparently joined the Knights of Labor as trade assemblies. These unionists made up at least half, and perhaps as much as two-thirds, of the total membership. District Assembly 53 became inactive in the late 1880s, although some of the trade assemblies continued to function, and some eventually affiliated with the Federated Trades Council and with national unions.[5]

Formed in 1882, the International Workingman's Association (IWA) took the name of Marx's First International to proclaim its socialist principles. The moving force of the IWA, Burnette G. Haskell, impressed historian Ira Cross as "erratic and brilliant." Educated as a lawyer, Haskell preferred the life of a publisher and radical organizer. His newspaper, *Truth,* appeared from 1882 to 1884, and it tended, like Haskell himself, to be dramatic, extravagant, even fantastic. Haskell and some IWA activists left the city to form a cooperative colony in 1886, and the IWA soon disappeared. During its brief existence, it provided an important meeting ground for the city's radicals, and IWA members influenced the course of the San Francisco labor movement for the next decade or more. They helped organize the Coast Seamen's Union, the brewery workers, and the Federated Trades Council in 1886.[6]

Growth of Organization, 1886–1893. The Federated Trades Council was an ambitious attempt to create a central body for the entire Pacific Coast. Some unions and councils outside San Francisco affiliated with the new council, but delegates who came regularly all had their bases in San Francisco. Roney became the first president, and the first officers included a number of IWA activists. In the beginning, the council concentrated on opposition to the Chinese in a fashion reminiscent of the defunct Trades Assembly. In the prosperous 1880s, however, ability to win improvements in wages and hours soon supplanted the race consciousness of the late 1870s. Anti-Chinese efforts gave way to more direct organizing activities, promotion of the union label (not the white-labor label), and boycotts of nonunion products. The council maintained a lobby in Sacramento that opposed convict leasing or convict-made goods and fought for legal protection of union labels, the secret ballot, and various inspection and licensing acts. Roney served three terms as president of the body, and, according to Cross, Roney and the council "brought renewed life to the labor movement in California." The council affiliated with the new American Federation of Labor (AFL) and tried to persuade its affiliates to do likewise. Alfred Fuhrman, a key figure in the organization of brewery workers, served as council president in the late 1880s and early 1890s. Under his leadership, the brewery workers disaffiliated from their national union; the AFL, in turn, suspended the Federated Trades Council for refusing to expel the now-independent brewery workers' union.[7]

During Fuhrman's presidency, the council supported a large number of boycotts and strikes—more, apparently, than it had the capacity to handle effectively. Fuhrman's sometimes high-handed tactics as president caused additional dissatisfaction with the council. In 1891 a number of construction unions withdrew from the Federated Trades Council to affiliate solely with a new body, the Building Trades Council. Other unions withdrew from the council because they disliked Fuhrman's leadership, or the suspension by the AFL, or the council's many unsuccessful boycotts and strikes. The council clung tenaciously to life (Walter Macarthur of the Sailors' Union of the Pacific later said it "couldn't grow and wouldn't die") until a conference of union representatives created a new central body, the San Francisco Trades and Labor Council, shortened in 1893 to the San Francisco Labor Council.[8]

Open-Shop Efforts and Depression in the Mid-1890s. Much of the advance of union activity in the 1880s came to a halt in 1892 and 1893 when employers launched a citywide open-shop drive and the nation plunged into a serious depression. The Board of Manufacturers and Employers of California, formed in late 1891, announced their intent "to promote the manufacturing interests of the Pacific Coast . . . [and] to peacefully settle all disputes that may arise between employers and employees." Usually called the Manufacturers' and Employers' Association, the group committed itself to the open shop and set out to roll back the union tide of the previous decade. By the association's third anniversary, its president could announce:

> Among the industries of San Francisco there remains but one single union which enforces its rules upon its trade. That union is the Typographical Union. The reason why this union still continues to dictate terms is because the employing printers have never combined to resist its demands.

In both brewing and sailing, the gains of the 1880s were swept away when the association provided assistance to the Brewers' Protective Association and the Ship Owners' Association. The open-shop drive and the economic depression brought San Francisco labor to a fifteen-year nadir by the mid-1890s. Although membership in the Labor Council fell to only fifteen unions by 1897, both the council and a number of unions survived the hard times.[9]

The revival of prosperity in the late 1890s, the discovery of gold in the Klondike in 1896, the development of the state's fruit-growing regions, and the acquisition of Hawaii and the Philippines in 1898–1899 all helped to stimulate the city's economy and the expectations of its business community. The Hay-Bunau-Varilla Treaty of 1903, authorizing American construction of a canal across the isthmus of Panama, added a dream of cheaper and faster water transportation to an already heady vision of a bay filled with ships bearing Klondike gold, Alaskan fish, Hawaiian sugar, California fruit, and goods from China and Japan. The city's business leaders dared to dream of surpassing New York as the nation's metropolis by the end of the twentieth century, and they ushered in the new century to a symphony of optimism and ambition.

The first flush of returning prosperity, from the initial movement of prospectors and supplies to the Klondike in 1897 and continuing through the war months of 1898, brought little union activity. But rising prices in 1899 prompted workers to seek higher wages, and employers initially granted many of these requests. The city experienced the beginning of an unprecedented boom in union membership. Brewery workers recovered ground lost in 1892, printers secured the eight-hour day from the city's newspapers, sailors won wage increases, and the Building Trades Council began to enforce the closed shop. The next year, 1900, witnessed the unionization of even more workers, including the teamsters. The return of prosperity brought a burst of union activity, which can only be compared with that of the 1930s in its scope and impact. By October 1901, the Labor Council counted ninety-eight affiliates and soon established its own weekly newspaper, the *Labor Clarion*. By 1904 San Francisco had 180 local unions, forty-two of them affiliated only with the reorganized Building Trades Council.[10]

BUILDING TRADES COUNCIL

The San Francisco Building Trades Council (BTC) during its heyday, the quarter-century from 1896 to 1921, became perhaps the most powerful labor organization in the country. BTC affiliates directly determined wages, hours, and work rules for their members. If a local wanted to change some work rule, the BTC leadership first gave its consent, then announced the new "law" to employers. Individual employers had ninety days to protest the change. If no one protested or if the BTC refused to accept the employers' complaints, BTC business agents enforced the new rule. The BTC did not advocate collective bargaining, at least as conventionally defined. BTC secretary Olaf A. Tveitmoe, in 1912, referred to contracts as "shackles by which the workers have locked their own hands" and "signed away the only right they have—the right to quit work when and where they please." BTC president Patrick Henry McCarthy told the U.S. Commission on Industrial Relations in 1914: "We believe we have a right to frame our own laws."[11]

Building trades workers could frame their own laws regarding wages, hours, and working conditions because they possessed the power centralized in and exercised by the BTC and, more specifically, by BTC president McCarthy. Born in Ireland, McCarthy learned the carpenter's trade there and came to America at the age of seventeen. He lived for a time in Chicago, moved to St. Louis and became a member of the Carpenters' Union, then carried both his trade and his trade unionism to San Francisco in 1886. He joined Carpenters' Local 22, soon became president of the local and then BTC president (in 1898, at age thirty-five), and won reelection every year for the next quarter-century. Handsome, with dark hair and an imposing handlebar mustache, McCarthy used his talents to build a base of great economic—and, ultimately, political—power. Tveitmoe joined him in 1900 when he became BTC recording secretary and editor of the BTC's weekly newspaper, *Organized Labor.* Born in Norway, Tveitmoe had taught school in Minnesota before coming to San Francisco in 1897. He worked as a cement worker and quickly became an officer in that union and its president in 1899. McCarthy and Tveitmoe helped to form the State Building Trades Council in 1901 and held corresponding offices in it. Others from the San Francisco BTC also held state or national offices in their unions. While some opposed McCarthy's reign as BTC president, no one could defeat him. Those who tried usually received vindictive treatment. Within the BTC and within the construction industry, McCarthy held final authority on all matters from 1898 to 1921. A visiting AFL official marveled in 1910: "Defeat was unknown."[12]

McCarthy, Tveitmoe, and the BTC dominated the construction industry in San Francisco by a simple and direct method: they required all workers in the industry to carry a union working card, a device described by Tveitmoe as "the keystone of the BTC's stability and success as an organization." All union members bought a quarterly card with their dues, and the card served as both a sign of union membership and a passport to employment. Shop stewards—union members working on each building site—and full-time union business agents policed each work site, maintaining a constant vigil for nonmembers. *Every* worker on a job site had to have a card if *any* union member was to work at that site. Most foremen had to be union members: to maintain their membership, they followed a rule that only union members be hired. As a result of these intensive organizing efforts, Tveitmoe could boast in 1905 that there "was nothing more to organize in the building industry." Only lumber and millwork from union mills, carrying the BTC label, were allowed on construction sites. BTC business agents had free access to all job sites where they checked for violations of BTC rules. The BTC held final authority to decide conflicts between employees and contractors over the enforcement of work rules. The president of the San Francisco Building Exchange, S. H. Kent, explained the system succinctly in 1905: "We have no labor troubles. . . . We give the men what they want."[13]

The basic organizational structure of the BTC—a number of autonomous locals of various trades affiliated with different national unions, united in an industrywide council to which the locals surrendered some of their autonomy—existed in other industries and in other cities. Other unions also relied on the closed shop, the union label on materials, and the use of business agents to police job sites and seek violations of union rules. The San Francisco BTC, however, used these techniques more successfully than others within San Francisco and elsewhere. The concept of an industrywide body, taking in all the local unions within the city in a particular industry, was well established in San Francisco by the turn of the century. The Iron Trades Council and the Allied Printing Trades Council, like the BTC, took in locals from different national unions. Other councils united the locals of one national union across the lines of jurisdictional differences, for example, the Joint Council of Team Drivers, the Joint Local Executive Board of Hotel and Restaurant Employees and Bartenders unions, and the District Council of Retail Clerks.[14] In 1901, the formation of a council of waterfront unions helped to precipitate one of the city's major labor conflicts.

THE SECOND PERIOD: 1901 TO 1919

San Francisco's economy in the late nineteenth and early twentieth centuries depended heavily on the waterfront. The men who worked aboard ship, loaded and unloaded cargo, and transported goods to and from the docks had few skills; most were young and single. Just as sailors found work through boardinghouse keepers, so longshoremen turned out for the "shape-up," in which potential workers assembled at a pier when a ship was to be loaded or unloaded, and the foreman hired some for that job. For sailors and longshoremen, work was temporary and typically performed under conditions of harsh discipline and low wages. Although the first recorded sailors' strike came in 1850 and longshoremen struck the next year, most early efforts at unions were short-lived.[15]

Waterfront Unions. Sailors established a more permanent union in 1885 when they formed the Coast Seamen's Union with assistance from the International Workingman's Association. This group merged with the Steamship Sailors' Union in 1891 to produce the Sailors' Union of the Pacific (SUP), and the SUP soon established itself as one of the largest labor organizations in the western United States. Paul Scharrenberg, editor of the SUP's weekly newspaper, *Coast Seamen's Journal,* described the SUP to the Commission on Industrial Relations in 1914 as "a real 'one big union' " for sailors. "It covers the entire Pacific coast. There are no locals. A man who is a member of that union can sail anywhere between here and the coast of Africa. That is the jurisdiction of the seamen's union of the Pacific coast." The SUP maintained branch offices up and down the coast and eventually in New York, and it helped organize not just sailors, but also marine firemen, cooks and stewards, and Alaska fishermen.[16]

Andrew Furuseth, born in Norway and conversant in English, German, Dutch, French, and the Scandinavian tongues, led the SUP for nearly fifty years. Furuseth served as secretary (initially the only paid position in the SUP) from 1887 to 1892 with some interruptions for returns to the sea, and then without interruption from 1892 to 1936. He helped create the International Seamen's Union and served as its president in 1897–1899 and from 1908 to his death in 1938. Walter Macarthur, born in Scotland, edited the *Coast Seamen's Journal* from 1895 to 1913, and Scharrenberg, Macarthur's successor as editor and secretary-treasurer of the State Federation of Labor after 1911, worked closely with Furuseth.[17]

The early longshore unions lacked such durable leadership, but they had existed on the waterfront since the 1850s and 1860s. One of them, the Riggers' and Stevedores' Union, survived from 1853 until the 1920s, but employers controlled it for a time in the late nineteenth century. A number of longshore workers' unions emerged in the 1880s, notably the Longshore Lumbermen in 1880, two stevedores' groups in 1886, and a brick-handlers' union and stevedore engineers' union in 1887. In 1888, these groups joined with three seamen's unions, three unions of ship repair workers (riggers, caulkers, and shipwrights), and a union of wharf builders to form a short-lived Council of Wharf and Wave Unions. Although this effort at coordinated action lasted only a year, the membership included all the organized trades on the waterfront at the time. Another short-lived effort at a council in 1891 included most of the same unions.[18]

In February 1901, the City Front Federation united the SUP, the longshoremen's unions, and the new Teamsters' Local Union 85, posing the potential for arresting the city's economic heartbeat should they ever vote to shut down the waterfront. An Employers' Association appeared two months later, led by prominent merchants and manufacturers. The association kept its membership, financial resources, and governing board secret but publicized its commitment to the open shop and its guiding principle: disputes between employer and employee should be settled "without interference from the officers or members of any labor organization." Association bylaws specified that no member could settle with a union without permission from the association executive committee. Centralized power now faced centralized power. At this juncture, the Epworth League, a Methodist young people's association, contracted with a nonunion drayage company to haul convention baggage, and that company subcontracted part of the task to a unionized company. The Teamsters' Union agreement with the Draymen's Association specified that no teamster was to work for a draying company not a member of the association. Teamster adherence to this contract became the immediate *casus belli* for San Francisco's "labor war" of 1901.[19]

The 1901 Strike. Initially, many of the draymen supported the teamsters' action, but when the Employers' Association formed the Merchants' Drayage and Warehouse Company to compete with the Draymen's Association, they swung against the union and yielded full control over events to the Employers' Association. One draying company after another locked out their workers for refusal to haul goods of the nonunion company. Eventually the Teamsters voted that all their members should strike. When unionized beer bottlers refused to handle goods delivered by nonunion drivers, their employers declared an open shop. Other firms also discharged employees who refused to load or unload wagons driven by strikebreakers. The teamsters and their sympathizers, locked out and on strike, joined several strikes already in progress: restaurant cooks and waiters, bakers and bakery wagon drivers, metal polishers, and the fourteen-union Iron Trades Council, striking as part of a nationwide effort against the National Metal Trades Association. Earlier in the summer there had been strikes of butchers and carriage workers; the latter settled only when the Teamsters' Union had threatened to stop deliveries to nonunion carriage companies.[20]

Most union leaders of 1901 remembered vividly how the Manufacturers' and Employers' Association of 1891 had decimated union after union. Determined to prevent a recurrence of those events, convinced (in Furuseth's words) that the "employers are determined to wipe out labor unions one after another," the city's labor leaders took stock of their resources, realized they could never hope to match the estimated half-million dollars raised by the Employers' Association, and understood that the BTC would never join if the Labor Council called a general strike. Concluding that the survival of the Teamsters—and many other unions as well—depended on labor's ability to convince the Employers' Association to back down, the City Front Federation voted to shut down the waterfront.[21]

From July 30 to October 2, during the height of the harvest season, the City Front Federation remained on strike. Mayor James Phelan tried to mediate but quickly discovered that the Employers' Association discouraged his efforts. "The vital principle involved in the present controversy," the association announced, "is that of non-interference by the labor unions, or their representatives, with the conduct of the business of employers." Mediation would compromise this principle. The association continued: "The principle thus involved may be surrendered by the employer, but it can not be compromised." The association remained convinced that the only acceptable labor relations were those between employers and individual employees. Mike Casey, leader of the teamsters, responded: "That is plainly saying to us that we may have 'smokers' or something of that sort as a result of the existence of unions, but that we shall not utilize the organization for the purpose they have been designed to serve."[22]

From the beginning, the Employers' Association used strikebreakers. These nonunion drivers immediately became the focus of strikers' antagonism; the hoots and jeers thrown at them were accompanied at times by bricks and stones. City police, assigned to ride the wagons driven by nonunion drivers, occasionally assisted the inexperienced drivers. The Employers'

Association soon replaced city police with private guards given the status of special police. Strikebreakers and employers secured permits to carry concealed weapons. According to the *Examiner,* the only daily newspaper sympathetic to the strikers, police were told to "make no arrests but use your clubs." The continuing importation of strikebreakers and their protection by the police eventually had their effects. The City Front Federation had brought 60 percent of the city's business to a standstill when the unions went out on July 30. By September 20 the strikebreakers had restored the waterfront to a semblance of normal operation. Special police continued to be prominent, and a gun battle on Kearny Street involving special police brought increasing calls for the militia to restore order. Governor Henry T. Gage soon arrived in the city and met with Father Peter Yorke, a strike sympathizer whose support in 1898 Gage had considered essential to his election. The governor then brought the Draymen's officers together with union leaders but excluded representatives of the Employers' Association. The two principals arranged a settlement within an hour, and teamsters returned to work with union buttons on their caps. During the two months of the strike, five people had died and more than three hundred had been injured.[23]

The employers claimed a victory, but in retrospect, the opposite conclusion seems unavoidable. Walter Macarthur wrote in 1906 that the "City Front Federation had vindicated the 'right to organize.' " Paul Scharrenberg, more than fifty years later, saw the 1901 strike as a crucial event that "established the unions in San Francisco permanently." According to the Employers' Association's own definitions, the settlement represented a defeat, for they had insisted that *any* agreement would amount to a surrender of their most vital principle. The Employers' Association soon disappeared, and unions, at least briefly, had virtually an open field. One other consequence of the strike, the election of a Union Labor party mayor (see Chapter 7), guaranteed that city police powers would not again be used as they had been in 1901. Two and a half years after the strike, muckraker Ray Stannard Baker wrote that in San Francisco, "unionism holds undisputed sway."[24]

Extension of Unionization, 1901–1916. The survival of the Teamsters and the waterfront unions, their ability to secure recognition and signed agreements governing working conditions, the disappearance of the Employers' Association, and a sympathetic administration in city hall all contributed to a unionization surge that extended through the winter of 1903–1904. Unionization not only included the skilled trades typical of unions throughout the nation's cities but also bootblacks, gravediggers, chorus girls, dishwashers, fish cleaners, janitors, poultry dressers, stablemen, wool sorters, and other workers who lacked unions in virtually any other part of the country. Most organized themselves into federal locals because there was no national union for their occupation. Experienced union officials warned the new unions to "go slow" and to take advantage of the moment's "peace and prosperity," to prepare for worse times certain to come when economic downturn or revival of the open-shop movement might bring a crisis. Industrywide bargaining and trade agreements became a common feature in some areas of the city's economy, but the employer associations that developed rarely held together as well as the unions. Many, instead, were loose, informal, short-lived, and often limited to a minority of the firms in the industry.[25]

The open-shop movement came back to life in the winter of 1903–1904 when the Citizens' Alliance formed a San Francisco branch. The Citizens' Alliance, a national organization with branches in most major cities, attracted little initial attention in San Francisco. When Herbert George (an experienced antiunion organizer) arrived, the city's labor movement took notice. George, a veteran of Colorado's war on the Western Federation of Miners, found a key difference between Colorado and San Francisco. In Colorado, the state government played an active role in the suppression of the miners' union; in San Francisco, city government paid deference to the unions, and the state government stayed out of city disputes.[26]

George undertook to build an employers' organization in the vacuum left by the demise of the Employers' Association, and he found eager recruits in some of the defunct association's most active supporters. The Citizens' Alliance attempted to use proven union weapons against the unions: it developed an open-shop label for its members to use on their printing, urged members to boycott union-label products, and picketed union shops with placards demanding the open shop. The group made frequent use of injunctions against picketing and hired private guards to protect nonunion workers. Through such tactics, the alliance did post a few victories. It broke the Stablemen's Union and established the open shop in stables, helped to break a strike by leather workers, and enforced the open shop in retail meat markets. The open-shop campaign failed to make much other headway, however, and most city unions maintained their previous status. In 1905, the alliance focused on the restaurant industry, and the culinary unions lost a number of union-shop agreements and eventually found themselves restricted to small working-class eating houses. In the 1905 election, George and the Citizens' Alliance made an effort to defeat the city's Union Labor party mayor, but he won even more decisively than before. In the aftermath of the earthquake and fire in April 1906, the Citizens' Alliance rapidly receded from the public eye. By 1907, the group still represented employers in a dozen industries, but George had been replaced, and the organization acquired a more low-key profile.[27]

These three efforts at uniting city employers had all strongly stressed that they did not oppose unions per se. The pattern began with the Manufacturers' and Employers' Association in 1891, which defined itself as opposed only to the unions' "arbitrary spirit" and to strikes and boycotts. "The boycott," they claimed, "is a crying evil of our times." They pointed to business agents who had been bribed (presumably by businessmen) to institute boycotts of "competitors." The Employers' Association in 1901 publicized the following description of their principles:

> We recognize the right of labor to organize to ameliorate its conditions, and we as employers will not trespass upon that right by refusing employment to anyone solely because he does or does not belong to any labor organization.

The Citizens' Alliance proclaimed a similar commitment, promising that "so long as the Union remains within legal rights it will find the Citizens' Alliance friendly." Recognizing that "the public at large, and in fact many of our own members" mistakenly believed the alliance intended to "disrupt and destroy labor Unions," they insisted instead that "our policy is embodied in the expression OPEN SHOP, which means that every man has the right to work and to the protection of the law." Acknowledging that "public opinion always has and will always support the Unions when they demand what is right," the alliance added that "when through violence, an attempt is made to secure that to which they are not entitled, the Citizens' Alliance will exert its full strength and power to defend those who are attacked, whether employers or employees." The Citizens' Alliance emblazoned these two central objectives on their letterhead as "Law and Order" and "Industrial Peace."[28] "The open shop" and "law and order" would remain the rallying cries for employers' associations from 1901 through 1934.

Unions, of course, responded to these arguments by questioning the employers' actual commitment to unionization. In 1908, the *Labor Clarion* quoted the definition of the open shop offered by Mr. Dooley, the fictional saloonkeeper created by Finley Peter Dunne, the most widely read political satirist of the day:

> Whut is th' open shop? Shure, 'tis a shop where they keep th' dure open t' accommodate th' constant sthream of min comin' in t' take jobs cheaper thin th' min what has th' jobs.

Andrew Gallagher, president of the Labor Council, defended the union shop in direct terms in 1914:

> We as workers don't believe that the employer has any right to ask us to work alongside of the man who bears none of our burdens, who shares none of our troubles, who will take upon himself none of the duty of enforcing any of the ideals that we stand for. . . . If he comes among us and refuses to become one of us, we reserve the right to cease work with him if necessary.[29]

Most unionists understood the call for the open shop as an assault on union power to enforce work rules or as an attempt to guarantee that some workers would remain on the job in the event of a strike. Professions of regard for unions fell especially flat on the ears of the veterans of 1891–1892 or 1901. Most unionists probably would have agreed with Mr. Dooley's oft-repeated analysis:

> "But," said Mr. Hennessey, "these open shop min ye minshun say they are for the unions if properly conducted."
> "Shure," said Mr. Dooley, "if properly conducted. An' there ye are. An' how wud they have them conducted? No strikes; no rules, no contracts; no scales; barely any wages, an' dam few mimbers."

Unions denied the predictable charges that they had incited violence and lawlessness, although Gallagher did acknowledge that the use of strike-breakers caused problems: "We are very often met on our side with over-anxious sympathizers. Sometimes they are union men and sometimes they are not." John O'Connell, secretary of the Labor Council, denied that union-ists were any more violent than employers, but noted in 1901: "If a dog got run over in the middle of Market Street the teamster would be blamed for killing him." O'Connell flatly denied that the teamsters were responsible for violence in 1901, attributing the violence instead to "the thugs, the gunmen of the employers' association."[30]

Labor's City, 1906–1916. Both "the open shop" and "law and order" took a back seat among businessmen after the earthquake and fire of April 1906. In the rush to rebuild, many San Francisco employers agreed to wage increases and improvements in working conditions as a necessary part of maintaining and expanding their work forces.[31] By one estimate, union wage scales advanced 20 percent in the year following the earthquake. There were, however, a number of union reverses after 1906 as well. Although the BTC saw its affiliates' membership nearly double, some unions did not survive the destruction of 1906 at all because some factories were not rebuilt or union members were scattered to new places of employment.[32] Despite gains among construction unions, the membership of Labor Council affil-iates remained steady.

The half-dozen years after the earthquake also saw several employers undertake antiunion drives, albeit without material support from any city-wide coalition. The most notable, the 1907 strike against the United Rail-roads, which ran nearly all the city's streetcar lines, brought strong and united support for the Carmen's Union from all parts of the labor move-ment including the BTC. Between May 1907 and March 1908, six men died of gunshot wounds, twenty-five people were killed in streetcar accidents, and more than a thousand were injured in accidents or in incidents between strikers and strikebreakers. In the end, the union acknowledged a defeat and turned in its charter. A much shorter and less violent strike against the Pacific Telephone and Telegraph Company brought a similar defeat for that union. The unions of the city also suffered embarrassment beginning in late 1906 and continuing for the next four years when the city's news-papers carried report after report of graft and corruption among the labor party officeholders elected in 1905. Patrick McCarthy himself ran for mayor in 1907 but lost. He came back to win the office in 1909. The years from 1907 to the outbreak of war in Europe brought stable times for the city's labor movement with few major conflicts and no strong open-shop cam-paign among the city's employers.[33]

By World War I, San Francisco had acquired a reputation as the most unionized city in the nation: a "closed-shop city." Despite the union shops established by the BTC, the SUP, Teamsters, culinary workers, and others, the city did not deserve its "closed-shop" reputation. Many sectors of the economy remained only partially organized, and others totally lacked unionization. While the BTC, Molders, SUP, and a few other unions may have included all—or nearly all—those in that trade as members, other unions had difficulty in organizing more than a small part of their potential membership. The culinary workers had a union-shop agreement with some restaurant owners, but many restaurants were not party to the agreement.

Three culinary unions had varying degrees of success in recruiting members in 1910.[34]

	Census count of white and black workers in the city	Total union membership	Percentage of white and black workers in union
Bartenders	2,177	681	31.3
Waiters	2,828	1,215	43.0
Waitresses	945	447	47.3

Even in the construction industry, two contractors remained immune to the power of the BTC and used only nonunion labor. Entire sectors of the city's work force lacked representation on the rolls of unions, notably office and clerical workers. Of some four thousand women employed as stenographers and typists, only ten or so were union members in 1912, and they worked in union offices or in establishments with a union shop rule. The other ninety members of the Office Employees' Union were men, and they represented fewer than 1 percent of the male office and clerical workers in the city. Nearly all white-collar occupations lacked unions, and the few that did exist—actors, hospital stewards and nurses, draftsmen—struggled to keep their small memberships. Among public employees, only streetcar workers had organized before 1917; by mid-1919, teachers, federal employees, letter carriers, and post office clerks had also formed unions. Although unions existed for most blue-collar female workers, black and Asian workers had none. In 1910, black workers made up 0.5 percent of the total work force. That year, the Labor Council resolved, by a narrow margin, that all affiliated unions should admit qualified black workers, but the resolution was largely symbolic. A few unions had national restrictions. Most trades had few, if any, black workers. Neither the Labor Council nor individual unions undertook major efforts to organize the few black workers in the city. The culinary unions led an effort, also in 1910, to reverse the long-standing prohibition on recruitment of Asian workers, but they lost overwhelmingly.[35]

The Law and Order Committee, 1916. San Francisco business leaders, from the earthquake of 1906 through World War I, had other priorities than confrontation with unions. As reconstruction of the city proceeded apace, the Panama Canal seized the imagination of many. Described by one booster as "the most important geographical fact since the discovery of America," the canal seemed to pose "imperial possibilities" for San Francisco, prompting one business leader to predict that "before the end of the twentieth century San Francisco shall have superseded New York as the imperial city of America." The bankers' journal discerned but one cloud on this boundless horizon: "the possibility of a labor war, with the open shop as an issue, in this the most strongly unionized city in the country."[36]

Conflict seemed imminent in 1914 when a group of businessmen formed a Merchants' and Manufacturers' Association that absorbed the remnants of the Citizens' Alliance. No open-shop drive was launched that year or in 1915, however, due to fears for the success of the Panama Pacific International Exposition. Most business leaders saw the exposition as crucial to attracting new manufacturing and developing a tourist industry. In mid-1916, however, the San Francisco Chamber of Commerce, the city's leading business organization, undertook an antiunion drive. Though interrupted briefly by World War I, this campaign ultimately destroyed many of the city's most potent unions.[37]

Frederick Koster, a key person in the formation of the Merchants' and Manufacturers' Association in 1914, became president of the Chamber of Commerce in May 1916, just as the economic impact of the war in Europe was becoming more and more apparent. High demand for American goods, a relative shortage of labor, and rising prices all combined to encourage unions to make wage and hour demands. June 1 marked the beginning of a coastwide strike by the International Longshoremen's Association (ILA). On June 22, the Chamber of Commerce resolved that the strike constituted "an unwarranted coast-wide combination and effort to interfere with the commerce of the Port of San Francisco," charged the ILA with "indirect and unlawful . . . enforcement of closed shop conditions," and castigated the union for its "spirit of ruthlessness" against "helpless" shipowners. Denying any opposition to organized labor, the Chamber insisted on "the maintenance of law and order in labor disputes" and on "the right to employ union or non-union workers, in whole or in part, as the parties involved may elect." The Chamber pledged "its entire organization and the resources it represents" to the open shop and the defense of law and order, and served notice that it would oppose "any effort . . . to throttle the commercial freedom of San Francisco." Soon after, Koster and a Chamber delegation asked Mayor James Rolph to hire five hundred special policemen for the waterfront; Rolph instead ordered the regular police to search all strikebreakers for concealed weapons. Koster thereupon called a special meeting of all city businessmen, and, by the Chamber's count, two thousand responded.[38]

Koster addressed this crowd, asking them for action to eradicate "that disease permeating this community." He denied that the Chamber had any intention of destroying labor unions and claimed that the "law abiding union man of the most radical type" need not fear the Chamber "in the slightest." Contrasting the "immediate selfish interest" displayed by some unions to the "communities [*sic*] interest," he called for a campaign to defend not just "capitalistic industrial San Francisco" but also "the rights of the man who wants to work." The assembled businessmen adopted a series of resolutions supporting the sanctity of contracts, the maintenance of law and order, and the open shop; created a five-person Law and Order Committee; and pledged themselves "to support this movement to the fullest extent." The group pledged $200,000 in five minutes, and the committee raised $1 million in a few weeks.[39]

From July 1916 until April 1917, the Law and Order Committee dominated industrial relations in San Francisco, raising the hue and cry against radical unionists following the bombing of the city's Preparedness Day parade on July 22 (see Chapter 8), assisting the Restaurant Men's Association in breaking a strike by the culinary workers' unions, establishing the open shop in retail lumberyards, and securing passage of a strict antipicketing initiative

in November 1916. The committee hired four hundred telephone operators to call every voter in the city and urge support for the ordinance.
Thereafter, picketing of any sort became illegal, punishable by fifty days in
jail.[40]

THE THIRD PERIOD: 1919 TO THE MID-1930s

For San Francisco, as for the rest of the nation, the war brought increases
both in union membership and in bargaining agreements. Spurred by a
high level of inflation, unions demanded wage increases, and unionization
spread among workers not previously organized. Metal trades workers struck
in late 1917 and, with the assistance of federal mediators, won substantial
pay increases. Federal mediation prevented or ended strikes throughout
the war period, but an effort to organize the city's streetcar workers failed.
The culinary unions rebounded from their earlier defeat and even managed to secure recognition from the city's most prominent hotels for the
first time. During the war years, the Chamber of Commerce preferred to
play a less prominent role in labor relations, limiting itself largely to statements against an anti-injunction bill, praising the governor for vetoing it,
and publicizing former president Taft's remarks on labor relations.[41]

In 1914, the formation of the Merchants' and Manufacturers' Association
had seemed to herald a labor war with the open shop as the employers'
object, but the imminence of the Panama Pacific International Exposition
had dissipated that threat. In 1916, the formation of the Law and Order
Committee of the Chamber of Commerce had seemed to hold similar portents, but war had intervened. In 1919, the long-anticipated open-shop drive
finally materialized, with the first major successes by employers coming on
the waterfront and in the metal trades. San Francisco was not the only city
to experience labor conflict in 1919. Throughout the nation, unions that
had waxed strong during the war now sought to bring their members' wages
into line with ever-increasing prices—dubbed "HCL" (high cost of living)
in the newspapers of the day. This push for wages coincided, in San Francisco as elsewhere, with growing fears of bolshevism in Europe and radicalism in the United States.

All these elements came together in a strike by the Riggers' and Stevedores' Union, Local 38–33 of the International Longshoremen's Association. The union had, for some years, included a sizable contingent of radicals, sympathetic to the Industrial Workers of the World. A strike by the
union in 1916, in violation of its contract, had been the catalyst in the formation of the Law and Order Committee. In 1919, the union struck again,
demanding not just wage increases but also representation on the boards of
directors of the companies involved, a 10 percent interest in the ownership
of the companies, and a quarter of all future dividends. The strike vote
violated procedures specified in the local's constitution, and the employers
refused to bargain, declaring that no faith could be placed in any agreement
with radicals. The employers then assisted in forming the Longshoremen's
Association, called the "Blue Book" union. Only through this company union
could work be secured on the waterfront from 1919 through 1934. The

Riggers' and Stevedores' Union, the oldest union in the city, expired, the first major casualty of the postwar open-shop campaign.[42]

Soon after the longshoremen voted to strike, the Bay Cities Metal Trades Council also walked out, striking shipyard employers throughout the area. The Labor Council supported this action fully, appealing nationwide for funds and contributing $100,000 itself to the cause, but to no avail. After six months, the Metal Trades Council acknowledged defeat, and the open shop became standard in the metal trades.[43]

Birth of the Industrial Association, 1921. In 1921, the open-shop drive reached the very heart of union strength, the Building Trades Council. The struggle between the BTC and contractors gave birth to the organization that would dominate industrial relations in the city for the next decade and a half— the Industrial Association of San Francisco. During 1919 and 1920, building contractors' associations slowly merged and evolved until, by October 1920, the Builders' Exchange had developed a degree of centralization comparable with that of the BTC. In February 1920, the Builders' Exchange and the BTC entered into an agreement tying wage increases to the cost of living, but in September the Builders' Exchange ordered all employers to refuse any wage increases. Amidst threats of strikes and lockouts, Acting Mayor Ralph McLeran requested the Industrial Relations Committee of the Chamber of Commerce (successor to the Law and Order Committee) to bring about a settlement. The Industrial Relations Committee suggested that both sides submit wage disputes to an arbitration board. Faced with the alternatives of arbitration or lockout, the BTC reluctantly agreed to arbitrate, convinced that failure to do so would bring the city's bankers and businessmen into the fray on the side of the employers. When the arbitration board recommended an across-the-board wage *reduction* of 7.5 percent, the BTC refused to accept the finding. The Builders' Exchange accused the BTC of backing out on a commitment and declared a lockout. The Chamber of Commerce called a mass meeting (like that of 1916) at which the bankers and businessmen of the city pledged support for the Builders' Exchange. When the BTC remained adamant, the Builder's Exchange announced that the lockout would be ended by the establishment of the open shop. BTC president McCarthy thereupon convinced the BTC to adopt the arbitrators' award, but the Builders' Exchange would not back down from their commitment to the open shop. BTC unions struck but eventually returned to work in defeat, under open-shop conditions, with a 7.5 percent wage reduction, "elimination of those rules which hitherto have tended to reduce output and increase costs," and no access to construction sites by BTC business agents.[44]

Under the auspices of the Chamber of Commerce, a Citizens' Committee was formed in mid-1921 to support the Builders' Exchange and to promote the open shop elsewhere. Of the $1 million that was raised, about a third came from only thirty firms. Standard Oil of California and the Southern Pacific Company led the list of contributors, with $30,000 each, followed closely by the J. D. and A. B. Spreckels Company with $25,000. The city's sixteen banks donated a total of $137,362; the Anglo and London Paris

National Bank, the Bank of California, Crocker Bank, and Wells Fargo Bank each gave $15,000. Associated Oil, Pacific Gas and Electric, the Santa Fe Railroad, and Union Oil Company also contributed $15,000 each. Thirteen companies with interests in Hawaiian sugar gave a total of $84,000, led by C and H Sugar's contribution of $25,000. Eleven companies contributed $10,000 each, and 1,500 firms and individuals gave amounts ranging from $5 to $10,000. Members of the Citizens' Committee and of the Industrial Relations Committee of the Chamber of Commerce, groups with overlapping memberships, soon created the Industrial Association of San Francisco, a permanent body dedicated to the open shop and committed to "efficiency in industry," "the right of an employer to engage or dismiss men individually on merit," and "the public interest."[45]

Civic Patriotism and the American Plan. Those who led the Industrial Association (IA) were cut from similar cloth. Members of the IA board of directors also held directorships in the most significant companies in San Francisco and elsewhere on the Pacific Coast. Virtually all the major companies of the city appeared on the IA board at some time, including Pacific Gas and Electric, the Southern Pacific Company, Matson Navigation, California Packing Company, Fireman's Fund Insurance, D. Ghirardelli Company, Haas Brothers, Levi Strauss and Company, Mailliard and Schmiedell, American-Hawaiian Steamship Company, Alexander and Baldwin, and the major department stores. The IA board also counted representatives of several national companies, including U.S. Rubber, Westinghouse, Bethlehem Shipbuilding, Pierce-Arrow, General Electric, and General Cigar. The advisory board consistently included representatives of the Bank of California and the various Fleishhacker interests (Anglo-California Trust Company, Anglo and London Paris National Bank, Anglo-California Bank).[46]

Leaders of the IA filled active roles in the city's Chamber of Commerce and some took similar roles at state or national levels. They belonged to the most exclusive clubs in San Francisco and some held similar memberships in Los Angeles and New York. They helped to found or direct the city's symphony, opera, and Art Association, and they provided similar leadership for everything from the Community Chest to Stanford University, from the Boy Scouts and YMCA to the California Historical Society, from Children's Hospital to the Republican party.[47] For them, the IA occupied only one small niche in busy and complex lives, and they defined its nature and objectives in a fashion consistent with their other civic activities.

Early in the history of the IA, spokesmen defined its victory over the Building Trades Council as "more a contribution to civic patriotism than to anything else." They called their magazine *American Plan* and their newsletter *American Plan Progress*. IA leaders, they assured the world, "have dedicated their best to this community development, and their only reward— and surely there could be no greater—has been the satisfaction of seeing San Francisco once again a free city in every sense of the word, in which capital can safely invest." "We are all San Franciscans," said IA president Colbert Coldwell in 1927, "with a common point of view—the welfare of the city." He portrayed the IA as the key to establishing "a trinity of interests

... that will insure our industrial peace and prosperity for the years to come," a trinity composed of labor, employers, and the public—represented by the Industrial Association.[48]

The "American Plan" meant more than just the open shop. The IA established the "impartial wage board" as the means of setting wages. Periodically throughout the 1920s and early 1930s, the IA convened boards to compare the rate of pay in the building trades in San Francisco with those in other cities and to make recommendations for adjustments. The IA's American Plan package also included apprenticeship schools, an employment agency, and work permits. The apprenticeship schools were the IA's solution to the scarcity of skilled workers. By training more workers, the IA sought to avoid "the fallacy of seeking to meet a labor shortage by giving the same mechanics higher wages." According to the IA, these schools represented a genuine community service: "We have taken some of these lads who were utterly unskilled and unfit for anything except driving automobiles, and made of them useful mechanics commanding a high wage, and splendid citizens of this community."[49] In addition to the schools, the IA also operated an employment agency. According to the IA, the placement agency paid no regard to union or nonunion status. In fact, in the construction industry at least, no work site ever had more than 50 percent union members.[50]

Union Opposition to the American Plan. Problems arose, to be certain, in maintaining the open shop. Iron molders kept up opposition to the IA throughout the early 1920s. The IA accused the molders of using a roving "wrecking crew" and of "regularly shooting down or otherwise assaulting in the most cruel and brutal manner defenseless American Plan foundry workers."[51]

When the Carpenters' Union struck in 1926, the IA charged them, too, with "slugging and killing." In fact, the carpenters' strike posed the most serious challenge to the IA between 1921 and 1934. The strike began on April 1 at the prompting of the national headquarters of the United Brotherhood of Carpenters and Joiners; the national officers took a direct hand in strike planning from the beginning. The IA portrayed the effort to regain the union shop as a power play by the union, aimed at American Plan carpenters: "It is not a strike against employers or capital, but a strike of carpenter against carpenter, with the public and the prosperity of the city threatened."[52]

The strike lasted for more than nine months, affecting between four and five thousand workers. Violent encounters took place almost daily. The IA hired strikebreakers from outside the Bay Area and maintained a boardinghouse for them. Strikers waylaid nonunion workers and attacked them, both verbally and physically. Several unionists formed a "wrecking crew," roaming the city at night and demolishing the work on nonunion sites. The Board of Supervisors initially sided with the unions and ordered police to withhold protection from nonunion work sites. The IA pushed the Police Commission and other public officials to jail strike leaders for conspiracy to riot, but San Francisco juries refused to convict those charged. As the strike wore on and as violence and vandalism continued, the IA hinted that a return to vigilantism might be necessary. In late October, a nonunion carpenter died of injuries received in a beating. The strike finally came to an end in mid-January, following the first formal agreement between union officials and contractors since 1921, but the agreement implicitly recognized the continuation of the open shop.[53]

The IA portrayed the molders' and carpenters' strikes as unusual, reflecting the "gory record of a handful of defeated union gangsters who captured union leadership." Strikes, claimed the IA, had actually become unnecessary: "There is nothing reasonable that San Francisco unionism wants that it cannot have under the liberty and freedom of the American Plan." Constant vigilance was necessary, however, because "exploiters of labor, posing as leaders, are watching and working night and day for the chance to rule or ruin San Francisco's industry and progress." The IA kept before the community the constant menace of "the labor bosses and racketeers" and the continuing need to "keep the way open for the future prosperity of industry and business."[54]

The Labor Council charged the IA with other activities in addition to those for which the organization so quickly took credit. According to the Labor Council, the IA "hired sluggers who are sent out armed with blackjacks to beat and maim inoffensive San Francisco workingmen for the terrible crime of exercising their American right to be identified with a labor union." Not limiting charges to rhetoric, the Labor Council produced affidavits from an IA inspector and from an employee of the detective agency retained by the IA. These men acknowledged that the head inspector of the IA had sent them to a job site to seek out a worker who "preached unionism to the non-union men." They "struck [him] over the head with blackjacks which each one of us then and there had in our possession." Similar affidavits, apparently never published, implicated the IA's detective agency in the shooting of the business agent of the Iron Molders' Union and two other molder activists, one of whom died. To the Labor Council, the American Plan—which they sometimes referred to as the "un-'American Plan' "—represented only the "falsely labeled longing of a few arrogant men for absolutism in industry."[55]

Despite the success of the IA in instituting or maintaining the open shop in construction, the metal trades, on the waterfront, and elsewhere, most unions survived and many survived with contracts. The IA failed to establish a foothold in a number of industries. In 1931, after ten years of the American Plan, the largest local in the San Francisco Labor Council was Teamsters' Local 85, with 2,700 members. The musicians' local stood very close to that number with 2,500. The city's four culinary unions claimed a total of 5,245 members; other large unions in 1931 included Typographical Local 21, the chauffeurs' local (despite the open shop enforced by the IA in several leading taxi companies), the Alaska fishermen, federal employees, ferryboatmen, and carmen (streetcar workers). The Sailors' Union of the Pacific, however, had only 250 members, and there were no longshoremen's unions affiliated with the Labor Council. Membership in construction trades unions had fallen drastically. The heart of the city's economy—the waterfront, food processing, iron and steel, construction—was under the American Plan.[56]

Waterfront interests, agricultural processing firms, and those companies that combined both by shipping Hawaiian agricultural products had long taken prominent roles in the open-shop movement, both in the IA and in its predecessors. Because of the perishable nature of some of their products and because of the central importance of water transportation to the processing and distribution of their products, they opposed unions and strikes more vigorously than most other segments of the city's economy. These and other open-shop proponents, through the IA, helped maintain the open shop in construction when many contractors expressed willingness to continue union-shop arrangements. By keeping unions weak or on the defensive throughout the city, open-shop advocates felt that they reduced the political power of unions and thus protected themselves from the political pressures that had aided union organizing during the heyday of the Union Labor party. Open-shop advocates elected some sympathetic city officials but never dominated city government.[57] When the IA finally suffered defeat in 1934, it was primarily because of political changes a continent away, over which the business community of San Francisco could exercise little influence.

□   □   □

The growth and development of labor unions and employers' associations over the period from 1880 to 1931 display a number of common elements. First, and so obvious as to scarcely require mention, is the emergence and development of *organization* as the basis for labor relations. After 1901, no employer group publicly denounced the concept of unionization itself, and no labor group suggested that employers ought not to join with one another. Conflict occurred not over the notion of organization but over the aims and conduct of the organizations. Both unions and employer groups recognized the benefits of organization, and both pursued the concentration of power and the centralization of decision making that organization made possible. Although slow to develop strong associations, employers ultimately proceeded further in the direction of centralization than did unions.

Jealous guardianship of local autonomy often formed the shoals on which labor central bodies foundered, notably on the waterfront. The Labor Council, largest and most visible central body in the city, had virtually no leverage over its members except the power of persuasion. A local that chose not to accept the advice of the Labor Council could not be forced to do so—witness the action of the Riggers and Stevedores in 1919 when the Labor Council urged them to abide by their own constitution. The Building Trades Council had much more power, but only over those unions in the construction industry. By contrast, citywide employers' associations on several occasions required employers to lock out their employees even though the employers preferred not to do so, for example the draymen in 1901 or some specialty contractors in 1921 and 1926. "The autonomy of each trade," a fundamental AFL principle, translated in practice into a more decentralized structure among unions than existed among employers, especially after 1921.

Centralization also meant, at times, the extension of disputes to larger arenas in an effort to mobilize more resources than one's opponent. The

City Front Federation strike in 1901 and, later, the general strike of 1934 provide examples of such broadening from the union side, and the activities of the Citizens' Alliance and the Industrial Association supply others from the side of the employers.

Within these general parameters of an acceptance of organization, the concentration of power, and the centralization of decision making, a variety of other patterns assume importance. A crucial one has to do with willingness—or unwillingness—to engage in conflict. In some instances, especially in industries with many small-scale entrepreneurs, success in achieving accommodation seemed to breed more of the same, for example, the close relationship between the teamsters and draymen both before and after the conflict of 1901.

In other industries, a high degree of concentration of decision making—either through monopolistic or oligopolistic corporations or powerful employers' associations—seemed to encourage conflict as employers calculated their abilities to stockpile materials, hire strikebreakers and guards, and outlast the workers. San Francisco Labor Council leaders, after 1901, tried to avoid conflict and seek accommodation and repeatedly counseled new unions not to take risks. When conflict developed, both sides often justified their positions in terms broader than those of the immediate dispute at hand. Both, during the 1920s especially, accused each other of arrogance and narrow self-interest; both presented their position as the one best suited to advance the interest of the community. Such justification in terms of the "public interest" reflects a pattern that goes back beyond the 1920s, to 1901 at least and perhaps before.

Both sides in time of conflict understood the central importance of mobilizing the power of the government on their side, and of denying that ally to the other. Throughout the period from 1901 onward, labor in San Francisco rejected the dictum to avoid politics. San Francisco unions instead undertook active attempts to control—or at least to neutralize—the power of city government. Employers, too, understood the importance of city government, and the most dramatic conflict of the period, the strike of 1901, came when employers successfully mobilized city police in protection of strikebreakers.[58]

Aside from drink and vice, and the calamities
of vice, there is no deep poverty here.
—SARAH INGERSOLL COOPER, ca. 1889

Chapter 5

Culture and the Moral Order

Economist David Wells, puzzled by what he called the "sociological sequences" accompanying industrial capitalism, took up his pen during the late 1880s to analyze the impact of the new economic forces on the distribution of wealth and the well-being of society. Violent clashes between labor and capital seemed to grow as rapidly as the nationwide railroad network. Frightening episodes of urban crime seemed to multiply as quickly as the streetcars that fostered city growth. Armies of unemployed men tramped threateningly throughout the country, and men, women, and children living in miserable poverty filled the almshouses and the older, more congested districts of the cities. San Franciscan Henry George decided in 1879 that "social difficulties . . . are, in some way or another, engendered by progress itself" and argued that the Single Tax provided the only solution. Ten years later, thousands of Americans joined the "Nationalist" movement after reading Edward Bellamy's *Looking Backward* and after agreeing that abolition of corporate property and nationalization of industry would be necessary preludes to social harmony and individual security.[1]

Bellamy's proposals, like George's Single Tax, attracted ardent supporters, but David Wells came closer to the typical attitude of the country's political and social leaders when he recommended careful, incremental, cultural reform as an antidote to crisis. Social disorder, he argued, would be temporary and should be regarded as an inevitable manifestation of evolutionary stress, but social activists could intervene to humanize the process. Society, he concluded, has "become a vastly more complicated machine than ever before—so complicated, in fact, that in order to make it work smoothly, all possible obstructions need to be foreseen and removed from its mechanism."[2]

SCHOOL REFORM

The ethic of social engineering prescribed by Wells found echoes throughout the nation by the 1890s and the first years of the century. Moral control
legislation, including the use of schools to inculcate social morality and the
use of urban planning to ensure civic loyalty, emerged as something of a
panacea.[3] The superintendent of the New York City schools summed up
what had become a national consensus when he told the National Education
Association convention in 1890 that "the most important business of government . . . is the development, intellectual, moral, and physical, of the
individual. In these facts lies the *raison d'être* of public education. The government that does not educate must either give place to a better government, or it will inevitably fall before a worse." Twelve years later, in a popular
manual for reformers published by Columbia University Press in 1902,
Frank Rollins argued that because diverse ethnic groups had filled the cities
and the population had become more heterogeneous, the need for the state
to oversee the education of its citizens had never been more critical.

> In cities so largely foreign in population (the city population by itself is quite
> un-American) American customs and institutions must be preserved for the
> sake of national unity; and American residents, especially of the poorer and
> middle classes, must be assured of conditions among which they may give their
> children respectable homes and a suitable education.[4]

Protestant reformers had no monopoly on patriotism during this period,
for Irish and Italian Catholics and German Lutherans and German Jews
demonstrated their devotion to the importance of correct moral guidance
by establishing private schools that operated parallel to the public systems.
Nonetheless, public schools did serve thousands of children in American
cities, and in San Francisco they also possessed a potential for the assimilation of Chinese and Japanese children. Control over the administration
and curriculum of public schools thus served as an important symbol of
cultural power.[5]

Controversy between Protestants and Catholics over cultural policies played
as important a role in San Francisco during the 1850s and 1860s as it did
in other centers of immigration such as St. Louis, New York, and Boston.
Like San Francisco's business leadership, the school administration and school
board were top-heavy with Yankees from New England. These men shared
the belief of Massachusetts state superintendent Horace Mann that the state
should enlist the schools to bring order to the society. John Swett, who
played an active role in San Francisco cultural politics for two generations,
exemplified their philosophy when he announced that "nothing can Amer-
icanize these chaotic elements and breathe into them the spirit of our institutions but the public schools." The city's first high school principal declared
that "the formation of an upright, Christian character is the great business
and success of life." In 1852, the first superintendent of schools observed
that "a large majority of the children have just now for the first time entered
American schools. Many of them are of foreign parentage, and both parents
and children are unacquainted with our manners and customs, as also with
our institutions." He warned readers of his report that policymakers would

need "great wisdom to control the multifarious elements and to bring order out of so much confusion."[6] But the two most popular superintendents, John C. Pelton (elected for two terms) and James Denman (elected for three terms), rejected the assimilationist policies of the New England model. "Both Pelton and Denman," according to Victor Shradar, "viewed themselves as servants to all the public and saw the necessity of representing the needs of all their constituents rather than catering merely to the Protestant, Yankee elite of the city."[7]

James Denman's third term as superintendent of schools (1873–1876) coincided with a period of labor surplus and high unemployment that peaked in mid-1877. Philanthropic cultural reformers from San Francisco's Protestant community reacted like their counterparts in New York, Philadelphia, and Chicago to the thousands of men who tramped the roads looking for work or who had to be dispersed by city police when they blocked the streets while lining up for jobs. Ragged bands of rootless and discontented young men vented their frustration by harassing the Chinese and smashing business property; they seemed to portend a generalized social breakdown. Rising numbers of destitute migrant families sought relief from hunger and sickness; they appeared to be bringing San Francisco a new class of vagrant children who threatened the future order of society. Newspaper editors, like many city officials, expressed alarm at the prospect of the spreading social malaise. Preachers often suggested a remedy: an education that taught respect for social institutions and encouraged the young to accept the available roles in the working class. Keep in mind, Reverend Noble of Plymouth Church explained in 1874, that "all the world over it is the ignorant classes who are the lawless, dangerous classes."[8]

Reverend Noble's association of ignorance and criminality and his conviction that schooling offered an alternative to anarchism fit a rhetorical pattern that became typical during the insecure years of Gilded Age America. The cycles of economic boom and bust that persisted throughout the last quarter of the century also affected San Francisco. The city experienced some return of prosperity in 1881 and early 1882, but by the end of the year unemployment increased. The iron and steel industries had an especially hard time whereas the building trades fared the best. Although the 1886–1892 period witnessed improvements, wages never rose above the cost of living, and employment remained unsteady. The year 1892 brought renewed increases in unemployment, and by June 1893 the eastern financial panic began to take its toll on California. One estimate put the number of unemployed at thirty-five thousand, and the *Coast Seamen's Journal* reported that the "destitution, misery and suffering" had not been so severe for a generation.[9]

Persistent economic insecurity and the accompanying social turbulence of the 1880s and 1890s helped guarantee that those San Franciscans who regarded the making of the schools into an institutional remedy for disorder would find rich opportunities for reform activities. The reformers, however, faced considerable opposition from representatives of the city's Irish, German, and Italian residents who found such social control formulas repugnant to their own more pluralistic versions of the good life. Further complication came from the fact that the Democrats dominated the city school board for most of this period, and the Democratic party catered more to the huge ethnic vote than to the smaller native-born group (by 1878, the city had 21,097 foreign-born voters and 16,818 native-born voters).[10] Not surprisingly, when Democrats constituted the majority on the school board, foreign-born membership rose the most. During the 1871–1873 period, when 75 percent of the board members represented the Democrats, immigrants made up 58 percent of the board. During the 1883–1890 period, Democrats controlled 66 percent of the seats on the board, and foreign-born membership averaged 29 percent. Two-thirds or more of the immigrants who served on the Board of Education during the 1865–1895 period had achieved the relatively high economic status of owners of businesses or professionals.[11]

Even before the social turmoil of "the terrible seventies" brought the issue of public school policy to center stage in San Francisco, controversy over the preferred mode of Americanization surfaced in connection with debates about the teaching of foreign languages. John Pelton, Democratic school superintendent between 1865 and 1867, broke with tradition by establishing German, French, and Spanish classes. Foreign-born Democrats had lobbied for such classes, and Pelton acquiesced. He believed that "the object of our Public School system, its true policy and leading idea, is to meet all reasonable educational demands." The new schools would serve the needs of immigrant families who could not afford private language teaching, "yet they were unwilling to permit their sons and daughters to grow up to maturity, and remain forever ignorant of their mother tongue."[12] By 1871, one-third of the city's children attended these Cosmopolitan Schools, as they were called, where German and French were taught along with English. Pelton's successor, James Denman, disliked these schools because he thought they would "perpetuate the evils of caste distinction." Denman could not discontinue an institution that had quickly become a popular feature of the city's cultural life, but he appointed an investigating committee that urged teachers to put foreign-language instruction to work as a vehicle for Americanization. Once enrolled, foreign-born students would follow the regular curriculum and have contact with American children, which would—he hoped—provide prompt assimilation. Eventually, school boards with fewer Democratic and foreign-born members cut foreign-language instruction to a maximum of one-half hour per day.[13] After the peak period of popularity in foreign-language classes during the early 1870s, both total enrollment and the number of schools offering the classes declined. Although opponents failed to push a bill through the state legislature prohibiting the use of public money for special language teaching in 1878, hard times led to cutbacks in the financing of "nonessential" courses such as French and German.[14]

The depressed conditions of the 1870s also moved reformers throughout the country to agitate in favor of state compulsory attendance laws. Whereas labor unions supported these coercive laws to prevent competition from child labor, philanthropists and cultural reformers saw them as a way to "save the child" and protect the state. The laws particularly appealed to reformers in states troubled by industrial upheaval, and sixteen out of thirty-eight states had passed them by 1885.[15]

California's legislature, with Republicans mainly supporting and Democrats mainly opposing, passed a compulsory attendance law in 1874. Prior to passage of the law, Democratic state superintendents had opposed it whereas Republicans cited the link between pauperism, crime, and the lack of education as compelling reasons for supporting the measure. In 1878, following the violent "July Days" of 1877, San Francisco's superintendent, A. L. Mann, argued that the city police should arrest truant children because it would be cheaper "to educate people at the public expense than to pay the cost of their arrest, conviction, and imprisonment for crime." The San Francisco school board, like the majority of city boards elsewhere in the country, made no serious attempt to enforce compulsory attendance during the nineteenth century. Neither teachers nor administrators cared much for the prospect of teaching unwilling truants along with other students, especially when the lack of spaces meant that even those who enrolled voluntarily could not be accommodated. The San Francisco board eventually adopted a policy of eliminating students if they missed eight days of school in any one month as a way of meeting the demands of parents who wanted their children placed. Compulsory attendance legislation thus appears to have played a largely symbolic role in San Francisco: placed on the books by reformers determined to use the schools to reinforce social order, the laws remained there as testimony to the high status of the reformers' ideals.[16]

Just as the city's Protestant cultural reformers sought to protect the state and the society by keeping children in school, both Protestant and Jewish reformers believed the future would be more secure if slum children from poor families could be attracted to school at an earlier age. Fewer than a dozen kindergartens existed in the United States before 1870, but by 1880 over four hundred operated in thirty states. Kindergartens in San Francisco owed their beginnings to a group of Jewish philanthropists and charity workers led by Judge Solomon Heydenfeldt and merchant Samuel Levy. Heydenfeldt and Levy had attended lectures by Felix Adler, founder of the New York Ethical Cultural Society, during his visit to San Francisco, and they decided to try out his ideas about the benefits of free kindergartens. With a name (the Public Kindergarten Society) and $130 in pledges, they asked prominent reformer and suffragist Caroline Severence (who had recently moved from Boston to Los Angeles) to recommend an instructor. Kate Wiggin, a young friend of Severence, also from New England and recently graduated from a kindergarten training school operated by German-born Emma Marwedel, quickly accepted the offer to come to San Francisco. Toward the end of 1878 Wiggin opened the Silver Street Free Kindergarten in the Tar Flats area south of Market Street. One year later Sarah Cooper, born in upstate New York in 1835 and already a resident of San Francisco for a decade, established the city's second kindergarten on Jackson Street in the infamous Barbary Coast district.[17]

Altruism and the control of social disorder provided the rationale for the work of Cooper, Wiggin, and their supporters and followers. Wiggin shared Cooper's belief that it was "far better that we plant kindergartens and organize industrial schools and educate the young for work, than to let them grow up in such a manner as to be good for nothing else than to form Jacobin clubs and revolutionary brigades." Cooper believed, along with Wiggin, that the kindergarten provided a way to "plant a child-garden in some dreary, poverty stricken place in a large city, a place swarming with unmothered, undefended, undernourished child-life."[18] An estimated one thousand educators, writers, society people, and curiosity seekers came to observe the Tar Flats class in the first year and a half. Cooper believed strongly in what she called "Christian activity," and the kindergarten seemed an ideal vehicle. In addition, kindergartens nicely fit her concept of "preventive charity," for "the pliable period of early childhood is the time most favorable to the eradication of vicious tendencies, and to the development of the latent possibilities for good." By 1884, her Golden Gate Kindergarten Association operated six classes on an annual income of over $10,000.[19]

By this time both Cooper and Wiggin had put their association on a permanent footing by gaining the financial support of women from some of the city's wealthiest families. Inspired by contemporaries in New York and Boston, Mary Crocker, Phoebe Hearst, and Jane Stanford stood at the center of charitable work in San Francisco. According to historian Carol Roland: "Their dynamic leadership and extensive generosity in a wide range of educational and cultural endeavors reinforced the idea that wealth carried with it a responsibility to promote social and civic betterment."[20] Charles Crocker's daughter, Harriet Alexander, became president of the board of Silver Street and along with her mother, Mary Crocker, contributed over $12,000 for the school's operating expenses over a decade's time. Adolph Sutro and James Fair, of Comstock fame, also provided substantial support. Sarah Cooper's supporters included Miranda Lux, wife of Charles Lux, one of the city's ten richest men. Jane Stanford gave Cooper $4,000 to establish a Leland Stanford, Jr., Memorial Kindergarten in 1884, and over the years she increased her donations to the point where she supported six kindergartens. Cooper first secured Phoebe Hearst's support in 1883 when Hearst agreed to finance a Union Street class. By 1906, her contributions had amounted to over $80,000. By 1895, as forty free kindergartens enrolled 3,588 children, most from poor and immigrant homes, San Francisco claimed to have the largest privately funded kindergarten system in the nation.[21]

MORAL REFORM

The presence of "self-made" men like millionaires Sutro and Fair on the boards of the kindergarten associations reinforced the widely held belief that California offered success to any American willing to work hard. San Francisco kindergarten supporters, like their colleagues elsewhere, distinguished between "the worthy poor" (down on their luck due to sickness, accident, or death) and "paupers" (malcontents who avoided honest work and drank in saloons). The kindergartens could help turn children away from the temptations offered by "the 3,300 gin shops and corner groceries of the city, and the use of opium." After an interview with Cooper, journalist Milicent Shinn argued in the *Overland Monthly* that "drunkenness and laziness are the real cause of poverty in San Francisco" and "the lowest poverty may be said to belong to the foreign classes." This was significant, in her view because the "population is more than half foreign; with more saloons and open vice of any sort than any other city in the Union." Reformers argued that if the poor would withstand "the monster evil intemperance" and similar temptations, they stood a much better chance of prosperity in San Francisco than in eastern cities. Protestant and Jewish reform groups generally supported Sarah Cooper's belief that "aside from drink and vice, and the calamities of vice, there is no deep poverty here."[22]

Catholic charity organizations, influenced by the theory that poverty was an unavoidable part of the human condition, took issue with the concept that the causes of poverty could be isolated like germs and cured by properly administered social reform medicine. The head of the Sisters of Mercy, a group active in dispensing charity in the South of Market area, agreed that alcoholism aggravated the troubles of unemployed workers and their families but insisted that the more basic problem was a shortage of jobs. The Mother Superior refused to accept the contention that immigrants and their children brought their troubles on themselves by their lack of motivation and their addiction to harmful substances. In her view, the Irish and other immigrant groups should not be blamed for lack of motivation, for many who wanted to work could find no jobs.[23]

Differing viewpoints about poverty did not stop Catholic, Protestant, and Jewish moral reformers from joining together to abolish the city's red light district. San Francisco's "purity crusade," like its counterparts in other cities, raised the banner of Judeo-Christian morality and family respectability against the satanic cunning of white (and Asian) slavers and the profligacy of men who preferred to purchase their sexual pleasure. In 1895, Father M. Otis began a campaign to close the brothels in a Chinatown alley across the street from St. Mary's Church. In 1897, a grand jury report publicized some of the lurid details of the houses along Pacific Street in the Barbary Coast area. Then Father Otis intensified his campaign by joining forces with the Reverend R. C. Foute of Grace Episcopal Church. Soon Father Terence Caraher, pastor of the Church of St. Francis in North Beach and chairman of the Committee of Morals of the North Beach Protective Association, became a leader in the campaign to shut down the Barbary Coast brothels. He was joined in 1912 by J. C. Westenberg, an uncompromising evangelist who headed the Whosoever Will Rescue Mission located in the thick of the Barbary Coast on the 400 block of Pacific Street. Westenberg announced that he would tour the nation under the auspices of the American Purity Association calling for a boycott of the upcoming Panama Pacific International Exposition unless the Barbary Coast was out of business by 1915. He threatened to "photograph every dive and brothel . . . and send copies to every news-paper and periodical, religious and secular in the world."[24]

Westenberg's demand for immediate abolition of the vice district met with considerable sympathy among like-minded members of the city's Protestant, Catholic, and Jewish congregations. At the same time, many dissenters opposed the purity crusade, and this more tolerant group argued for a continuation of the policy of regulated vice that had been established in San Francisco by 1912. Clayton Herrington, a prominent judge in the city, expressed their point of view when he argued that "San Francisco is no worse than other large cities; it is better than a great many I have seen in other parts of the world."[25] Mayor James Rolph himself, in a vehement letter to Westenberg that he never mailed, expressed the "live and let live" point of view that many San Franciscans shared:

> In replying to you who seem, from your letterheads, to be the principal repository of all righteousness, I reply to all the self-advertising pharisees and all the well-meaning hysterics who have been agitating so loudly to reform other people's morals. I propose, in this administration, to draw the line carefully between vice and amusement, no matter how humble that amusement may be. Many of the people who are now calling for intolerant restrictions would not be satisfied until they destroyed all the amusement and entertainment that have given San Francisco life and character throughout the world.
> We are the Portola City.
> We ask the world to come here and revel.[26]

Despite his personal views, Rolph ultimately adopted a more conciliatory position, and he approved measures that led to the closing of the "wide open" vice district in February 1917. After the nation declared war in 1917 and San Francisco became an active military port, the Police Department created a morals squad to suppress the prostitution that continued to flourish. Purity crusaders were pleased with its work. One irate citizen, however, describing himself as "an unmarried man for very good reasons," informed Mayor Rolph that "these dirty sneaking skunks of the Morals Squad are a stench in the nostrils of all manly men."[27]

Closing down the Barbary Coast made social purity official policy, but the city's demand for illicit pleasure kept its flourishing "underworld" alive during the 1920s and 1930s. Private detective and former FBI agent Edwin N. Atherton's report to the grand jury in March 1937 dramatized the extent to which the social purity policy served purely symbolic purposes. The Board of Supervisors hired Atherton's firm, and it spent sixteen months investigating vice and police corruption. City newspapers emphasized the sensational finding that bail bondsman Peter P. McDonough and his brother deserved the title "fountainhead of corruption." The McDonough brothers were at the center of an underworld empire of approximately 135 "regular, old established" houses of prostitution, regular violations of closing hours by saloons, abortion mills, operations for the fencing of stolen property, and extensive gambling operations, including bookmaking, lotteries, slot machines, and gambling houses. Atherton estimated that the police received at least $1 million in graft each year, and he implicated sixty-seven police officials and twenty-four other government officials by name. Atherton's report led to the revocation of McDonough's bail bond license and toppled him from his position as the "fountainhead of corruption."[28]

Atherton himself took pains to remind the grand jury that "police graft has its origins in prostitution, gambling, and other illegal activities" and recommended that San Francisco legalize all such businesses. Unhappy with the "absence of any continuous, active support from prominent citizens or groups" and at the "somewhat synthetic beginning" of the investigation, Atherton also criticized Mayor Angelo J. Rossi for what appeared to be lack of leadership. The investigator pointed out that "when we were employed, we were informed this investigation was not intended to be a moral crusade in the sense that it should bring about the closing of unlawful businesses, as such a course was contrary to the desires of the great majority of San Franciscans." Atherton agreed to this policy "and adhered strictly to it throughout the investigation." "We were aware," he wrote, "that the bulk of the people wanted a so-called 'open town' and that the history of San Francisco reflected a public attitude of broad-mindedness, liberality and tolerance, comparable probably to only two other American cities, namely New York and New Orleans." He was unhappy at one of the by-products of the constraints imposed on him when his project "unfortunately, became known as the 'Atherton investigation' instead of being recognized as a civic enterprise." As long as official San Francisco prohibited vice but allowed it to flourish, proclaimed purity but tolerated license, the city could not reduce graft. "Punitive action will not cure the evil condition. The cause must be removed." "Those persons who think that prostitution and gambling are stopped because of prohibitive legislation, must be likened to the ostrich of popular repute."[29]

Twenty-two years earlier, a prominent leader in the national antiprostitution movement foreshadowed Atherton's argument by observing that "the law is an instrument much more difficult to use than is commonly supposed."[30] Paul Boyer recently has shown that the nation's "great coercive crusades" against the brothel and the saloon "ultimately failed." Well-to-do "patricians and business leaders" all over the country, convinced of the need for "the creation of greater moral cohesiveness in the sprawling and heterogenous cities," agreed in principle with Father Caraher even when, as in San Francisco, they adopted a laissez-faire attitude. Nonetheless, beginning in the 1890s, "they channeled their real energies into less explicit social control efforts involving the beautification and enrichment of the city's physical environment."[31]

CIVIC BEAUTIFICATION

San Francisco was no exception. The force of the "City Beautiful" movement struck San Francisco between the late 1890s and 1910 when James Phelan and the Association for the Improvement and Adornment of San Francisco worked to implement their belief that the redesign of the city's physical environment would increase social harmony and enhance San Francisco's prosperity and growth. Phelan believed that San Francisco needed statues, monuments, parks, parkways, great plazas at the focal points of grand boulevards, and stately public buildings in the Beaux Arts style in order to dramatize its potential as "the capital of an empire."[32] Phelan's convictions grew out of his experiences as president of the Bohemian Club and the San Francisco Art Association, his vice-presidency of the California World's Fair Commission in 1893, and his service as the manager of the

California exhibition at the Chicago World's Fair. He also helped inaugurate
the Mid-Winter Fair in San Francisco (1894).

In 1899 Phelan unsuccessfully put his influence as mayor behind a proposal to extend the Panhandle of Golden Gate Park downtown to the intersection of Van Ness Avenue and Market Street. Five years later, no longer
mayor, Phelan and the presidents of the Bohemian Club, the Pacific Union
Club, and the Art Association organized the Adornment Association, which
published a list of planning objectives for the city. The formation of the
association coincided with Reuben Hale's proposal that San Francisco host
a world's fair and with growing public discussion within the business community about San Francisco's need to maintain its attractiveness to tourists
and prospective investors in the face of competition from southern California. Even before Phelan began his term as first president of the association, he asked Daniel H. Burnham, the nation's leading city planner, to
provide a comprehensive design as the basis for a campaign to secure public
support for an "imperial" San Francisco along the lines of Athens, Paris,
and Washington, D.C.[33] Judd Kahn has shown that "founders of the association, by and large, were longtime San Franciscans and members of the
city's social and economic upper crust." The Burnham plan that they commissioned included measures to reduce traffic congestion, increase commercial efficiency, and enhance aesthetic pleasure. In addition, elements in
the plan provided citizens, in the view of the architect himself, "a lesson of
order and system, and its influence on the masses cannot be overestimated."[34]

Burnham's belief in the uplifting potential of his proposals never received
a test. Neither the strongest supporters of the plan nor its staunchest opponents would agree that city government ought to exercise the sweeping
powers over private property necessary for the implementation of a comprehensive city plan. Unwilling to trust the electoral process because they
could not control the outcome, Phelan and his fellow reformers probably
decided "to leave the Burnham plan as an inspiring ideal at which to aim
[rather] than to try to enact it by a political process that might weaken the
very basis of social stability."[35]

Although the Burnham plan had come and gone by 1910, well-to-do San
Franciscans continued to support policies designed to provide cultural uplift
by contributing to the establishment and the support of public museums,
art institutes, libraries, and concert orchestras. Like Phelan and the Adornment Association, and like their counterparts in New York, Boston, and
Chicago, San Francisco's leading cultural philanthropists turned to cultural
policy primarily for social purposes. As Helen Lefkowitz Horowitz has put
it in describing the Chicago case: "Disturbed by social forces they could not
control and filled with idealistic notions of culture, these businessmen saw
in the museum, the library, the symphony orchestra, and the university a
way to purify their city and to generate a civic renaissance."[36]

In San Francisco, as elsewhere, only a small proportion of individuals
carried out the bulk of the cultural philanthropy. In San Francisco, as elsewhere, philanthropists exuded self-confidence as they assumed leadership
roles that they regarded as properly their own. They turned to cultural
policy with certainty in their conviction that the best people should shape
the city's culture rather than with anxiety about their status as arbiters of

taste.[37] San Francisco did depart from the norm in the relatively large proportion of Roman Catholics and Jews who played key roles in the development of major cultural institutions. Chinese, Japanese, and black San Franciscans, however, played no more active a role in shaping the city's cultural policies than they did in other American cities, and racial exclusion remained the norm throughout the period in this as in other aspects of public policy formation.[38]

During the early period of San Francisco history—as in the case of western cities generally—the development of the arts followed patterns similar to those east of the Rockies. In San Francisco, as in the other leading cities of the West in 1880, no sharp distinctions separated places of entertainment from places for the appreciation of the arts. Beer gardens, lecture halls, and twelve theaters flourished in the city, and the Grand Opera House stood at the social and cultural heart of San Francisco. Two thousand people in formal evening dress attended special events there amid ornate splendor. Chinatown had its Chinese Royal and Chinese Grand theaters. Other San Franciscans from all walks of life flocked to the four-thousand-seat pavilion at Woodward's Gardens. Support for arts and entertainment came from private sources during the period of robust expansion and economic ups and downs between the gold rush and the 1890s. All kinds of city government expenditure earned the scrutiny of politically active San Franciscans, and the dominant laissez-faire ideals of the period discouraged public spending to support art activities of any kind.

By the 1890s, San Francisco's dominant position on the Pacific Coast was challenged by Los Angeles, Portland, and Seattle. Then the serious depression between 1893 and 1897 convinced the city's business community of the need to bolster the image of San Francisco and to improve its reputation by enhancing its prowess as a cultural center. Such cultural development required cultural philanthropists to develop new relationships among private associations, city government, and the arts. The events leading to the establishment of the M. H. de Young Memorial Museum illustrate the beginnings of these new arrangements. De Young, proprietor of the *Chronicle*, served as a commissioner and vice-president of the 1893 Columbian Exposition in Chicago. He believed that San Francisco should announce its intention to prosper despite the depression by presenting a "Mid-Winter Fair" advertising the climatic advantages of the city and California. A committee of activists from business and the professions, not the city government, created a fund-raising drive that raised $361,000. The committee elected de Young head of the fair, and over two million attended by the close of the gates in July 1894.

The fair earned a profit of $126,991, which was used to finance the conversion of the Fine and Decorative Art Building and the adjacent Royal Bavarian Pavilion into a permanent museum. This Mid-Winter Fair Memorial Museum was inaugurated and administered by the Park Commission in March 1895. The Park Commission exercised jurisdiction over the museum from 1895 to 1926; the name changed to the M. H. de Young Memorial Museum in January 1921 when the Park Commission accepted the deed of trust.

The museum's history between 1895 and 1921 illustrates the complex combination of private initiative and public support characterizing the origins of several arts policies during this period. De Young made his private collections gifts to the city; the Park Commission provided the funds for expansion in 1897; donations and wills from other private individuals helped pay building costs for expansion from 1917 to 1921. De Young's belief that "when the people have a little leisure time, they do not go downtown, where the streets are dead and there is no life. They go to their parks. And that is the logical place for a museum," helped ensure that Golden Gate Park would house one of the city's major cultural institutions. His conviction that the museum should be open every day of the week free of charge helped ensure its popularity and high attendance rates.[39]

M. H. de Young celebrated his seventy-fifth birthday in October 1924 at a gathering hosted by the Downtown Association, the David Scannel Club of firefighters, and members of the Police Department. The popularity evinced by these and other tributes helps to explain the widespread support generated by the de Young Endowment Committee in its drive to amend the city charter to make the de Young Museum a separate city agency under the control of a self-perpetuating board of trustees rather than a part of the Park Commission. The amendment committed the Board of Supervisors to appropriate not less than $40,000 annually for the support of the museum; de Young himself provided a bequest of bonds worth $150,000 from his estate. By the November 4, 1924, election, Proposition 29 had won endorsements from the Civic League of Improvement Clubs and Associations, the Downtown Association, the San Francisco Club, the Chamber of Commerce, the Real Estate Board, the Bureau of Governmental Research, and the Labor Council.[40]

Proposition 29 passed by wide margins in all of the city's assembly districts, with support dropping below 60 percent only in the Bayshore and North Beach areas where voters nonetheless voted 58 and 57 percent in favor. In 1924 just over half the registered voters supported the new policy to establish a separate city subsidy for the de Young Museum and to place it under a self-perpetuating board of trustees. In the same election, 54 percent of the voters approved Proposition 28, amending the charter to accept the California Palace of the Legion of Honor as a gift from Adolph B. and Alma de Bretteville Spreckels and to require the Board of Supervisors to provide "sufficient funds" for its annual maintenance as a museum. As in the case of Proposition 29, the assembly districts that polled the highest majorities above the citywide average were in middle- and upper-middle-class areas.[41]

The few percentage point differences among the various parts of San Francisco should not distract attention from the general voter support for city government to assume financial responsibility for the de Young and the Palace of the Legion of Honor under a new policy. The concept that public funds would be turned over to and administered by self-perpetuating boards of trustees received substantial majorities in all parts of the city.[42]

Two years later, in 1926, voters, by more than three to one, authorized the city to accept from the U.S. War Department a deed to the property occupied by the Palace of Fine Arts (originally part of the 1915 Panama

SAN FRANCISCO UPPER CALIFORNIA
IN 1847.

San Francisco, with Yerba Buena cove in the foreground and Telegraph Hill on the right, in 1847. During that year, the mayor authorized the first survey, laid out the rectangular street pattern, and opened bidding for private purchase of waterfront lots. (Photo courtesy of the Bancroft Library, University of California, Berkeley)

Above left, the Montgomery Block in 1856. Entrepreneur Henry W. Halleck, later Union general-in-chief for President Lincoln, built this office block in 1853. Law offices, the city's first law library, offices of the U.S. Army Engineer Corps, the *Alta California, Daily Herald,* the Adams Express Company, and the Bank Exchange Saloon made this one of the city's chief business centers. Merchants met here to organize the Vigilance Committee in 1856. (Photo courtesy of the Bancroft Library, University of California, Berkeley)

Above, William C. Ralston. This memorial, with Ralston surrounded by pictures of the Bank of California, the Palace Hotel, the California Theater, and a half-dozen of his other investments, appeared in the *San Francisco Newsletter* shortly after his death in 1875. Although he did not live to see the opening of the Palace Hotel, Ralston had already earned heroic stature for making, in the words of his eulogist, "California a synonym for princely hospitality and generosity to the utmost bounds of the universe." (Photo courtesy of the Bancroft Library, University of California, Berkeley)

Left, William T. Coleman. One of the city's most successful commission merchants, this Kentucky-born, college-trained engineer controlled assets of over $100,000 by 1860. Merchants chose the popular and respected self-confessed admirer of Napoleon president of the Vigilance Committee of 1856 and the Committee of Safety of 1877. (Photo courtesy of the Bancroft Library, University of California, Berkeley)

Gustave Niebaum, Lewis Gerstle, and Louis
Sloss in the offices of the Alaska Commercial Company at 310 Sansome Street.
Founded in 1868 by several San Francisco
Jewish merchants and non-Jewish eastern
entrepreneurs, the firm owed its prosperity
to seal hunting, fur trapping, salmon fishing and canning, and land speculation.
(Photo courtesy of the Western Jewish History Center, Judah L. Magnes Museum)

The Nathan-Dohrmann Company. Organized in 1884, the firm supplied crockery, silver, glass, and chinaware to well-to-do San Franciscans. Co-founder Frederick W. Dohrmann helped organize the city's Merchants' Association in 1894, assisted in James D. Phelan's mayoral campaign in 1896, and led the drive for the reform charter of 1898. (Photo courtesy of the Bancroft Library, University of California, Berkeley)

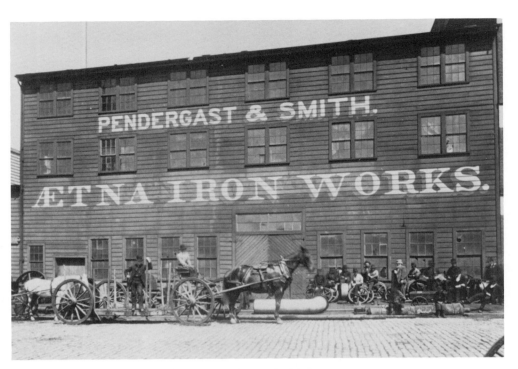

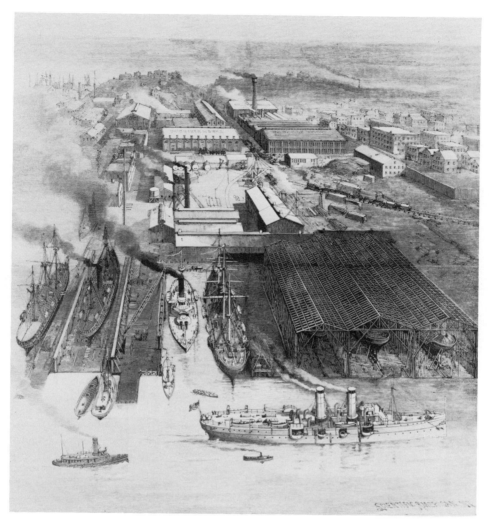

San Francisco's manufacturing economy
thrived on a base of food processing and
the production of tools and machinery from
the 1860s to 1900. Firms such as the Aetna
Iron Works, above left, and Robert F. Bunker's meat-packing company, below left,
while less celebrated than the "Great Pacific
Coast Shipbuilding Plant" of Prescott, Scott,
and Company (the Union Iron Works,
above), typified the city's industrial activities
for a half-century. (Photos to the left courtesy of the Bancroft Library, University of
California, Berkeley; drawing from *Scientific American*, July 2, 1892)

Market Street, looking east toward the Ferry Building, in the year of the Panama Pacific International Exposition. The busy retail shopping district between Powell Street and Grant Avenue (the north side, at left) and Fifth and Third streets (the south side, at right) is visible in the foreground. When the Chamber of Commerce boasted of the city's "commercial supremacy" in a booklet published for the exposition, it singled out landmarks such as the Flood Building, housing the general offices of the Southern Pacific Railroad (left side of street in photo); the Ferry Building (in the distance); the Claus Spreckels Building, also known as the *Call* Building (first tower to the right of the Ferry Building); the Humboldt Bank Building (second tower); and the Emporium (far right of photo). (Photo courtesy of the Bancroft Library, University of California, Berkeley)

The Market, Post, and Montgomery streets intersection in the 1920s. San Franciscans had begun calling Montgomery "the Wall Street of the West" by this time, and the Crocker Building (left), the First National Bank Building (center), and the Wells Fargo Nevada National Bank Building (right) stood across Market Street from the Palace Hotel (left, out of sight) at the gateway to the financial district. The four tracks of the two streetcar lines are visible in the foreground. The Municipal Railway used the outside tracks, and the private Market Street Railway used the inside tracks. Complete four-track service connecting the new southern and western lines to the ferries commenced in mid-1918. (Photo courtesy of the Library of Congress)

Ferry Building, late 1890s. This photograph must have been taken shortly after the opening of the Ferry Building, for there are no automobiles in the picture. Constructed between 1895 and 1903, the building saw peak ferry traffic of 170 boats a day, bringing commuters from around the bay and depositing them at the foot of the city's major thoroughfare. The large streetcars in the photograph are those of the Market Street Railway, later the United Railroads; smaller, horse-drawn cars can also be seen, operating on the outside tracks. In stark contrast with the grandeur of the Ferry Building's tower, inspired by the Giralda Tower of the Cathedral of Seville, the building in the central foreground advertises baths for 12½ cents. Such facilities were a fixture of the area along the waterfront, catering to sailors, longshoremen, and other young, single males. To the south of the Ferry Building (toward the right side of the photograph) stood several blocks of sailors' boardinghouses. (Photo courtesy of the Library of Congress)

Great piers protruded into the bay along the waterfront, forming the heart of the city's economy. For sailors and longshoremen, hours were long, and work was hard, with frequent periods of unemployment between jobs. Longshoremen's work (upper photo) relied primarily on human muscle power, supplemented only somewhat by mechanical assistance; much the same was true for sailors. The Sailors' Union of the Pacific maintained headquarters on the waterfront (lower photo), from where it exerted a powerful force in the shipping industry from the 1890s through the early 1920s. (Upper photo courtesy of the California Historical Society, San Francisco; lower photo courtesy of the Bancroft Library, University of California, Berkeley)

Part of the South of Market area, about 1885.
The luxurious Palace Hotel, completed in
1875 as the centerpiece in William C. Ralston's scheme to draw the business district
southward, dominates the upper right of
this photo. In the left foreground is Howard Street, unpaved and with wide wooden
sidewalks. The spire of St. Patrick's rises in
the distance, down Mission Street. The
densely packed working-class area on
Tehama Street, described in Chapter 3, was
a block to the south (left in the photo). (Photo
courtesy of the California Historical Society, San Francisco)

Small-scale manufacturing flourished in the
South of Market area. The man in the photo
is wheeling out a casting from the Whyte
and De Rome Foundry, 128 Main Street,
probably in the early 1890s. The castings in
the foreground are marked for the battle-
ship *Oregon*, Cruiser No. 6, and the monitor
New Jersey. All these vessels were constructed at the Union Iron Works shipyard;
this foundry must have subcontracted some
of the brass castings. (Photo courtesy of the
Bancroft Library, University of California,
Berkeley)

Left, two South of Market refugees pose outside a tent, perhaps their temporary refuge from the destruction of the 1906 earthquake and fire. Despite the trauma of the devastation, they face the camera with a smile and a look of jaunty confidence. Irish women in the South of Market area, like these refugees, were more likely to be employed for wages than any other group of women in the city. (Photo courtesy of the Bancroft Library, University of California, Berkeley)

Above, Mission Street, with Third Street in the foreground, about 1909. Streetcars, freight wagons, carriages, a bicycle, and pedestrians vie for space at this busy intersection. A policeman stands at right center. By 1909, this part of the South of Market area had been rebuilt following the destruction of 1906 and had become largely a commercial and manufacturing district, with housing pushed further west. (Photo courtesy of the San Francisco Archives, San Francisco Public Library)

The street running from right to left across the foreground of the photo is identified as Folsom on the gas light on the left, but the unidentified cross street in this 1886 photograph could be anywhere from 10th to 26th. Streetcar tracks are visible along unpaved Folsom Street, and the crowd across the street may have been waiting for a streetcar when the photographer attracted their attention by setting up photographic equipment.

This part of the Mission District was similar to the block on Bartlett Street described in Chapter 3: skilled workers, small shopkeepers, and a scattering of professionals serving their neighbors. Throughout the late nineteenth and early twentieth centuries, the Mission District formed a stable, working-class area with large numbers of Irish and Germans, but with Irish increasingly prominent in the early twentieth century. (Photo courtesy of the San Francisco Archives, San Francisco Public Library)

Mission Street at 22nd, 1905. A construction crew for the United Railroads has torn up the brick paving to install a streetcar intersection. The crew has stopped work to pose for the photographer, who has also captured a policeman on the right. Small neighborhood stores and shops share the street with single-story homes and sets of flats. (Photo courtesy of the San Francisco Archives, San Francisco Public Library)

Twenty-fourth Street at Diamond, June 1909. When paving finally came, it was typically brick, as in this photograph. The sign on the grocery store on the right advertises steam beer, a San Francisco specialty. The bakery on the left is run by Christian Kolb; Germans outnumbered all other groups among bakers in the late nineteenth and early twentieth centuries. Storekeepers and shop owners often lived behind or above their stores. In the distance rise the slopes of Twin Peaks, not yet breached by streetcar lines and, therefore, not yet the site of residential construction. (Photo courtesy of the San Francisco Archives, San Francisco Public Library)

Mission Street at Ocean in the 1920s. By the 1920s, automobiles had come to share the street with the streetcars, and motion picture theaters had appeared among the neighborhood shops and stores. The ethnic and economic composition of the Mission District, however, showed slight change from the turn of the century until after World War II.

This shopping district in the Outer Mission looks much like those closer to downtown. One of the "white-front" cars of the Market Street Railway passes a neighborhood theater featuring *Uncle Tom's Cabin*. Asphalt has been laid over the brick paving to provide a smoother surface for the automobiles' pneumatic tires. (Photo courtesy of the San Francisco Archives, San Francisco Public Library)

California Street between Divisadero and Scott, probably in the late 1880s. These four houses are typical of those constructed in the Western Addition in the 1880s. Unlike many of the working-class residences of the Mission District, these upper-middle-class homes boast small front yards surrounded by iron fences. (Photo courtesy of the California Historical Society, San Francisco)

Temple Sherith Israel, the oldest Jewish
congregation in the city, which relocated
from downtown to California and Webster,
between the Western Addition and Pacific
Heights, in 1905. This photo was taken
shortly after the earthquake and fire, and
the sign over the side entrance identifies
Sherith Israel as the temporary site of the
superior court; here Abraham Ruef was
indicted and pled guilty. (Photo courtesy of
the San Francisco Archives, San Francisco
Public Library)

The 1000 block of Fillmore Street, the major shopping area of the Western Addition, about 1910. Businesses include Dresner Tailors, Zobel's, Brake and Shenker, and Nate Levy, Union Tailor. For a brief period after the earthquake and fire, Fillmore Street threatened to replace the downtown area as the city's major retail area. (Photo courtesy of the San Francisco Archives, San Francisco Public Library)

Horses munch their oats on Geary Street,
between Laguna and Buchanan, about 1910.
By then, a small portion of the Western
Addition had become the city's center of
Japanese settlement. Note how the front
yards of the 1870s and 1880s became the
small shops and stores of the early twentieth
century. (Photo courtesy of the Bancroft
Library, University of California, Berkeley)

An upper-class residence at the corner of Sacramento and Van Ness, June 1887. This part of Van Ness boasted a number of elaborate mansions, and similar homes were beginning to be built to the west in Pacific Heights. Upper-middle-class rowhouses can be glimpsed east down Sacramento Street (to the right), and another Van Ness mansion can be seen to the north (left). The absence of paving in the 1880s knew no class: both Sacramento and Van Ness were unpaved at the time of this photograph. (Photo courtesy of the Bancroft Library, University of California, Berkeley)

California Street, looking west from Mason—the crest of Nob Hill—about 1890. Once construction of the California Street cable-car line made the top of Nob Hill more easily accessible, the city's economic elite began to buy out previous residents and to accumulate complete city blocks for the construction of elaborate mansions. The white frame house in the center was built in 1872 by David D. Colton, an associate of the Southern Pacific Railroad's "Big Four," and was sold to Collis P. Huntington (one of the "Big Four") a decade later. James Flood brought Connecticut sandstone (known to New Yorkers as brownstone) all the way across the nation for the construction of his house, on the right, in 1885. The second house from the left is that of Charles Crocker, another of the "Big Four." The photo was taken from the home of Mark Hopkins (still another of the "Big Four"), described by architectural historian Randolph Delehanty as "by far the most elaborate pile of carved-and-sawn redwood California ever saw." Others living in the vicinity included Leland Stanford (the final member of the "Big Four"), George Hearst, the Tobins (of the Hibernia Bank), and others who dominated the economic life of the western part of the nation. Of these monuments to ostentation, only the Flood mansion survived the earthquake and fire in 1906. Gutted by the fire, it was rebuilt in 1912 and has since housed the Pacific Union Club. (Photo courtesy of the Library of Congress)

Above, Dupont Street (renamed Grant Avenue in two stages, in 1907 and 1908), about 1908. The cross street visible in the center foreground is California Street, just three blocks down the hill from the Flood mansion. Although some business and civic leaders tried to move Chinatown to Hunter's Point following the devastation of 1906, the area was quickly rebuilt, much of it with salvaged bricks. The two buildings on the left were both built in 1908, the center one for the Sing Chong Company and the one on the left for the Sing Fat Company. The pagodalike embellishments represent an effort by San Francisco architects to blend the standard commercial buildings of the day with what the city's leading architectural journal called "the fantasy of the Far East"; the style proved popular and was adopted for other Chinatown buildings. (Photo courtesy of the Bancroft Library, University of California, Berkeley)

A Chinese peddler, about 1890. The two large baskets were carried by a pole balanced over the shoulder. Inside the large baskets were a variety of smaller baskets, holding a variety of vegetables and fruits, and perhaps seafood as well. Visits by the Chinese peddler are described through children's eyes in Chapter 3. (Photo courtesy of the Society of California Pioneers)

The photo below is of the Presidents of the Six Companies, about 1900. These wealthy merchants were the de facto government of Chinatown. Only two favored Western dress styles, the others keeping to more traditional garb. (Photo courtesy of the Society of California Pioneers)

The north side of Broadway, in the 1920s. Broadway and Columbus formed major thoroughfares for Italian North Beach. Stores along this part of Broadway included Moretto's Drugs, Giglio Hot Lunch, and Dante Billiards. Above the stores and shops can be seen the crowded Italian residential area on the slopes of Telegraph Hill. (Photo courtesy of the San Francisco Archives, San Francisco Public Library)

The Italian community included many small
food-processing enterprises, including Italian food specialties. The photo above shows
premier pastrymaker Mario Gallo taking an
order from tenor Beniamino Gigli. (Photo
from G. M. Tuoni, *Attivita' Italiane in America* [n.p., 1930], p. 157)

Parducci and Domenici's San Francisco Sausage Factory, 505 Davis Street. (Photo from G. M. Tuoni, *Attivita' Italiane in America* [n.p., 1930], p. 169)

Italians came to dominate fishing and truck farming by the early twentieth century. The photo shows feluccas, Italian fishing boats with lateen sails, at Fisherman's Wharf. (Photo courtesy of the Bancroft Library, University of California, Berkeley)

Cultural reform, in San Francisco as in other major American cities, owed much of its momentum to the individual efforts of Protestant women. Above, Donaldina Cameron photographed with a group of Chinese girls who lived under her care at the Presbyterian Mission Home at 920 Sacramento Street in Chinatown. (Photo courtesy of the Society of California Pioneers)

Except for Chinese and Japanese parents, whose children had more limited, segregated, facilities, San Franciscans took full advantage of expanded public school curricula during the period from 1900 to 1930. While the reformers who established programs of vocational training (below right) and school gardens (above right) typically recommended such innovations as vehicles for "Americanization" and "social efficiency," parents typically regarded the experiences as useful background for their children's personal and occupational success. (Photos courtesy of the Bancroft Library, University of California, Berkeley)

Golden Gate Park, above, built on a sandy, windswept site declared by architect Frederick Law Olmsted to be "impossible," took shape between 1870 and the 1930s as a typical example of combined public and private urban development. The city bought the land, and its Park Commission and park superintendent controlled design, maintenance, and expenditures. Private philanthropy provided the most popular attractions. The Children's Playground, the first built in a public park in the nation, was established in 1886 with a bequest from Comstock financier and U.S. senator from Nevada William Sharon. (Photo courtesy of Joseph A. Grandov)

Above right, the statue of Ulysses S. Grant and the Fine Arts (later de Young) Museum. The museum, built for the 1894 California Mid-Winter International Exposition, became the city's fine arts museum largely through the efforts of Michael de Young, publisher of the *San Francisco Chronicle.* Below right, the Music Pavilion. The bandshell and concourse, gifts to the city from "Sugar King" Claus Spreckels, were constructed in 1899. (Photos courtesy of the Bancroft Library, University of California, Berkeley)

When sandlot orator Denis Kearney was arrested and jailed repeatedly for using incendiary language and inciting to riot in 1877, he became a martyr in the eyes of his working-class supporters. Upon his release for lack of evidence, the Workingmen's Party of California (WPC), Kearney's political vehicle, organized a triumphal procession and drew Kearney through the streets on a drayman's wagon decorated with flags. The WPC illustrated the potential for class-based politics, although its program consisted largely of demagogic harangues against the Chinese and the wealthy. (Drawing from a photo, published in E. Benjamin Andrews, *The History of the Last Quarter-Century in the United States: 1870–1895,* 2 vols. [New York, 1896], 1:374)

San Francisco City Hall and Hall of Records, 1900. Begun in 1871, completed in
1898, and occupied in 1900, this neoclas-
sical monument was demolished by the
earthquake in 1906. Built on the site of the
first cemetery of Yerba Buena village,
between Market, McAllister, and Larkin
streets, the cost of the structure escalated
from an original estimate of $1 million to a
final tally of $8 million. Shea and Shea, the
construction firm that initially promised to
complete work in two years, managed to
distribute regular kickbacks during the thirty
years it took to finish the job. Most San
Franciscans regarded such "honest graft" as
a normal feature of municipal government
and prided themselves on their city's imposing official edifice. (Photo courtesy of the
Bancroft Library, University of California,
Berkeley)

Above, Adolph Sutro, entrepreneur, engineer, philanthropist, and mayor of San Francisco (1894–1896). Prussian-born and Jewish, Sutro disliked religious ritual and considered himself a freethinker. In the 1860s and 1870s, Sutro defied the "Silver Kings" and built a tunnel to ventilate and drain the mines of the Comstock Lode. Moving to San Francisco after selling the tunnel in 1879, Sutro made a fortune from his investments in city real estate, operated the Cliff House, built the swimming pools at Sutro Baths, and planted trees on a barren hill that became Sutro Forest. In the 1890s, his campaign against federal funds for the Southern Pacific Railroad endeared him to the Populist party, on whose ticket he successfully ran for mayor. (Photo courtesy of the Bancroft Library, University of California, Berkeley)

Left, James Duval Phelan, banker, patron of the arts, reform mayor of San Francisco (1897–1901), and Democratic senator from California (1915–1921). Son of the founder of the First National Gold Bank, Phelan was raised in a devout Irish Catholic home, received private tutoring, and graduated from St. Ignatius College (later the University of San Francisco). He emulated his father and insisted that strict Christian ethics must govern private and public business, and his

conviction that "order and security . . . flowed from good government" made him the ideal spokesman for the business reformers of the 1890s. His vigorous advocacy of legislation to exclude Japanese immigrants earned him the support of those white workers who shared his disdain for Orientals and disliked their competition in the labor market. (Photo courtesy of the Bancroft Library, University of California, Berkeley)

Above left, Eugene Schmitz, violinist, director of the Columbia Theater orchestra, president of the Musicians' Union, and Union Labor party mayor of San Francisco (1902–1907). A native San Franciscan of Irish and German ancestry, Schmitz was also a Roman Catholic. First elected in 1901, he gained reelection twice, and as the city's chief executive he conscientiously pursued a pro-labor policy. After his conviction during the graft trials (overturned by the state supreme

court), he served a number of terms as a popular member of the Board of Supervisors beginning in 1917. (Photo courtesy of the San Francisco Archives, San Francisco Public Library)

Above right, a picket, about 1904. During the early twentieth century, picketing became a common sight on San Francisco streets as unions urged their sympathizers to boycott companies that refused to recognize unions. "The Owl" on this sign refers to the Owl drugstore chain, object of a long organizing campaign by Drug Clerks Union Local 472. (Photo from *McClure's*, February 1904)

Mayor Eugene Schmitz as motorman of the first streetcar to operate after the 1906 earthquake and fire. Schmitz endeared himself to working-class voters by his dedication to the cause of organized labor, but San Francisco's ensuing reputation as the city where "Unionism Holds Undisputed Sway" so galled James D. Phelan, Rudolph Spreckels, and other businessmen-reformers that they financed the graft prosecution as the means to depose the Union Labor party. (Photo courtesy of the San Francisco Archives, San Francisco Public Library)

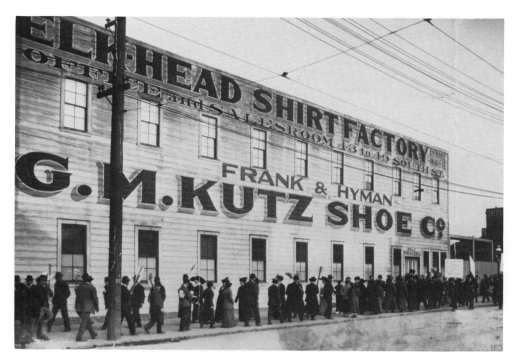

Picket line, about 1915. The pickets appear
well dressed and orderly in this photograph
from the files of the San Francisco Chamber of Commerce, but an antipicketing
ordinance was approved by voters as a result
of an initiative campaign led by the Chamber in 1916. (Photo by Gabriel Moulin,
courtesy of the California Historical Society, San Francisco)

"The Four Million Dollar Meeting" (above left), 1910, took place in the Great Hall of the Merchants' Exchange. This mass meeting of the city's leading business figures launched the Panama Pacific International Exposition (PPIE) with an intense fundraising effort, which produced promises of $4 million in less than two hours. The PPIE, in turn, became a major force for civic unity in general and especially for unifying the business community.

The exposition achieved a sense of stylistic harmony and unity by assigning each prominent architect an enclosed courtyard rather than a separate building and by giving control over the use of a color to a single designer. The photograph at left (below) is of a luncheon in the Court of Abundance. (Photos from Frank Morton Todd, *The Story of the Exposition,* 1:24 and 3:6)

Panama Pacific International Exposition vice-presidents. Clockwise from top left, William H. Crocker, banker with diversified investments throughout the western United States; Reuben Brooks Hale, department store owner; Michael H. de Young, publisher of the *San Francisco Chronicle*; James Rolph, Jr., then president of the Merchants' Association, later mayor; Leon Sloss, president of the Northern Commercial Company, successor to the Alaska Commercial Company; and I. W. Hellman, Jr., president of Union Trust and director of several other banks. These six men, representing a variety of views on other contemporary issues, set aside their differences to create a common front in support of the exposition. (Photo from Frank Morton Todd, *The Story of the Exposition,* 1:94)

Completed in late 1915, city hall (left foreground in the photo above; opposite, viewed from across the plaza) was designed by San Francisco architects John Bakewell, Jr., and Arthur Brown, Jr. Sally Woodbridge, an architectural historian, has described the building as the nation's "only really first-rate example of French High Baroque Revival carried out in detail and with loving care." To its right stands the Civic Auditorium, built by the Panama Pacific International Exposition for use in its activities in 1915. Across the plaza from the Civic Auditorium is the State Office Building, under construction in this photograph and completed in 1926. Facing city hall across the plaza is the public library, completed in 1916.

The broad thoroughfare running from lower right to top center is Market Street. The central business district is in the upper left; South of Market manufacturing and residential areas are in the upper right. Piers line the waterfront on either side of the Ferry Building. (Photo courtesy of the Library of Congress)

Civic Center, 1922. Planned with a concern for architectural unity and harmony, the San Francisco Civic Center was one of the most impressive accomplishments of the "City Beautiful" movement. Mayor James Rolph deserves major credit for the planning and completion of the Civic Center. For Rolph and his growth-minded supporters from business and labor, the buildings—especially city hall—symbolized the spirit of civic unity they hoped would energize San Francisco urban development. (Photo courtesy of the Bancroft Library, University of California, Berkeley)

Above, the California delegation to the 1920 Republican National Convention with candidate Warren G. Harding on his front porch in Marion, Ohio. From the right: California governor William D. Stephens, Harding, William H. Crocker, Wallace Alexander, and Patrick H. McCarthy. Business leaders such as Crocker and Alexander used their state and national political influence to maintain and enhance San Francisco's economic position vis-à-vis other cities. They also played major roles in organizing the Industrial Association in 1921 and thereby helped to end the twenty-year ascendancy of McCarthy's Building Trades Council. (Photo by Edmonston, Washington, D.C., courtesy of the California Historical Society, San Francisco)

In the photo to the left stand Angelo Rossi (on the left) and James Rolph, Jr. (on the right). Rossi, a successful businessman and prominent leader of the Downtown Association, served as a supervisor through much of the 1920s. When Rolph was elected governor in 1930 and had to resign the mayoralty in 1931, Rossi was chosen by the Board of Supervisors as his successor. The political styles of both men emphasized boosting the city and smothering controversy with urbane good humor. (Photo courtesy of the San Francisco Archives, San Francisco Public Library)

Above, Herbert Fleishhacker (center), long-time political confidant of Mayor Rolph, joins Mayor Rossi (right) in holding a check for $24,000 to be used for rehabilitation of the Palace of Fine Arts, the only building to survive from the Panama Pacific International Exposition, 1931. Fleishhacker was one of the most influential leaders of the conservative wing of the California Republican party throughout the 1920s.

Sheriff Tom Finn (right), 1911, from a campaign card issued during his reelection effort. A founder of the Stablemen's Union, Finn was originally elected sheriff as the Union Labor party candidate in 1909. He lost in 1911 but regained the sheriff's office in 1915 and held it until 1927. During Hiram Johnson's administration as governor, Finn emerged as a major Republican leader, playing an influential role in moving the unions into Johnson's organization. He remained a power in Republican politics until his death in the 1930s. (Photos courtesy of the San Francisco Archives, San Francisco Public Library)

San Francisco, June 1, 1930. The previous decade saw the proliferation of skyscrapers. Industrial Association publications delighted in publishing photographs of the city's new "American Plan" skyline. The Ferry Building is slightly to the left of center in this photograph, and the headquarters of the Southern Pacific Company appears just to its left. The skyscraper farthest to the left is the Pacific Telephone and Telegraph Company Building, the largest corporate office building on the Pacific Coast at its completion in 1925. The large building with a pyramidal cap, right of center, is the Mark Hopkins Hotel, located on Nob Hill on the site of the Mark Hopkins mansion and completed in 1925. By 1930, the central business district had already begun to take on some of the physical characteristics of a mini-Manhattan. (Photo by Gabriel Moulin, courtesy of the Library of Congress)

Pacific International Exposition). Although fewer than half of the registered voters participated in this decision to amend the charter, the high majorities (only one assembly district returned a yes vote below 70 percent) suggest widespread voter approval of an earlier Board of Supervisors decision to spend $100,000 on rehabilitation of the building and to continue city government maintenance.[43]

Interaction among individual "cultural entrepreneurs," art interest groups, municipal government, and the voting public not only shaped city policy toward the de Young Memorial Museum, the California Palace of the Legion of Honor, and the Palace of Fine Arts, but also guided the establishment of the War Memorial Opera House and the San Francisco Museum of Art. Both the Musical Association of San Francisco and the San Francisco Art Association participated in a 1918 proposal to build a structure to house a symphony hall, opera, and art museum. A memorial court, dedicated to the Arts of Peace and the military forces of World War I, was to be included. John Drum chaired a fund-raising committee composed of William H. Crocker, Charles Templeton Crocker, Milton Esberg, Herbert Fleishhacker, Emanuel Heller, Walter Martin, and John McKee. By the spring of 1920 the committee had collected subscriptions and pledges for $1,625,000 and purchased a building site opposite city hall.[44]

The original committee was expanded by representatives of the American Legion, who were interested in the suggestion that the building contain quarters for the Legion. With the participation of the Legion, a new fund-raising drive opened with a well-publicized rally in May 1920, but only about $370,000 additional subscriptions followed.

William H. Crocker, at the time a regent of the University of California, advised the committee that the War Memorial would be tax-exempt if the project became part of the university. The regents agreed to enter into a trust agreement with representatives of the San Francisco Art Association (Walter Martin and Charles Templeton Crocker), representatives of the Musical Association (John McKee and Emanuel Heller), representatives of the American Legion (Charles Kendrick and Frank F. Kilsby), as well as Milton Esberg, Herbert Fleishhacker, William H. Crocker, and John Drum. The War Memorial Trust Agreement, dated August 19, 1921, became the legal foundation for the War Memorial project.

During the next nine years, a number of issues concerning the building of the War Memorial developed. These issues and the pattern by which the parties involved settled them illustrate again the nature of the interaction between the groups involved in the creation of the city's arts policy. In 1923 the trustees made a proposal to the city to build an opera house, an American Legion building, and an art museum that would be part of the Civic Center. The city would purchase the land (the original lot was sold in 1924 because it seemed too small) with funds provided by the trustees and then refund half of the money to the trustees. The city acquired the site of the War Memorial buildings between 1923 and 1925 after the Board of Supervisors approved the proposal.

After the trustees found an architectural team in 1926, they decided that additional funds would be necessary beyond those already subscribed.

Not wanting to pare down the plans, they decided to use the existing funds and request a supplement from the voters. They met with a United Veterans Council War Memorial Committee, publishers of the major city newspapers, and the Board of Supervisors and decided to build only two buildings instead of the original three. There would be an opera house and a "Veterans and Arts Building." The Board of Supervisors agreed to submit a $4 million bond issue to the public in the spring of 1927, and all five newspapers endorsed the measure.

Only 31 percent of San Francisco's registered voters expressed a preference on the War Memorial bonds, with 70 percent approval. All assembly districts gave majorities favorable to the bonds, with the lowest majority being 64 percent in the Bayshore District. The other bond issues that required a two-thirds vote did not obtain high enough majorities, but the War Memorial passed with a comfortable two-thirds.

Between spring 1927 and fall 1928, differences of opinion developed between some of the veterans' groups and the War Memorial trustees. The University of California regents notified the Board of Supervisors in September 1928 of their intention to transfer the trust funds to the city. Concerned that they might not receive sufficient space under the new plans, in 1928 the veterans campaigned against a charter amendment to create a new city board of trustees for the War Memorial, accusing the original trustees of mismanagement and waste of the privately subscribed funds, and the Board of Supervisors held up the $4 million bond issue until the veteran organizations were satisfied with the plans. The parties finally reached a compromise by November 1930 when the board approved the transfer of funds to the eleven "Trustees of the War Memorial," which voters had approved in the November 1928 election.[45]

Interest groups with a large citywide constituency—like the veterans' organizations—could influence the outcome of arts policy issues on the ballot, but smaller groups influenced arts policy largely by cooperative interactions with city officials. The eventual resolution of the differences between the San Francisco Art Association and the San Francisco Museum of Art (the museum was the agency created by the Art Association to operate the museum part of the War Memorial) and the veterans' organizations depended on gradual adjustment involving the mayor, the Board of Supervisors, the city attorney, and the representatives of the organizations rather than on public participation by voters involving widespread publicity and debate.

Close and cooperative association among groups with a direct interest in the arts, city officials, and municipal reform organizations such as the Commonwealth Club and the San Francisco Bureau of Governmental Research provided the impetus for the inclusion of an Art Commission in the revised city charter that was prepared in 1930 and passed by voters in 1931 (see Chapter 8). Sections 45 and 46 of this charter, concerned with the composition of the Art Commission and its powers and duties, came almost word for word from the recommendations of the art sections of the Commonwealth Club.[46]

In February 1931, after the charter had been drafted but before voter approval in March, members of the groups that claimed credit for the insertion of the Art Commission in the new city charter formed the San Francisco Federation of Arts. This group defined its purpose as "setting up of machinery for the nomination of members of the Commission of Arts as proposed in the new Charter of San Francisco and such other duties as may be determined later."[47] One month after voters approved the charter, the new organization formally inaugurated its activities. Believing that "it is obvious that those actively occupied with the arts are in the best position to know who in the community is qualified to serve in this capacity," the organizing committee went on to say that "this subject [nominations to the mayor for the art commissioners] affords but the immediate incentive for organizing the proposed Federation. We are confident that it will quickly prove its utility in all matters arousing the common interest of local arts groups, or calling for their united action." The following groups received invitations for the June 1931 meeting: San Francisco Art Association, San Francisco Opera Association, Musical Association of San Francisco, San Francisco Musicians Club, San Francisco Society of Women Artists, Roxburghe Club of San Francisco, Bohemian Club, The Book Club (Northern California Chapter), American Institute of Architects, American Federation of Musicians (Local No. 6), and American Society of Landscape Architects (Pacific Coast Chapter). The other art organizations of the city would be welcome once the federation had established itself as an information advisory group for the mayor, Board of Supervisors, and the Art Commission.[48]

The organizers of the federation sought to shape San Francisco arts policy according to a model derived from New York. On April 27, 1931, the chairman wrote to the secretary of the Fine Arts Federation of New York for copies of its constitution and bylaws "and any other data that would assist us in the formation of this Federation." The federation regarded its role as a necessary corrective to time-consuming methods of policy making that occurred as the result of debate, disagreement, conflict, and compromise. The controversies among the veteran organizations, the Art Association of San Francisco, and the trustees over the War Memorial plans had generated delays of four years, and some unresolved issues would continue to create friction until the late 1930s. Chairman E. Spencer Macky of the federation described the goals of the new organization in a way that specified its members' perception of its proper political role:

> We do need some united action in this city in matters pertaining to art. We feel that such an organization can do a great deal to unify public opinion, and bring political pressure to bear through its united membership in the political support of art in this city.

The public announcement distributed after the formal inauguration of the federation also explicitly referred to the federation's political nature:

> Hitherto situations demanding common action between the various arts or between various organizations in the same field have had to be met by some sort of improvised co-operation, with the attendant delay and inefficiency that this implies. The new federation provides permanent and organized means for meeting these situations as they arise.[49]

The federation met on November 19, 1931, to select its nominees to the mayor for the Art Commission, and the commission held its first meeting on January 21, 1932.

The new charter preserved the independence of the M. H. de Young Memorial Museum and the California Palace of the Legion of Honor from the Board of Supervisors and the mayor. Because they had self-perpetuating boards serving indefinitely, these cultural institutions would develop policies independently of political currents within San Francisco. The Art Commission, on the other hand, received a mandate to "exercise all reasonable supervision of policy connected to the arts as may hereafter be assigned to it by ordinance or executive action." The charter also gave the Art Commission power to "supervise and control the expenditure of all appropriations made by the Board of Supervisors for music and the advancement of art and music." These charter provisions allowed the Art Commission to develop interpretations of its responsibilities both by influencing and by being influenced by mayors and supervisors, as well as by interest groups outside city government. The charter also required the Art Commission to approve works of art in buildings on city property and designs for buildings, bridges, and other structures on city property.[50]

Development of San Francisco's cultural policies after World War I raised numerous questions about power and influence. The ways in which informal accommodation and electoral politics resolved these questions demonstrated the distance between the cultural reform movements of the late nineteenth century and those of the 1920s. Working-class militancy posed threats to San Francisco's social and economic order with relative frequency during the period from 1865 to 1906. But after the waterfront strike of 1901 and the earthquake and fire of 1906, successful challenges to existing patterns of economic power became increasingly limited by a growing consensus grounded on culture and the moral order. Kindergartens and schools nurtured social cohesion and cultural conformity. Urban planning and civic design stimulated cultural nationalism and local pride. Institutionalization of the city's museums, symphony, and opera as treasures of all the people encouraged personal identification with the city's stature as a "world class city." Patrick McCarthy, mayor from 1910 to 1912 and a symbol of respectability for the city's stable working-class population, generally supported such public cultural reforms, as well as the parallel ethnic cultural institutions that provided a vehicle for the private aspirations of striving families. At the same time, McCarthy—like Mayor Rolph (1912–1931)—paid deference to his constituents' ethnic loyalties and defended San Francisco's ethnic and cultural diversity as a civic resource rather than as a dangerous threat. The patriotism and Americanization fervor of World War I provided a boost to a cultural process long under way. By the early 1920s, San Francisco possessed a mainstream culture that tolerated literary bohemianism but frowned on political radicalism, lived in peace alongside unconventional lifestyles but drew the line at militant dissent.

*Fate was kind to the Californians in sending
them a demagogue of a common type, noisy and
confident, but with neither political foresight
nor constructive talent.*
—JAMES BRYCE, on San Francisco politics
in the 1870s

*The game of politics is not a branch of the
Sunday School business.*
—CHRISTOPHER A. BUCKLEY,
on San Francisco politics
in the 1880s

Chapter 6

Politics in the Expanding City, 1865-1893

In the midst of San Francisco's years of explosive growth following the Civil War, James Bryce described California as having "more than any other [state] the character of a great country, capable of standing alone in the world." He saw San Francisco as the "capital" of this country, "a commercial and intellectual centre and source of influence for the surrounding regions, more powerful over them than is any Eastern city over its neighborhood."[1] Removed from other urban centers by half a continent or more, San Francisco's politics—with few exceptions—differed in degree, not in kind, from the politics of New York or Chicago. Before exploring the major exception, the Workingmen's party of the late 1870s, some of the elemental structures of politics must be surveyed.

THE GAME OF POLITICS

On any election day, in any American city in the late nineteenth century, similar scenes unfolded. Large crowds of men stood outside every polling place (politics was a distinctly male pastime) eagerly importuning voters to accept long, narrow pieces of paper called "tickets." This ticket (in fact a ballot) carried the names of candidates for various offices. Until the adoption of the secret ballot (1891 in California), each political party provided ballots for the use of voters. The "party ticket" carried the names of that party's candidates only. Voters wishing to cross party lines first accepted a party ticket, then scratched out the names of candidates they wished to avoid, and finally wrote in the names of their favorites. To make this easier, candidates sometimes distributed "pasters"—strips of paper with glue backing, imprinted with the candidate's name and designed to be stuck over the name of his opponent. No secret booths existed for this activity. Instead, voters accepted a ticket from a party worker, then walked into the polling place and placed that ticket in the ballot box, all under the watchful eye of party retainers. Shrewd party leaders made scratching difficult or impossible by making tickets narrow, taking up all the space on them with either candidates' names or decoration, and sometimes using miniscule typeface to prevent the use of pasters.[2]

Political success, given such a system, required at the very least a corps of faithful party workers, enough to staff every polling place and distribute tickets, plus sufficient financial resources to print a supply of tickets. Campaigning usually became a matter of identifying one's supporters and mobilizing them on election day. Here, again, parties relied on a large corps of workers. The politics of mobilization implied as well the politics of organization. Organization began at the grassroots, with political clubs scattered throughout the neighborhoods of the city. Often located above or in back of a saloon, clubs included a range of social activities along with those of a political nature. All clubs affiliated with—and were sometimes created by— one of the major political parties. Sometimes clubs had geographic jurisdictions; others claimed ethnic or occupational constituencies. Still other organizations remained informal, based on a set of personal contacts at a place of work or recreation. Firehouses, militia companies, and neighborhood saloons all typically served as foci for political organizations.[3]

The county committee stood at the apex of this organizational structure in San Francisco, and it centralized decision making and directed party efforts throughout the city. In the nineteenth century, politics and parties were essentially synonymous. Balloting and mobilizing voters were but two of the many functions performed by parties. Nominations for office came from party conventions, held at the city level for city and county offices and within the various districts for members of the assembly, state senate, and House of Representatives. A "primary," in which voters (or club members) chose delegates, preceded each convention. Access to elective office thus came entirely through the channels of party organization, from primaries through conventions to the printing of ballots and mobilizing of voters. Those who wished to break with the party organization usually did so by forming an independent party, complete with all the accoutrements of established parties. Candidates, if elected, usually remained attentive to the party leaders, who provided the necessary support for electoral success. Just as access to elective office came through the channels of the party, so too did parties typically guard the door to appointive positions. Appointive positions—patronage—provided much of the nourishment for the armies of campaign workers. Contracts and franchises—also forms of patronage— often flowed to those whose contributions helped to make success possible. Candidates themselves typically contributed 10 percent of their annual salary (or the annual salary of the position to which they aspired).[4]

One New York political leader of the late nineteenth century explained his personal prosperity by saying: "I seen my opportunities and I took 'em." Ample opportunities existed for the political entrepreneur, as many as for the businessman of the day. Wealth and power awaited the shrewd and resourceful. The political system remained as unregulated as the economy and contained as many opportunities for manipulation. In a system based on maximizing voter turnout, the man who could provide voters commanded attention. Proprietors of sailors' boardinghouses thus stood high in organizational councils, for each boardinghouse held as many as a hundred potential voters. No matter that most were usually away on a voyage—they often managed to vote anyway through careful planning by party leaders. On one occasion, it is alleged, even the crew of a foreign man-of-war tied up in the San Francisco harbor marched to the polls to take part in a city election. The system encouraged the appearance of "price clubs," groups claiming to represent a particular constituency, which made endorsements from among the nominees of the regular parties and then offered, for a donation (a "price") from each nominee, to print up tickets and distribute them to the constituency in question. Some such groups were undoubtedly legitimate, but others—like the Independent Democratic Liberal Republican Anti-Coolie Labor party—most likely sprang from the imaginations of small-scale entrepreneurs who assumed the candidates would pay the price requested rather than run the risk of alienating potential backers.[5]

PATTERNS OF CITY POLITICS BEFORE 1877

Throughout the late 1850s and 1860s, San Francisco politics was dominated by the heirs to the vigilantes, the People's party. Between 1856 and 1875, only one Democrat won the mayoralty. After the Civil War, however, memories of the events of 1856 receded ever further from mind. Thousands of newcomers poured into the city—many of them Irish and German immigrants—and the Democratic party began to emerge as the majority. Democrats won the mayoralty in 1875 and 1877, carried the city for their gubernatorial candidate in 1875, and usually could command a majority until the turn of the century. Arranging the city's wards according to their mean Democratic vote between 1873 and 1877 (measured by voting for mayor, governor, and president) produces the following:

Ward	Mean Democratic Vote (%)
1	59.8
7	55.2
10	52.6
9	51.7
11	51.1
3	48.6
4	47.0
2	46.0
12	44.7
5	44.2
8	39.3
6	37.4
City	48.6

Map 2 identifies ward boundaries. As can be seen, the Democrats' strength came from working-class sections of the city—the waterfront and South of Market, disproportionately of foreign stock (especially Irish) and Catholic. Democrats were weakest in the middle-class and upper-class areas north of Market Street, home to merchants, professionals, and others in white-collar occupations, also heavily of foreign stock but with a tendency to be German and Jewish rather than Irish and Catholic. The sixth ward, including Nob Hill, was the wealthiest area in the city and was least likely to vote Democratic. The second, third, and fourth wards were more heterogeneous, including a variety of occupations, ethnic groups, and lifestyles.[6]

In his description of California, James Bryce observed: "The most active minds are too much absorbed in great business enterprises to attend to politics." Prominent San Franciscans, to be certain, found themselves "much absorbed in great business enterprises" throughout the three decades following the Civil War. Their interests ranged from the Comstock Lode to the wheat fields of the interior valleys, from Promontory Point to Los Angeles, from Alaskan fur and fish to Hawaiian sugar. The most prominent San Franciscans, those with mansions atop Nob Hill or on the peninsula, rarely involved themselves in city politics. They left the rough-and-tumble of club meetings, voter mobilization, and patronage distribution to others, characterized by Bryce as "the inferior men."[7] But the lords of the Comstock and the masters of the Pacific railway did not, by any means, absent themselves from politics. On the contrary, they involved themselves thoroughly and sought constantly to involve the government as an active partner in their enterprises. They paid little attention to city government, relatively powerless because of the Consolidation Act, but turned instead to those governments with real power, those in Washington and Sacramento and—occasionally—Carson City and Honolulu.

The Politics of Business. The best-known partnership between government and private enterprise in the nineteenth century must surely be the construction of the transcontinental railways. The companies that became the Southern Pacific received more than 10 million acres of land, yielding a net revenue of $10 million over the first half-century of the line's existence, in addition to federal bonds that netted nearly $21 million. The California state legislature, in 1864, assumed the interest on $1.5 million in railroad bonds, at 7 percent for twenty years, a commitment worth $2.1 million on its face. In 1863 and 1864, the legislature authorized three counties and the cities of Sacramento and San Francisco to provide further subsidies for railroad construction. The quartet in command of the railroad plunged deeply into the politics of legislative activity. Collis Huntington usually represented the line in Washington. Leland Stanford, president of the company, won election as governor in 1861 and served as head of the Republican party in California while Republicans in Congress ladled out generous subsidies for his railroad. He also proved willing to approve subsidy bills coming from the California legislature.[8]

Although the legislature authorized several counties and cities to subsidize railroad construction, voters in each had to approve the bond issues.

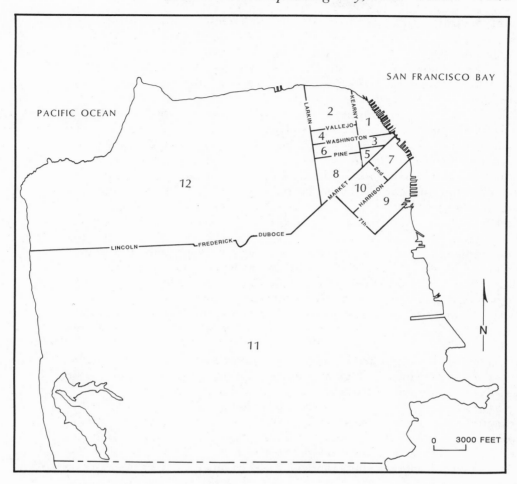

Map 2.   Ward Boundaries, 1856–1900

In most instances, approval came routinely, but not in San Francisco. San Franciscans viewed the railroad with suspicion. A Sacramento-based corporation (headquarters did not move to San Francisco for another decade), headed by Sacramento merchants, it might break the position San Francisco held as chief entrepôt to the Pacific Coast. In 1863, the city's legislative delegation split five to five on the question of authorizing a $1 million bond issue to subsidize railroad construction. City voters, on election day, produced a majority in favor of the bonds, but opponents quickly claimed that the majority resulted from the activities of Philip Stanford, brother of the governor, who circulated among the city's polling places distributing five- and twenty-dollar gold pieces and urging voters to approve the bond issue. When the Board of Supervisors refused to issue the bonds, the railroad went to court to claim its due, and the state legislature told the supervisors to compromise the claims. In June 1864, a committee of supervisors met with Stanford and agreed to pay $600,000. Even then, the mayor and the city's fiscal officers refused to issue the bonds until ordered to do so by the state supreme court.[9]

After the mid-1860s, the railroad no longer sought direct cash subsidies, but other efforts to secure assistance continued. In 1868, a state senate committee recommended giving to the railroad nearly seven thousand acres along San Francisco's southern waterfront, constituting total control over the area from Channel Street south to Point San Bruno in San Mateo County. The lands were all submerged, and the railroad was to pay about $100 per acre for them. This acquisition would provide the railroad with access to the San Francisco docks and with a location for the terminus of the transcontinental line. Furthermore, the railroad could fill in the submerged lands, construct a seawall, monopolize the southern waterfront, and simultaneously bar any other railroad from access to the city's piers. The proposal brought a storm of criticism from San Francisco business leaders, and a much-diluted compromise finally granted sixty acres for railroad terminals and a right-of-way. In the early 1870s, the city granted use of several streets as sites for track construction. Although the railroad failed to acquire control over the San Francisco waterfront, it did achieve a monopoly over the Oakland waterfront, and only intense opposition from San Francisco diverted a proposal to give the railroad complete control over Goat Island (now Yerba Buena Island).[10]

The railroad continued to invest large amounts of both time and money in political activities throughout the late nineteenth century. Huntington represented Southern Pacific interests in Washington whenever Congress was in session, and Stanford carried out similar duties in Sacramento. Huntington was remarkably candid in describing his attitude toward officeholders: "If you have to pay money to have the right thing done, it is only just and fair to do it." He concerned himself with the composition of the San Francisco delegation to the House of Representatives, giving directions on one occasion that John K. Luttrell—whom Huntington characterized as "a wild hog"—should be defeated, preferably by denying him renomination. On another occasion he issued orders to defeat William A. Piper, whom he deemed "a damned hog" and "a scavenger." By 1890, however, Huntington complained that "things have got to such a state, that if a man wants to be a constable he thinks he has first got to come down to Fourth and Townsend streets [Southern Pacific headquarters] to get permission." Huntington committed himself first and last to the Southern Pacific, and party politics took second place with him. Stanford, by contrast, helped to organize the Republican party, ran for statewide office as a Republican in both 1857 and 1859 (before his involvement with the railroad), and won the governorship for that party in 1861. Throughout the 1870s and 1880s, Stanford kept his hand in state politics, making campaign speeches and lobbying on behalf of the Southern Pacific. In 1885, he won election to the U.S. Senate.[11]

When Stanford took his seat in the Senate, he joined fellow Republican, fellow San Franciscan, and fellow businessman John F. Miller. When Miller died a year later, George Hearst, another Nob Hill resident (albeit a Democrat), replaced him. During the mid-1880s, San Franciscans held not just the two California Senate seats but also one from Nevada. In 1874, the city provided two of the three leading candidates for the Nevada senate seat open that year. William Sharon, chief Nevada representative of the Bank of California, maintained a legal residence in Nevada although he lived in San Francisco after 1872. Adolph Sutro, the other San Francisco candidate, had left the city for Nevada's silver mining region in 1860, but his family continued to live in the city until the early 1870s, and his children attended school in the Bay Area while their father sought election to the Senate from Nevada. Sharon won the election, but took over both the Palace Hotel and the Bank of California the same year and lived in San Francisco during most of his term. Sutro's family returned to the city in 1879, although Sutro made another try to defeat Sharon in 1881. The victorious candidate that year, however, was James Fair, a partner in San Francisco's Nevada Bank. Fair bought a home in San Francisco shortly after his election, but his wife divorced him and received the mansion as part of the settlement. Fair lived in Washington when the Senate was in session and at other times in the Lick House in San Francisco, one of his many investments in city real estate.[12]

San Franciscans saw Nevada as a satellite on the east and took a similar view of Alaska to the far north. In 1870, several San Francisco firms submitted bids for an exclusive franchise to take seal pelts on the tiny Pribilof Islands off the coast of Alaska. Congress had not yet created a territorial government for Alaska, but its potential as a source of furs was well known. John Miller, erstwhile Collector of the Port of San Francisco, prominent Republican, and president of the Alaska Commercial Company, won the contract. Senator Cornelius Cole, a former business partner of Miller's, and Senator William Stewart of Nevada, a close associate of Louis Sloss (who both preceded and succeeded Miller as company president), provided important assistance in securing the contract. Miller himself went to the U.S. Senate in 1881. The Alaska Commercial Company rapidly extended operations to the mainland fur trade, established a virtual monopoly there, and operated with virtually no restraints. Until 1884, Alaska had no real government. Some insisted, in fact, that the San Franciscans who ran the company and their Washington lobbyist exercised a veto power over political development in Alaska.[13]

The men who dominated the financial and commercial life of San Francisco in the nineteenth century knew their way about the corridors of power. They understood that the economy was political, and they realized that success for their far-reaching business concerns required a firm grasp of politics. No other city in the nation could boast of having three residents sitting simultaneously in the U.S. Senate! City politics was a penny-ante game compared with the stakes for which these men ordinarily played. Further, they knew the limitations on city government imposed by the Consolidation Act of 1856. In an effort to prevent corruption, that document granted few powers to the Board of Supervisors, made appropriating funds difficult, prohibited debts and liabilities, and reduced the mayor to little more than a presiding officer. The intent—and to a large extent the effect— was to reduce city government to administration, with little potential for initiative. John P. Young, in 1912, characterized the result as "dry rot." In the 1860s, the legislature removed the waterfront, heart of the city's economy, from control by city government and transferred it to a state commission. The most routine city business required approval by the state legislature. Even the widening of Kearny Street, undertaken in 1866, needed prior legislative authorization.[14]

William Ralston and the Politics of Urban Development. The widening of Kearny Street inspired William Ralston to a more grandiose scheme to revise the city's streets. He proposed extending Montgomery Street, an important commercial thoroughfare, straight south across Market, slashing through those blocks (all diagonal to the proposed new street) and providing access to the industrial area developing south of Market. Ralston presented this proposal to the supervisors in late 1866, and, after lengthy hearings, the supervisors accepted the plan by the narrow margin of seven to five. When this brought a mayoral veto, the seven-to-five margin changed to the two-thirds necessary to override. The surveying generated so much controversy that the project ground to a halt. In the meantime, John Middleton won election to the state legislature in order to secure authorization for a massive cut through Rincon Hill. The cut produced a nearly level grade for Second Street from Market to the docks at the foot of First and Townsend, an area where—not coincidentally—Middleton held property interests. Ralston abandoned his Montgomery South plan and embraced a less drastic alternative. He and Asbury Harpending proposed to create a new street that would run parallel to Second and meet Montgomery at Market. New Montgomery Street involved both a new commercial thoroughfare from Market to the docks and the leveling of Rincon Hill. The legislature authorized the scheme after (according to Harpending's memoirs) payment of $35,000 to Sacramento vote brokers, daily restaurant bills of $400, and intense lobbying in both Sacramento and San Francisco. When the legislature later repealed the authorization, Ralston and Harpending constructed two blocks of the new street using their own land. They then sought to pull the financial and commercial center of the city southward toward their new street by constructing the Grand Hotel, on New Montgomery at Market, and then the Palace Hotel, facing the Grand across New Montgomery.[15]

Ralston wanted the Palace to be the world's finest hotel, and he hoped it would revitalize his New Montgomery Street Real Estate Company. But the construction of the Palace further drained his already depleted resources, and he turned in desperation to a scheme to sell water to the city. Ralston, like most San Franciscans, knew that dissatisfaction with the service provided by the Spring Valley Water Company, the city's source of water, had convinced the Board of Supervisors to buy out that company. Unlike most San Franciscans, Ralston also knew that an engineer had recommended that the city acquire the Calaveras watershed near San Jose as an additional source of water. He and an associate concocted a bold plan. They bought the Calaveras watershed for $100,000, then began to acquire Spring Valley stock. Ralston's tight financial situation meant that they could not pay cash. Instead, they offered more than the going price for the stock but paid with certificates promising that price plus interest. They soon "owned" more than half the stock in the company (without having had to pay for it) and used their control to sell the Calaveras watershed to the Spring Valley Water Company for more than $1 million—a profit of more than $900,000. Its assets augmented by $1 million, the company was now worth about $10 million. Ralston and his partner then offered to sell the entire company to the city for $15 million—another $5 million profit, enough to bail out Ralston's other faltering enterprises. The proposal brought a tidal wave of opposition, and the supervisors refused. Undaunted, Ralston looked to the upcoming city elections and began organizing a slate of supervisorial candidates favorable to his scheme. Before election day, however, Ralston's financial juggling act faltered. Forced to resign the presidency of the Bank of California, he died during his daily swim in the bay. His slate also failed, and the Spring Valley Water Company remained a private corporation until well into the twentieth century.[16]

THE WORKINGMEN'S PARTY OF CALIFORNIA

Ralston's resignation as bank president came on the heels of a run on the bank that had become a virtual panic. At the same time that the Bank of California closed its doors, silver mining stocks fell sharply. Many who had succumbed to the mania for silver stock speculation lost heavily. By 1876, seven thousand San Franciscans received assistance from the city's benevolent associations. The following year the nation plunged into a depression, compounded in California by declining yields from the Comstock and by a drought that caused the failure of the grain harvest. This, in turn, reduced the need for labor both for harvesting and for loading on the docks. Unemployment affected at least 15 percent of the city's work force, perhaps more. In July 1877, a railroad strike in the east and announcement of wage cuts for California railroad workers prompted a mass meeting sponsored by the Workingmen's party of the United States, a small socialist group. Held on the "sand lots"—open, sand-covered building sites near city hall—the meeting attracted eight thousand. Before long, the socialists lost control of their meeting and the crowd became a mob, roaming the city, attacking Chinese laundries, and beating those Chinese unfortunate enough to come within the mob's reach.[17]

Anti-Chinese Antagonism. Antagonism toward the Chinese did not spring full-grown from that mob in July 1877. On the contrary, it had developed and gathered force for more than two decades. State legislation aimed at Chinese miners appeared in 1855. With the increase in unemployment following completion of the transcontinental railroad, anti-Chinese meetings took place on San Francisco sandlots as early as 1870. "Anticoolie" organizations appeared at about the same time, sponsored initially by the Knights of St. Crispin, an organization of shoemakers. San Francisco public officials responded to this growth of anti-Chinese sentiment by passing a series of discriminatory ordinances. They closed down the Chinese school but denied Chinese children access to the public schools. They defined the carrying of baskets on a pole across the shoulders as a misdemeanor, an action aimed at Chinese peddlers. They required all lodging houses to have 500 cubic feet of air for each resident and made tenants equally culpable with landlords for violations. Police never enforced the ordinance outside Chinatown, but enforcement in Chinatown soon produced such crowding of the city jails as to put them in violation of the ordinance. Supervisors thereupon passed the "queue ordinance," requiring that the hair of all jail inmates be cut to within an inch of their scalp (depriving the Chinese of their queues) in an effort to encourage payment of a fine rather than serving a jail term. Mayor William Alvord, elected as a candidate of the Taxpayers' and Republican parties, vetoed the queue ordinance in 1873 when it first passed; Mayor Andrew Jackson Bryant, a Democrat, signed it into law in 1876. Another 1873 ordinance levied high license fees on laundries that made deliveries on foot, a measure intended to harass Chinese laundry operators. Supervisors passed this ordinance over the mayor's veto. In 1876, rising unemployment again brought mass meetings aimed at the Chinese— the largest drew twenty-five thousand people—and a revival of the anti-coolie clubs. Just as in 1870, these brought in turn municipal actions aimed at pacifying the citizenry by enforcing the cubic air ordinance, reviving the queue law, and discriminating against Chinese laundries in the granting of laundry licenses.[18]

By July 1877, mass meetings at which speakers declaimed against the supposed evils of Chinese immigration had become staples of San Francisco life. The appearance of an anticoolie club at the socialists' rally in July 1877 surprised no one, but the riot that followed added a new element. Many in the mob knew that in Pittsburgh a crowd recently had put the torch to cars and buildings of the Pennsylvania Railroad. In San Francisco, the mob tried to burn Chinatown; they had been told for a generation that the Chinese caused low wages and unemployment. Although the mob failed to reach their objective, they frightened the city's commercial and political leaders. The next day a large group of the city's business elite met with the mayor and police chief. William Coleman, leader of the Vigilance Committee of 1856, took the chair. Mayor Bryant announced that city police could not cope with the emergency, and Darius O. Mills, head of the reorganized Bank of California, proposed a Committee of Safety under Coleman's leadership. Faced with illegal actions by a mob, the city's commercial leadership responded as it had twenty years before—it undertook extralegal action of its own. The committee rapidly enrolled 5,500 members, collected more than 2,000 rifles and carbines, and secured pledges of $75,000; Coleman also had 6,000 hickory pick-handles converted into impromptu police clubs. After patrolling the city for a few days, the Pick-Handle Brigade disbanded, considering its immediate work complete.[19]

Denis Kearney and the Workingmen's Party. A month later, Denis Kearney, one of the members of the Pick-Handle Brigade, tapped the emotions that had motivated the July mob in order to build a political movement with himself at its head. Kearney, an Irish-born drayman, later stated that he had no sympathy with the July meeting because he was "opposed to strikes."

Drawn into politics, by his own account, because the deplorable condition of city streets made his draying business difficult, in August he took a leading role in the formation of the Workingmen's Trade and Labor Union of San Francisco, a group intended initially as a "price club." The organization expanded in October as Kearney harangued crowds at sandlot meetings, his message usually the same: the rich used the Chinese to drive down wages, workingmen suffered from both the millionaires atop Nob Hill and their minions in Chinatown, monopolies must be destroyed, and—always his closing—"The Chinese must go." Not the first to advocate burning Chinatown or destroying the docks where Chinese immigrants entered San Francisco, Kearney repeated slogans long popularized by members of the city's political establishment. Kearney, however, tied anti-Chinese rhetoric to attacks on the city's business elite and gathered huge crowds who seemed eager to do his bidding. The police repeatedly arrested him for inciting to riot, and martyrdom increased his fame. By early 1878, the Workingmen's Party of California (WPC) had become a major political force, both in San Francisco and elsewhere in the state.[20]

The WPC reached the height of its state power in mid-1878 and remained a potent force in city affairs through the end of 1879. In January 1878, the new party elected its candidate to fill a vacant assembly seat across the bay in Alameda, won another assembly seat the next month, swept municipal elections in Sacramento and Oakland in March, and scored victories in other municipal elections in April and May. In June, the entire state voted to elect delegates to a constitutional convention. Throughout the state, Republican and Democratic party leaders coalesced on a joint slate, termed "nonpartisan" but in reality bipartisan and anti-WPC. Nonpartisan delegates formed the largest group in the convention, numbering eighty-one of the 152 delegates; the WPC counted fifty-one, and the rest wore various party identifications. Of those not aligned with the WPC, a number affiliated with the Grangers, who held antimonopoly views similar to those of the WPC. Although the WPC and the Grangers might have formed a majority, they achieved no real coalition. The convention met for some five months and produced a document that Henry George described as "a mixture of constitution, code, stump-speech, and mandamus." George felt it was "anything but a workingman's Constitution" because it disenfranchised transitory workers, levied a poll tax, and entrenched vested rights in land. Conservative groups, however, reacted with alarm to provisions on taxation and corporations. The new constitution also contained many restrictions on the Chinese and on the right of corporations to employ Chinese workers, sections quickly declared contrary to the U.S. Constitution and hence void. The ratification election in the spring of 1879 saw intense efforts on both sides, with the WPC and Granger groups working for approval and business groups and traditional political leaders opposed. Large majorities favoring ratification in agricultural sections of the state overcame opposition of urban areas, and the constitution took effect.[21]

September 1879 saw elections for both state officials and San Francisco city officers. The WPC and the Republicans shared in the victories statewide, the Republicans taking the governorship and the WPC candidate winning as chief justice of the state supreme court. The San Francisco city election, like so many events in the late 1870s, seemed almost a return to the chaotic 1850s when politicians settled with gunshots controversies they could not resolve through politics. The WPC chose Isaac S. Kalloch, pastor of the Baptist Metropolitan Temple, as its candidate for mayor. His nomination provoked strong opposition from Charles de Young of the *Chronicle*, which had previously been the only paper in the state even mildly supportive of the WPC. De Young published repeated attacks on Kalloch, likened him to "an Unclean Leper," revealed he had once stood trial for adultery, and added other charges. Kalloch used his pulpit to reply in kind, labeling the de Young brothers "moral lepers [leprosy seemed a popular charge] . . . hybrid whelps of sin and shame, . . . [and] hyenas of society." He brought the de Youngs' mother into the fray by referring to their "bawdy house breeding" and "guttersnipe training." The next day Charles de Young shot Kalloch in the chest and side, but the minister survived and won the election from his sickbed. Undaunted, de Young published a pamphlet repeating charges of Kalloch's licentiousness, and in late April 1880 Kalloch's son shot and killed Charles de Young. A jury acquitted young Kalloch when a witness—later convicted of perjury—claimed de Young had fired first. Kalloch, as mayor, faced a hostile majority on the Board of Supervisors (Republicans held three-quarters of the seats), and by the time he left office, the WPC itself had died.[22]

The WPC and the Voters. During its heyday, the WPC commanded the loyalty of half the voters in San Francisco. James Bryce ascribed this success to support

> by the Irish, here a discontented and turbulent part of the population, by the lower class of German immigrants, and by the longshore men, also an important element in this great port, and a dangerous element (as long ago in Athens) wherever one finds them.

Bryce added, however, that Kearney also drew support from "the better sort of working men, clerks, and small shopkeepers," no doubt the group Henry George referred to when he wrote that Kearneyism attracted "people who never joined the clubs or visited the sand-lot . . . people who were so utterly disgusted with the workings and corruptions of old parties as to welcome 'anything for a change.'" The Democratic party virtually disappeared in San Francisco—"scarce a grease spot was left to mark its place," according to one prominent Democrat—as the WPC seized the support of normally Democratic voters. Bryce, George, and others agreed that the WPC benefited greatly from the attention given it by the newspapers, especially the *Chronicle*, which supported the movement until Kalloch's nomination.[23]

If the vote to ratify the constitution and Kalloch's vote for mayor are used to analyze the base of WPC support among the voters, patterns emerge that verify the observations of both Bryce and George. Table 7 summarizes the WPC strength by ward and also includes the mean Democratic vote for 1873–1877.[24] The WPC clearly drew the bulk of its support from the same

TABLE 7

Voter Support for the Workingmen's Party, by Wards,
1879, Including Comparison with Support
for Democratic Candidates, 1873–1877

Ward	*Vote to Ratify the Constitution, 1879*	*Vote for Kalloch for Mayor, 1879*	*Mean Democratic Vote, 1873–1877*
1	61.0%	57.6%	59.8%
7	62.8	66.5	55.2
10	57.1	58.8	52.6
9	61.2	63.5	51.7
11	56.7	59.0	51.1
3	42.6	44.7	48.6
4	44.8	50.5	47.0
2	46.0	51.1	46.0
12	36.2	38.4	44.7
5	27.0	31.8	44.2
8	27.1	31.5	39.3
6	26.9	29.3	37.4
City	48.0	50.6	48.6

SOURCES: San Francisco, Board of Supervisors, *Municipal Reports* (San Francisco, 1872–1873), pp. 558–559; ibid. (1874–1875), pp. 768–775; ibid. (1875–1876), pp. 750–751; ibid. (1876–1877), pp. 1042–1043; ibid. (1878–1879), pp. 523–526, 758–807.

areas that had given the Democrats majorities before 1879, and the WPC did poorly in areas that had been—and remained—Republican. In nearly every instance, however, the WPC provoked a more cohesive response than had the Democrats. In working-class areas along the waterfront and south of Market Street, the WPC received a larger share of the vote than had the Democrats; in middle-class and upper-class areas, the WPC did worse. The sharpening of class antagonisms by Kearney cut through some of the non-economic bases for party affiliation that had previously operated.

By August 1881, Kearney himself admitted that "there is no Working-men's Party now." The WPC plunged to its nadir as rapidly as it had soared to its zenith. The reasons for the party's decline include the Kalloch–de Young shootings, splits within the WPC leadership over party policy and over alliance with the national Greenback party, and general disappointment over the outcome of the WPC agitation. Kearney, most observers agreed, lacked the ability to build a permanent organization, and, equally serious, he lacked the depth to propose and implement measures that would relieve the economic suffering that gave him his South of Market base. Henry George, as early as 1880, understood that Kearneyism posed no serious threat to the political order. He found the new constitution "destitute . . . of any shadow of reform which will lessen social inequalities or purify politics." WPC candidates, he felt, "have been no more radical than the average of American politicians." Most important, Kearneyism contained no viable alternative to the economic and social factors that produced both the July Days and Kearney. The WPC proposed instead, George wrote, "merely the remedy which their preachers, teachers, and influential newspapers are constantly prescribing to the American people as the great cure-all—elect honest men to office and have them cut down taxation." At the same time that the WPC suffered schisms and the younger Kalloch stood trial for shooting de Young, the elder Kalloch faced a hostile majority on the Board of Supervisors, the economy of the city slowly improved, and the level of unemployment fell. The WPC had fed on the distress of depression, and the unemployed and destitute had thronged to the sandlots to hear Kearney speak. With the return of more prosperous times, Kearney proved unable to attract the crowds of earlier days, and the WPC lost even this base.[25]

Despite the sound and fury of Kearneyism and the WPC, within two years it signified but little for the city's politics. Bryce expressed surprise at the ease with which such volatile political currents returned to familiar channels:

> The game of politics between the two old parties goes on as before. . . .
> The city government of San Francisco is much what it was before the
> agitation. . . . After all, say the lawyers and bankers of San Francisco, we are
> going on as before, property will take care of itself in this country, things
> are not really worse so far as our business is concerned.

"Neither," Bryce continued, "are things better," and for a time in the 1880s, they became worse.[26] San Francisco politics during the 1880s differed from previous patterns in one major regard: power was concentrated more than before (or after) in the hands of one person, Christopher Augustine Buckley.

CHRISTOPHER BUCKLEY AND THE POLITICS OF URBAN GROWTH

Buckley was born on Christmas Day in 1845 in New York City, the son of Irish immigrants, his father a stonemason. At the age of sixteen, young Buckley and his family moved to San Francisco. He worked briefly as a streetcar conductor but soon found a more congenial place as a bartender working for Tom Maguire. One of the premier saloonkeepers and political figures of the day, Maguire had worked closely with David Broderick in the 1850s. In one particularly controversial transaction (perhaps a forerunner of Ralston's water plan), Maguire sold a theater to the city for use as a city hall. Maguire's bar provided a political education for its eighteen-year-old bartender, an education augmented by William Higgins, a powerful Republican who took Buckley under his tutelage for a brief period in the late 1860s. By the time he was twenty-one, young Buckley struck out on his own as a saloonkeeper, later established a brief partnership with Maguire, then moved to Vallejo for two years.[27]

Buckley returned to San Francisco in 1873, a convert to the Democratic party. He began to work with a number of leading Democratic organizers, emerging slowly as a significant figure in his own right. Though blind by the late 1870s, Buckley did not miss a stride in his march toward power. In 1880 he convinced Kearney to swing the WPC organization behind Winfield

Scott Hancock, the Democratic candidate for president, then claimed the credit for carrying California for the Democrats for the first time since the Civil War. The same year, Buckley and other members of the Yosemite Club took over the local Democratic party. Within two years, most city politicians agreed that Buckley held sway as boss of the San Francisco Democratic party and that the Democrats could usually mobilize a majority on election day. Buckley dominated local politics for almost a decade before meeting defeat in the early 1890s.[28]

Buckley and the Democratic Party. When Buckley converted to the Democrats in 1873, he joined a party that had spent most of the previous twenty years in the political wilderness. From the Vigilance Committee of 1856 onward, only one Democrat had sat in the mayor's chair, and Democratic supervisors usually found themselves in the minority. In 1875, in part because of Ralston's water scheme and in part because of a third party's brief entrance into city politics, Democrats won all city offices and most legislative seats. Led by Mayor Bryant, they repeated the sweep in 1877. These victories inaugurated a quarter-century during which Democrats usually won the mayoralty and majorities on the Board of Supervisors. The victories sometimes came only by narrow margins, and they were punctuated by a number of defeats: in 1879 (by the WPC), in 1881 and 1890 (by Republicans), in 1892 (by an independent candidate), and in 1894 (by Adolph Sutro, running as a Populist).[29]

Buckley's title, "boss"—bestowed, to be certain, by his opponents—came not from any public office he held nor from any formal position in the Democratic party structure. His power derived instead from his stance in the center of a complex set of personal relationships that reached out to many parts of the city and to many of the city's Democratic voters. During the early 1880s, Buckley customarily operated from his Alhambra Saloon on Bush Street; after he sold the Alhambra in 1885, he met with supporters in various saloons and later in the Manhattan Club, a Democratic organization for which Buckley bought a Nob Hill mansion. His organization always had a feudal quality about it—Buckley might be king, but he reigned because of the loyalty of several great nobles who had power bases of their own. At times, some of these other Democratic leaders rose in revolt and tried to seize the reins of power from Buckley, but throughout the 1880s he quashed such rebellions.[30]

Buckley chose Democratic candidates carefully. William Bullough, Buckley's biographer, has provided the following description of Buckley's tickets:

> Slates presented by the Buckley organization were not composed of party hacks and incompetents but rather of members of the middle echelons of the business community, individuals of sufficient talent and respectability to appeal to voters throughout the city. Tickets were also persistently cosmopolitan, including nominees whose surnames identified them with politically potent Irish, German, French, Jewish, and Italian communities.

Washington Bartlett, Buckley's choice for mayor in 1882, had arrived in the city in 1849, became a journalist and publisher, then switched to the law, business, and real estate. A veteran of the Vigilance Committee of 1856, Bartlett had served three terms as county clerk, elected on the People's party ticket, and two terms in the state senate. As mayor, Bartlett distinguished himself primarily by holding down tax rates and city spending. His successor, Edward Pond, was cut from similar cloth. Despite some disagreements, Buckley gave both men Democratic nominations for governor. Bartlett won in 1886, but Pond lost in 1890.[31]

The Politics of Urban Growth.   Bartlett and Pond presided over a city undergoing rapid growth during the prosperous 1880s. New one- and two-family houses, exuberant local variants of prevailing styles, marched up the hills and through the valleys of the Mission District and spilled westward across the Western Addition. The new housing stimulated extension of streetcar lines, street lighting, water, and other utilities. Some of the most controversial, and potentially lucrative, political decisions of the 1880s dealt with franchises to private utility companies. Demands for streetcar franchises produced twenty-six grants in 1879 alone. When Buckley's slate proved victorious in 1882, he found himself popular not just with would-be traction magnates but with many other businessmen as well. In Buckley's words: "It was surprising to see how universal was the desire among men of substance, firms and corporations, to get on the right side of politics." Between 1879 and 1884, the Market Street Railway Company (owned by members of the Southern Pacific's Big Four) acquired the basis for a near-monopoly on streetcar transportation.[32]

Granting of franchises continued during 1885–1886 when Bartlett served his second term teamed with a Republican Board of Supervisors. With Republicans occupying eleven of the twelve supervisorial seats, franchise seekers turned their charms upon Buckley's Republican counterparts. Martin Kelly later recalled that one particularly lucrative veto override brought him and each of the Republican supervisors $5,000 apiece. The Spring Valley Water Company already had a monopoly but struggled—successfully—throughout the 1880s to prevent lower water rates. Annual battles also erupted over contracts for street lighting, with electric companies increasingly challenging the near-monopoly of the San Francisco Gas Light Company.[33]

Like his New York counterpart, Buckley saw his opportunities—he called them "certainties"—and he took them, emerging from his years of power independently wealthy, with a portfolio full of bonds (including Spring Valley Water Company, gas and electric companies, and streetcar companies), real estate investments throughout the state, and partnerships in a number of firms doing business with the city. By 1890, he was worth an estimated $600,000. Despite this wealth, Buckley's biographer avers that "Chris Buckley did not corrupt municipal polity in San Francisco."

> It already had been corrupted, if not by individuals certainly by the historical process of urbanization which rendered government under the Consolidation Act of 1856 and its maze of amendments both ineffectual and obsolete. The Blind Boss and his organization . . . brought a rough form of rudimentary

order to the chaos existing in municipal affairs and provided an interim—if extralegal—government that perhaps facilitated otherwise impossible civic development.[34]

Bullough might have added two further observations. First, San Francisco had long become accustomed to "extralegal" approaches to government, from the Vigilance Committee of 1851 and then 1856, through the latter's apotheosis by the People's party, to the Pick-Handle Brigade of 1877. Buckley's organization, of course, differed from these others. They all were organized by and supported by the city's leading merchants. Lower-middle-class businessmen, especially saloonkeepers, created Buckley's organization, and its power base stood squarely in the working class. Second, "civic development" in the 1880s most often proceeded along the lines of least resistance—and least cost. Franchises cost the city treasury nothing (they even generated modest revenue), and they benefited many—the company, the consumers, and the city officials who voted right. Buckley and the Democratic mayors of the 1880s reduced both the city's tax rate and its assessed valuation, resulting in substantial tax savings for property owners. As one result, school construction lagged far behind the growing school-age population. Contracts were awarded in 1871 for construction of a new city hall, but it was incomplete when Buckley came to power in 1882. Niggardly appropriations throughout the Bartlett and Pond administrations kept construction at a snail's pace. By the early 1890s, the still unfinished building—tagged "the new City Hall ruin"—stood as testimony to the priorities of city government: civic development would come through private enterprise, not through expenditure of public funds.[35]

Buckley's Fall from Power. Despite success in stabilizing city finances (largely by collecting back taxes from utility companies) and in reducing taxes, Buckley always had to battle with opposition to his regime, both within his party and outside it. The major outside opposition came from the Republicans, led by William Higgins, Martin Kelly, and Phil Crimmins. Their approach to politics differed only slightly from that practiced by Buckley. Buckley's opposition within his party also included some whose approach to politics differed from Buckley's only in that he was boss, and they wanted to be. In 1882, Buckley's opponents included the elder James Phelan, George Hearst, and a few other notables in addition to the remnants of the group the Yosemite Club had defeated for party leadership in 1880. Eventually Hearst reconciled himself to Buckley and went to the U.S. Senate with the boss's support. Anti-Buckley organizations came and went throughout the 1880s, including the improbably named Anti-Boss Anti-Monopoly Lone Mountain Democratic Club of San Francisco. In 1886, opposition included not only some who had long opposed Buckley but also a few members of his own organization. Charged with responsibility for virtually every fault in the city, Buckley usually shrugged off such accusations; he once said that "in the boss business you have to let it go." By the late 1880s, scandals in the schools combined with other issues to provide opponents with ample ammunition against the boss. Many Buckley opponents coalesced in 1890 as the

Reform Democracy and soon helped to give birth to the Committee of 100, which included the younger James Phelan, William Coleman, former mayor Pond, Gavin McNab, some erstwhile Buckley supporters (one of whom decided the boss had become "too heavy a load to carry"), and personal enemies of Buckley.[36]

In 1891, Buckley came under the scrutiny of a grand jury. William Bullough described the investigation as conducted by a "biased judge" and ten "hostile jurors." After months of widely publicized testimony, the state supreme court ruled that the grand jury had been constituted in violation of both the state constitution and the city charter. Buckley, taking no chances, made an extended trip to Canada, returned briefly to the city, then departed for England. The 1892 primary, conducted during his absence, saw reformers rout the organization, using tactics as manipulative as those of any boss. They printed their ticket, for example, on paper that could be read even when folded and so thin that several ballots might be held together. This "isinglass ticket" and similar maneuvers led Martin Kelly to confess: "When I saw what was within the scope of a reformer's vision, it was with sadness and humility that I realized the narrow limits of my own imagination."[37]

This disarray of the Democrats during the early 1890s found reflection in city politics. In 1890, lavish expenditures by Leland Stanford guaranteed both his own reelection to the U.S. Senate and a Republican sweep of city offices. Reformers accused Buckley and Senator Hearst of cutting a deal with Stanford, allowing a Republican victory in 1890 in return for a Republican washout in 1892 when Hearst would need a Democratic legislature to secure another Senate term. By 1892, however, Hearst was dead and Buckley was out of the country. Anti-Buckley Democrats managed to carry most city offices, but the two leading candidates for mayor came from neither major party. The same situation recurred in 1894 when Adolph Sutro won mayoral office as a Populist. Not until 1896, when James Phelan won the mayoralty as a Democrat, did the two major parties' candidates recover the top spots in the returns. By then, Buckley remained useful to the reformers as a straw man but could not recover his lost power. The new "boss" of San Francisco's Democratic party was Gavin McNab. Born in Scotland, McNab worked as a hotel manager before being admitted to the bar in 1901. His organization, the Junta Democrats, were largely professionals and businessmen, but they included a few former Buckley associates, a former WPC activist, and a number of federal patronage appointees.[38]

Politics in the Early 1890s. In comparing the patterns of voting during the early 1890s with those before and after, the most obvious difference lies in the strong showings of independent or third-party candidates. Beginning in 1888 and continuing through 1896, C. C. O'Donnell ran as an independent candidate for mayor; he secured about 30 percent of the vote on his first four tries, and he finished a close second on several occasions. A forceful speaker who had taken a prominent part in the WPC throughout its existence, O'Donnell drew his support largely from South of Market, the Mission, and the northern waterfront, all districts where the WPC had done well and all with substantial numbers of workers and Irish. O'Donnell's strong showing substantially reduced support for the Democratic candidate to the point where O'Donnell led the Democratic candidate several times. Not until 1896, when James Phelan (Irish and Catholic) carried the Democratic banner, did the Democrats recover their base South of Market and in the Mission. That year, O'Donnell did poorly in those areas, but Phelan got more than half their votes.[39]

Third-party candidates won the mayoralty in 1892 (when the secret ballot was used for the first time) and in 1894. In 1892, Levi R. Ellert ran on the Nonpartisan ticket, a group dominated by businessmen from both major parties. Ellert won on the strength of support from the Western Addition, Pacific Heights (where he took half the total vote in a four-way contest, his best showing), the upper-middle-class residential district just west of the central business district, and the more middle-class areas of the Mission District. The *Morning Call* characterized Ellert's support as coming from "the precincts where the better class of people have their homes." O'Donnell led South of Market, in the Mission, and downtown, the same areas where the Democratic candidate made his strongest showing. The Republican candidate did best in the same areas that gave Ellert his margin of victory. Similar patterns prevailed in 1894. Adolph Sutro, well known both for his large landholdings in the western part of the city and his recurring fights with corporations, became San Francisco's first Jewish mayor by defeating Ellert (running for reelection as a Republican), who placed third behind O'Donnell. Elected as the candidate of the Populist party, Sutro ran most strongly in the same areas that had elected Ellert two years before but added considerable support in working-class areas—the Mission, the northern waterfront, and South of Market, where he matched or even slightly exceeded O'Donnell's vote. James Phelan, running in 1896 as a Democrat and Citizens' Nonpartisan, swept to victory with a coalition that cut across these previous patterns. His best showings came in upper-class and working-class areas—Pacific Heights and the northern waterfront (he got 60 percent or more in both) and South of Market and the Mission (where he got more than half the votes). Phelan ran more poorly in the Western Addition and the residential area west of the central business district, middle-class areas where both Ellert and Sutro had done well. Even in those districts, however, Phelan ran well ahead of his Republican opponent (his closest challenger), securing margins as large as two to one. Buckley's last hurrah as a political leader came that year; his candidate, nominated by the Populists and Anti-Charter Democrats, ran fourth in all parts of the city, far behind Phelan both south of Market and in the Mission.[40]

The ticket splitting of the early 1890s resulted in part from the nature of the issues and candidates and in part from the disarray of the dominant Democrats. Another important element was the new Australian (secret) ballot law, which guaranteed that every voter could choose among all the declared candidates without having a party retainer peering over his shoulder. The 1891 legislature approved the new ballot law only after a long battle, led by the Democrats and the San Francisco Labor Council. Republican leaders in the legislature delayed until virtually the last minute, then finally yielded to the pressures from the minority Democrats and the virtually unanimous press. The Australian ballot law was an important chink in the armor of the parties. Now a corps of party workers did not need to stand outside every polling place. A candidate with only a weak party organization but a high degree of personal popularity—Sutro is a good example—could win overwhelmingly even though the remainder of his party ticket had no significant support. Even though the Australian ballot law helped to elect Sutro in 1894, in most other ways parties remained as formidable as before. Parties still controlled access to office, through the primary and convention system, and the Australian ballot law did not apply in those intraparty affairs—witness the devious methods used by reformers and regulars alike in 1892. Even the use of secret paper ballots in a party meeting could produce surprising results; in the 1895 Democratic general committee meeting, the 292 committee members present cast 338 ballots, 184 for the reform candidate and 154 for the candidate of the regular faction.[41]

With a few exceptions, basic patterns of politics after the defeat of Buckley remained much as they had been before. Much of the process of campaigning still consisted of identifying and mobilizing one's supporters, and South of Market boardinghouses still formed potent centers of political support. For South of Market residents, politics remained a diversion, a social activity, and a potential channel of mobility. Neighborhood political clubs still provided, on occasion, "clam bakes, bull-head breakfasts and the like" and still sought to act as "an employment agency on the most wholesale scale possible." Chris Buckley had vividly demonstrated how politics could lift a stonemason's son to riches, and many working-class young men knew that through campaign work "a good fellow could gather in a few simoleons without overtaxing his strength." Politics could still produce patronage positions for the fortunate few. Newspapers had publicized the fact that when Buckley's slate entered city hall in 1883, his father became principal office deputy for the superintendent of streets, his nephew entered the police force, a cousin by marriage was named chief assistant to the head of the carpenter shop in the school system, and his bodyguard became superintendent of the House of Correction.[42] Politics, for the South of Market working class, could also be an instrument of protest, as shown by the WPC in the late 1870s. Although South of Market provided the bone-and-sinew of party organization, direction came largely from lower-middle-class businessmen: saloonkeepers like Buckley, Higgins, and Maguire, hotel clerks like McNab, draymen like Kearney.

Businessmen and professionals of the upper-middle and upper classes seem rarely to have understood the political value of clam bakes and bull-head breakfasts. Most would have been awkward and uncomfortable performing what Martin Kelly described as essential duties in his work:

> He must swagger into a saloon, slap down a twenty, call up the house and tell the bar-keeper to freeze onto the change. . . . He must dispense the cold bottle and the hot bird. . . . He must never forget his lowly retainers, for whom he must find jobs, kiss their babies, and send them Christmas presents.[43]

Nor did the residents of Nob Hill or the Western Addition value politics as a channel of mobility. Most of them already had a greater degree of material prosperity and higher social standing than they could possibly achieve through politics. Nonetheless, some of them did take part in politics. For some, participation came grudgingly and out of a sense of party loyalty. In 1880, George Hearst bought the *Examiner* to provide the city with a Democratic daily newspaper, and he subsidized it continually for the next several years.[44] For some, as well, there were abstract principles and issues that usually reinforced their party loyalties and often kept their political attention fixed on Washington and Sacramento.

Beyond and in addition to party loyalty and principle, businessmen and professionals seem to have entered politics for three main reasons: a quest for preferment, a defense of their enterprises, and a desire for status. Many of these directed their attention away from city politics. Quests for preferment took the form of subsidies (usually state or federal), franchises (at any level), or contracts. Such preferments had the potential for turning modest fortunes into sizable ones. The Big Four stood as the leading examples, but others could be found without effort—the Slosses and Gerstles of the Alaska Commercial Company; Claus Spreckels, who secured important concessions from King Kalakaua of Hawaii and turned them into a sugar fortune; or Adolph Sutro, whose tunnel franchise in the Comstock made him a wealthy man. Once secured, preferment had to be protected against those who might overturn it. Regulation was virtually nonexistent, but threats of regulation or even government ownership posed constant dangers. The status of high office, especially in the U.S. Senate, allowed one to combine party loyalty, high principle, quest for preferment, defense, and membership in the nation's most exclusive club. If competition in California became too intense, there was always Nevada, a route to the Senate taken by Francis G. Newlands, who moved to Nevada in 1888, was elected to Congress in 1892, and to the Senate in 1903, following in the footsteps of his father-in-law, William Sharon.[45]

For members of San Francisco's upper class who sought preferment, had to defend their turf, wished to demonstrate their party loyalty, or hoped for the status of high office, the customary method of participating in politics in the late nineteenth century was not the hustle of South of Market politics, but the rustle of greenbacks and the clink of gold. One English visitor to the city in 1877 wrote that "it would, *in reality*, be no exaggeration to state that men (voters) are standing on the public sidewalk, with the price of their votes marked on their sleeves." Abraham Ruef, a young lawyer cutting his political eyeteeth in 1890, recalled that in that election "five dollars was said to be the ruling rate for single votes [for Stanford-pledged legislators], though as high as ten dollars was paid for voting the 'straight' tickets." Officials, like voters, charged for their support. Martin Kelly justified such behavior in the case of franchises:

> When men of wealth came to us for gifts which meant golden fortunes for themselves, does any fool suppose we didn't ask for a modest "cut"? Of course we did. Was it not equitable and just?

Just as Huntington believed it "just and fair" to buy a vote in order "to have the right thing done," so bosses and officeholders felt it "equitable and just" to charge for the services they could deliver.[46]

Closely contested elections and controversial legislative decisions rarely passed without someone—usually on the losing side—attributing the outcome to the purchase of votes. The claims appeared so frequently and gained such wide publicity that many assumed that the purchase of votes was inherent in the system. Some looked to the dominance of political parties as a major part of the problem and began efforts to break that power. The Australian ballot law marked the beginning of the attack on the power of parties, but the full-scale assault did not come for another two decades.

Some reformers sought to solve urban problems through the improvement of education, hoping to produce an educated and responsible electorate. Many hoped that the problems of the city could be solved simply by replacing corrupt officeholders with honest ones. Others hoped to induce respect and orderliness in the public through construction of imposing and inspiring civic edifices. Some condemned the saloon and brothel as agents of corruption in the body politic and demanded their abolition as essential to civic and social purity. One group of reformers sought changes in the structure of city government, finding the source of corruption in the weakness of the mayor, limits on the supervisors, and the consequent need to centralize decision making outside the formal process of city government. The new state constitution of 1879 had provided that San Francisco might draft a replacement for the Consolidation Act, and three proposals for new charters were placed before the voters, in 1880, 1883, and 1887. Buckley opposed these efforts, and voters defeated all three. Few reformers, however, addressed the central question posed by Henry George in 1880:

> When, under institutions that proclaim equality, masses of men, whose ambitions and tastes are aroused only to be crucified, find it a hard, bitter, degrading struggle even to live, is it to be expected that the sight of other men rolling in their millions will not excite discontent?

His answer was equally disquieting:

> The political equality from which we can not recede, and the social inequality to which we are tending, can not peacefully coexist.[47]

This city is not made up entirely of merchants
and does not exist for the well-to-do alone.
—FATHER PETER YORKE, 1896

I will be the mayor for the whole city, and not
the mayor for any particular section. I will try
to wipe out all dividing lines on the map of
San Francisco.
—JAMES ROLPH, JR., 1911

Chapter 7

Progressive Politics, 1893-1911

By the early 1890s journalists routinely pointed out that "the heart of the Democracy" throbbed in "the laboring district" South of Market Street. More careful observers would have distinguished between the "Regular" Buckley supporters and the backers of the "Reform Democracy." Though led by a millionaire banker of Irish Catholic parentage and a corporate lawyer who preached an ideology of honesty and efficiency in government, the reform faction used its own techniques of "honest graft" to depose Buckley. Party politics during the early 1890s thus contained an unstable mixture: "military-style" election time adventure (especially attractive to the action-seeking working class) existed alongside appeals for businesslike government (highly tempting to the stable working class).

Although the reform faction that forced Buckley from his leadership position in the Democratic party used "packed" grand juries and crooked nominating conventions as freely as "the Boss" had done, its goals were quite different. The reformers aimed at the eventual creation of a stable, dependable party organization capable of routinely capturing office without having to depend on the unruly, adventuresome, election-day foot soldiers from the South of Market who had been an important part of Buckley's electoral army. Like the regime of "Honest John" Kelly in New York City, whose purge of the more rowdy, undisciplined, "dangerous" elements from the Democratic party has led Martin Shefter to describe him as the man who made "democracy safe for capitalism," the junta of Gavin McNab in San Francisco brought together stable, home-owning, upwardly mobile ethnic working-class voters and the city's wealthy younger mercantile and financial capitalists.[1]

These business leaders, typified by banker James Phelan and by the San Francisco Merchants' Association (1894), acted from the conviction that the city's future economic prosperity required promotion of business by means of municipal fiscal encouragement, as well as protection from both confiscatory taxation and capricious expenditures.[2] They regarded city government as too important to be left to the undisciplined outcomes of urban political conflict. The businessmen-reformers characteristically fitted their economic development interests with a "legal-rational" philosophy of municipal government that illustrated their increasing unease with the "traditional" point of view that had dominated nineteenth-century urban politics. The traditional approach—as practiced most effectively by Buckley—emphasized personal relationships and deemphasized both institutional structure and specialized training. The legal-rational approach, by contrast, laid stress on the importance of both structure and method. Charter revision in the 1890s provides a vivid illustration of such concern with the structure of urban government. The new politics of "businesslike" municipal government favored methods avowedly scientific, based on careful research designed to discover the "best" (usually meaning most efficient) way of accomplishing a task. The legal-rational approach to politics usually emphasized the importance of expertise and sought to recruit specially trained analysts.

THE CHARTER REFORM MOVEMENTS

Reformers made unsuccessful attempts in 1880, 1883, and 1887 to modernize the city charter, but their successful campaign of the 1890s began at the end of the depression winter of 1893–1894 and coincided with the first anniversary of the Labor Council of San Francisco. In April, some fifty members of the city's business elite formed the Merchants' Association, which was dedicated to the application of business principles of management and nonpartisanship to municipal government. (See Table 8 for the social composition of participants in charter reform politics.) Soon the association succeeded in obtaining the city contract for street sweeping, and its campaign to improve sales by beautifying sidewalks prompted journalists to hail its work as "the sign of a municipal awakening."[3]

In October, with unemployed workers flocking to the city in anticipation of another hungry winter, the association assumed the leadership of a charter reform campaign. During their meeting that month, the members of the association heard the president of the Pacific Coast Technical Society applaud "the impulse among businessmen and commercial bodies to cure the loose methods and lack of business principles in the expenditure of their money for benefits, privileges and enjoyments for which they pay but which they do not receive." A charter grounded in the principles of business would improve the situation in San Francisco where, "as in so many of our large cities, the village system of dealing with some of the most vital problems bearing on domestic comforts and commercial prosperity has obtained too long."[4]

The fifteen members of the Board of Freeholders elected in November agreed with the Merchants' Association version of municipal reform, and they too called for efficiency, an end to waste, strengthening the power of

TABLE 8

Social Standing of Charter Reform Activists, 1896–1898

Group Affiliation	Percentage Listed in Social Register or Blue Book
Officers of the Citizens' Charter Association (1896)	100
Board of Freeholders (1896)	86
Officers and directors of the Merchants' Association (1896)	75
Board of Freeholders (1898)	53
Committee of 100[a] (1897)	43
Officers of the Central Trades and Labor Alliance (1896)	0
Officers of the San Francisco Labor Council (1896)	0

SOURCES: San Francisco, Board of Supervisors, *Municipal Reports* (San Francisco, 1897–1898) p. 304. *San Francisco Chronicle*, Aug. 3, 1897, Sept. 5, 1896, Aug. 13, 1896; San Francisco Merchants' Association, Minutes of the board of directors, Feb. 3, 1897, California Historical Society; *Voice of Labor*, Aug. 8, 1896; *Langley's San Francisco Directory, 1895–1898* (San Francisco, 1895–1898), *Crocker-Langley San Francisco Directory, 1900* (San Francisco, 1900); *The San Francisco Blue Book* (San Francisco, 1896–1900); *San Francisco Social Register* (New York, 1908).

[a]The Committee of 100 had twenty-one subcommittees. Persons listed in the *Social Register* or *Blue Book* comprised the majority on half of the subcommittees and a balance of power in two-thirds. Also, 91 percent of all committee members came from business or the professions, and 63 percent worked as attorneys or owned or managed business firms.

the mayor, and an appointed Board of Education. Even physician Jerome A. Anderson, elected on the Populist ticket, believed that the best way of "making somebody responsible" was to make the city "run like any other great corporation." At the same time, Anderson wanted municipal ownership of public utilities. He thereby expressed a seemingly contradictory, but frequently espoused, goal: favoring the corporate ideal for municipal decision making along with desiring popular control over the production of necessary municipal services.[5]

Shortly after the freeholder election, the California superintendent of schools announced the essentials of a program for school centralization that would guide discussions for the next four years. He held up the record of "reform" city superintendents in eastern cities as the model for the West, and he urged the creation of small nonpartisan school boards accountable to central city officials rather than neighborhood ward voters. A program of centralization appealed to the San Francisco Teachers' Club as well, but before advising the freeholders, the teachers consulted "prominent educators" and studied the "leading Eastern cities." They suggested a five-member nonpartisan board appointed from the career teachers with at least five years of experience in the city's schools. They also called for strict separation of the business and teaching functions of the school system.[6]

That same day, a *Chronicle* editorial on "good city government" argued for the application of "modern theory" to San Francisco: "Curtail the number of elective officers," for the resultant system of "power coupled with the strictest responsibility offers the best possible solution for the evils of bad and inefficient government." For the *Chronicle*, good government meant efficient government, and efficient government meant a municipal order modeled on corporate outlines: "The Board of Freeholders is composed of businessmen, and they should apply to the creation of a charter the rules of business with which they are familiar. All the good and respectable people of San Francisco will favor a charter framed on the general plan suggested."[7]

Walter Macarthur, editor of the *Coast Seamen's Journal,* assumed no such automatic harmony among businessmen, business interests, and the interests of the city's "good and respectable people." He had hinted at quite a different conception of ideal urban government in his remarks to those assembled at a meeting of the reform-oriented Civic Federation earlier that week. With financier I. J. Truman (one of the freeholders) as president, the federation passed resolutions demanding an end to election fraud and called for the beginning of home rule. Macarthur put the Labor Council on the side of the federation's goals, but he warned that the council "believes that the real beginning of this movement goes deeper than these things and that the workingmen themselves must have the opportunity to work for fair wages and get justice in the courts." Macarthur's qualified support for the Civic Federation matched that of M. M. McGlynn, editor of the *Voice of Labor,* the organ of the Labor Council. McGlynn also urged home rule, and he especially opposed fraudulent use of public money for private gain and corporate profit. From McGlynn's perspective "as a trades unionist, it was particularly pleasing to see the eminently respectable gentlemen of the cloth or the law advocate the very same measures that ten years ago they called the trades unionists anarchists for advocating."[8]

If Macarthur and McGlynn drew connections between class and politics in their remarks on the Civic Federation, so did its president, I. J. Truman, in his remarks on the need for civil service measures in the new charter. "The City Hall," he said, "has many men who would be a success as bricklayers, blacksmiths, farm hands, etc., but who are out of place as clerks and accountants." From Truman's perspective, working-class officials could not be expected to possess the wisdom necessary for decision making in municipal government. Nor could working-class voters be expected to exercise intelligence in selecting members for the school board. The mayor should appoint board members, for "it is more likely he will appoint parties fitted by education and moral standing in the community."[9]

When the Civic Federation adopted its permanent constitution, organized labor was absent from the roster of participating groups, and the bylaws included a clause requiring a three-fourths majority for the admission of new members. At the same time, the ties between the Civic Federation and the Board of Freeholders were strengthened when two more of the freeholders became officers of the federation. The remarks of freeholder W. F. Gibson—that although a large board of supervisors "is more in harmony with the democratic form of government," the "sentiment of the city is at present opposed to that idea"—may well have been based on his perception of the Civic Federation as constituting the legitimate representative of "the sentiment of the city."[10]

The close connections among the Merchants' Association, the Civic Federation, and the Board of Freeholders helped yield a charter strong on centralization, civil service, and corporate principles in general. The charter contained no provisions for municipal ownership of public utilities, and, except for its inference that the working class lacked expertise and should be kept far from power, it promised no solution to the problem of private abuse of the public trust.

The 1896 Charter Fight. The *Voice of Labor* immediately criticized these weaknesses as it opened an intensive campaign to defeat the charter in the election of 1896. Centralization would "wholly fail to stem the tide of municipal corruption," and "what we stand for and insist upon is our right, as a city, to make our own laws, by popular vote, upon such subjects as properly belong to city government." One month later, at a citywide convention of labor reformers and trade unionists called by the Labor Council, the audience heard a variety of speakers condemn the document. The Merchants' Association, on the other hand, gathered the questionnaires it had sent to the members of the city's business associations and other "clubs of social, commercial or political importance" and proclaimed that "public opinion is overwhelming" on behalf of civil service, business methods, and the new charter. The Citizens' Charter Association introduced the term *progressive* into San Francisco's political vocabulary in 1896 when it described the kind of voter that "may be counted on as a friend of the new Charter":

> Those who wish for a City Government conducted on business principles, and free from reference to national or state politics; . . . merchants who want to have this city made the equal of other large cities of the United States in public improvement, cleanliness of streets, attractiveness to visitors, as well as in commerce and enterprise; . . . [those] whose interests require that the industrial activity of our municipality should be encouraged, public buildings erected, private real estate improved and increased in value . . . and in general, all the progressive elements among the voters of San Francisco.[11]

For a year, while the newspapers published copies of the charter and speculated about its chances, the alignment remained stable. Merchants' Association, Civic Federation, and freeholders stood on one side; organized labor lined up on the other. Then in late June 1896, the chancellor of the archdiocese of San Francisco, Peter Yorke, added the influence of the *Monitor,* the official paper of the archdiocese, to the side of labor. The Central Trades and Labor Alliance had charged that the charter included "provisions directly against the rights and interests of labor" and "does not provide for the initiative and referendum, proportional representation, or any other means whatever of insuring government by the people instead of by bosses." Yorke now charged that the freeholders had ignored the evolutionary nature of municipal government in their "attempt to turn out governments for cities as men turn out sausages." The *Voice of Labor* had argued that the charter "displayed the determination to curtail and minimize the rewards of labor" and that anyone who supported it "must regard property above flesh and blood." The *Monitor* now scored the charter as "supremely vicious" because "the trail of the APA [the nativist American Protective Association] is visible across it." Singling out the provision for hiring teachers as his major target, Yorke suggested that its requirement that public school teachers be public school graduates "means that if a parent wishes to educate his child where he believes best, he is to be punished by having that child debarred from teaching in the public schools."[12]

As James Walsh has recently pointed out, Yorke's defense of Catholicism against the APA had mainly symbolic importance and resulted in little more than the silencing of several strident orators. The nativist organization never possessed social, political, or economic power in San Francisco, and even the possibility shrinks given the fact that active Catholics outnumbered church-going Protestants by about five to one. Although the APA may have posed little threat to San Francisco Catholics, the mobilization of Catholics against the charter created doubts about its success, for the Irish constituted the most highly politicized ethnic group in the city.[13]

At about the time the Merchants' Association asked the San Francisco Election Commission to place the charter at the top of the ballot, Yorke intensified his opposition. Then he accused the Merchants' Association of nativism and demanded that they explain "why they are doing the dirty work of the APA."[14]

The Labor Council met one week after this attack and, perhaps stimulated by the priest's opposition, elected a slate of officers even more opposed to the charter than the previous leadership. They then voted to decline the invitation to the charter convention called by the Merchants' Association, and they decided instead to prepare a pamphlet against the charter for distribution to the city electorate.[15]

The Merchants' Association in the meantime asked James Phelan to preside over a Citizens' Charter Association of San Francisco that would meet every two weeks until the election. The choice of Phelan, a member of the association and a wealthy Catholic of Irish stock, may have been calculated to placate potential Catholic opposition. The charge by former mayor and state senator Frank McCoppin that "religious sentiments of the people are being played upon for the purpose of making votes against the charter" may have been intended to discredit the validity of Yorke. But any support gained by the choice of Phelan probably was offset when the merchants chose Horace Davis for vice-president. Davis had led a union-busting merchants' protective association in 1892, and organized labor warmly disliked him for his comment in 1894 that since much of the power of the unions had been destroyed, "capital will now flow into our city like water."[16]

The charter convention met for the first time on August 12, with Frederick Dohrmann, head of the Merchants' Association, as temporary chairman. Before introducing Phelan, Dohrmann explained one part of the strategy that he hoped would secure the victory of the charter. The association would use the already existing neighborhood organizations that represented "the best element and the best class of our citizens" to build a network of activists throughout the city. The other part of the campaign plan was discussed at a meeting of the directors of the Merchants' Association. After director Maurice Rothchild reported on his visit to Peter Yorke and explained the priest's opposition, the directors decided to appropriate $1,000 to support the campaign and to send a delegation to "visit the *Chron-*

icle, Report and such other newspapers as they may select to secure their cooperation for the charter."[17]

Except for an acceleration in the pace of the battle, the general character of the conflict continued into September according to the pattern set by the end of August. The *Chronicle* published several exposés of municipal corruption consistent with the charter supporters' goals. The secretary of the Merchants' Association published the official pamphlet urging voters to regard the charter as modeled on "the most Progressive cities of the United States" and to see that its public school clause was actually a device to ensure that "education must be practical."[18]

By late September, several events introduced new complications into the situation. Public school teachers opposed to the charter adopted a newly militant position and held several meetings to protest the school clause. Apparently, teachers stood about equally divided on the charter, but the opposition (probably Catholic in large part) charged that it represented "a vicious attempt to do away with the tenure of office of teachers." At about the same time, the city's political party system lumbered into action in anticipation of the election. Regular and reform factions vied for legitimacy within both major parties, and their mayoralty nominations revealed the strength of the ethnic divisions rending the city's politics.[19]

The regular Democrats, successors to the now greatly weakened "Blind Boss" Buckley, billed themselves as the "Anti-Charter Democrats" and appealed to voters with language already made familiar by the Labor Council and Peter Yorke. Challenging the Buckley Democrats, but still within the councils of the party, the reform faction nominated Phelan for the mayoralty but carefully avoided making a direct endorsement of the charter. On the Republican side, the business and good-government faction nominated a popular city merchant, Charles Laumeister. Like Phelan, once he became a candidate, Laumeister avoided taking a public stand on the charter, but he did stress the need for a city government responsive to the needs of trade and commercial interests. Opposed to the reform Republicans stood the regulars under the guidance of John Spreckels, whose alleged links to the APA provided additional fuel for the already intense ethnic dimensions of the election. The Spreckels faction's nominee, Charles S. Taylor, tagged by the *Monitor* as "the nominee of the APA convention," also avoided mention of the charter.[20]

The parties could no more contain the ethnic divisiveness that generated these alignments than they could the class conflict that accompanied them. The chairman of the meeting for the charter on October 22 found himself confronted with "hisses, howls, hoots and cat calls" that lasted ten minutes when a speaker mentioned the name of the APA mayoralty candidate. Walter Macarthur, representing the Labor Council at the same meeting, argued that "there are but three classes in the city—the working class, the begging class, and the thieving class. Of these only the first has a right to be represented." Macarthur "denied that the charter would bring home rule" and saw it instead as a device for imposing what he called "class rule."[21]

The Labor Council made a similar argument in its pamphlet that Macarthur had helped to write. While "the confessed purpose of the proposed new system of government is centralization," it was also the case that "the assumption which underlies the Charter is that the people at large cannot be trusted to elect an honest government." Voters should see the charter as "a system retrogressive in every particular, representative of class despotism and absolutely unalterable." Urging reform in methods of accountability rather than a change in the principle of representation, the Labor Council argued that "elective government must be retained, and if possible enlarged, as the only safeguard of popular government." The pamphlet provided a thorough critique of the charter, but the council concluded with an affirmation of its interest in honest municipal government and home rule and called for a new, more representative, charter convention.[22]

San Francisco voters defeated the charter some two weeks after Macarthur attacked it as a vehicle for class rule, even though they chose Phelan for the mayoralty (voters gave about two votes to Phelan for every one that went for the charter). Phelan had been swept into the mayor's office on a platform of responsible municipal administration modeled after corporate management. Prosperity after 1897, Phelan's skillful use of patronage (for example, he cultivated Patrick McCarthy, head of the Carpenters' Union, and eventually appointed him to the Civil Service Commission), and factional fights within the labor movement complicated the political situation.

The Campaign for the 1898 Charter. Peter Yorke immediately supported the Labor Council's demand for a more representative "charter of compromise." "This city," he argued, "is not made up entirely of merchants and does not exist for the well-to-do alone. The laboring man, the tradesman, the artisan, have as much at stake here as the merchant prince. Therefore any association which is working for the good of the city must open wide its ranks and gather in all these classes."[23]

The Merchants' Association quickly reassembled its ranks and planned a new campaign, explaining that "we do not want a class charter, but it must be for the people and for all the people." One of the directors admitted that "we have begun at the wrong end and tried to make a charter for the people without first finding out what they wanted."[24]

By the time Phelan presented his inaugural address on January 4, 1897, the Merchants' Association had begun a campaign to centralize the neighborhood improvement clubs into a weapon for the charter. Phelan, having kept silent about the charter during his campaign, assumed leadership in his capacity as mayor, regretted that "the city does not possess a more scientific and satisfactory charter," and called for a Committee of 100 to draft another document. Phelan also brought the question of school reform into the center of attention and argued for "the necessity of practical trade and technical education. . . . This has been a source of prosperity to numerous cities, for by improving the technical skill of the artisans and mechanics, the product of their labor finds sale in the markets of the world." He then asked the grand jury to investigate "extravagance" in school spending, thereby putting into motion a year-long campaign of exposé.[25]

Three days later, Phelan walked into the office of the Merchants' Association and asked its secretary "to prepare a list of names from which the

Committee of 100 might be selected." The Merchants' Association then worked closely with Phelan throughout the first half of 1897. By the time the Committee of 100 met for the first time in July, the association had also begun to put the public schools in the forefront of the campaign.[26]

As the gradual improvement of business conditions in 1897–1898 brought the promise of renewed prosperity, organized labor demanded that its interests be represented in the Committee of 100. Having hoped for a committee of elected members, labor found that "one man has selected from among his personal friends and political supporters such men as he thought would give the convention the appearance of having a representative character." Trade unions "represent at least one-third of the population . . . and should have had at least one-third of the delegates, whom they should have been permitted to select." Instead, "four men alone were selected from their ranks, and those were taken without the authority of the unions." The procedure was not "likely to create confidence in the brains of the city's workers."[27]

Similar concerns emerged when the subcommittee on education met with teachers and principals to draft the school clause of the charter. The subcommittee had invited the principal of each school, as well as one elected teacher from each school, but a number of teachers complained of their reluctance to vote for a school clause. They pointed out that "they had been chosen rather to be present and report back proceedings than to vote on behalf of those who had chosen them." The vote proceeded, with about half of the teachers abstaining, the resolutions for centralization passed, and the dissenters returned to their colleagues to report the *fait accompli*.[28]

The Committee of 100 also exercised considerable skill in dismissing the point of view of dissident members of the small minority representing labor. Only the insistence of the one socialist member saved the suggestions of the Trades and Labor Alliance from being buried in committee without a reading. They gained a hearing, but nothing more.[29]

The socialist member remained isolated from the other labor members as well as from the business and professional majority. The most vocal trade unionists—Walter Macarthur of the *Coast Seamen's Journal* and Patrick McCarthy of the Carpenters' Union—stayed at opposite sides of the political spectrum from the start. One reporter went so far as to describe McCarthy as "more conservative than any of the millionaires." The same observer noted that while the minority had no power, "the sincerity of the radicals is appreciated and humored by the conservatives." "Indeed," he continued, "these theorists have never had such a thoughtful audience to work upon and the capitalists are quite as responsive and interested as the men who have neither property nor possessions to hazard by experiments in State control and communism."[30]

This vocal but ineffectual minority provided the support for the proposal for a board of eighteen supervisors elected by ward, a plan, noted the *Voice of Labor*, that "would have carried with it all that element in the community which favors democratic organization of municipalities." The proposal actually chosen by the committee, described by one newspaper as "the American plan of concentrating executive functions in the hand of the mayor," had "its strongest adherents among the property holders and the conservative elements of the convention."[31]

By the time the Committee of 100 finished its draft for a charter, the majority had decided against its original plan of presenting the voters alternatives on the most contentious issues such as mayoralty power, control over public utilities, public school governance, and direct democracy measures such as the initiative and referendum. The Merchants' Association continued to advertise the committee as "thoroughly representative," despite the continued cries of labor to the contrary, and the neighborhood improvement associations in the newer areas of the city had formed a citywide organization. This new San Francisco Improvement Association then declared its intention to follow the example of the Merchants' Association in its campaign for a charter.[32]

The late December election of the Board of Freeholders, which would officially present a charter to the electorate for approval, rekindled the factional fighting that had split the city's party system during the election of 1896. The Committee of 100 fielded a slate taken from its ranks (with McCarthy the only member from the labor contingent) that earned the prompt endorsement of the reform elements of both major parties. The regular Democrats joined with the Populists in a "fusion ticket," and the Socialist Labor party presented its own nominees.[33]

One week before the freeholder election, the chairman of the Election Commission, William Broderick, asked Phelan to explain "why it was that, in making up the Committee of 100, only six were selected from six of the leading Democratic districts and three large Democratic districts were entirely overlooked. I have an interest in the Democratic Party and I would like to know why the Democracy south of Market Street was not considered worthy of more representation."

> The making of a charter is not a matter of geography, replied the Mayor. It certainly is a matter of judgement, responded Broderick, and it certainly would have been better to have had the Democratic party represented. The committeemen were selected with reference to their occupation rather than their location, said Phelan.
>
> I am of the opinion, said Broderick, that it was constructed on other lines, and the list was fixed up by you and a few others in a back room.[34]

Broderick made a valid argument when he observed that the assembly districts with the largest representation on the committee were the wealthiest areas of the city. He could also have pointed out that the working-class districts of the city held only eighteen seats. The middle- and upper-class districts held the balance of the positions in the committee.[35]

The Catholic press contained no criticisms of the ethnic makeup of the committee, and in the issue of the *Monitor* published two days before the election, Peter Yorke announced that the slates seemed nonpartisan and, therefore, satisfactory. The APA issue had receded in importance, and the priest's opposition did not reappear.[36]

About one-third of the registered voters came to the polls on December 26, 1897, and they chose by a small margin the freeholder slate nominated by the Committee of 100. Highest turnout occurred in the assembly districts that had been best represented in the committee whereas the lowest turnout came from the working-class districts South of Market and in the Mission.[37]

Phelan, the Merchants' Association, and the freeholders lost no time in renewing their campaign. Three days after the election, Andrew S. Draper, former Cleveland superintendent of schools and a leading educational reformer, described the ingredients of "a desirable school system" at a meeting called by the mayor. Draper reviewed the usual litany of "formidable difficulties" facing city school systems and presented the standard list of remedies by means of centralization. The elements of Draper's centralization program informed the final school clause of the charter. Perhaps the freeholders had, like the *Chronicle,* "watched school proceedings with amazement and disgust" during some six months of charge and countercharge between grand jury and school board members over nepotism and personnel problems. Nonetheless, they offset their proposal for an appointed school board with a concession to critics in the form of an elected superintendent.[38]

If centralization succeeded as the basis for the public school clause, it also succeeded in the section on the Board of Supervisors. At the final meeting of the freeholders, with Phelan attending, a vote was taken to consider an earlier proposal that the charter should provide an eighteen-member board with two from each of nine districts elected by district. This proposal was defeated, and the freeholders decided to recommend what was described as a "radical change" to a Board of Supervisors nominated and elected at large.[39]

With only a month remaining before the special May 26 election for the charter, the Labor Council met to consider its merits. McCarthy, the only labor member of the Board of Freeholders, took the offensive and argued that the working-class interests had been fully considered. Another speaker agreed, saying that "every responsible suggestion emanating from labor leaders had been carefully considered and granted, and valid and satisfactory reasons had been given for not granting other demands from the same source." Other members argued otherwise, that "the charter was framed in the interest of capital and that the rights of labor had been entirely ignored." This division among Labor Council activists continued onto the pages of the *Voice of Labor.* Its editorial writer informed readers that although the charter could have contained a stronger initiative and referendum clause, it possessed good features as well as bad, and he would be "satisfied to abide by [the voter's] judgement." At the same time, the paper continued to print attacks on the charter.[40]

The *Monitor* refused to take sides on the charter, for Yorke now saw it "purely as a political instrument" and "entirely free of bigotry and injustice." If Yorke proved unwilling to raise the ethnic issues, Phelan, speaking to a rally of workers in the South of Market two days before the election, showed no such reluctance. Here, millionaire Phelan shared the platform with carpenter McCarthy, the one the son of Irish parents, the other an Irish immigrant. Phelan announced that "the charter would give the city what the people of Ireland have been fighting for and what the boys in blue are now going to the front to win—home rule." McCarthy explained that the charter's provision for two dollars per day and an eight-hour day for city laborers made it "a charter that would benefit the common people. Isn't that enough for the working people?" he asked.[41] In an editorial in the *Coast Seamen's Journal* the same day, Macarthur answered that it remained far from being enough.

> This is, in effect, a proposition that labor should be willing to vote for any old system of government as long as that part of it that works for the City Hall gets eight hours and $2 per day. If the new Charter will run any risk at all by this insinuation that the working man of San Francisco is a sheer ass its chances of adoption are pretty slim.[42]

Macarthur's differences from McCarthy stemmed from deep-seated disparities in their perceptions of the needs of the labor movement. Working-class voters may also have noticed another difference: Macarthur was a Scotsman, and Scandinavians constituted 40 percent of his union (the Sailors' Union), but the Irish made up the largest group both in the city and in the labor movement.[43]

Several events in April and May could have influenced the judgment of voters as much as newspaper arguments and ethnic loyalties. Augustus Widber, city treasurer, absconded with over $100,000 in public money, only to be caught and convicted. Charter supporters lost no time pointing to ways the charter, with its provisions for efficient professional city management, could help ensure against such criminal behavior. Then the Merchants' Association stepped up its campaign after Phelan warned them against allowing a false sense of security to lull them into defeat. The charter supporters also decided to begin "addressing the workmen at the mills and foundaries" and distributed 22,500 copies of the May issue of the Merchants' Association *Monthly Review* devoted especially to the charter.[44]

When the polls closed on May 26, some 26,969 of the 73,410 registered voters had cast their ballots on the charter, giving it a victory of 14,389 to 12,025. According to Macarthur in the *Coast Seamen's Journal* and a journalist in a San Francisco newspaper, the *Report,* the low turnout occurred because the polls closed two hours before sunset in violation of both state law and public announcements by the freeholders. Macarthur argued that the election commissioners thus tricked many workers into what "practically amounted to the disfranchisement of large numbers of voters." Whatever the case, the turnout for the special election (37 percent) had dropped by four percentage points from the turnout on the charter of 1896 during the general election when the charter vote had lagged far behind the vote for mayor and national candidates, during a period in which the mean turnout was 84 percent.[45]

The *Report* accurately observed that "the strength of the adverse vote was from the districts of small residences." In fact, only six of the city's eighteen assembly districts mustered a majority against the charter, and four of them (waterfront districts 28, 32, 44, and 45) housed the seamen and dock workers most likely to have been swayed by Macarthur and the *Coast Seamen's Journal.* The other two opposition districts (31 and 43) yielded such close votes that a handful of switchers could have shifted them into the other column, but they too ranked high in working-class populations. These districts teemed with unskilled and transient workers who lived where small homes, boardinghouses, and hotels huddled together intermixed with commercial and industrial firms and where only small proportions of the population owned their homes.[46]

The greatest support for the charter came from what were still called the suburban residential areas in the western and southwestern parts of the city where most residents owned substantial homes, from the residential area just west of Nob Hill, and from the only two working-class districts where appreciable numbers owned their homes. The greatest support derived from the areas of the well-to-do, including those filling up with what Robert Wiebe has called "the new middle class" and the districts of the skilled workers with steady employment.[47]

With the vote so close in most of the eighteen assembly districts, we can learn more by grouping them according to ethnic criteria and then noting the characteristics of those falling above and below the citywide vote of 55 percent for the charter. The newer and well-to-do districts that gave the charter substantial support ranked highest in old-stock and ethnic residents. The working-class districts that registered a lower yes vote than the city as a whole—including the eight districts that would soon provide the Union Labor party with its base of support—also happened to hold the lowest proportions of old-stock population in the city.

The reform charter of 1898 thus emerged as the product of a campaign by organized business led by the Merchants' Association rather than the result of a personal crusade by Mayor Phelan. Phelan did play an important role in the campaign, but it began when, as a member of the Merchants' Association, he supported the charter in his capacity as a private citizen. Organized labor played a crucial role in the battle for the charter, even though it displayed considerably less unanimity on the desirability of the reform than did business. The two groups together, displaying varying degrees of conflict and coalition, generated a political process that was also continually beset with overtones of ethnic consciousness.[48]

The participants themselves described the issues in language charged with class consciousness. Dismayed because "labor had been absolutely without representation" during the drafting of the charter and unimpressed by the fact that "a pretense was made at giving labor a seat," the editor of the *Coast Seamen's Journal* wrote that "the whole proceedings, from inception up to the present moment, have been controlled by one influence, i.e. Business." The *Monthly Review,* mouthpiece of the Merchants' Association, expressed "pardonable pride" in its ability to "justly claim to have inaugurated the movement that gave birth to the new Charter." The legal framework for the governing of San Francisco would now be "based upon the platform first enunciated by the Merchants' Association."[49]

Class consciousness and class conflict definitely shaped the course of the charter campaign, but they did so to the accompaniment of ethnic tensions. Solidarity among labor against the proposed charter helped ensure its defeat in 1896, but so did the determined opposition by Yorke because of its alleged dangers to the interests of Catholics. Divisions between workers over the proposed charter helped condition its victory in 1898, but so did the decision by the Catholic press that the new measure contained "no provisions which will operate against any citizen or class of citizens because of their faith."[50]

The new charter pleased the Merchants' Association and Mayor Phelan because it strengthened the powers of the city's chief executive: the mayor now had undivided authority to appoint and remove members of city boards and commissions; he could make charges against elected officials and suspend them while they awaited trial; he could veto ordinances of the Board of Supervisors, and the votes of fourteen of the enlarged eighteen-member board were necessary to override a veto. The provisions for at-large election of supervisors and for civil service pleased the business leaders more than the clauses permitting the city to utilize the initiative and referendum, establish publicly owned utilities, and initiate minimum-wage and maximum-hour provisions for city employees. The Merchants' Association and Phelan accepted the latter, more populist, measures as a necessary cost of successful implementation of the structural reforms of the executive and legislative branches of municipal government. Martin Schiesl has recently described the nationwide movement for reform of municipal government, and his characterization fits San Francisco as well:

> If they were to be successful their organizations had to be as efficient as the machine and . . . designs to reorganize municipal government had to be complemented by practical schemes to gain and keep political power. Such conditions produced the search for controls which would centralize authority in the executive branch of local government.[51]

THE PHELAN ADMINISTRATION

Phelan put together his policy recommendations for municipal projects with the cooperation of the Merchants' Association.[52] During his first campaign in 1896, he had argued that San Francisco should be "the capital of an empire," and in the 1899 Democratic party municipal platform he wrote that the "great and varied resources of the Pacific Coast behind us and the vast ocean before us point unerringly to the greatness of San Francisco."[53] Phelan stressed the need to "act with confidence." The Merchants' Association applauded the mayor's sentiments and spurred him on to more aggressive leadership on behalf of the city's commercial priorities. "The fact is," argued former Merchants' Association director Herbert E. Law, "there is nothing inevitable about . . . the city's growth, about density, about future greatness, about natural center and inevitable control of commerce."

> There has never been an organization in this city approximating the present organization of the Merchants' Association. There has never been a time when the merchants were in so close union, so strongly cemented together, so single in their purpose, and so resolute as they have shown themselves to be during the past year [1898] . . . but in comparison with the possibilities, the effort has been but that of a child.

The organized business community needed "a careful leader, who will train every force in the direction it is needed" and "give San Francisco a great future."[54]

Phelan promoted San Francisco business from his position as head of municipal government while arguing that the necessary spending would benefit the entire population by increasing population and tourism. Terrence McDonald's study of city expenditures shows an "across-the-board increase in expenditure over that of the machine [1883–1892] period." Placing a higher priority on accountability and efficiency than on fiscal conservatism and budgetary stringency, the Phelan administration, in consultation with organized business, "sought to bend the power of politics to their own tasks, broadly conceived, in line with a new notion of urban political economy."[55] A similar spirit informed the administration's approach to bonded indebtedness. With encouragement and urging from the neighborhood improvement associations and the Merchants' Association, the mayor proposed bond issues for a new sewer system, city hospital, city hall, park extensions, schools, and port improvements. In 1899, voters approved an issue for the sewer system, a new hospital, seventeen schools, and two new parks. Although taxpayer suits blocked some and the courts invalidated others, Phelan eventually secured approval to increase the city's total indebtedness from $186,000 in 1897 to $11,025,000 in 1901.[56]

The San Francisco Labor Council differed with Phelan on the need for public improvement bonds, just as it had earlier disagreed with his advocacy of the new charter. The mayor nonetheless attracted substantial support among the city's working-class voters by helping to raise money for striking miners, by endorsing a demonstration against the use of federal troops against strikers in Idaho, and by participating in Labor Day parades. "Mr. Phelan has made a good mayor," according to the *Voice of Labor*; "San Francisco has had few if any that were better." Even when the city's trade unions took advantage of the post-1897 return of prosperity to demand union recognition and the closed shop—novel measures considerably beyond the usual proposals for "pure and simple" improvements in wages, hours, and conditions—Phelan expressed sympathy by adopting a "hands-off" policy.[57]

Phelan's attempts to draw together both business and labor behind a program of municipal reform and city development, a strategy he had successfully pursued as the leader of the 1897–1898 phase of the charter campaign, worked until the summer of 1901. Then, during a bitter two-month-long strike, which pitted a recently organized and militantly anti-union Employers' Association against a City Front Federation representing some sixteen thousand teamsters and waterfront workers, Phelan found himself forced to side with the employers. Now, instead of praising the mayor, the labor newspapers carried articles alleging that Phelan had advised workers to return to their jobs if they wanted to avoid being clubbed. Instead of passing out prizes during a Labor Day parade, the mayor presided over an administration in which police officers protected strikebreakers. The evidence suggests that Phelan tried to arbitrate, but employers refused to cooperate. The mayor announced his intention to preserve order and refused to defend what he considered the destruction of private property by strikers. He refused to intervene or countermand the orders of his police commissioner. The commissioner, George Newhall, who served as president of the San Francisco Chamber of Commerce, ordered officers to clear strikers off the streets along the waterfront, guard drivers of nonunion wagons, and disperse picket lines. The Iron Trades Council, involved in a separate strike, argued that Phelan and his administrators had lent "their official aid to assist a small wealthy combination of capitalists to override and tyrannize every citizen of the city" and had consequently violated their oaths to use their office for the good of all San Franciscans. Their solution: use the next municipal election to vote for a city administration made up solely of union members.[58]

THE UNION LABOR PARTY

Mayor Phelan had announced that he would not seek reelection even before the strike by teamsters escalated into the waterfront conflict, but the pervasive perception among working-class voters that both the mayor and the Democratic party had betrayed them stimulated the organization of a labor party during the summer. Members of unions affiliated with the American Federation of Labor, delegates to the County Labor Council, and Socialist Labor party activists founded the Union Labor party. Political broker Abe Ruef emerged as the power behind the scenes by the time of the nominating convention in the fall. A University of California graduate and a lawyer from the city's Jewish mercantile elite, Ruef had aspirations for national political prominence. Frustrated in his attempt to unseat "regular" Republican leaders with his own Republican Primary League in the August 1901 primary elections, Ruef nonetheless had faith in the concept of coalition politics that Phelan and the Merchants' Association had used so successfully in the charter campaign. Walton Bean has pointed out that Ruef's strategy consisted in choosing directors for the Republican Primary League from "every religion and creed, and from labor, capital, merchant, practical politician, and professional man. Each was to be given equal prominence."[59]

Three weeks after he had failed in his bid to take over the city's Republican party, Ruef and several labor associates from the Republican Primary League successfully introduced what became the official platform of the Union Labor party. Sensing a leadership vacuum in the movement to create a municipal labor party, Ruef moved quickly and wrote what he described as a platform "true to every principle of labor, yet conservative." One historian has described the document as "a masterpiece of equivocation," but nonetheless it fit nicely into the coalition strategy. Ruef also successfully proposed his friend and one-time business associate Eugene Schmitz as the Union Labor party nominee for mayor. Schmitz, a native San Franciscan, could likewise appeal to a multiethnic and interclass coalition because he was a Catholic homeowner, with both German and Irish roots, and besides being president of the Musicians' Union, he also had experience as a businessman and employer.[60]

Despite the tradition of political independence among trade unionists that fostered a distrust of either partisan endorsements or labor parties, Andrew Furuseth, head of the Sailors' Union of the Pacific, overcame his long-standing opposition to "a class government." "I found," he said, "that we had a class government already and inasmuch as we are going to have

a class government, I most emphatically prefer a working-class government." Both the Labor Council and the Building Trades Council, however,
refused to endorse the Union Labor party. The Building Trades Council,
with some vehemence, described the party on election eve as a "stench in
the nostrils of all law-abiding citizens."[61]

Steven Erie and Jules Tygiel have analyzed the voters who sided with
Furuseth to give Schmitz a victory with 42 percent of the vote, taking the
plurality from his Republican and Democratic opponents, Asa R. Wells and
Joseph S. Tobin, respectively (see Table 9 for the Union Labor party vote,
1901–1911). Schmitz ran especially well in the South of Market area, the
waterfront districts, and in the family neighborhoods of the skilled artisans.
"The votes," Tygiel concludes, "were distinctly distributed along class lines,"
and "the correlation between the ULP vote and working-class residence by
ward was an extremely high .84."

> The election provided, in a sense, a referendum regarding the policies of the
> Employers' Association and the right of unions, not merely to organize, but to
> establish the closed shop. In choosing Schmitz over Wells and Tobin, the San
> Francisco electorate had demonstrated its support of the labor movement. The
> second, and more important issue, was one of who should control the city
> government, labor or capital. As indicated by Furuseth's reasons for support-
> ing the party, workingmen had come to realize that "class government" did
> exist in San Francisco, and that elections were a battle over which class would
> achieve power. The extreme polarization of the vote demonstrates that these
> issues were clearly perceived by the San Francisco electorate and that the
> struggle was fought and decided along class lines.[62]

While Schmitz received only a third of the votes in the well-to-do areas
of the city that had given the charter its greatest support, his opponents
granted him a period of grace and adopted a wait-and-see attitude. Mayor
Phelan charged that the Employers' Association had erred in adopting an
intransigent position during the waterfront conflict. He also affirmed the
right of working-class voters to take their protest to the polls and concluded
that the election had been "a splendid object lesson in popular government."
City attorney Franklin K. Lane predicted that Schmitz would "surprise the
decent moneyed people and anger the laboring people with his conservatism." Neither Schmitz and his supporters nor Phelan and Lane realized it
at the time, but the ability of the Union Labor party to elect a mayor and
three of the eighteen supervisors ushered in a period of partisan instability
and political turmoil that lasted until November 1911.[63]

DECADE OF CONFLICT

This decade of conflict, dramatically punctuated by the earthquake and fire
of 1906, divided itself into four phases. From January 1902 to the end of
1905, the Union Labor party made its debut, and the Schmitz administration adopted a pro-labor stance. In April 1902 the Carmen's Union struck
against the United Railroads, blocked streetcar tracks, and jammed downtown traffic. The general manager tried to intimidate the strikers by hiring

TABLE 9

Percentage of Vote in San Francisco Assembly Districts for
Union Labor Party Mayoral Candidates, 1901–1911

Assembly District	1901	1903	1905	1907	1909	1911
28	59.1%	50.1%	70.0%	50.9%	62.0%	51.2%
29	59.3	60.5	73.0	50.3	65.6	53.7
30	51.6	58.4	71.8	48.0	69.0	54.1
31	56.6	63.5	71.8	43.3	64.1	54.6
32	66.0	54.4	66.9	43.8	60.7	48.2
33	51.5	61.0	71.2	46.3	59.9	48.2
34	45.4	42.5	56.2	30.4	47.3	39.0
35	43.3	36.2	50.0	29.8	46.7	32.7
36	44.6	48.4	63.5	36.2	52.9	42.8
37	29.1	29.2	41.3	20.4	33.8	25.5
38	28.5	32.3	50.2	24.5	42.0	29.5
39	29.0	43.7	51.6	22.8	33.9	25.1
40	24.3	21.5	33.7	15.0	30.5	20.1
41	29.3	34.4	44.4	22.1	29.7	22.1
42	28.6	36.0	49.4	20.1	28.9	18.9
43	29.4	30.6	41.1	22.6	28.3	17.3
44	45.1	35.5	55.9	33.1	46.8	28.2
45	40.9	54.0	70.9	48.2	57.0	37.6
City	40.7	43.5	56.5	30.2	45.2	34.2

SOURCES: 1901: *San Francisco Chronicle*, Nov. 7, 1901; 1903: *San Francisco Chronicle*, Nov. 5, 1903; 1905: *San Francisco Chronicle*, Nov. 8, 1905; 1907–1911: San Francisco election records, Registrar of Voters, City and County of San Francisco.

armed guards to ride the streetcars, but Mayor Schmitz refused to issue permits to carry weapons. The daily newspapers likewise supported the strikers, as did many local employers, and the union made a favorable settlement after only a week on the picket lines. Schmitz kept his seat in the 1903 election, but the Union Labor party managed to elect only two supervisors that year, one of whom also had the Republican party nomination. By the end of 1905, several developments had begun that would shape the party's later history. Phelan, chagrined at a boycott against a labor party issue of municipal bonds in the national financial market, and his friend and business associate Rudolph Spreckels, had begun to show interest in the muckraking exposés of graft in the Schmitz administration that Fremont Older included in the *San Francisco Bulletin*. As managing editor of the paper, Older had increased its circulation and made himself something of a guardian of the city's morality by printing sensational stories of protection provided to prostitutes and gamblers by the Union Labor party administration. At the same time, however, the Citizens' Alliance had launched a particularly aggressive open-shop campaign (without the sympathy of Phelan and more pragmatic capitalists), a campaign that convinced Patrick McCarthy (head of the Building Trades Council) to give official support to the party as a way to ensure the survival of the skilled trades unions.[64]

The second phase of the decade of conflict lasted from the end of 1906 to the end of 1907. The aggressive head of the antiunion Citizens' Alliance made the open shop a political issue in an incendiary speech during the

1905 campaign, and McCarthy's endorsement brought to the labor party even more votes from the city's primary-sector working class. For working-class voters, a vote for the party now meant a vote for a city administration dedicated to the defense of labor against the open shop and its consequences. Mayor Schmitz and every labor party candidate, including the entire Board of Supervisors, took their offices in early 1906 with large majorities behind them. Schmitz maintained his policy of refusing police protection to strikebreakers or to the property of employers when he refused to increase police forces on the waterfront during the lockout against the Sailors' Union of the Pacific in 1906. The newly elected supervisors, however, regarded themselves as independent of organized labor, as well as impervious to the reputed stature of Abe Ruef as their "boss." A series of careless deals involving payments to the new supervisors by businessmen hungry for franchises allowed another segment of the business community (led by Phelan and Spreckels) to expose the Union Labor party, bring its officials to trial, and remove them from office. In the middle of 1907, a plan to nominate a replacement mayor by means of a joint convention of the Labor Council, Building Trades Council, Merchants' Association, Chamber of Commerce, Board of Trade, Real Estate Board, and Merchants' Exchange broke down. Three members of the "graft prosecution" team then chose Dr. Edward R. Taylor, a member of the city's social elite, as interim mayor. The three-man team then required the eighteen members of the Board of Supervisors to make Taylor's position official by electing him. Then those who had confessed to bribery resigned, at which point the new mayor appointed replacements. The new Board of Supervisors was thereby purged of representatives from organizations of the working class. Patrick McCarthy, free from any association with the disgraced government, in an attempt to preserve what was left of the labor party, ran as the party's candidate in November 1907 against Taylor. But Taylor, running on a nonpartisan "Good Government League" ticket supported by Phelan, Spreckels, and those members of the business community anxious to bury the Union Labor party, kept his office.[65]

The two years between the election of Taylor in 1907 and McCarthy's successful second campaign as the Union Labor party candidate in 1909 constitute the third phase of this period. As the sensationalist exposés of 1906 and 1907 hardened into predictable and tedious legal moves and countermoves in 1908 and 1909, the city's newspaper editors lost interest in the moral crusade. Businessmen Patrick Calhoun, Thornwell Mullally, Frank G. Drum, John Martin, W. I. Brobeck, and others were indicted for bribery, and the socially prominent business elite members of the Pacific Union and Bohemian clubs lost patience with muckraking and the graft prosecution when the spotlight turned in their direction. The leaders of the city's various trade associations and booster organizations complained of lost business from customers who disliked the climate of uncertainty. McCarthy's victory in 1909 rested on a coalition between businessmen opposed to the continuation of the graft trials and dependable regular supporters of the labor party in the working-class neighborhoods. In the words of James Walsh: "Ethnic-labor politicians joined Nob Hill capitalists to forge a new coalition against the prosecutors who were still trying to convict the bribe-giving [business] executives." Using a typical "business unionism" appeal grounded in the concept of harmony between capital and labor, McCarthy promised to bring to city hall an administration dedicated to classless, conservative, businesslike government.[66]

McCarthy proved a disappointment to the Merchants' Association, the Chamber of Commerce, and other backers from the business community. Always uneasy about his independent base of support and concerned that his live-and-let-live philosophy regarding saloons, gambling, and prostitution would compromise their campaign for an international exposition, business leaders dropped him for a more predictable candidate. The San Francisco Labor Council had endorsed the third-party philosophy of the Union Labor party, and some of its leaders had consistently opposed McCarthy; they also refused to support his candidacy in 1911.[67] The years 1910 and 1911, therefore, make up the fourth and final phase of a decade of political turmoil marked by the rise and fall of the Union Labor party. By this time, San Francisco, like cities all over the country, had reached the limits of "the discovery that business corrupts politics." As Richard McCormick has shown, muckrakers like Fremont Older of the *Bulletin* filled their pages with "facts and revelations," but "these writings were also dangerously devoid of effective solutions." In California, as elsewhere, the "passions of 1905–06 were primarily expressed in state, rather than local or national politics," and usually "the policy consequences were more favorable to large business interests than local solutions would have been."

> Criticism of business influence in government continued to be a staple of political rhetoric throughout the Progressive era, but it ceased to have the intensity it did in 1905–06. In place of the burning attack on corruption, politicians offered advanced progressive programs, including further regulation and election-law reforms. The deep concern with business corruption of politics and government thus waned.[68]

The demise of the San Francisco graft prosecution, particularly the deflection of blame away from the corporations that had offered the bribes, including Pacific Gas and Electric, Pacific Telephone, and the United Railroads, had come about partly because the Merchants' Association and the heads of the city's largest banks waged a decisive campaign to turn discussion about municipal politics away from issues of class conflict and business graft toward issues of city development and economic progress. The high point of the graft trials coincided with both the city's recovery from the earthquake and fire and the nation's recovery from the banking panic of 1907 that created a widespread clamor for corporate regulation. San Francisco financial institutions suffered less than some others, but the sobering experience tended to draw the city's bankers into self-conscious organization just as it did elsewhere.[69] The first step involved creating a favorable public image for business. The editor of the new journal *Coast Banker* described in October 1908 the need to counteract the "proposition that is generally in the minds of the public" that "the public-service corporation is the enemy of the public." Corporations "should be protected from rash and ill-considered action on the part of the people."[70]

John A. Britton, president of San Francisco Gas and Electric Corporation and first vice-president of Pacific Gas and Electric, admitted that "the original sins of the corporations themselves" were "equivalent to the action of get-rich quick concerns." At the same time, he criticized "the present attitude of the press" because "it will rarely, except in its advertising columns for pay, give the corporation side of any argument." Britton urged the organized business community to adopt "a new method of treating the public" in order to restore corporations "to the favor in which they were once held."[71] Frank Anderson, president of the Bank of California, urged both the press and the students and faculty in a University of California speech to remember that although "the communal conscience has changed" and "some things regarded right or proper twenty years ago are frowned upon today," it would be "better even that abuses should continue for a time longer than that they should be corrected by injustice and by the infliction of hardships upon those who are wholly innocent." Calling for cooperation among all segments of the community interested in progress, Anderson praised his listeners for "whatever high and honorable ideals you may have formed. . . . You need have no apprehension that they will be scorned in the business world or that you will have to put them away to win success."[72]

Anderson, Britton, and the *Coast Banker* all advocated regulatory legislation as an antidote to the kinds of business graft that Fremont Older and his colleagues had uncovered in the course of the graft prosecution. "Regulation," according to Britton, "is needed for protection" from a sensationalist press and vote-hungry politicians.[73] Like the advocates of charter revision in the 1890s, the supporters of regulatory legislation during the next decade favored administrative solutions and executive powers of government over legislative bodies. They trusted expertise and centralized decision making and regarded both voters and elected legislators with grave suspicion. "What," asked Britton in April 1909, "can a body of men chosen from the masses, know in the generally farcical investigations made, of the detail of a business that calls for the highest skill in finance and engineering." His preferred mode of accountability involved administrative structures of government. Legislatures "have neither time, patience, or opportunity to legislate for such control as is needed, but should only be empowered to delegate to an executive body especially organized for that purpose, such regulation and control after a calm, and unbiased presentment of the case as each issue becomes involved."[74]

Britton's position as president of San Francisco Gas and Electric and first vice-president of Pacific Gas and Electric gave him a direct interest in the question of the regulation of San Francisco corporations. He also maintained an active interest in city development and served as a director of the Panama Pacific International Exposition. Like so many executives of San Francisco's largest corporations, Britton saw no conflict of interest between the progress of his firm and the progress of his city. Once the proper regulatory commissions began their work, the public ire would dissipate, and Britton urged newspaper editors to stop making "political heat" and instead "engage in a campaign to better and uplift."[75] Russell Lowry, assistant cashier of the American National Bank, reminded San Franciscans that they

owed their economic well-being to the fact that it was the banks and corporations that had made their city the Pacific Coast's leading metropolis.

> A remarkable feature of this condition is that the accumulation of wealth has
> not been alone in the hands of a few rich men, but the stream has been widely
> diffused and distributed among all classes and occupations. As the rich have
> become richer, the poor have also become richer, and there are few cities in the
> world of its size so free from slums and tenements as San Francisco; few where
> the workers have been so uniformly prosperous, so able to live in comfort with
> a minimum of hard work and put by a little something against the day of
> adversity.[76]

The Merchants' Association, convinced that San Francisco would lose its
premier position if it did not modernize port facilities, recruit new residents, attract conventions, strengthen architectural safety standards, and
adopt professional accounting procedures for city government, moved
aggressively in 1910 and 1911 to regain the leadership role it had played
during the charter campaign in 1894–1898. M. H. Robbins, Jr., an engineer
trained at Yale University who served as Pacific Coast manager of the Otis
Elevator Company, assumed the presidency of the organization in June
1910. Possibly influenced by the model provided by Boston, where the Merchants' Association had merged with the Chamber of Commerce the pre-
ceding year, Robbins gave direction to the "growing feeling in the community that more effective work could be done by the various commercial
organizations in San Francisco if they were consolidated into one large and
powerful association."[77]

Between mid-1910 and the end of 1911 when a reorganized San Francisco Chamber of Commerce began life after a merger of the Merchants'
Association, Downtown Association, Merchants' Exchange, and Chamber
of Commerce, Robbins and the Merchants' Association initiated a wide-
ranging series of proposals for San Francisco urban development. These
included a ten-year local improvement bond issue, charter amendments
allowing the city to construct the Twin Peaks and Stockton Street tunnels,
and a plan for more efficient accounting systems for the municipal government. The association also helped organize a Convention League, which
secured twenty-three conventions for the city in 1911, and it began several
projects designed to increase access to and movement on the southern
waterfront. "We aim," said Robbins at the formal inauguration of the new
Chamber of Commerce, "to establish by the influence and work of a united
citizenship the power necessary to San Francisco's advancement, at a rate
commensurate with her greatness. It requires only sufficient local patriotism to substitute order for disorder; and reason, common sense and action
for negligence, indifference, and inertia."[78]

Determined to rid San Francisco's reputation of the smell of scandal that
remained from the years of Union Labor party administrations and graft
investigations, the organized business community moved into electoral politics.
Convinced that intense partisan conflicts produced instability, they supported a successful charter amendment in November 1910 that established
nonpartisan municipal elections. Besides prohibiting party affiliations of
candidates on the ballot, the measure strengthened the role of the chief

executive by extending the mayor's term of office from two to four years. The amendment also specified that any candidate who received a majority of votes at the primary would automatically be elected. When Congress announced at the end of January 1911 that San Francisco had defeated New Orleans and other rivals in the competition to host the 1915 international exposition, organized business pulled its resources together and planned a campaign to elect a businessman-mayor who would guarantee political stability and social harmony by appealing to as many segments of the electorate as possible.[79]

THE MAYORAL CAMPAIGN OF 1911

In April 1911, attorney Henry U. Brandenstein and twenty businessmen and professionals, members of both parties, organized a Municipal Conference for the purpose of nominating James Rolph, Jr., for mayor. They also drew up a slate for all city elective offices and pledged to carry out an aggressive campaign. Except for six attorneys and three physicians, the members of the Municipal Conference were leading businessmen, twelve rated listings in the *Blue Book,* three served as Chamber of Commerce officers, and four belonged to the Merchants' Association. Half of the group had at least one parent who had been an immigrant.[80]

Rolph had seemed an ideal candidate for mayor as early as 1909 when both the Republican County Committee and the Municipal League of Republican Clubs had unsuccessfully solicited him as a nominee. Two friends, Gavin McNab, long-time Democratic party strategist, and Republican Matt Sullivan, law partner of recently elected Governor Hiram Johnson and a Johnson appointee as chief justice of the state supreme court, kept up the pressure on Rolph to run for the office. McNab and Sullivan had good reason to think that Rolph might be able to create the kind of coalition that Phelan had attracted in 1896 and 1898. Like three of every four San Francisco men, he was the son of immigrants. Like the majority of wage earners, he had grown up in a working-class district, and like those workers who voted in largest numbers, his father (a bank clerk) had achieved respectability by means of steady work and devotion to his family. Rolph himself remained in the Mission District of his youth all his life, despite his well-publicized self-made journey from newsboy to millionaire.[81]

Owner of both a shipping firm and a bank, Rolph served three terms as president of the Merchants' Exchange and twice as a trustee of the Chamber of Commerce. He boosted home manufactures as president of the Mission Promotion Association, and he played a leading role in the creation of the reorganized Chamber of Commerce. Employer of both seamen and shipyard workers, Rolph served as president of the Shipowners' Association and helped negotiate the first formal contract with the Sailors' Union of the Pacific. He resigned from the Shipowners' Association when it supported the open shop during the waterfront strike of 1906.[82]

If his business record and his sympathy with the principle of collective bargaining attracted both labor and capital, Rolph's civic work endeared him to those San Franciscans who believed that future growth and development depended upon a progressive alliance between business and government. After the earthquake and fire, Rolph established the Mission Relief Association, with his home as headquarters, and he successfully fed tens of thousands of homeless people. He served as an officer of the Portola Festival of 1909, and he played an active role on the Committee of Six that successfully lobbied to have San Francisco picked as the site of the Panama Pacific International Exposition.[83]

When he announced, "I am not a politician," upon accepting the Municipal Conference nomination, Rolph gave notice that his appeal to voters would be based on a call for civic unity by a man who stood above partisan loyalties. His battle cry, as the *Examiner* called it, dramatized this unity theme: "I am for all the people."[84] The Municipal Conference platform, endorsed by both parties, constituted a straightforward extension of the reform Democratic principles of the Phelan campaigns of 1896 and 1898, the doctrines of the charter reformers, and the lessons learned by organized business from the political strife of the Union Labor party period. Rolph pledged to repudiate patronage and extend a rigorously enforced civil service, especially in the fire, police, and school departments. Liquor licensing would be reformed in order to end the alleged favoritism of the McCarthy administration. Not surprisingly, the platform included municipal ownership of utilities, Hetch Hetchy water for the city, the purchase of the Spring Valley Water Company, modernization and extension of the streetcar system, and harbor improvements—all measures of long-standing interest to both business and labor advocates of urban development. Rolph favored complete freedom for unions to organize, and he pledged himself to a policy of noninterference in conflicts between management and labor.[85]

Carole Hicke has described how in all of Rolph's speeches "the event upon which he was able to hang all of his principles was the coming of the Exposition."

> Did the city need new harbor facilities? The Exposition provided the rationale, for many visitors would arrive by water. Was public transportation a problem? The need must be answered, the system improved and expanded, to prepare the city for the Fair tourists. Was industrial conflict liable to become serious? A moratorium on all such conflict must be declared until the Exposition was over.[86]

The strategy of referring to the exposition served to dramatize Rolph's conviction, and that of his sponsors, that the interests of the city as a whole took precedence over those of any particular district, neighborhood, or faction. In this respect, Rolph and his supporters aligned themselves with what Samuel Hays has called the "cosmopolitan" point of view, or as Rolph himself put it: "I will be the mayor for the whole city, and not the mayor for any particular section. I will try to wipe out all dividing lines on the map of San Francisco."[87] To working-class audiences, Rolph appeared as "just plain Jim Rolph of the Mission, your neighbor. I believe in labor unions and have long been a friend of labor." To national-origin groups, like the Scandinavian American Political Club, Rolph could say: "I feel at home with Scandinavian people. I am in the shipping business and have come in contact with men of Norway and Sweden." His message to the organized business community reiterated his dedication to administrative government:

> I am aware that the principal usefulness of the Mayor consists in the work which he may be able to do as the executive head of its business affairs, looking upon the city not so much as an integral part of the state, but as a business corporation of which the citizens are the responsible shareholders.[88]

Rolph refused to make accusations against the incumbent mayor, but his chief campaign aides launched a blistering attack on McCarthy, who, they claimed, had ignored the needs of the various interest groups in the city and "whose only political creed is to perpetuate himself in power or climb to higher achievement." Rolph's endorsers and speechmakers included several influential leaders of the city's labor movement who preferred him both because of his repudiation of the open shop during the 1906 waterfront strike and because of their long-standing aversion to Patrick McCarthy. Andrew Furuseth, head of the Sailors' Union of the Pacific, once again abstained from his rule against involvement in electoral politics and made a pro-Rolph speech just before election day. Walter Macarthur spoke frequently on Rolph's behalf, as did James De Succa of the Iron Molders' Union, James H. Roxburg of the Print Pressmen, and Edward J. Kirwin, who had served on the Union Labor party county committee. The labor leaders drove to and from Rolph rallies in a large touring car, capable of carrying a dozen people, that reporters dubbed "the Union Labor special."[89]

None of the charges made against McCarthy could be proven, and the similarities between his platform and Rolph's made it hard for voters to distinguish between their policy positions. McCarthy came out in favor of woman suffrage and said he wanted San Francisco to be a closed-shop city, and these forthright stands may have lost him some support. McCarthy suffered more from the loss of backing from several organized groups, including the 3,100-member P. H. McCarthy Businessmen's Association that had supported him in 1909. Rolph, on the other hand, attracted the endorsements of the Democratic and Republican parties, the Non-Partisan Voters League, and the San Francisco Civic League.[90] An "Irish-American Club," announcing that "we do not support candidates for reasons of race or religion," campaigned for Rolph under the leadership of George A. Connelly. Connelly argued that the key issue in the campaign should be the fact that the "demoralized state of our affairs is fast destroying the world confidence San Francisco has richly earned," and Rolph was the "man to restore our credit and insure an era of prosperity."[91] A group called the Municipal Conference Campaign Committee, composed of three hundred men, organized the rallies and publicity for Rolph. The group included Edward Taylor, the former mayor; A. H. Giannini, brother of the head of the Bank of Italy; Adolph Spreckels; Theodore Roosevelt, Jr.; and Francis V. Keesling, wealthy attorney and vice-president of the West Coast Life Insurance Company; as well as Walter Macarthur and a handful of labor leaders. "They were mainly upper and middle class, middle-aged businessmen and professionals. Ethnicity of the group reflected the San Francisco population's characteristics, with a somewhat higher percentage of northern Europeans."[92]

The steady growth of Rolph's coalition between April and September 1911 signified the gradual dissolution of McCarthy's political base. The mayor refused to acknowledge the weakness of his position, however, and ten days before the election he could still proclaim: "Wherever I go, I am acclaimed with cheers. It will be a landslide, pure and simple, for the entire Union Labor ticket." McCarthy could not have been more mistaken. Rolph received 47,427 votes to McCarthy's 27,067 on September 26. The Socialist party candidate took 3,893.[93] Once again, as in the vote on the reform charter in 1898 and every mayoralty election from 1901 to 1909, the vote in 1911 showed the importance of both class and ethnicity. As Hicke has aptly put it, although the "most significant characteristic that can be identified city-wide was whether the voter was foreign born or native born," the "more transitory, possibly unskilled working class tended to vote for McCarthy, while the more stable, family-oriented workers tended to vote for Rolph."[94]

The editor of the *Coast Banker* made his own analysis of the vote in the October issue of the journal. Rolph owed his nearly two-to-one victory to the fact that he "stood for common sense, decency and protection of personal and property rights." But "a large part of the more intelligent men of San Francisco, by reason of their living in the suburbs, do not vote in the city proper. It is roughly estimated," he wrote, "that had Oakland, San Rafael and other suburbs voting power in San Francisco the vote in favor of the people's candidate, Mr. Rolph, would have been over three and one-half to one."

> The greatest good that will come to San Francisco by reason of the results of the election is the rehabilitation of the reputation of the city, which throughout the entire world had practically been lost. Naturally . . . property values have been materially strengthened by the election.[95]

By the time Rolph took office in January 1912, Governor Hiram Johnson and the state legislature of 1911 had begun the passage of pro-labor legislation that would earn it a reputation for progressivism among the San Francisco electorate. Labor Council activists now placed their support behind the progressive program, just as some of them had stood behind the Rolph candidacy, and the city's rank-and-file working-class voters followed their lead. As the South of Market electorate became a smaller proportion of the working-class vote, these voters also moved to the right politically, demonstrating by their votes for both progressive statewide candidates and for Mayor Rolph their belief in the possibility of a municipal government "for all the people."

Common scolds and obstructionists are
the curse of San Francisco.
—JAMES ROLPH, JR., 1913

Chapter 8

Politics During the Reign of Rolph, 1911-1932

Toward the end of James Rolph's unparalleled nineteen-year tenure as mayor of San Francisco, the story was told that he began an address to a group of San Francisco males with the salutation: "Brother Knights [of Columbus] and fellow Masons." Whether true or not, Rolph must have delighted in the telling of it, for he dearly loved being "mayor of all the people." A critic in 1929 admitted that "he attempts, and usually succeeds, to be all things to all people." While some have dismissed Rolph's style as glad-handing and baby kissing designed to catch votes, most of his closest associates described him as genuinely gregarious, deeply committed to democratic values, and sincere in his efforts to be mayor of all.[1]

Rolph's first term as mayor included an impressive array of accomplishments—the Panama Pacific International Exposition, construction of the Civic Center, initiation of service on the Municipal Railway, and important steps toward ensuring an adequate water supply. In each case, Rolph closely identified himself with the accomplishment, held up the project as a benefit to the city as a whole, and sought to realize a vision of civic unity based on toleration, a harmony of interests, and symbols of progress achieved through commitment to common goals. Throughout his first term, Rolph brought all his considerable energy to bear on the attainment of unity and progress. He did so in a context considerably different from that of his predecessors, and a brief look at this changed context must precede more detailed treatment of the Rolph years as mayor.

ROLPH AND PROGRESSIVISM

Rolph's inauguration coincided with nationwide reforms in the structure and function of government at all levels—local, state, and federal. Taken together, these changes make up a part of progressivism. San Francisco had already witnessed a number of typically progressive reforms before Rolph became mayor, notably the new charter and the graft prosecution. Several other changes in city government came during Rolph's tenure. In some of those changes, Rolph played the role of initiator or proponent; for others, he was little more than an interested bystander. One set of changes that Rolph did little or nothing to bring about, but which he embraced and came to personify, involved substantial reductions in the power and influence of organized political parties. Changes in the process of balloting, creation of a strong Civil Service Commission, restrictions on the number of patronage positions available for party loyalists, and charter amendments making city offices nonpartisan, all weakened political parties prior to Rolph's election in 1911. State legislation in 1911 and 1913 extended nonpartisan status to other offices, and other state legislation in 1909 and after established and extended the direct primary.[2] As a result, the once-mighty empire of party organization stood in disarray by the midpoint of Rolph's first term.

Rolph, in 1911, became San Francisco's first nonpartisan mayor, but that distinction did not proceed solely from the new charter provision. Registered as a Republican, Rolph received endorsements in 1911 from both the Republican and Democratic parties. Later, in 1918, he sought both the Republican and Democratic nominations for governor under the provision of the California primary law that permitted cross-filing. Rolph emerged the victor in the Democratic primary, based on a strong showing in San Francisco and elsewhere in northern California. He also did very well in the Republican primary in northern California but lost in southern California and lost the plurality statewide. Rolph smothered partisanship with his hearty conviviality and effusive love for his city. Of all San Francisco's mayors, Rolph stands out as most effective in practicing the politics of personality. At the end of his term as mayor, one journalist noted that Rolph "would rather shed a cheerful light than slay dragons." Always nattily dressed, with a boutonniere (he preferred gardenias), he exuded urbanity and affability. Partisanship seemed alien to his soul, and he never acquired the sort of organization that would qualify as a machine.[3]

Rolph forms a bridge between the two patterns of political thought and behavior described in Chapter 7 as the traditional and the legal-rational. Whereas Rolph's hand shaking and baby kissing mark him as a highly effective practitioner of the traditional politics of personal relationships, in his decision making he often turned to the advice of experts. In designing the new Civic Center, building the Municipal Railway, and improving the water supply, Rolph first secured the advice of experts, then threw his energy and ability into the political fray in defense of their decisions. During Rolph's first year in the mayor's office, San Francisco even acquired a new agency, the Bureau of Efficiency, headed by E. R. Zion, who set out to find "what methods give the best results and what give the poorest." Once the best methods were found, through survey and analysis, they were to be extended to all parts of the government to produce the maximum efficiency.[4]

When Rolph took the oath of office for the first time in 1912, he carried into city hall a philosophy of government that the Merchants' Association and James Phelan had articulated in their call for charter reform twenty years before. The Rolph coalition rejected the narrow definition of municipal government and refused to limit the city government's role merely to the provision of some essential services (police, fire, education, sewage disposal, paving) and to the franchising of private companies to provide other necessary services (water, gas, electricity, transportation). Rolph's supporters, like Phelan's, denied that the city's proper role in expansion and development was limited to securing land titles, surveying streets and boundaries, and providing (or franchising) necessary services. The charter of 1898–1900 had extended definitions of essential services in allowing for the city to take over municipal transportation and water systems. Even though the city rejected the elaborate planning involved in the Burnham plans of 1905 and 1909, the increased role of the city in directing development, when added to the increased reliance on expertise, inevitably led to formalization of the city's role in the planning of expansion and development. The Panama Pacific International Exposition generated demands for planning for its conclusion, and the supervisors approved an ordinance. Rolph did not implement the ordinance until after some revisions, however, and he did not appoint the city's first planning commission until late in 1917.[5]

THE PANAMA PACIFIC
INTERNATIONAL EXPOSITION

The Panama Pacific International Exposition (PPIE) had stood at the center of Rolph's election campaign in 1911. The PPIE also stood at the center— sometimes literally, sometimes only figuratively—of many of the other civic accomplishments of the period before World War I. It reflected many prevailing patterns of political thought, notably a quest for civic unity, a reliance on expertise and planning, and a melding of private and governmental activities in the promotion of development.

The first steps toward the exposition came in 1904, and the company that oversaw the project filed articles of incorporation in 1906. In 1909 a mass meeting took place on the floor of the Merchants' Exchange. All San Franciscans were invited to hear inspirational oratory and endorse the selection of a nominating committee. Gavin McNab, one of the leaders of the city's Democrats, gave the principal address and sounded the tocsin of civic unity:

> ιn the presence of this inspiring occasion, all differences among our people will pass away. In its place will rise the genius of municipal unity, a spirit capable of marvels. We shall be only San Franciscans—one for all and all for one, and all for *San Francisco*.

A second mass meeting in 1910, also in the Merchants' Exchange, brought together the results of extensive solicitation and spontaneous enthusiasm to create an impressive demonstration of commitment to the project. Two thousand participated, and they pledged more than $4 million in an hour and fifty minutes.[6]

Two more mass meetings later in 1910 and a door-to-door canvass of the business district brought the total funds to over $6 million and also pro-

duced a resolution—introduced by McNab—to secure a city bond issue of
$5 million. A special session of the legislature, engineered by McNab,
authorized the city to vote on a bond issue, and added a $5 million sub-
scription by the state. Both required approval by the electorate. The state
voted 77 percent in favor, and city voters gave the subsidy an incredible 95
percent margin. A massive lobbying blitz of Congress defeated an effort to
designate New Orleans as the official site of an exposition celebrating the
opening of the canal, and in early 1911 President Taft officially signed the
resolution designating San Francisco as the site for the official celebration.
Planning shifted into high gear, and the exposition opened in early 1915,
the first major American exposition since 1876 to open without delays resulting
from incomplete construction.[7]

The Exposition and the Quest for Civic Unity. The PPIE epitomizes many of
the dominant values of the city's business community at that time, all of
them transferred to city government in one form or another. The quest for
civic unity, dramatized by Gavin McNab in 1909, reached a high degree of
fulfillment. Businessmen laid aside old quarrels, systematically assessed
themselves all they could afford, and gave of their time as well as their
money. The PPIE board of directors counted a broad cross-section of the
city's business and professional community, with P. H. McCarthy added as
a representative of both labor and city government. For president they
chose an engineer, Charles Moore, head of a firm with branches throughout
the West and a member of several boards of directors. The six vice-presidents included William H. Crocker, Reuben Hale (secretary-treasurer of a
major department store), Isaias W. Hellman, Jr. (president of Union Trust,
director of other banks), M. H. de Young (proprietor of the *Chronicle*), Leon
Sloss (president of Northern Commercial Company, successor to the Alaska
Commercial Company), and James Rolph, Jr. (not yet mayor but president
of the Merchants' Association).[8]

The PPIE board of directors and committee members read like a list of
the leaders of the business community, and the PPIE experience taught
them that they could work together in a way they had never done before.
By contrast, the earthquake and fire had produced a brief sense of civic
unity, but it had soon disintegrated in disputes over proposals to plan the
rebuilding. The graft prosecution had divided the business community,
some siding with Spreckels, Older, and Phelan, some taking the side of
Calhoun and others accused of giving bribes. But the PPIE brought the
business community together and gave them a model for united action that
was soon translated into other areas—witness the merger of all four of the
city's leading business associations in 1911. The unity created by the PPIE
extended, at least symbolically, beyond the business community. The Building Trades Council subscribed $5,000 to the fund, and the Labor Council
and Building Trades Council pledged to relax many of their work rules
and not to demand changes in wages, hours, or work rules. In return,
business leaders quashed the developing Merchants' and Manufacturers'
Association, thus preventing any open-shop drive during the period when
the PPIE was under construction or in progress.[9]

The city's united support for the PPIE had stood forth clearly in the vote on the subsidy. The city again dramatically demonstrated its support on the exposition's first day. On February 20, 1915, everyone in the city was invited to walk down Van Ness Avenue to the exposition grounds, led by the mayor. An estimated 150,000 turned out, nearly one-third of the city's population. According to the PPIE's historian: "Merchants, bankers, clerks, stevedores, high-salaried corporation managers, factory hands, all marched in the same columns, in the same ranks. . . . Every distinction was forgotten except that of being part of the parade that was going out to open the Exposition." The grounds they entered "rested on a new and great principle of architecture harmony. . . . All chance of discord had been eliminated, and a harmony created that had never been seen on any such scale before." At the exposition grounds, the Catholic bishop, a leading rabbi, and the Episcopalian bishop all offered prayer; Governor Hiram Johnson, Mayor Rolph, William H. Crocker, and others made short speeches. Then President Wilson, in Washington, used a wireless to activate the machinery of the exposition grounds, and the PPIE was open.[10]

The Exposition as Epitome of Legal-Rational Values. The administrators of the PPIE embodied many of the other legal-rational values of the day. They rankled at any suggestions of patronage in hiring; indeed "it was ultimately recognized that the best way not to get a job with it [PPIE] was to set 'pull' in motion." Experts were sought throughout the nation. The Architectural Commission included leading local architects—several trained at the École des Beaux Arts—and representatives of major New York firms including Carrére and Hastings, McKim, Mead, and White, and Henry Bacon. Jules Guerin, a New York artist, was given control over the use of all color on the buildings. Frederick J. V. Skiff, director of the Field Museum in Chicago and an experienced exposition planner since 1891, became an all-around consultant with the title Director-in-Chief of Foreign and Domestic Participation. Alfred Esberg, prominent tobacco importer and cigar merchant and member of the PPIE board of directors, spent weeks in research at the Library of Congress and returned to San Francisco with a set of statistical relationships between the size of the host city and the attendance level at all ten of the expositions held in the United States between 1876 and 1909. This research and analysis, characterized as the foundation for "a science of expositions," provided the basis for surprisingly accurate predictions of both total attendance and average daily attendance. Based on these estimates, PPIE directors drew up their budget and determined the size of the exhibit palaces and grounds. Budget control was tight and highly centralized.[11]

Planning at all levels extended much further than at previous expositions. Moore banned political maneuvering from PPIE deliberations, accepting the presidency only on condition that "there be no intrigue. conspiracy, or star-chamber proceedings, and that friendliness and frankness between Directors exist at all times and that the members do not frame up pools of votes; that there be no factions." Concerned about maintaining "continuity of policy and hence continuity and unity of management," most PPIE subscribers agreed to vest five trustees with their rights to vote annually for the board of directors. The trustees were expected to maintain the same administration and thereby to avoid

> duplication or triplication of effort, waste of funds, confusion of policies, conflicts and abandonments of plan, letting of contracts without regard to the money in hand, general failures in execution . . . a hodgepodge of unrelated buildings and discordant physical features and an operating force without coördination or discipline . . . [which] hideous features . . . have, in the past, characterized the development of cities all over the United States.

Many of these same business leaders, it need hardly be noted, made similar arguments in 1910 in favor of extending the term of mayor from two to four years.[12]

The first four-year mayor was, of course, James Rolph, Jr., a vice-president of the PPIE. Rolph gloried in the exposition and claimed—in verse—to have attended each of its 288 days:

> I've attended all the days;
> I've sung every nation's praise;
> I've watched them give a million plaques away.
> I've helped you celebrate,
> Every country, town and State,
> And worn my high plug hat three times a day.
>
> I've collected souvenirs
> From Alaska to Algiers,
> From Cuba to the beach of Waikiki.
> But no matter where I am,
> Be it Sydney or Siam,
> San Francisco, you're Home, Sweet Home to me.

Rolph loved to lead parades from the exposition auditorium in the new Civic Center to the PPIE grounds, and he delighted in greeting the wide range of visiting dignitaries, from Camille Saint-Saëns to William Jennings Bryan, from Thomas Edison to former presidents Roosevelt and Taft. Rolph identified himself closely with the PPIE during his 1911 campaign, and he lost no opportunity to continue that identification during the years following. Nonetheless, the city had virtually no role in the planning, construction, and operation of the PPIE, beyond contributing $5 million. But just as Rolph succeeded in transferring some of the PPIE's aura of unity and achievement to himself, so did the PPIE inspire and inform a number of major undertakings by the Rolph administration.[13]

THE CIVIC CENTER

The most dramatic of these PPIE-related undertakings was unquestionably the development of the new Civic Center. The first proposal for creation of a Civic Center appeared in 1899, incorporating the city hall just completed, the new federal building on Seventh Street between Mission and Market, and the auditorium of the Mechanics' Institute. Daniel Burnham drafted an ambitious city plan in 1905 and revised it in 1909. Both envisioned monumental civic centers. Even though the city clearly required a new city hall to replace the one that collapsed in the earthquake and fire, a bond issue to build one failed to win approval in 1909. When Rolph took office as mayor in 1912, nearly six years after the earthquake and fire, San Francisco did not have a permanent city hall, had no plans for one, and had no financial capability to build one.[14]

In his 1911 campaign, Rolph had promised to build a new city hall. In his inaugural address he pointed to "three important measures appealing to immediate attention [which] are: A new City Hall, A public water system [and] Improved street car transportation." Even before taking office, Rolph appointed an advisory committee of experts—five architects and an engineer—to advise in initial planning for a city hall. Once in office, Rolph designated a board of three consulting architects to undertake further planning and then supervise construction. By this approach, he hoped to depoliticize planning and building by bypassing the politically controversial Board of Public Works, still headed by Union Laborite Mike Casey. To head the consulting architects, Rolph chose John Galen Howard, president of the local American Institute of Architects. A Berkeley resident, Howard presented impeccable credentials: he had attended the Massachusetts Institute of Technology and the École des Beaux Arts; he had worked for the two most prominent firms in the country, H. H. Richardson and McKim, Mead, and White; and he had been planner and professor of architecture at the University of California.[15]

In March 1912, the city voted on a bond issue to build a city hall and begin the Civic Center. Rolph spearheaded an exhaustive campaign, sought to transfer his own popularity to the bond issue, and tied the bond issue to the success of the PPIE. In proper progressive fashion, bond issue supporters adduced elaborate statistical arguments to justify the financial expenditure. They promised labor that construction would employ only hometown workers. Voters responded with the same unity they had earlier demonstrated in support of the PPIE subsidy: the bond issue carried by an eleven-to-one margin.[16]

The plans for the Civic Center were complete soon after the election. The new city hall would occupy two city blocks and would face an open plaza on its east. Directly across the plaza would be a library and an opera house. Facing the plaza on the south would be an auditorium, and a state office building would form the north side of the plaza. Smaller buildings would fill each of the corners. As Joan Draper has indicated in her study of the Civic Center, this design—together with the architectural styling of the buildings—was intended "to achieve a strong sense of visual unity." Virtually the last burst of the "City Beautiful" movement of the turn of the century, the San Francisco Civic Center embodies many of that movement's central characteristics: dignity, unity, harmony, and order on a monumental scale designed to inspire feelings of respect and reverence. Fulfillment of the plan proceeded rapidly.[17]

The bond issue of 1912 provided only for acquisition of land and for construction of a city hall, but the PPIE directors stood willing to construct an auditorium. An auditorium was, in fact, crucial to their plans, for they intended to stimulate attendance by convincing associations to hold their annual conventions in the exposition city. The PPIE scored a high degree of success, claiming a world's record of 928 conventions in 288 days; one reason for this success lay in their offer of free meeting-hall facilities, both in the auditorium and on the exposition grounds. Because of the needs of the PPIE, the auditorium was the first Civic Center building to be completed, in January 1915. Rolph had presided over groundbreaking for the city hall in the spring of 1913, following a design competition won by John Bakewell and Arthur Brown, Jr., and he presided over the dedication in late December 1915.[18]

The new city hall fulfilled every expectation. It was impressively big—Rolph delighted in telling visiting dignitaries that the dome was higher than that of the national capitol—and it exuded a sense of imperial grandeur. Not only was the building visually stunning, but San Franciscans could also boast that "it was built within the appropriation and, what is more, *it was built without any scandal and without any graft.*" Three-quarters of a million dollars from Andrew Carnegie allowed construction of a library, dedicated in early 1917. Opera lovers pledged another three-quarters of a million dollars to construct an opera house, with subscribers to get first choice of seats. The city would provide the site and utilities—a proposition closely parallel to those for the auditorium and library, except for the privileges granted to the subscribers. Rolph, however, vetoed the proposal as "undemocratic" and as promoting "aristocratic pretensions." The state opened a design competition for a state office building in 1916, but the war and other problems intervened, and construction was not completed until 1926.[19]

Rolph had promised a first-class exposition, and the PPIE had certainly fulfilled that promise, although Rolph could hardly claim he had been responsible. He had promised a new city hall and had delivered in a most convincing fashion. Before the end of his first term, he had dedicated both the auditorium and the city hall and had broken ground for the library.

THE MUNICIPAL RAILWAY

Rolph's promises for extension of the Municipal Railway also saw fulfillment before the end of his first term. The charter that went into effect in 1900 had included the possibility of municipal ownership of public utilities:

> It is hereby declared to be the purpose and intention of the people of the City and County of San Francisco that its public utilities shall be gradually acquired and owned by the City and County.

In fact, discussion of public ownership of the water system dated to the 1870s and might have occurred then had not William Ralston attempted so audaciously to profit from the transaction. Although the water system had been considered for decades as the prime candidate for municipal acquisition, the streetcar system proved the first focus of attention by municipal ownership advocates.[20]

At the turn of the century, most of San Francisco's residents lived within a block or two of a streetcar line. In 1902, one corporation, the United

Railroads, acquired control of nearly all these lines, counting 226 miles of track and nearly one thousand cars. Three-fourths of the trackage and almost half the cars drew their power from overhead electric lines. Cables powered most of the rest, primarily in the downtown areas. A few were still horse-drawn, and one line was steam-driven.[21]

The United Railroads, under the leadership of Patrick Calhoun after 1905, sought permission from the city to convert all their lines to electricity, but the supervisors—prodded by beautification proponents led by Rudolph Spreckels—resisted until after the Union Labor party sweep in 1905. Then the counsel for the United Railroads and Abraham Ruef agreed that $200,000 would be sufficient to secure the board's consent. Ruef told the graft prosecution of this bribe in early May 1907, and by mid-May the full account had appeared in the city's newspapers. Two days after Ruef's statement to the prosecution, the Carmen's Union struck the United Railroads, demanding three dollars a day and an eight-hour work day. Calhoun vowed no surrender, imported strikebreakers and armed guards, and broke the strike and the union. Labor historian Robert Knight characterized the strike as "the most violent streetcar strike ever seen in San Francisco, or probably in any other American city." On May 7, Calhoun's armed guards opened fire on a group of strikers, killing two and wounding twenty, including several bystanders. The ten-month casualty list among strikers and strikebreakers stood at six dead and 250 injured, with another twenty-five dead and 900 injured among streetcar passengers.[22] While Calhoun's strikebreaking earned him plaudits among open-shop advocates, it also brought the undying enmity of organized labor. His brazen purchase of the Board of Supervisors created similar sentiments among Spreckels and the reformers.

With Calhoun as convenient bête noire, efforts to secure municipal ownership of some part of the streetcar system drew increased support. Voters had rejected bond issues in 1902 and 1903, and an appropriation by the supervisors in 1907 failed to pass judicial scrutiny. Another bond issue, in the spring of 1909, failed by only a few votes. Success finally came in December 1909 when voters gave a three-to-one majority to two bond issues, to acquire the independent Geary Street line and convert it to electric cars and to extend the line down Market Street from Geary to the Ferry Building. With their passage of these bond issues, voters gave birth to the Municipal Railway, the first municipally owned streetcar line in the nation.[23]

Creating the Municipal Railway. Approval of the bond issue only started the process of building. Mayor P. H. McCarthy and his head of Public Works, Mike Casey, vowed that all labor for rebuilding of the line would be union labor, paid union wages. Control of construction remained with the Board of Public Works. Criticism circulated that employment on the project came only to those loyal to the Union Labor party and that those employed had to contribute to the party. Rebuilding of the line moved at a glacial pace. Only a bit over two miles—mostly unconnected—were complete when McCarthy left office.[24]

Immediately upon taking office, Rolph invited Bion J. Arnold, a nationally prominent traction expert, to advise the city. President of the American

Institute of Electrical Engineers and of the Western Society of Engineers, Arnold had advised Chicago, New York City, Kansas City, Los Angeles, and Denver on their transportation systems. He and Rolph determined to depoliticize construction by changing to the contract system rather than continuing under the Board of Public Works. The remaining 3.5 miles of track were completed in less than six months, at a total cost only slightly more than the price of the 2.1 miles built under McCarthy. In late December 1912, Rolph personally piloted the first car out to the end of the line and back, then spoke briefly and extemporaneously:

> We all should feel pleased that we have today started out in the great work of municipal ownership . . . let us all work together for the public good. In unity there is strength. Let us all stand together.

Rolph used the new streetcar line, like the new city hall and the PPIE, to promote a sense of unity and accomplishment, and he welded these feelings of unity and accomplishment to his own personality.[25]

Completion of the Geary Street line did not directly affect the holdings of the United Railroads at all. The next step in extending municipal ownership involved the monopoly that the United Railroads held on Market Street. Arnold drafted a lengthy charter amendment proposing a partnership between the city and the corporation; the proposal appeared on the ballot in December 1912. Rolph was wary, however, and stayed out of the city during the crucial days of the campaign. The proposal lost. Soon after, in early 1913, Rolph and Calhoun's successor agreed on terms whereby the Municipal Railway would have access to Market Street. Rudolph Spreckels found this compromise unacceptable, however, and used the referendum to force a public vote. Rolph plunged into the campaign enthusiastically, scourging Spreckels with a burning letter:

> A ratification of the lower Market Street agreement means actual public ownership of a municipal railroad to the ferry, at once. This, your people are opposing: I doubt their good faith. . . .
>
> The professional agitators who are backing your association, financially and otherwise, never built any roads, and never will build any. . . . They oppose everything and suggest nothing. . . . Their sole aim and object in life seems to be, to acquire notoriety by preventing anything being done. . . .
>
> You cannot ride on a law-suit or on a speech. . . . Common scolds and obstructionists are the curse of San Francisco.

The voters sided with Rolph by almost two to one, and Rolph soon took the reins to drive the last horse-drawn car down Market. A few months later, he again plunged into another campaign, this time for a huge bond issue to build Municipal Railway lines to serve the PPIE. Rolph spoke at as many as ten meetings a day promoting the bond issue. Voters approved by a margin of 80 percent, and Rolph soon donned a motorman's cap to drive the first car over the new tracks.[26]

HETCH HETCHY

Rolph's ability to deliver on his campaign promises extended as well to the fourth major concern, water. As in the case of the Municipal Railway, Rolph built upon foundations laid by others but threw his considerable energies into the project and—in concert with other prominent San Franciscans—managed to secure federal consent for construction of the Hetch Hetchy reservoir.

Efforts had begun in 1900–1901, toward the end of Phelan's administration. Phelan, the city engineer, and the Board of Public Works agreed that the Hetch Hetchy valley—a canyon with near-perpendicular granite walls rising 2,500 feet above a flat meadow floor, located in the Sierra 170 miles east of San Francisco—held important advantages over other sites. Phelan left office before any claims could be made and—indeed—before the decision had become public. City officials decided to keep the Hetch Hetchy decision secret "in order to prevent private parties and corporations, speculatively inclined and more mobile than city authorities . . . from forestalling the city's actions." Acting as a private citizen, Phelan applied for the rights to use Hetch Hetchy as a reservoir in April 1902. The city engineer announced the city's intent in July 1902, and soon after, Phelan transferred his claim to the city. Unfortunately, the U.S. Secretary of the Interior had denied Phelan's claims the month before.[27]

For the next ten years, four different Interior secretaries seesawed back and forth in denying, granting, and modifying grants to allow use of the Hetch Hetchy valley as a reservoir. Chief opposition came from two quarters: John Muir, the Sierra Club, and other preservationists, on the one hand, and the Spring Valley Water Company, on the other. The company claimed that its watersheds and reservoirs were sufficient to supply the city's needs for the foreseeable future and correctly saw the Hetch Hetchy proposal as the first move toward municipal ownership of the city's water system.[28]

Although Phelan remained committed to the Hetch Hetchy project throughout the ten-year contest for permission, his successors in the mayor's office did not always share his enthusiasm. Abraham Ruef convinced Eugene Schmitz that water sources could be found nearer to home, in the Bay Cities Water Company—which had offered Ruef one-third of an estimated $3 million profit from the sale of its holdings to the city. The city's interest in Hetch Hetchy revived under reform mayor Edward Taylor, and repeated conferences between city officials and Spring Valley officers produced an agreement to sell the company's holdings to the city for $35 million. The bond issue, coupled with another to construct the Hetch Hetchy system, came before the voters in 1910, by which time McCarthy sat in the mayor's chair. McCarthy favored the Hetch Hetchy construction but opposed purchase of the Spring Valley holdings on the ground that the price was too high. The Hetch Hetchy bonds passed by 95 percent, but the Spring Valley bonds secured only 65 percent, slightly less than the two-thirds needed for approval.[29]

The Raker Act. When Rolph took office in early 1912, the city still did not have permission to construct the reservoir. Rolph listed water as one of his major priorities, tied the city's needs to the PPIE (which would, he claimed, greatly increase the need for water), and took charge of the city's lobbying efforts in Washington. Soon after, he appointed a new city engineer, Michael M. O'Shaughnessy, Irish-born and educated, with nearly thirty years of experience that included railroad, mining, and hydraulic projects, as well as town site planning in California and Hawaii. For a generation of San Franciscans, O'Shaughnessy would come to epitomize the engineer-as-city-official as he extended his responsibilities from designing structures to planning and promotion.

By early 1913, proponents of the Hetch Hetchy plan concluded that the only hope for federal permission was through an act of Congress. The time was propitious. Woodrow Wilson had named, as his secretary of interior, Franklin Lane, a California Democrat, long-time Phelan associate, and supporter of the reservoir. Rolph's city attorneys drafted a bill, Democratic Congressman John Raker (another political ally of Phelan, whose district included Hetch Hetchy) introduced it, and San Francisco turned out a full force of lobbyists: Phelan and Rudolph Spreckels both went at their own expense, and Rolph, O'Shaughnessy, city clerk John S. Dunningan, and others from the Rolph administration all made one or more journeys to Washington. Wilson signed the Raker Act late in 1913. From the first draft of the bill, and through its various revisions, it prohibited the city from selling water (and, through a later amendment, electrical power) from Hetch Hetchy to "any private person, corporation, or association" intending to resell it.[30]

Building Hetch Hetchy Reservoir.   In retrospect, the ten-year struggle to secure federal permission to build the Hetch Hetchy reservoir must have seemed like the easiest part of the project. Construction began during the summer of 1914 and ultimately involved a sixty-eight-mile-long railroad, eighteen miles of tunnels through granite, and several dams, the largest completed only in 1923—named O'Shaughnessy Dam. The name was appropriate, for the project had become O'Shaughnessy's in almost every way, from design to finding buyers for the city bonds. Simultaneously, Rolph sought to buy out the Spring Valley Water Company. His first try, in 1913, failed when the supervisors refused to place it on the ballot. A second effort, in 1915, went before the voters proposing payment of $34.5 million. Rolph and O'Shaughnessy strongly supported the measure, but Spreckels played his usual role, urging the voters to reject the measure because the price was too high and the properties old and inadequate. Only 54 percent of the voters voted in favor, far short of the two-thirds required. Thus, by the end of his first term as mayor, Rolph could point to the Raker Act and the beginnings of construction in the Sierra, but additional water supplies for the PPIE had to come from other sources.[31]

FROM CIVIC UNITY TO POLITICAL POLARITY

When Rolph took his oath of office in 1912, he told the supervisors that "our city may little note nor long remember what we say here, but let us so conduct our administration that it can never forget what we will have done here." In four years he had done much. He seemed a whirlwind of motion energetically promoting first one bond issue, then another, leading a parade, presiding at a groundbreaking, initiating a new streetcar line, laying a cornerstone, greeting visiting dignitaries, dedicating a new building. Constantly in the public eye, he had a phenomenal memory for names and faces. An instinctive democrat, he disliked the pretensions of those who considered themselves to be "the best people" or "right-thinking business-men." He especially questioned the commitment of the Chamber of Commerce to work for "the benefit of all the people" and did not belong to the organization that had been created in 1911, even though he had held high office in two of the organizations that had been merged into it. He strongly and repeatedly supported the right of workers to unionize and to bargain.[32] Through hard work, careful selection of subordinates, reliance on expertise and planning, and his own out-going personality, he succeeded in creating—briefly—a high degree of unity based on pride of accomplishment and on himself as symbol of the city. It was an extraordinary feat, given the strife of the decade from 1901 to 1911. But the "Era of Good Feelings" was also short-lived.

Europe plunged into war in August 1914, and the specter of that conflict hovered over the PPIE, preventing some nations from attending and limiting the participation of others. The war acted as a catalyst, provoking reactions that eventually plunged San Francisco into what one prominent Republican called "a violent class war." Portents appeared during the PPIE. On July 5, William Jennings Bryan spoke in favor of peace and international friendship. "The world," he said, "has run mad," and he urged the United States to look "toward better things than war." Theodore Roosevelt spoke fifteen days later, vehemently denigrated "the professional pacifists, the peace-at-any-price, non-resistance universal arbitration people," and advocated an increased army and universal military training.[33]

The war not only divided San Franciscans over the question of preparedness; it also prompted unions to seek wage increases to match rising prices. By early 1916, the city seemed poised on the verge of the long-threatened labor war, for the close of the PPIE signified the end of the truce between the unions and the open-shop advocates. Unions marked some gains in both wages and hours in early 1916, but a waterfront strike in the summer brought the Chamber of Commerce into the fray as a proponent of the open shop. Emulating PPIE tactics, a Chamber-sponsored mass meeting of businessmen established a Law and Order Committee and pledged funds—a half million dollars within a week, one million dollars by year's end—to restore "peace and quiet" on the waterfront. The waterfront strike ended a week later, on July 17.[34]

Preparedness Day and the Mooney-Billings Case. By then, preparedness advocates were busily preparing a massive Preparedness Day parade, modeled on one held in New York in May. At the head of the parade committee sat Thornwell Mullally, nephew of Patrick Calhoun and his executive assistant at the time of the Ruef bribe and the strike of 1907, former member of the PPIE board of directors, and a leader of a volunteer cavalry troop, which included most of the polo team of the Burlingame Country Club. Others on the parade committee included William H. Crocker, Herbert Fleishhacker, M. H. de Young, and other city business leaders. The Labor Council urged workers to boycott the affair. The Building Trades Council absolutely prohibited participation by members and tied preparedness to Homestead, Ludlow, Coeur d'Alene, and the "skulls of working men, women, and children, shot, murdered and burned to death by militia men." On July 20, an antipreparedness demonstration brought together some of the city's labor leaders, reformers, socialists, and pacifists. Rudolph Spreckels condemned the organizers of the parade as grafters, and Paul Scharrenberg of the California State Federation of Labor denounced them as "industrial vampires."[35]

On July 22, Rolph and Mullally, leaders of the parade, started down Market Street at 1:30 P.M., a half-hour behind schedule. Behind them came more than twenty thousand of the city's businessmen and professionals, their wives in a separate women's division, and veterans of past wars. At 2:04 P.M., a bomb exploded on Steuart Street near Market, killing nine and injuring forty. As the parade continued and ambulances took away the injured, souvenir hunters, police, and volunteers vied in collecting fragments and evidence. The search for those responsible quickly narrowed to a small group of radical union members and anarchists. Authorities soon arrested five suspects: Warren K. Billings, recently released from Folsom Prison where he had served two years for illegally transporting dynamite; Thomas J. Mooney, an iron molder, socialist, would-be union organizer, and chief suspect in the dynamiting of a power line south of San Francisco; Rena Mooney, a music teacher who had assisted her husband Tom in an abortive streetcar strike the week before the bombing; Edward D. Nolan, a machinist and anarchist, from Machinists' Lodge 68; and Israel Weinberg, a jitney driver and officer of the Jitney Bus Operators' Union, whose son took piano lessons from Rena Mooney.[36]

Once the suspects were in custody, police and city district attorney Charles Fickert focused their attention exclusively on building a case against them, discarding or ignoring contrary evidence or testimony. Billings was tried first, convicted, and sentenced to life in prison. Mooney came next, was convicted, and sentenced to death. Then the defense began to discover indications of perjury and subornation; key witnesses did not appear in the trial of Rena Mooney, and the jury found her not guilty. Weinberg received a similar verdict, and Fickert dropped charges against Nolan. Fifteen years later, researchers for the Wickersham commission drew up a report on the cases and presented the following conclusions:

> There was never any scientific attempt made by either the police or the prosecution to discover the perpetrators of the crime. . . . There were flagrant violations of the statutory law of California by both the police and the prosecution. . . . Immediately after the arrest of the defendants there commenced a deliberate attempt to arouse public prejudice against them, by a series of daily interviews given to the press by prosecuting officials. . . . Witnesses were permitted to testify at the trials, despite such knowledge in the possession of the prosecutor of prior contradictory stories told by these witnesses, as to make their mere production a vouching for perjured testimony. . . . Witnesses were coached in their testimony to a degree approximating subornation of perjury. . . . After the trials, disclosures casting doubt on the justice of the convictions were minimized, and every attempt made to defeat the liberation

of the defendants, by a campaign of misrepresentation and propaganda carried on by the official who had prosecuted them.[37]

At first, the defense drew support almost solely from a small group of radicals and anarchists, among them Alexander Berkman, who had been publishing an anarchist journal—ominously titled the *Blast*—in the city since January 1916, and Emma Goldman, who was in the Bay Area delivering a lecture series in July 1916. Radicals in the labor movement, especially those involved in the International Workers Defense Fund, also took prominent roles in raising funds and agitating. When indications of subornation and perjury began to mount, after Tom Mooney's trial and before that of Rena Mooney, Frederick Koster of the Chamber of Commerce condemned criticism of Fickert, and the Law and Order Committee offered to assist Fickert in the Rena Mooney trial.[38]

By July 1917, the U.S. district attorney reported to Washington that "the community is at fever heat and deadly divided on the cases. . . . [I]t was taken up by the Law and Order Committee of the Chamber of Commerce as a chance to suppress the Unions, and the Unions evidently took up Mooney's side of it in order to counter-move against the action of the Chamber of Commerce." Chester Rowell, a leader of the progressive faction of the state's Republican party, wrote to Theodore Roosevelt of "a violent class war on in San Francisco which is becoming nearly as bitter as was the schism over the graft prosecutions ten years ago." In December 1917, Fickert's opponents forced a recall election, but Fickert's battle against anarchism won him endorsement by Theodore Roosevelt and support from the Chamber of Commerce and most of the business community. The opposition had the support of the Labor Council and many ministers upset over Fickert's tolerance of vice interests. Fickert secured more than three-fifths of the votes after a bomb demolished part of the governor's mansion the night before the election.[39]

Demonstrations against Mooney's execution took place worldwide in 1917 and 1918, but efforts to secure a new trial failed. Attempts to secure a pardon from the governor enlisted the support of President Wilson, but failed too; instead, Governor William D. Stephens commuted Mooney's sentence to life imprisonment, guaranteeing a continuation of the struggle to free both him and Billings. Their long battle for freedom came to a successful close only in 1939, and Billings did not secure a pardon until 1961.[40]

Throughout the latter half of 1916 and into 1917, as the Mooney case continued to make headlines week after week, other events also contributed to the feeling of "class war." The Law and Order Committee established itself as the leader of an open-shop campaign, succeeded in breaking the culinary unions despite efforts by Rolph to bring about arbitration, broke a strike against retail lumberyards, and tried to break the Structural Iron Workers' Union but failed when Rolph had police remove private armed guards from construction sites and also canceled city contracts with firms insisting on the open shop. In November 1916, the Law and Order Committee convinced the city's voters to adopt a strict antipicketing ordinance, and in 1917 the Chamber of Commerce persuaded the governor to veto an anti-injunction measure.[41]

Rolph's Retreat from Leadership. By the crisis of mid-1916, Rolph had already begun to trim his activities. He suffered what his aides described as "a temporary breakdown" in January 1916, requiring "complete rest" in "a local sanitorium." He also had an appendectomy at that time. Thereafter, he cut back his exhaustive schedule. The war brought Rolph serious financial reverses. Between 1915 and 1918, the mayor had made impressive additions to his already considerable wealth by investing in ships and ship construction, but the war ended with three ships partially built and no buyer. By 1921, his export-import firm had gone into liquidation, and Rolph owed $1 million. Much of this debt was due Herbert Fleishhacker of the Anglo and London Paris National Bank, who emerged in the 1920s as a key Rolph political adviser.[42]

During the war and throughout the 1920s, as Rolph won term after term, he continued to be highly visible. William Hines preserved the following picture in early 1929:

> Rolph . . . will order the siren on the Ferry Building blown, or the streets decorated with flags and bunting, on the slightest provocation. Hardly a week goes by without a parade up Market Street with Rolph leading the show. Most of the time it is a motion picture actress up from Hollywood.

Hines claimed that "the highest dignitary of the nations of the world might be visiting San Francisco and, if paraded up Market Street, Rolph will take as many bows with his silk hat as the dignitary." Hollywood, especially, seemed to attract Rolph, and he delighted in associating with motion picture celebrities, especially attractive actresses. According to Hines, Rolph's leading of parades constituted virtually his sole exercise of leadership.

> With a charter that gives the mayor of San Francisco extreme powers, Rolph has practically turned the reigns of government over to the chairman of the finance committee [Franck Havenner]. They are bitter enemies, but the leading banker of San Francisco [Herbert Fleishhacker] has found it advisable to make the lion and the lamb lie down together.[43]

These observations coincide with those of Andrew Gallagher, member of the Board of Supervisors throughout much of the 1920s and a personal friend of Rolph. In an interview in 1960, Gallagher recalled that "as the years passed the Mayor gave a decreasing amount of his attention to the problems of administration, and he relied increasingly on his capable secretaries, advisors, and political supporters to attend to the day-by-day problems of government."[44] As Rolph retreated from the active leadership style of his first term, as he came increasingly to preside (perhaps "reign" would be more appropriate), the politics of the city became increasingly factious. Some projects begun during the period before the war continued almost as if they had a life of their own; other political issues closely reflected the labor-management conflicts of the decade; and in still other political arenas the locus of decision making shifted away from city government to private associations claiming to act in the public interest.

CONTROVERSY OVER PUBLIC OWNERSHIP

The Municipal Railway and the Hetch Hetchy project continued to occupy a prominent place in the politics of the war period and the 1920s. By the time of the PPIE in 1915, the Municipal Railway had grown to a system of ten lines and the close of the exposition did not bring a slackening of streetcar construction. City Engineer O'Shaughnessy, usually with the political support of Rolph, worked to implement most of the suggestions in Bion Arnold's comprehensive report of 1912. The construction of the Stockton Street tunnel in 1914, financed by assessments on the property owners benefiting from improved service, provided a model for the financing of the Twin Peaks tunnel, the longest streetcar tunnel in the world. Arnold acted as consultant, O'Shaughnessy was engineer, and Rolph proudly drove the first car through the completed bore in 1918. Rolph's dedication speech candidly linked municipal enterprise—termed "socialism" by the *Illustrated World* in 1915—with urban development:

> With the coming of the rails and the operation of streetcars through the Twin Peaks Tunnel, it will no longer be necessary to move down on the peninsula or across the Bay to Marin or Alameda Counties to find suitable home sites. Enough will be provided west of Twin Peaks.

Real estate agents came in force to the dedication exercises, ready to take celebrants to prospective homesites in the southwestern third of the city. Arnold had long since pointed out that a commuter could travel from across the bay to downtown San Francisco as quickly and cheaply as from the southwestern third of the city, and he was not alone in attributing the undeveloped state of that area to inadequate transportation and water. Municipal enterprise—socialism only in the eyes of the most conservative—remedied those deficiencies, and the postwar period saw a construction boom west of Twin Peaks, including creation of such exclusive areas as St. Francis Wood and Forest Hill. By 1928, construction of the Duboce tunnel and the Judah Street line marked the virtual completion of the Arnold plan of 1912.[45]

Stalemate over Streetcars. Expansion of the Municipal Railway and efforts to buy the holdings of the Market Street Railway Company generated intense political controversy throughout the 1920s. In 1917, with the Twin Peaks tunnel complete but no tracks yet laid in it, the supervisors clashed over the use of the tunnel. Some advocated that it be the exclusive property of the Municipal Railway, others that the United Railroads be allowed to use it, and still others that the United Railroads be given exclusive right to use it. Rolph insisted on municipal ownership of the tracks and won, but only after a stormy meeting. As Rolph retreated more and more from leadership, O'Shaughnessy increasingly filled that role, planning extensions and promoting new projects. In 1927, he was the major proponent of a $4.6 million bond issue, but voters rejected the proposal.[46]

An effort to sell the Market Street Railway (MSRy) to the city came in 1922, shortly after the United Railroads' bankruptcy forced reorganization. John Francis Neylan claimed that the architect of this scheme was Gavin

McNab, acting for bankers and "insiders," and that the asking price of $34 to $40 million was—by the admission of Fleishhacker—$10 million too high to be realistic. In 1925, an initiative measure proposed city acquisition of the MSRy for a total of $36 million. Neylan again saw McNab and Fleishhacker as responsible for the proposal and felt Rolph's closeness to both made the mayor unreliable in representing the city's interests. When voters rejected the measure, the MSRy was sold instead to the Standard Power and Light Company. Everyone involved knew that most MSRy franchises would expire in 1929, at which time 60 percent of the company's holdings would become the property of the city. In 1927, over the opposition of both Rolph and O'Shaughnessy, the Board of Supervisors hired a nationally prominent consultant, Delos F. Wilcox, to survey the city's streetcar situation. Wilcox recommended a purchase price of $20 million and, failing that, that the city plan to take over all the expiring franchises in 1929. Caught among an unsympathetic Board of Supervisors, voters who refused to pay the company's price, and expiring franchises, the Market Street Railway found relief in a charter amendment in 1930, implemented by the supervisors in 1931, granting a twenty-five-year operating permit in return for promises to improve service and to build a new line. There matters remained until 1944 when voters approved the purchase of the railway for $7.5 million.[47]

Defeat of Public Power. The Hetch Hetchy project, like streetcar expansion, continued throughout World War I and the 1920s and, like the Municipal Railway, generated intense political conflicts. By 1918, San Francisco owned a 68-mile-long railway in the Sierra, but pouring of concrete for the major dam in the system did not begin until 1921. Dedication of O'Shaughnessy Dam in 1923 marked completion only of the first major step. Next came the construction of a powerhouse and power lines (completed in 1925), an aqueduct 156 miles long (including 85 miles of tunnels, the last done in 1934), and acquisition of the reservoirs and distribution system of the Spring Valley Water Company. By 1924, the first $45 million bond issue had been exhausted, and another bond issue of $10 million came before the voters. O'Shaughnessy took the central role in promoting the bonds, promising: "Give me the ten million now and I'll be back in a couple of years for twenty-three million more to finish the job." Because of his constant advocacy of bond issues, whether for water or streetcar work, some suggested that his initials, M. M., actually stood for "More Money." The total cost, when Hetch Hetchy water finally flowed from city faucets in 1934, was about $100 million.[48]

While the cost of the Hetch Hetchy project itself generated political controversy, much greater controversy swirled around the disposition of the power generated at the dam. For nearly five years in the mid-1920s, the power issue held the central place in the city's politics, and the echoes from that struggle still occasionally reverberate through the city's politics. The federal Raker Act specified that water and power realized from the Hetch Hetchy project could not be sold to private interests for resale. Conflict began when O'Shaughnessy pushed the electrical generating plan to early completion in order to produce revenue to help offset future construction costs. Funds from the initial bond issue were fast diminishing, however, and

O'Shaughnessy could not extend the transmission line across the bay and into the city. In February 1923, acting at the prompting of the Labor Council, Supervisor Eugene Schmitz (the former mayor) introduced a resolution favoring municipal ownership of a power distribution system. Lengthy deliberations ensued, but the supervisors unanimously approved the resolution in July. Soon after, O'Shaughnessy outlined four options for implementation: (1) construction of a distribution system to compete with private companies; (2) purchase of the existing systems owned by Pacific Gas and Electric or Great Western Power; (3) sale of power at wholesale rates, an option seemingly foreclosed by the Raker Act; or (4) power distribution through the facilities of a private company. By the fall of 1923, the approach of municipal elections allowed Neylan of the Hearst press to push Rolph and other candidates to demonstrate their commitment to municipal ownership as a precondition to endorsement. In September, the supervisors declared themselves "unalterably and unequivocally opposed" to distribution through a private company, and Rolph created a five-member advisory committee "one hundred percent" favorable to public ownership, headed by former mayor James Phelan. Rolph received the Hearst endorsement and won his fourth election.[49]

In early 1924, the supervisors began discussion of a recommendation from the advisory committee that the city begin construction of a step-down station. Members of the business community opposed this as a step to more elaborate construction and expenditures; some argued that the cost would imperil prompt completion of the water project. By March, two options came under official consideration: sale of power to a private company, with the company to act as the city's agency for distribution; or construction of a transmission line and step-down station as the first stage of direct city distribution. One newspaper proposed a third alternative, no power generation until a municipal distribution system was in place, but that option did not receive serious consideration. Throughout the first half of 1924, various proposals appeared for separate bond issues for water and power construction, a combined bond issue, or construction of a step-down plant through direct appropriation and the gradual development of a distribution system in the same fashion. In the late spring of 1924, the power companies (Pacific Gas and Electric and Great Western) put their position in writing to Neylan. After conversations with Wigginton Creed of Pacific Gas and Electric and Mortimer Fleishhacker of Great Western, Neylan concluded that they wanted to keep "the city out of the power business forever insofar as competing with them is concerned." Fleishhacker frankly told Neylan "that they were concerned about the city entering the power business for the reason that he knew once the city got into competition with the private corporations the city would cut rates and render their enterprises unprofitable." The power companies proposed that Pacific Gas and Electric would receive all Hetch Hetchy power on the east side of the bay, would transmit power to the city for street lighting and municipal streetcars, and would purchase all the other power for approximately $2 million per year.[50]

Throughout the remainder of 1924, little action took place on the power issue. In accord with a decision of the supervisors in January, the state

Railroad Commission carried out a valuation of Pacific Gas and Electric and Great Western properties as the first step in condemnation proceedings, but estimates of completion in a year's time proved far too optimistic. By early 1925, some action became essential, for the generating plant was virtually complete. In March 1925, Rolph vetoed a measure to allow the temporary sale of power through a private company, but negotiations with the power companies bogged down. The advisory committee insisted that any contract for distribution through a private company had to specify that certain customers be designated as the city's customers, but Pacific Gas and Electric refused. Finally, after a tense fourteen-hour supervisors' meeting, Rolph and eleven supervisors accepted the power companies' terms. The *San Francisco News* headlined the action as "SOLD OUT," and the minority of seven supervisors who opposed the contract appealed to the Interior Department to declare it a violation of the Raker Act. Rolph got Commerce Department Secretary Herbert Hoover to intercede on behalf of the majority, and the contract was approved.[51]

In the fall elections, Rolph gave strong support to every member of the majority up for reelection, but voters retired them all, including such popular figures as Ralph McLeran, Angelo Rossi, Eugene Schmitz, and the board's first woman, Mary Morgan. A "clean-out" slate of candidates for supervisor and city attorney swept to victory with the support of the Hearst press, the unions, and the progressive faction of the Republican party, headed by Sheriff Thomas F. Finn. The new majority, led by Franck R. Havenner (a former aide to Hiram Johnson), used income from the contract with Pacific Gas and Electric to set up a special fund to build a transmission line to the city, but a taxpayers' suit defeated this effort. In 1927, Havenner led support for a bond issue to construct a transmission line, but it went down to defeat. The valuation proceedings were finally completed in 1929, and voters faced four bond issues totaling $68 million in 1930; again, all failed. Despite sporadic revival of the issue later, the repeated defeats in 1925, 1926, 1927, and 1930 meant that public power would never again occupy so central a position in the city's politics.[52]

Buying Out the Spring Valley Water Company. Efforts to secure voter approval to buy the holdings of the Spring Valley Water Company were more successful. Despite defeats in 1910 and 1915, proposals appeared on the ballot in 1921, 1927, and 1928. Rudolph Spreckels continued his opposition into the 1920s. The 1928 effort, led by O'Shaughnessy, Rolph, Phelan, and Havenner, finally produced a majority of 80 percent in favor. The final purchase price of $41 million was up from the $35 million voted on in 1910, the $34.5 million proposed in 1915, or the $38 million in the 1921 and 1925 issues. Although the bond issue finally won voter approval, the city soon discovered that it could find no purchasers for the bonds. The same problem plagued the Hetch Hetchy bonds approved at the same time. In December 1929, A. P. Giannini of the Bank of Italy had his bank buy $4 million of the Hetch Hetchy bonds and led a syndicate that took the entire $41 million Spring Valley bond issue. The Board of Supervisors created the San Francisco Water Department in early 1930 as a division of the Board of Public Works to operate the system as a municipal corporation, to be self-financing, and to be responsible for liquidation of the bond issues involved in its creation.[53]

PARTY ORGANIZATIONS IN A REPUBLICAN CITY

Conflict over municipal ownership formed one major aspect of city politics throughout the 1920s. Another was the virtual disappearance of political parties and the emergence of several factions organized around key political leaders, most of them Republicans. Throughout the 1920s, Tom Finn and Peter McDonough vied for control of the Republican party of San Francisco. Finn, founder of the Stablemen's Union at the turn of the century, held several elective and appointive positions under the aegis of the Union Labor party between 1901 and 1909. Untouched by the scandals, Finn's grassroots organizing for the party led to his nomination for sheriff in 1909. Elected with McCarthy that year, he shared McCarthy's fate in 1911 as well but regained the sheriff's office in 1915. Finn threw his organization behind Hiram Johnson and rapidly emerged as a major leader of the Republican party, thought by many to have control over state appointive positions in the city. He kept a reputation for supporting progressives, maintained strong ties to organized labor, and could reputedly deliver the endorsement of the Union Labor party after it became the endorsing arm of the city's unions. Finn had briefly allied with McDonough but broke with him by 1920. Peter and Thomas McDonough inherited their father's saloon and branched out in the bail bond business in 1896. Peter gradually came to dominate the city's vice operations by his ability to protect his underworld clients through his contacts in city hall.[54]

Neither Finn nor McDonough was cast from the mold of a boss like Buckley, although both were called "boss." Finn came closer, acquiring a reputation as the person to go to for "an appointment or a job or something done," as "the most powerful vote dictator in the State who made and unmade United States Senators, Congressmen, elevated humble men to high office, smashed the dreams of those who would be mighty." McDonough, by contrast, looked and behaved like a businessman, protecting his operations, raising funds for political donations from the city's vice interests, and cultivating close contacts with police and politicians. Finn and McDonough locked horns repeatedly in the 1920s, with Finn usually backing candidates from the progressive wing of the Republican party and McDonough supporting conservatives. Finn's power declined a bit after 1927. That year, he delivered endorsements from both the Republican and Union Labor parties to former supervisor James E. Power, running against Rolph for mayor. Rolph accused Finn of bossism and put up a candidate against Finn for sheriff. McDonough reportedly offered ten dollars for every vote against Finn. Both Power and Finn lost, although Finn continued to be a power in the local Republican party until his death in 1938. Not until 1935 did McDonough's political clout wane, and then only after an exhaustive investigation labeled him "a fountainhead of corruption," and he lost his bail bond license.[55]

In addition to Finn and McDonough, the city counted many other factional leaders, power brokers, and political activists. Timothy A. Reardon, Rolph's choice as president of the Board of Public Works and a member of the Democratic County Committee throughout the 1920s, developed a reputation as the person to contact for support from the Democratic party. Reardon usually backed Rolph to the hilt, and some accused him of heading a Rolph "machine" centered in the Department of Public Works, but the evidence for such accusations is scanty. Other prominent Democrats included Gavin McNab and former Senator James Phelan. The Democratic party, however, suffered growing defections among voters. At the beginning of the decade, it claimed about a third of the city's registered voters, but it held only a fifth by 1930.[56]

The city seemed overwhelmingly Republican in the 1920s, and most would-be politicos belonged to that party or—like Paul Scharrenberg and other leaders of organized labor—moved into that party before the decade's end. The state Republican party divided into progressive and conservative wings throughout the decade, and San Francisco provided much of the leadership of both factions. The conservative faction of the city's Republicans included William H. Crocker, Herbert Fleishhacker, and M. H. de Young. The progressives, led by Hiram Johnson, counted fewer bankers, although A. P. Giannini played an important role in the 1926 Republican primary by supporting progressive C. C. Young against incumbent governor Friend Richardson. Neylan, another key leader of the progressive faction, maintained a private law practice at the same time he served Hearst as publisher of the *Morning Call* and determined editorial policy for all five Hearst papers on the West Coast. A staunch advocate of municipal ownership of public utilities, Neylan clashed frequently with Hearst over endorsements and politics but generally had his way with editorial policy through the 1920s. In 1923 and again in 1927, Neylan tried to use his power to stiffen Rolph's commitment to municipal ownership.[57]

A POLARIZED ELECTORATE

During the late teens and through the 1920s, San Francisco voters expressed their preferences on a variety of policy issues—charter amendments, bond issues, initiatives—as well as on candidates, and the results point to a sharply polarized electorate throughout the period. Tables 10 and 11 present representative examples of voting behavior illustrating the nature of the polarity. Table 10 summarizes voting on eight policy issues involving labor, municipal ownership, urban development, and planning. A dozen more policy votes might be added to the list, with patterns of support differing only in degree, not in kind, from these examples. Table 11 summarizes voting for eight candidates, and, again, a dozen or more others might be presented showing similar patterns. Table 12 summarizes census data for the same assembly districts used in Tables 10 and 11, and Map 3 locates these districts.

The first six assembly districts in the tables all lie south of Market Street (although part of 29 extends into the Western Addition), and these six make up a distinct political area. As indicated by the 1914 and 1916 votes

TABLE 10

Voting Behavior on Selected Policy Issues, by Assembly District, 1912–1930

Assembly District	Establishing Eight-Hour Day, 1914	Prohibiting Picketing, 1916	Transmission Line Bond Issue, 1927	Public Ownership of Trans-Bay Bridge, 1927	Airport Construction Bond Issue, 1926	Establishing City Planning Commission, 1912	Strengthening City Planning Commission, 1928	Extending MSRy[a] Operating Permit for 25 Years, 1930
21	65.1%	33.6%	63.8%	66.3%	77.7%	44.6%	47.9%	44.8%[b] }
22	61.0	29.5	58.0	59.0	71.6	32.3	37.7	
23	63.9	26.6	60.0	63.4	77.6	36.4	40.3	48.5
24	56.5	33.0	58.1	57.7	81.4	37.1	44.8	48.8
25	47.3	39.4	60.2	61.0	79.7	42.5	52.1	47.6
29	50.1	38.4	61.0	62.1	81.4	47.0	45.1	47.9
26	39.1	49.2	54.3	55.2	83.4	50.6	45.7	51.3
30	41.6	54.0	52.6	54.1	85.2	56.7	52.1	54.1
27	27.3	64.5	49.3	47.5	82.3	54.8	49.6	56.7
28	28.4	65.2	43.1	42.1	83.5	52.6	52.6	61.7
33	37.8	60.3	44.0	44.7	83.4	48.3	59.8	62.3
32	27.6	71.6	45.5	44.4	88.6	67.0	63.7	61.4
31	21.4	76.0	34.4	35.5	87.9	67.3	65.2	66.1
City	41.2	52.0	50.7	51.3	83.1	50.4	51.3	55.3

SOURCE: San Francisco election records, Registrar of Voters, City and County of San Francisco.

[a]Market Street Railway Company.

[b]Assembly districts 21 and 22 were combined between 1928 and 1930.

TABLE 11
Voting Behavior for Selected Candidates, by Assembly District, 1915–1929

Assembly District	James Rolph, Jr. (Mayor), 1915	Charles Fickert (District Attorney), 1919	Angelo J. Rossi (Supervisor), 1921	Hiram Johnson (U.S. Senate, Republican Primary), 1922	Robert La Follette (President), 1924	Mean Vote for "Clean-Out" Slate, Board of Supervisors, 1925	James Rolph, Jr. (Mayor), 1927	Angelo J. Rossi (Supervisor), 1929
21	38.2%	25.1%	34.7%	52.6%	64.4%	54.6%	39.2%	37.4%[a]
22	36.7	25.9	38.1	58.9	66.6	57.5	40.7	
23	32.1	19.1	37.1	59.5	67.7	59.7	42.9	35.6
24	41.4	26.7	42.0	56.3	57.4	55.3	51.3	43.0
25	47.4	32.7	41.8	56.5	61.2	59.2	50.2	42.1
29	44.6	30.3	39.2	54.9	60.0	56.7	48.2	39.4
26	55.3	37.5	45.5	52.5	48.6	53.1	52.7	44.2
30	56.4	37.6	44.3	47.6	47.9	49.9	53.9	47.5
27	66.4	43.5	50.2	47.1	35.4	45.9	61.3	51.8
28	67.1	48.5	53.6	41.9	29.6	41.3	62.1	53.1
33	49.1	47.4	63.8	44.4	37.6	40.2	53.6	56.8
32	68.6	55.4	55.6	39.8	27.6	38.0	63.5	59.3
31	72.1	60.6	64.0	32.5	24.3	33.3	66.5	63.5
City	53.7	39.1	47.6	48.3	44.8	48.3	55.3	48.6

SOURCE: San Francisco election records, Registrar of Voters, City and County of San Francisco.

[a] Assembly districts 21 and 22 were combined between 1928 and 1929.

TABLE 12

Social and Economic Characteristics of Assembly Districts, 1920 and 1930

Assembly Districts	Population Foreign Stock White		Population Born in Selected Countries, 1920			Families Owning Homes, 1930	Value of Housing Stock, 1930[a]		
	1920	1930	Ireland	Germany	Italy		Lower	Middle	Upper
22[b]	74.5%	62.7%	4.9%	4.1%	5.8%	40.9%	62.6%	28.6%	5.2%
23	76.4	68.3	4.7	4.0	8.4	67.1	48.4	43.0	7.3
24	70.9	59.7	6.7	4.5	2.9	64.7	36.3	37.8	24.4
25	65.8	60.8	5.1	4.4	2.6	22.8	33.7	47.7	14.5
29	63.9	55.7	4.3	4.2	1.7	10.3	31.0	48.2	16.9
26	64.7	61.6	4.2	4.4	1.5	28.6	26.8	50.9	19.3
30	59.7	52.2	3.0	4.4	1.3	12.7	34.9	43.2	16.4
27	56.7	53.7	3.6	3.8	0.8	50.3	11.4	42.8	43.5
28	58.1	57.9	3.5	3.7	1.0	45.9	8.6	35.7	53.8
33	63.7	48.0	0.8	1.5	18.8	8.3	42.6	30.7	21.1
32	55.6	49.8	1.4	2.8	3.0	6.1	10.2	41.3	36.6
31	55.9	52.0	2.9	3.1	3.8	20.8	9.1	24.3	58.9
City	63.7	56.7	3.6	3.7	4.7	36.7	25.8	39.0	30.5

SOURCES: Table 13, "Composition and Characteristics of the Population, for Assembly Districts of Cities of 50,000 or More: 1920," U.S. Bureau of the Census, Department of Commerce, *Fourteenth Census of the United States: 1920*, 11 vols. (Washington, D.C., 1922–1923), 3:127; Table 23, "Population by Sex, Color, Age, etc., for Cities of 50,000 or More by Wards or Assembly Districts: 1930," U.S. Bureau of the Census, Department of Commerce, *Fifteenth Census of the United States: 1930*, 6 vols. (Washington, D.C., 1932–1933), vol. 3, pt. 1, p. 287; Table 24, "Classification of Families, etc., for Statistical Areas of Los Angeles and Assembly Districts of San Francisco: 1930," ibid., 6:189.

[a]Lower includes owner-occupied houses valued under $5,000 and tenant-occupied housing renting for less than $29 per month; middle includes owner-occupied houses valued between $5,000 and $7,499 and tenant-occupied housing renting for $30 to $49 per month; upper includes owner-occupied houses valued over $7,499 and tenant-occupied housing renting for more than $49 per month. Totals do not add to 100 because of values not reported (4.7 percent citywide).

[b]Assembly district 22 includes data for assembly district 21 for the 1920 census. The districts were combined between the two census years.

(Table 10), these six districts formed the heart of labor's political strength, turning in solid majorities in favor of state laws regulating working conditions, a city ordinance requiring a union label on city printing jobs, and the recall of District Attorney Fickert. The same six districts also formed the core support for municipal ownership. Other parts of the city, at times, also registered high levels of support for particular municipal ownership issues, but the six labor districts stand out in the consistent nature of their support. These assembly districts—unlike other areas—favored municipal ownership even if it meant placing the city into competition with powerful private corporations like Pacific Gas and Electric.

The behavior of these six districts on policy issues carried over into voting for candidates. "Sunny Jim of the Mission" Rolph received majorities in all six districts only once, in 1919, when he was endorsed by erstwhile labor opponents Patrick McCarthy and Andrew Gallagher and when his only serious opponent was former mayor Eugene Schmitz. Tom Finn, by contrast, won the sheriff's badge in 1915 by building substantial majorities in these districts, and he increased the size of those majorities in 1919 and 1923, averaging nearly 70 percent in the districts south of Market Street. State and national politics activated similar voting behavior, with the southeast corner of the city providing Hiram Johnson's base in the city (after the pro-labor legislation of this first term) and support for Robert La Follette both in the 1912 primary and in 1924 and for Al Smith in 1928.[58]

At the opposite pole of San Francisco's politics from the six districts south of Market stood assembly district 31, the exclusive Pacific Heights and Marina area, where 60 percent of the homes fell into the upper ranges of value and rent. The south of Market districts voted two to one against the anti-picketing ordinance, but district 31 voted three to one in favor; the labor districts voted three to two in favor of a city-owned transmission line for Hetch Hetchy power, but district 31 voted two to one against. In instance after instance, knowing the behavior of one of these two areas allows prediction of the behavior of the other simply by inverting the ratios. Where the south of Market districts favored the presidential candidacy of Hiram Johnson in 1924, by voting three to one or four to one for delegates pledged to him (Tom Finn received the highest number of votes of any of the Johnson delegates), assembly district 31 gave a two-to-one backing to Calvin Coolidge (William H. Crocker received the highest number of votes of any Coolidge delegate). When Charles Fickert ran for reelection in 1919, despite strong suspicion of having suborned perjury and despite revelations of dealings with McDonough's vice interests, district 31 still gave him 60 percent of its vote, compared with only 40 percent of the vote cast citywide.

Six other assembly districts usually voted with district 31, although seldom in as high proportions. Five of these six had distinctly middle-class characteristics. Districts 26 and 30, the Western Addition, Eureka Valley, Dolores Heights, and part of Buena Vista Heights, developed in the late nineteenth century as middle-class or upper-middle-class areas, survived the earthquake and fire, and were becoming increasingly inhabited by tenants. Still, many indications of the middle-class nature of the area survived. Residents of German stock outnumbered those of Irish descent in both

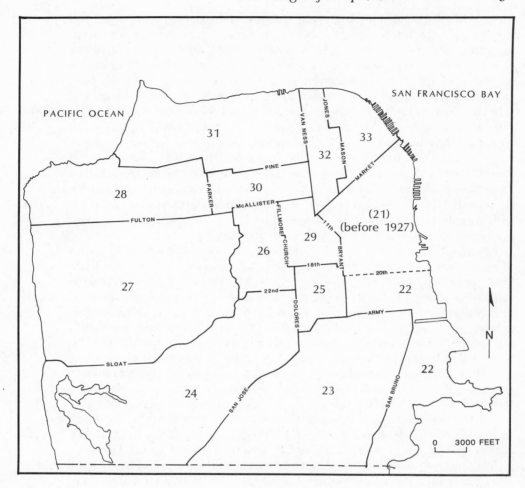

Map 3.   Assembly District Boundaries, 1912–1931

districts, and more than two-thirds of the housing stock fell into middle or upper value ranges. Districts 27 and 28, the Sunset and Richmond areas, newer middle-class suburbs, developed for the most part after 1906. Some parts of these two districts developed primarily because of the prior construction of Municipal Railway lines and tunnels. Half of the families there owned their own homes, and nearly half the homes fell into upper ranges in value. Both districts included upper-class enclaves—Forest Hill in district 27 and Sea Cliff in district 28. These four districts usually fell somewhere between the extremes of the labor districts and Pacific Heights in their voting behavior, with the older areas (26 and 30) usually somewhat closer to the patterns of the labor districts, and the newer areas (27 and 28) closer to Pacific Heights.

Districts 32 and 33, located downtown, usually behaved similarly on policy issues but showed somewhat greater diversity on candidates. District 32 included Nob Hill and the high-rent apartment district to its north, as well as the many apartment houses north of the Civic Center. Ninety percent of the housing stock was of middle or upper ranges, and 87 percent of the residents were over twenty-one years of age (compared with 75 percent citywide). Many of these apartment dwellers found employment in white-collar occupations in the downtown area. District 33 included the central business district, home to some businessmen and related clericals and professionals, but also included the Tenderloin (heart of McDonough's vice empire), Chinatown, and the Italian areas of North Beach. Nearly one of five residents had been born in Italy, and more than 30 percent were of Asian descent. Most of the housing stock fell into lower value ranges. District 33 behaved politically like district 32, rather than like a working-class district, perhaps because of very low rates of political participation. In 1931, with Angelo Rossi running for mayor, only 15 percent of the adults voted in district 33, compared with 32 percent citywide.[59]

In the factious and personality-oriented politics of the 1920s, as issues of public ownership criss-crossed with struggles to control the local Republican party, a private association called the San Francisco Bureau of Governmental Research (BGR) emerged as a major force representing the business community. Describing itself as "an incorporated nonpartisan citizens' agency to study public business, cooperate with officials and specifically work for economy and efficiency in municipal affairs," the BGR received the lion's share of its financial support from the Chamber of Commerce. The BGR grew out of an effort by the Real Estate Board's Tax Committee in 1916, when that group invited experts from the Bureau of Municipal Research of New York City to survey the structure of San Francisco government. As this survey progressed, a group of San Francisco businessmen incorporated the BGR in October 1916 as a local adjunct to the efforts of the New Yorkers. Thereafter, the BGR became a fixture in local politics, publishing a journal, *The City*, devoted to municipal issues. The Real Estate Board remained prominent in the leadership of the BGR, with Bruce Cornwall of Coldwell, Cornwall, and Banker serving as chairman of the board of trustees until the mid-1920s. His partner, Colbert Coldwell (a leader of the Chamber of Commerce and of the Industrial Association) was an officer of the group throughout the 1920s and early 1930s. Others prominent in the leadership of the BGR included E. Clarence Holmes of Holmes Investment Company, Daniel Koshland of Levi Strauss, and John H. McCallum of McCallum Lumber. William H. Crocker served on the board of trustees through the 1920s and early 1930s, and Herbert Fleishhacker served on the board briefly.[60]

Throughout the 1920s, the BGR, through *The City*, provided elaborate collections of data and analysis on a wide range of city issues, but certain issues stand forth as most prominent. The streetcar and water systems, of course, took a prominent place. In both instances, the BGR favored actions to foster urban development by the construction of new streetcar lines (whether by private or public capital) and creation of an adequate water supply. Demand for salary standardization became a recurring theme: "Development of equitable and impartial salary and wage fixing procedure, centralized for the whole municipal personnel, on a basis that will remove this question from the field of politics and place it on an equitable fact-basis for the whole service." The BGR linked its concern for low taxes to its criticism of the decentralized and "political" nature of municipal decision making. From time to time, the bureau advocated regional planning efforts and municipal ownership of garbage collection and disposal, presented extensive information on the political and engineering problems involved in construction of a bay bridge, and favored a charter amendment to shift zoning decisions from the supervisors to a commission appointed by the mayor.[61]

Charter Revision Efforts, 1916–1930. Throughout the period from 1916 to 1930, the BGR's most prominent objective remained a restructuring of "our illogical form of government." New York's Bureau of Municipal Research, in its 1916 *Report,* had recommended changes in city government

> so as (1) to make the mayor definitely responsible for exercising executive leadership; (2) to make the board of supervisors solely a legislative and reviewing body, which shall not exercise any administrative functions; and (3) to make both the mayor and the supervisors readily responsible to the people.

The supervisors, the *Report* emphasized, should "have no responsibility for leadership." The assumptions behind these recommendations carried into the 1920s the "progressive" philosophy of the 1890s:

> Any charter which is adapted to the successful management of a corporate enterprise, whether public or private, must contain provision for responsible leadership. . . . The only leadership which can be made effective is executive leadership. . . . No successfully managed organization which has an executive, as distinguished from its board of trustees or council of representatives, places on the members of the board responsibility for preparing and submitting plans.

Espousal of a corporate form of decision making, with policy making the prerogative of the president (mayor) and with the board of directors (supervisors) limited to scrutiny of executive initiatives, became a staple of BGR efforts over the next decade and a half. Although the precise features of the plan changed somewhat from time to time, the BGR remained at the center of attempts to reorganize the city government, to make it more "logical," that is, more like a business corporation.[62]

The *Report* came on the eve of American entry into the war, but the BGR revived interest in structural reform in 1921 by promoting a conference and involving a wide range of organizations, including the American Legion, Chamber of Commerce, and Labor Council. The Commonwealth Club provided a major impetus for the conference. The major speaker, Professor Edwin A. Cottrell of Stanford University, focused on the advantages of the then-popular city manager form of urban government. Meetings following the conference took up various aspects of city government and produced a series of recommendations including greater centralization, reduction of the authority of the supervisors, and adoption of the city manager plan. The Chamber of Commerce developed some limited interest in these developments, apparently under BGR prodding, but no further effort for extensive charter revision took hold until the late 1920s.[63]

Milton Marks, chairman of the 1921 Commonwealth Club conference, won a seat on the Board of Supervisors in 1925 and, as chairman of the Judiciary Committee, secured a board resolution in January 1928 to hold hearings to determine if the charter required fundamental change. The BGR, one of the many groups testifying, recommended adoption of the city manager form of organization as "the nearest counterpart in government to the best form and practice in private business, commerce and industry in this country." Describing the city as "one of the half-dozen largest corporate enterprises in the State," the BGR acknowledged that the city "probably has a wider diversity of functions than any private corporation in the State." The BGR urged a simplified scheme of government in which only the mayor, supervisors, and district attorney would stand for election, and most administrative responsibility would rest with the city manager. The BGR also called for centralization of utility management under an independent commission, creation of a city planning commission to make zoning decisions independently of the supervisors, a centralized pension system under an independent commission, and a centralized budget procedure under the city manager. Thirty-two charter amendments were submitted to the voters in 1928, including creation of a public utilities commission, a city planning commission (with the powers proposed by the BGR), and a War Memorial Board to oversee the as-yet-unbuilt music and art buildings. While the latter two were approved, the first was not.[64]

In the spring of 1930, the BGR created the San Francisco Charter Revision Committee (CRC), with the director of the BGR as the committee's secretary. The committee undertook charter revision in a manner reminiscent of the activities of the Committee of 100 in 1897, but opposition soon arose from supervisor Franck Havenner (closely associated with the Johnson wing of the Republican party, with labor, and with the municipal ownership advocates), the Labor Council and Building Trades Council, and the Hearst papers. The *Examiner* blasted the CRC as an attempt "to grab control of the city government," and others charged it with desiring to restrict municipal ownership and to implement a city manager. CRC advocates charged that the only other method of wholesale charter amendment— election of a Board of Freeholders—would mean that politicians would be in charge of charter reform, that the cost would be prohibitive, and that proceedings would be open to any number of wild theorists and cranks. On June 23, the same day the CRC voted in favor of a city manager plan, the Board of Supervisors resolved to elect a Board of Freeholders in August, at the same time as party primaries.[65]

Writing a New Charter, 1930–1931. Fifty-three candidates sought election to the Board of Freeholders, and of the fifteen successful, six had been part of the CRC, and one had also served as president of the BGR. Four freeholders carried the endorsement of the Labor Council, including two who had been on the CRC. Of the other two successful Labor Council endorsees, one was secretary of the Building Trades Council; the other had been president of the Labor Council but had lost that position in 1917 for his opposition to the campaign to free Tom Mooney. One of the freeholders, the sheriff's attorney, had strong support from city employees. In all, the fifteen included seven businessmen, six lawyers, one educator (owner of a private school), and one trade union official. There were no women, and all fifteen males were white. One study of the charter characterized the election of freeholders as "dominated by the conservative, propertied interests of the City," and the characterization seems an apt one.[66]

The new charter was ready for a public vote in March 1931, and it passed with 56 percent of the vote. It drew the opposition of the *Monitor,* the official newspaper of the archdiocese, because key officials were appointed rather than elected. The Labor Council strongly opposed it for similar reasons, and also because of limitations on city employees as well. City employees, both those in the Labor Council (firefighters and teachers) and those organized separately, opposed the charter because it restricted both their right to seek elective office and also their right to participate in municipal campaigns at all, a provision motivated perhaps by the rumors of a Rolph-Reardon "machine" among employees of the Public Works Department.[67]

Voters divided in their reaction to the new charter along the same axis that characterized most voting behavior of the period. The vote in favor of the charter, by assembly district, stood as follows:

District	Percentage
22	51.6
23	47.5
24	50.2
25	46.1
29	51.2
26	51.9
30	55.9
27	57.8
28	61.4
33	58.0
32	66.2
31	70.0

Although three labor districts returned slight margins in favor, the overall vote of the five was opposed, 49 percent to 51 percent.[68]

The Charter of 1932. The charter that was adopted with strong approval from the city's upper- and middle-class areas incorporated many of the proposals advocated by the BGR and similar business groups over the previous decade. Described as a cross between the strong mayor and city manager approaches to city government, the charter created two new positions, chief administrative officer and controller. These two included many of the duties—although not all—typically performed by a city manager. The chief administrative officer (CAO), to be appointed by the mayor, served for unlimited tenure subject only to suspension by the mayor, recall by the voters, or removal by two-thirds of the supervisors. The CAO supervised a wide range of city activities formerly under the mayor or under independently elected officials: the coroner, the department of public finance and records (including the public administrator, county clerk, registrar, recorder, and tax collector), the city purchaser, property director, director of public works (sewers, streets, building maintenance, and building inspection), the health department (including hospitals), the welfare director, and others. The controller became chief fiscal officer of the city, responsible for all funds, financial reporting, receipts, and disbursements; the controller also became responsible for the compilation of a centralized city budget, based on data from the CAO and other department heads. The mayor could cut any item or increase most items in this budget. When presented by the mayor to the supervisors, that body might cut any item but could not increase any items except for capital expenditures or public improvements. The mayor retained an item veto.[69]

Although the position of mayor under the new charter was described as a continuation of the strong mayor approach of the previous charter, in fact the mayor's office lost some of its power. The mayor, to be certain, had the power to appoint the CAO, but only when a vacancy occurred, which might well not happen during any given four-year term. The mayor was also to appoint members of the dozen or so policy-making commissions but could not remove commission members held over from previous administrations. Pay for the mayor was to be less than that of the CAO. Where the mayor formerly presided over the Board of Supervisors, the new charter allowed the board to select its own president. The number of supervisors was cut from eighteen to eleven, to be elected at large (as in the previous charter). The supervisors and the mayor were prohibited from involving themselves in any fashion with administrative services except for inquiry. This provision, designed to focus sole authority and responsibility in the various executive officers and commissions, contained a long list of expressly prohibited actions and defined violation of its provisions as grounds for removal from office.[70]

The old charter provided for twenty-one boards and commissions, some self-perpetuating, most appointed by the mayor, nearly all subject to control by the supervisors through their authority over budget making, appropriations, and auditing. Three of the twenty-one were abolished by the new charter, although one became an advisory board reporting to the CAO. The library board changed from self-perpetuating to appointive, but three others maintained their self-perpetuating nature. Thirteen boards remained essentially unchanged, except for occasional additions or deletions of a member; both the Board of Education and the War Memorial Board retained their previous peculiarities. Three new boards were created, for art, permit appeals, and public utilities. The BGR and others had long advocated creation of a public utilities commission, claiming that "under the old charter, responsibility for the management and the operation of city-owned utilities is divided between the board of public works and the board of supervisors." O'Shaughnessy had stepped into that situation to become de facto head of both Hetch Hetchy and the Municipal Railway. O'Shaughnessy's supporters claimed that some of the charter provisions had as their purpose deposing the city engineer, and that occurred immediately upon implementation of the new charter. O'Shaughnessy became only a consulting engineer, consulted by no one but his old friends. The Art Commission resulted from the initiative of the Commonwealth Club (see Chapter 5). The charter also provided for a harbor commission should the state ever relinquish control of the city's waterfront. With the exception of the three self-perpetuating boards, the school board, and the War Memorial Board, members of all other boards and commissions were to serve for overlapping terms of four years each. Thus, an incoming mayor faced a formidable array of policy-making bodies, most beyond his reach and most explicitly beyond the over-sight of either mayor or supervisors. Overruling a board was purposefully difficult, although not impossible.[71]

The charter of 1932 emerged from a decade and a half of discussion. By the time the freeholders met, the city's business community—led by the BGR—had developed a set of objectives aimed at restructuring city gov-ernment along the lines of corporate enterprise. Central to these objectives were the need for expert and nonpolitical planning, centralization of exec-utive decision making, and limitation of the supervisors to the approval or disapproval of executive initiatives. However, throughout the period, the office of mayor was itself being as thoroughly redefined by Rolph as the presidency would soon be transformed by Franklin Roosevelt. From the war onward, Rolph exercised less and less executive leadership, increas-ingly left administrative duties to others, often allowed the chair of the Finance Committee to function as acting mayor, and preferred leading parades and hosting starlets.

Throughout the 1920s, political campaigns rarely focused on issue dif-ferences between candidates (with a few exceptions) but consisted instead of rhetoric suggesting that the city was in dire danger of returning to the days of Ruef and Schmitz. Newspapers, at election time, ran stories recount-ing the graft prosecution findings. In 1927, Sheriff Tom Finn was the object of a clumsy attempt at entrapment. A few years before, former mayor Patrick McCarthy was revealed to have received $10,000 from Pacific Gas and Elec-tric in return for his opposition to a state proposition that the utility deemed harmful; it led, finally, to his removal from the leadership of the Building Trades Council. Accusations that Rolph (or any of a number of others) owed favors to the McDonough brothers were common political fare. This recur-ring focus on the potential for corruption suggested to many that additional safeguards were needed to prevent future imprecations.[72]

The result of these converging patterns was a charter that imposed numerous barriers to corruption, shifted administrative duties away from the mayor to a nonpolitical expert manager, limited the mayor to making appointments and adjusting the budget (and leading parades and greeting celebrities), removed much of city government from the immediate over-sight of elected officials in an effort to remove it from politics, and reduced the number of elected officials but continued the existence of numerous policy-making boards and commissions independent of both mayor and supervisors. Frederick Wirt has described the charter as creating "fractionated decision making," leading to "the lack of decision making," but the new charter did not cause decision making to fractionate, nor did it reduce policy making to incrementalism. Both patterns can be found throughout the decade of the 1920s. Although the new charter did not initiate these patterns, it contained nothing to counteract them and much to perpetuate them.[73]

End of the Rolph Era. James Rolph left the mayor's office while the freeholders were still in the midst of their work. He had won the Republican nomination for governor in the 1930 primary, defeating the progressive incumbent C. C. Young, and went on to an easy victory in November, winning 86 percent of the vote of his own city and 72 percent statewide.

The right to fill the vacancy in the mayoralty rested with the Board of Supervisors. The only other time the supervisors had exercised this power under the charter was in 1907 when the graft prosecution had dictated that they choose an outsider, Edward Taylor. In 1931, however, the supervisors made it clear that they intended to elevate one of their own. Several were interested, but Angelo Rossi soon emerged as the leading candidate. Rossi was, in many ways, cut from the same pattern as Rolph. Successful businessman, long-time active member and officer of the Downtown Association, he won election to the Board of Supervisors in 1921, was defeated for reelection in 1925, but came back to win again in 1929 with the highest vote of any candidate. He became chairman of the Finance Committee, the most powerful position on the board, in 1930. Rolph had followed his usual practice of designating the Finance Committee chairman as acting mayor during his many absences in 1930, and he soon made clear his preference that Rossi fill the mayoralty on a permanent basis. Rossi drew opposition from a number of supervisors, especially those with labor endorsements and those who saw themselves as candidates. No anti-Rossi coalition emerged, however, especially after Tom Finn joined the Rossi camp. Rossi won by fourteen to two, with one supervisor absent and with Rossi himself not voting. In office, Rossi quickly established himself as a carbon copy of his predecessor—always nattily dressed, with a fresh boutonniere, an inveterate booster of San Francisco, but more constitutional monarch than a prime minister.[74]

□   □   □

When Rolph first took the oath of office in 1912, he did so in a city without a city hall, a city still rebuilding from the disaster of 1906, a city divided over the proper role of unions and the political power of labor, a city in which the business community was just emerging from disputes over planning and the graft prosecution. Within a short time, Rolph initiated construction of a magnificent city hall and Civic Center, inaugurated the nation's first municipally owned streetcar system, launched the Hetch Hetchy project, and presided over the Panama Pacific International Exposition. While Rolph was very much at the center of all these, as initiator or energetic booster, his drive and enthusiasm failed to survive the Preparedness Day parade bombing, the war, and the labor strife that came in its wake.

In the absence of both mayoral leadership and political parties, city voters polarized between business and labor. Rolph found himself unable to accomplish his ideal of amicable labor relations achieved through collective bargaining, and the Industrial Association moved to cripple once-powerful unions. As Rolph behaved more and more like a chairman of the board rather than a corporation president, the movement to create a city manager grew, guided by the Bureau for Governmental Research. The bureau, the Industrial Association, the Panama Pacific International Exposition, and—of course—the Chamber of Commerce strongly expressed the unity and determination of the business community. While the business community never completely dominated city government, the paralysis of city government over key issues of municipal ownership not only produced outcomes acceptable to the business community but often created them.

Chapter 9

Conclusion: Politics, Power, and Urban Development in San Francisco

San Francisco from the end of the Civil War to the Great Depression of the 1930s provides a rewarding setting for the study of political decision making. In this study, as in studies of other American cities conducted during the past two decades, the central question concerns the nature of power. Is power concentrated or dispersed? Who wields power and for what purposes? Max Weber's approach has proven consistently useful, for he defined power as the ability of an individual or group to achieve their goals in the arena of public decision making even though others seek to block them or to accomplish other objectives.[1]

Because access to resources is crucial to the ability to succeed in politics, most studies of urban decision making have identified the social and economic resources held by individuals or groups in the community. This study described San Francisco's economic, social, and cultural institutions and located significant individuals and groups within this institutional context. Then it examined their impact on the structure, functioning, and development of city government. Individuals and groups use resources in a variety of institutional decision-making arenas. Governmental decisions, however, typically involve the largest number and widest range of participants, and governmental decisions usually carry far-reaching consequences. This study has focused on key political episodes as a means of understanding the interaction of individuals and groups and, most important, of understanding the power relationships among them.

APPROACHES TO THE STUDY OF POWER

The analysis of resources is an important element in understanding power relationships, but resources alone do not determine the outcome of the decision-making process. Besides possessing political resources, individuals and groups must use them to accomplish particular ends. At least a few of San Francisco's socioeconomic elite fit the classic example of the wealthy patrician who disdains politics in favor of cultural pursuits and who therefore has little or no actual political power despite a great potential for power. While some Pacific Heights aristocrats did eschew politics, their continued ability to do so stemmed from the close and continued political involvement of others of their social class. In San Francisco, no class with resources to engage in politics (and hence with resources to protect) disengaged from politics as a group.

San Francisco provides verification of long-standing observations that resources may take forms other than wealth, prestige, and control of economic institutions and that economic resources do not automatically produce power. From 1901 onward, unions successfully mobilized voters and thereby secured a sympathetic ear, and sometimes a supporting hand, in city hall. San Francisco also contained individuals who failed to translate wealth into political power. Rudolph Spreckels experienced a brief moment in the sun when he underwrote the graft prosecution, but shortly afterward he failed to rouse the public against Rolph's compromise with the United Railroads. Similarly, some San Francisco organizations failed to convert political power into the achievement of objectives outside the realm of local politics. For example, throughout the 1920s the Building Trades Council often counted a majority of the Board of Supervisors among its friends, but it could not use this political influence to regain union recognition. An assessment of the relative access to a variety of political resources held by participants in the decision-making process is vital for an understanding of the outcome of that process, but a mere measuring of resources does not explain who held power, the structure of power, and the uses of power.

Another approach to understanding power requires determination of the beneficiaries of public decision making. Some decisions lend themselves easily to this approach. When the struggle over Hetch Hetchy electrical power ended, the beneficiary was evident; no one could doubt the political power of Pacific Gas and Electric. The outcome of the graft prosecution produced a clear consensus as to those who had *not* benefited, although a list of beneficiaries might include a disparate array of upper-class good government advocates, antiunion employers, a few politically ambitious lawyers, and—perhaps—taxpayers. This difficulty in identifying beneficiaries points to the central problem of the "benefits" approach: the more complex the issue, the more numerous and disparate the beneficiaries. *Major* decisions, almost by definition, are or become complex, often stretching over a long period of time and involving a variety of participants, many of whom might be identified as receiving *some* benefit. For example, the creation of the Municipal Railway and the boring of the streetcar tunnels benefited commuters (many of them middle- and upper-income homeowners), downtown retail store owners (whose customers found it easier to shop), union labor (who built the lines and staffed the streetcars), real estate agents and developers (who viewed the opening of new lines and tunnels as unparalleled opportunities for showing choice building sites), and construction contractors and building trades craftsmen (who rapidly erected new neighborhoods along the tracks). A list of those benefiting from the construction of the Opera House and Veterans' Building is similarly wide-ranging: musicians and artists, opera-goers and music lovers, art museum patrons, veterans' organizations, the hotel and restaurant industry (which catered to the consumers of culture), construction contractors and building trades craftsmen, and those owning real estate or businesses in the vicinity of the Civic Center. Calculating the benefits from decision making can contribute to the analysis of power, but these two examples make it clear that some major decisions—indeed, many major decisions—do not lend themselves to easy determination of beneficiaries.

A third approach to the study of power is to examine the process of decision making and to draw conclusions regarding the effectiveness of the participants. Carl Harris, in his study of Birmingham, Alabama, and David Hammack, in his study of New York City, are among those who have examined the process of decision making.[2] This study, too, has sought to illuminate power relationships by studying episodes of public decision making. Its focus has been on highly visible and controversial decisions rather than on the rarely publicized decisions on more routine municipal functions, although our examination has been informed by Terrence McDonald's careful study of San Francisco municipal expenditures.[3] Study of the process necessarily involves consideration of the socioeconomic background of the participants, their political resources, and their motivation (and, thus, what they anticipated as benefits).

MODELS OF URBAN DECISION MAKING

The two classic models of the urban decision-making process remain those of Floyd Hunter, whose study of Atlanta revealed an elite of business leaders who dominated decision making in every significant arena, and Robert Dahl, who found in New Haven a pluralistic process. Dahl described many citizen groups moving into and out of the decision-making process depending on the issue, and he concluded that government decisions emerged from compromise among concerned interest groups rather than from the pronouncements of an elite.[4] Hammack's 1982 study of New York City presents a fragmented elite model, which acknowledges the elite character of decision making but denies the existence of a single, unified power structure.[5] Hammack's conclusions suggest a model incorporating elements from both Hunter's Atlanta and Dahl's New Haven, in which decisions emerge from interaction and compromise among various elite groups.

Roger Lotchin's studies of San Francisco and other Pacific Coast cities in the 1920s and 1930s suggest still a fourth model of decision making. Lotchin argued that the most important single factor in San Francisco politics and civic affairs was a Darwinian competition among West Coast cities, a struggle so intense as to create in San Francisco a unity that transcended intraurban differences in the common cause of besting Los Angeles. Lotchin's model suggests that leaders of business, unions, and civic affairs set aside their differences or compromised readily in the face of outside competition for the commercial primacy of the Pacific Slope, with the specter of decline and decay hovering over them should they fail.[6]

While Lotchin correctly points to competitiveness as an element making for civic unity, there were other powerful factors pushing in contrary directions. When San Francisco business leaders found competition with Los Angeles to be a convenient tocsin, they sounded it; when they found investment opportunities there, they put down their cash without a pang of conscience. The largest single developer in San Diego was a San Franciscan, John Spreckels. San Francisco's Bank of Italy provided important financing for the development of Hollywood's film industry. Standard Oil of California, the Southern Pacific Company, and other companies with corporate headquarters in San Francisco all invested heavily in southern California. Bay Area business leaders worked closely with their Los Angeles counterparts in a wide range of endeavors including the state Chamber of Commerce, the state Republican party, and various state commissions.[7] Similarly, in 1910–1911 Bay Area unions launched an ambitious drive to organize their counterparts south of the Tehachapi mountains. Although the bombing of the *Los Angeles Times* brought that effort to a halt, statewide labor organizations, notably the California State Federation of Labor and the State Building Trades Council, continued to provide forums for discussing common concerns and for coordinating activities.[8] Political struggles within San Francisco, for example, those over union organizing, Hetch Hetchy electricity, and the city charter, raged with hardly a suggestion of a united front against the *Angeleños*.

San Francisco politics after 1916 reveal a polarized pattern that fits none of the four models. A highly unified business community stood at one pole, arrayed against a unified labor force at the other. Voting behavior clearly illustrates these class divisions, with the South of Market area consistently expressing views directly contrary to the political attitudes of Pacific Heights. Other neighborhoods ranged between these poles, in proportion to their residents' tendencies to identify with business or labor.

BUSINESS UNITY

The sense of unity displayed by the city's business community evolved in a propitious setting. To an extent true only of New York among the nation's major cities, San Francisco enjoyed economic autonomy. Few distant corporations played a major role in the city until early in the twentieth century. Nearly all of the city's businesses were owned and operated by San Franciscans, whose interests ranged from Alaskan fisheries to Hawaiian sugar plantations, from Mexican mining operations to hydroelectric power plants in the Sierra Nevada, from logging in Washington to San Joaquin valley wheat fields. They operated on an imperial scale, but most of their corporate boardrooms were within a few blocks of one another. They ate lunch in the same Financial District restaurants or in exclusive club rooms, saw each other regularly at the meetings of corporate and civic boards, worshipped in a few prestigious churches and synagogues, and watched fondly as their children married the children of friends.

Membership on the same corporate and civic boards and in the same exclusive clubs did not automatically produce unity among the city's business leaders. Unity emerged slowly, beginning with efforts at improving transportation in the 1890s. The earthquake and fire of 1906 forged a unity born of shared adversity, although efforts for citywide planning fell victim to squabbling and to the desire to rebuild as quickly as possible. The graft prosecution unified the business community so long as the focus of the prosecution remained on Union Labor party supervisors who had received bribes; when the attention shifted to the corporate officers who had offered bribes, the business community divided sharply.

The Panama Pacific International Exposition went far to develop civic unity, especially within the business community; its board of directors was selected to represent all possible points of view, and Charles Moore became president because he was acceptable to both sides of the graft prosecution controversy. The PPIE provided an organizing model soon applied elsewhere; the launching of the Law and Order Committee in 1916 was a carbon copy of PPIE mass meetings and million-dollar subscription drives. By the 1920s, the San Francisco business community had produced a number of institutional expressions of its unity. The Industrial Association served as the business community's arm for labor relations. The Bureau of Governmental Research provided its liaison to city government. The Commonwealth Club offered a forum for public presentation of proposals. The Chamber of Commerce brought together nearly all the city's business leaders in support of growth and development. The Republican party—or, more properly, the wing led by William H. Crocker, Milton Esberg, and Wallace Alexander—provided focus for state and national politics.

The city's business community continued to exhibit differences and disagreements. Anti-Semitism kept Jewish business leaders from membership in the Pacific Union Club and a few other prestigious organizations. Personal animosities between individuals produced anecdotes still chuckled over by the participants' grandchildren. In the teens and twenties, however, individual feuds and institutionalized anti-Semitism did little to impede the momentum of civic unity. Bitter personal enemies, supporters and opponents of the graft prosecution, Jews and Pacific Union members, all joined in planning for the PPIE and served together on its board. Nearly all prominent business leaders celebrated the merger of the city's leading commercial organizations in 1911 by joining the Chamber of Commerce and making it, for a time, the largest in the nation. Many of them continued that cooperation into the Law and Order Committee of 1916 and the Industrial Association after 1921, and few voiced opposition to the policy recommendations of the Bureau of Governmental Research.

LABOR SOLIDARITY

San Francisco's unions, and its blue-collar families more generally, achieved a high degree of unity earlier than the business community. Robert Knight concluded his exhaustive study of San Francisco labor from 1900 to 1918 by citing sources of strength for unionization: the traditions and influences of earlier years, the composition of the local labor force, the structure of the economy and the city's isolation, the reluctance of labor leaders to push too far or too fast, the willingness of business leaders to seek accommodation rather than conflict, and the political potency of the working-class vote. Lucile Eaves in 1910 and Alexander Saxton in 1971 both proposed another major element: the unifying influence on white workers of two decades of anti-Chinese agitation. Saxton seemed to suggest that the unity of white labor could not have been possible without this racist experience, and Eaves anticipated his analysis by six decades: "Much of the present strength of the California labor movement is due to the sense of common interests, and the habit of unified action which were acquired in this great campaign." Eaves added, however, that "much additional discipline was necessary before it was possible to weld the differing groups into the effective central organizations of the present time."[9] The emergence of effective central bodies, as well as the development of strong local unions, came well after the zenith of anti-Chinese agitation and owned more to the experience gained in opposing employer associations in the 1890s, and again in 1901 and after, than to the organizational legacy of racism.

Union strength emerged from workers' neighborhoods as well as from confrontation between organized labor and employers. By the teens, both the Labor Council and the Building Trades Council had their own buildings, located near where the major South of Market thoroughfares curved south to become the major streets of the Mission District; both buildings contained ample office space for local unions as well as rooms on the ground floor for socializing. Unions sponsored picnics and other social affairs and formed a source of social life as well as work-site organization. Life in the South of Market and Mission districts also included churches, ethnic associations, sporting events, and political clubs. Owners of small businesses in working-class neighborhoods usually sided with their patrons, with whom they often socialized and worshipped. A handful of the city's most prominent businessmen could also be found among labor sympathizers even in the dark days of the Industrial Association.

As was true of the business community, workers and their organizations harbored antagonisms affecting both individuals and groups. P. H. McCarthy held his Building Trades unions at arm's length from the more heterogeneous Labor Council, sailors waged jurisdictional battles with longshoremen, and anti-Semitism occasionally surfaced in Labor Council meetings. Nonetheless, to a degree unusual in American cities, repeated conflict with employer associations fostered a unity that strengthened central bodies and individual unions and gave birth to the Union Labor party. The party, in turn, provided dramatic evidence of the political clout of unions and allowed the use of city government to support organizing efforts. Throughout the period after 1901, San Francisco labor promoted unity through the columns of its two major weekly newspapers, the Labor Council's *Labor Clarion* and the Building Trades Council's *Organized Labor.* Through those papers, union members learned of the need for solidarity with workers throughout the nation as well as elsewhere in the city; they also learned lessons of cooperation among all white workers, across the lines of ethnicity. Locals, central bodies, the labor press, and the Union Labor party formed the major institutions defining labor unity; they were bolstered by the efforts of sympathizers such as Peter Yorke and his *Leader.*

ETHNICITY AND CLASS

Among both business and labor, feelings of class unity submerged ethnic differences. Unlike eastern cities, no white group found itself excluded from the ladder of economic and social mobility. The Irish dominated trade-union leadership, but they also presided over major banks and manufacturing firms. Sons of Erin took prominent political roles of the most diverse sort: James Fair, Comstock silver king and U.S. senator from Nevada; Denis Kearney, sandlot rabble-rouser; Christopher Buckley, saloonkeeper and Democratic boss extraordinaire; Martin Kelly, Buckley's Republican counterpart in the 1890s; James Phelan, heir to a banking fortune, mayor, U.S. senator; Patrick McCarthy, building trades union leader and mayor. During the 1920s, Tim Finn led the progressive wing of the city's Republican party, the McDonough brothers operated within the Republicans' conservative wing, and Timothy Reardon was the acknowledged leader of the city's tiny band of Democrats.

Other ethnic groups exhibited a similar diversity. Jewish political figures included Max Popper, Democratic ally of Phelan in the 1890s; Adolph Sutro, bibliophile and Populist mayor; Julius Kahn, Republican stalwart as assemblyman and congressman; Abraham Ruef, *éminence grise* of the Union Labor party; Hugo Ernst, socialist and leader of the culinary unions; Milton Esberg and Herbert Fleishhacker, leaders of the conservative faction of the Republican party in the 1920s. Political figures of German descent included both Eugene Schmitz, union leader, mayor, and supervisor; and Rudolph Spreckels, the progressive gadfly who paid the bill for the graft prosecution that brought about Schmitz's downfall. Italians who began to achieve political prominence in the 1920s included Alfred Roncovieri, member of the Musicians' Union, superintendent of schools, and supervisor; Angelo Rossi, businessman, leader of the Downtown Association, and moderate-to-conservative supervisor and mayor; and A. P. Giannini, most prominent banker on the West Coast and occasional supporter of progressive Republicans. Protestants of old-stock American descent included conservative Republican magnates such as Crocker and Alexander, but also Fremont Older, the crusading editor; Isaac Kalloch, Baptist preacher and Workingmen's party mayor; and the Hearsts, father and son, strong advocates of the Democratic party and, in the son's case, of labor causes.

San Francisco prided itself on its tradition of tolerance for all, although the tradition included only white groups. Immigrants and their children remained largely immune to the wave of nativism that swept the nation in the late nineteenth century. The American Protective Association's anti-Catholicism gained few converts in a city predominantly Catholic and Jewish. Prohibition and other varieties of moral reform also found few supporters. In 1914, when California voted on Prohibition, 83 percent of San Francisco voters said no. This rejection of Prohibition showed no ethnically distinctive patterns. Assembly districts south of Market Street and in the Mission District with large proportions of Irish Catholics, staunchly pro-labor in their voting behavior, varied from 16 to 21 percent in favor of Prohibition; middle-class districts ranged from 17 to 19 percent, with no major differences between German Jewish areas and those more ethnically mixed; wealthy Pacific Heights (where old-stock Protestants were dispro-portionately represented) and the North Beach–Tenderloin area (with Italians most prominent) registered the lowest levels of support, 15 and 10 percent, respectively. A similar pattern appeared in a vote on a state nui-sance abatement proposition aimed at the brothels of the Barbary Coast. In other parts of the nation, sentiment on Prohibition and moral reform reflected underlying ethnocultural cleavages and proved powerful predic-tors of voting behavior; San Francisco voters' rejection of proposals for moral reform illustrates the city's reputation for toleration among white ethnic groups and underscores the preeminence of economic class as the primary determinant of political behavior.

EVOLUTION OF POLITICAL DECISION MAKING

San Francisco's polarized politics emerged from the fiery crucible of labor conflict in the 1890s and the violent waterfront strike of 1901. Patterns of political decision making regarding urban development evolved more grad-ually. Six major periods may be discerned, each different in significant ways from the period before and after:
1. 1856 to 1877, merchant dominance
2. 1877 to 1880, the Workingmen's party episode
3. 1880 to 1890, the era of Christopher Buckley
4. 1890 to 1901, heyday of the Democratic reformers
5. 1901 to 1911, the Union Labor period
6. 1911 to 1931, the era of James Rolph
While each of these periods has been described in detail already, a restate-ment of some of the central characteristics of each may help to indicate both the relationships between them and the changing relationships between municipal government and patterns of urban development.

Merchant Dominance. For twenty years after the Vigilance Committee of 1856, the nature of municipal policy was shaped by two influences: the strict limitations of the Consolidation Act and the political dominance of the city's merchants. Of the six mayors elected by the People's party and its successor, the Taxpayers' party, five were merchants and one was a lawyer.[10] The era was one of minimal government by any criterion. City government remained almost entirely in the hands of the political heirs of the vigilantes. Office-holders stressed their honesty and parsimony, and key decisions about urban development took place almost entirely outside the arena of city govern-ment. The emergence of a central business district north of Market Street and an area of light manufacturing south of Market resulted from decisions made by entrepreneurs such as William Ralston rather than through any exercise of the municipal polity.

The merchant politicos limited city government to the protection of life and property through police and fire departments, provision of an educational system (usually overcrowded and understaffed), maintenance of the streets (72 percent of the streets remained unpaved in 1880, another 11 percent were covered only with crushed stone, and few streets had gutters), construction of sewers (one-quarter of the city's houses were still not connected to a sewer in 1880), and the reserving of park lands (although the city's larger parks remained largely undeveloped until late in the nineteenth century). Private companies and individuals performed other essential services, typically through a franchise from the city, including provision of water and gas, collection of garbage and night soil, rendering, and street transportation.[11]

Although the six People's party mayors and the two Democratic party mayors of this period approached the role of city government similarly, they drew their support from quite different parts of the electorate. The People's party strength came in upper-class and middle-class sections of the city, areas with disproportionate numbers of old stock and Germans, Protestants and Jews. Democrats, by contrast, ran most strongly in working-class areas of the city, with disproportionate numbers of Irish and Catholics. The Democrats of San Francisco, in short, drew their support from the same ethnic and economic groups who provided the bulk of Democratic support in Boston or New York, in Illinois or Nebraska. Although voters divided in their party allegiances along lines of ethnicity and class, leaders of the two parties showed little difference in their attitudes toward the highly limited role of city government.

The Workingmen's Party. The Workingmen's party episode did nothing to change the role of city government, but it did demonstrate the potential for a class-based political movement. Support for the party followed the general pattern of support for the Democrats, but with support more pronounced in lowest income levels and less so at higher income levels. While Workingmen's party support had some ethnic dimensions, especially among the Irish, a comparison of the support for WPC and Democratic candidates indicates the extent to which Democratic support was moderated at both economic extremes by cross-cutting effects of ethnicity and class. The Workingmen's party and Kearney sharpened political class lines by simple-minded appeals based on racism and opposition to the wealth epitomized by Nob Hill. Beyond such antagonisms, the party offered no political program, neither one aimed at using city government to assist the depression-wracked WPC constituency nor one that differed in any particular from the limited role previously subscribed to by all major political leaders. The party, in sum, represented a demonstration of working-class political power bereft of any political agenda.

Buckley's Decade. At the end of Kalloch's term as mayor (1879–1881), the patterns of the 1870s resumed, with merchants in the mayor's office during four of the next five terms. Throughout most of the 1880s, as control of the dominant Democratic party rested with Christopher Buckley, he and the officeholders of that decade demonstrated no more of an agenda than had the Workingmen's party or the People's party. Voters repeatedly rejected efforts to alter the Consolidation Act, and city government continued in the highly limited role so thoroughly rehearsed before. Indeed, city government during the Buckley regime showed almost no change in patterns of city expenditures, unlike either the gradual increases of the People's party era (resulting from increasing population) or the sharp increases of the Phelan years (resulting from changing concepts of city government).[12] While voting behavior returned to the pre-WPC patterns of ethnicity and class, the nature and direction of urban development continued to be determined outside the arena of city government.

Phelan and Reform. The Democratic reformers who came to power in the 1890s and who looked to James Phelan for leadership challenged prevailing expectations regarding the structure and function of city government. In order that city government might be freed from the constraints of the Consolidation Act, Phelan led a group of businessmen-reformers who produced a new charter, implemented in 1900. Phelan's charter increased the authority of the mayor, dropped all semblance of a ward system in electing supervisors, and proposed eventual public ownership of utilities. In the reformers' view, municipal government was to do far more than provide police and fire protection, education, and streets and sewers. Self-styled "progressive citizens," the reformers hoped to use city government to provide direction for the very development of the city.

   Phelan and his associates also formed the moving force behind the drafting of the Burnham plan of 1905, an ambitious design to rearrange the city's streets and parks to create scenic vistas and ordered inspirations. Planning of the sort envisaged by the Burnham plan would have required strong centralized authority over the half-century or more required to complete the proposal.[13] Burnham adjured his devotees to make no small plans, but Phelan and the reformers needed no such urging. In their most ambitious moments, they saw the city as not just a commercial marketplace and manufacturing site, but also as a seat of learning and government, a place for recreation and inspiration, an organic entity worthy of celebration and devotion. While Phelan and his associates embraced a new concept of city government, they did not entirely dispense with past practices, when plans for urban development were created and implemented wholly outside the realm of government. Many of the Phelan group's initiatives, for example, the charter, the Burnham plan, or the Hetch Hetchy proposal (at least from 1901 to 1906), were nurtured *outside* government, then presented to elected representatives for adoption and implementation.

Union Labor Control. The Phelan Democrats lost their legitimacy with working-class voters after the bitter class conflict of the 1901 waterfront strike and the advent of the Union Labor party realized the potential of the Workingmen's party. Where the latter had lacked a program, however, the former not only mobilized voters along class lines but did so in support of a program. The reformers of the 1890s had used city government to implement a program conceived and developed among the business community. The Union Labor party used city government to protect existing unions and to promote unionization of workers not yet organized. Under the Union Labor party, municipal government moved to implement a program conceived and developed among the city's unions. The party proposed a much narrower program than that of the reformers, who wanted to use city government to transform the city itself. The party, created to save unions, largely failed to address broader concerns of urban development. The initiative in areas such as franchises fell by default to Abraham Ruef, whose approach owed more to Christopher Buckley and Martin Kelly than to James Phelan. Such methods of enlisting city government in support of development were no longer acceptable, however, and Ruef brought disgrace upon the Union Labor party. Patrick McCarthy, elected mayor in 1909, had the opportunity to redeem the party, but his program was only slightly broader than that of Schmitz and Ruef. In addition to protecting unions, McCarthy fostered construction of the Municipal Railway, but he saw the project as a means of supplying jobs at union wages to loyal union members.

The Era of Rolph. When James Rolph entered city hall in 1912, he brought back into the mayor's office the breadth of vision characteristic of the reformers of the 1890s, but he coupled it with a sympathy for labor and an appreciation of ethnic diversity. For a brief time, from 1912 to 1916, urban development came to rest squarely with the city government, as Rolph appointed experts to draw up plans for the Civic Center, the Municipal Railway, and the water system. Expansion of streetcar and water services, to be certain, was intended to aid privately planned development such as the Panama Pacific International Exposition and residential growth in the Outer Mission, Sunset, Parkside, and West of Twin Peaks neighborhoods. After World War I, Rolph's leadership waned and patterns returned to those more typical of the 1890s, as the business community formulated development plans and turned to municipal government for implementation. These patterns characterized disposal of Hetch Hetchy electrical power, extension of the Market Street Railway franchises, creation of the War Memorial Opera House and Veterans' Building, construction of the Bay Bridge and the Golden Gate Bridge, and charter revision in 1930–1932.

Unlike previous times, however, during the 1920s an opposition coalition emerged that went beyond mere nay-saying to advocate a different role for the city in development. The business community accepted municipal ownership of activities not in competition with private enterprise, but this new opposition, led by Franck Havenner, argued as well for municipal ownership of some enterprises directly in competition with private corporations. Both public ownership advocates and their opponents, however, found it easier to mobilize a majority to defeat proposals than to forge a majority to take action—witness the defeat of efforts to buy out the Spring Valley Water Company in 1910, 1915, 1921, and 1927, the defeat of all the incumbent supervisors who had voted against public ownership in 1925, or the defeat of public ownership bond issues in 1927 and 1930.

□   □   □

Max Weber's definition of power poses a question: which individuals or groups were able to succeed in their efforts in the arena of public decision making even though others sought to block them or to accomplish other objectives? Judged by the ability to elect public officials, both sides of San Francisco's polarized politics were able to succeed. Judged by the ability to win public support on propositions, again both sides could point to successes. Judged by access to campaign resources (workers, money, newspapers), both sides could command an array of support. Judged by the outcomes of public decision making on a wide range of issues, both sides could count victories as well as defeats.

While several measures of political success suggest that both sides shared in political power, another criterion suggests the contrary. Who initiated new issues and thereby set the political agenda? By this measure, the business community exercised far greater political influence than labor. For the most part, labor's political objectives were *defensive*, aimed at preserving hard-won gains and at extending them to other workers in the face of employer opposition. Employers, too, saw politics as having a potentially important role in labor relations, and they sought government assistance in breaking strikes. This development, more than any other, created and defined San Francisco's political polarity.

By contrast, after the 1890s, the business community also saw politics as one of several means for implementing urban development plans. Labor usually involved itself at first in such matters only when its primary concern of protecting its organization from assault coincided with or overlapped a development issue. Thus, outraged by the open-shop practices of the United Railroads, labor joined forces with proponents of residential development and with advocates of public ownership to create and extend the Municipal Railway. By the 1920s, public ownership issues usually featured the same political alignments as did labor issues, but the initiative rested with the business community, whether the question involved the role of the city government in the 1926 Carpenters' Union strike or the means of circumventing the public ownership provisions of the Raker Act. Even though labor could elect its own candidates to city office as often as not, even though labor-oriented voters could carry city referenda as often as not, even though labor supporters could win votes on the Board of Supervisors as often as not, almost all the labor victories (especially after 1911) were *reactive* or *defensive* because business defined the political agenda. In this larger sense, then, power was not shared but concentrated.

Men such as James Phelan or William H. Crocker, who sought to use the power of city government as one instrument among many to define or redefine the nature of the city itself, typically did not define their roles as involving the promotion of a class or group interest, nor did they tote up a balance to determine benefits. Their business and personal activities provided their understanding of the city: its neighborhoods and districts, its surrounding suburbs, its role in the economy of northern California, and its position as economic capital of a region stretching from the Bering Strait to the Isthmus of Panama, from the sugar plantations of Maui to the mines of Coeur d'Alene. Their organic sense of the city led them to the conclusion that a project that benefited the city would inevitably benefit all city residents in proportion to the investments each had made. San Francisco's business leadership held secure control over the city's development. They were certain that if projects were appropriately planned, if visions were sufficiently bold, if implementation was prompt and efficient, then benefits would naturally flow to all, although clearly not in equal proportions.

Postscript

From the Politics of Polarity to the Politics of Hyperpluralism

Although this study has concluded that San Francisco politics in the early twentieth century exhibited sharply etched polarities, students of more recent city politics have characterized them as pluralistic. Frederick Wirt, whose *Power in the City: Decision Making in San Francisco* appeared in 1974, characterized the city's politics as "hyperpluralism."[1] In 1980, Kevin Starr, author of *Americans and the California Dream,* described the city's politics in the *Examiner* as "an unseemly, inefficient species of village squabbling." The executive director of the San Francisco Charter Commission put it bluntly: San Francisco politics represented "pluralism run amok."[2] What happened in San Francisco between 1932 and the 1970s to transform the polarized politics of the early twentieth century into the hyperpluralist politics of the later twentieth century? A complete answer is not possible without a full-scale study, but a brief survey can suggest the central elements of continuity as well as the most important forces of change.

LABOR: FROM POLARITY TO PARTNERSHIP

Basic patterns of labor's involvement in politics have changed surprisingly little since the early twentieth century. Unions created the Union Labor party as a defensive move to prevent the use of city power against the emergent union movement. From 1901 through the implementation of the new city charter in 1932, labor rarely moved beyond a defensive approach to city politics. Although the city's labor relations underwent a major revolution in the 1930s, the nature of the relationship between organized labor and city government changed very little. The major impetus for change in labor relations came not from within the city but instead from the federal government. When Congress passed the National Industrial Recovery Act in 1933 and included section 7-a providing for collective bargaining, labor organizations in San Francisco, as elsewhere in the nation, launched organizing drives. Workers too read section 7-a as a call to organize, and groups of them walked the halls of the Labor Temple, the Labor Council's building, looking for the proper union to join.[3] In 1934, Mayor Angelo Rossi used city police to protect Industrial Association trucks carrying goods unloaded from ships by strikebreaking longshoremen; a battle between police and strikers left two unionists dead. Labor responded with a brief general strike, and striking maritime workers were able to use section 7-a to force some concessions.

In 1901, the use of city police to protect strikebreakers had earned Mayor Phelan the enmity of labor and had brought to birth the Union Labor party. Labor launched no political demarche in 1934; instead Rossi won second and third terms in city hall. Because the Wagner Act of 1935 protected the gains made under section 7-a and allowed their extension at the same time that it established a regulatory body that gave a legal structure to labor relations, labor's attention came to focus on Washington. Through the decade of the 1930s, San Francisco voters slowly changed their voting allegiances. In 1930, 82 percent of the city's voters registered as Republicans; ten years later, 65 percent were Democrats.[4]

Although San Francisco's union membership doubled between 1933 and 1940[5] and city voters moved from the Republican party to the party of Franklin Roosevelt, these changes produced no immediate impact in city hall. James Rolph's successors seemed cast from the same mold, though most lacked his charming veneer. Angelo Rossi (1931–1944), Roger Lapham (1944–1948), Elmer Robinson (1948–1956), and George Christopher (1956–1964) were all moderate-to-conservative Republicans, and all but Robinson made their mark as successful businessmen. The resurgent labor movement elected supporters to the Board of Supervisors, as it had done throughout the 1920s, and sent others to Congress (including Franck Havenner) or to the state legislature. If San Francisco labor from 1901 through 1932 had engaged in politics for defensive reasons, its later goals remained much the same: defense of the gains made under protection of federal legislation.

By the mid-1930s, leading employers had moved from a policy of suppression to a strategy of assimilation, stressing the mutual self-interest of business and labor so long as labor limited itself to collective bargaining over wages, hours, and working conditions. Those who presented a broader agenda for labor often found themselves the targets of red-baiting and efforts to remove them from influence. Havenner lost his congressional seat through such maneuvers, and Harry Bridges spent years in court fighting deportation efforts.[6] If anything, the federal protections for collective bargaining contained in New Deal legislation made San Francisco labor less active than before in city politics, as some unions came to consider their previous defensive politics as unnecessary and others came to view politics solely in terms of their own jobs. By 1982, for example, the Electrical Workers, and the Building Trades more generally, provided strong leadership in committing the Labor Council *against* a proposition to study the feasibility of public ownership of electrical-generating and distribution systems on the grounds that federal protection of bargaining rights was preferable to that available to city employees.

URBAN DEVELOPMENT

Patterns of decision making in the area of urban development also showed little change from the 1920s. One union official in 1970 defined his union's role in development controversies as only to "supply the workers and assure their rights," but environmentalist efforts to limit high-rise development propelled Building Trades unions into a political coalition with the city's business leadership, for they both adamantly opposed limits on growth.[7] The most ambitious proposals for urban development in San Francisco since the 1930s have followed the pattern marked by the Burnham plan advocated in 1905. For example, in 1953, the Board of Supervisors designated the South of Market area as a possible location for a redevelopment project. Real estate developer, hotelier, and Democratic party activist Benjamin Harrison Swig soon produced the San Francisco Prosperity Plan to transform the area into a convention, sports, and office complex. Discussion ebbed and flowed during the 1950s, but by the early 1960s the business community united behind the Swig proposal and converted city officials to their views.

Operating through both private organizations and government agencies, a revised version of the Prosperity Plan lumbered into being, generating more than a decade of lawsuits and political controversy, but ultimately producing the Moscone Convention Center. As the municipal redevelopment effort slowly neared realization, private capital transformed the environs of the convention center from a collection of hotels for transients, small manufacturing companies, and low-income residences into a high-rise extension of the Financial District.[8] By the time the Democrats met in Moscone Center in July 1984 to nominate Walter Mondale for president, new office structures stretched from the waterfront to the convention center, marking the transformation of fully half of the South of Market District. Similar initiatives from the business community, operating through private organizations and public agencies, produced both the Bay Area Rapid Transit system and an underground route for the Municipal Railway along Market Street.[9]

As San Francisco's business community began to transform its central business district into a mini-Manhattan, critics of high-density development emerged and began to gain support. In 1959, a test of strength came when plans for a freeway across Aquatic Park and the Marina Green sparked a "freeway revolt," which led the Board of Supervisors to halt the freeway's progress. Six years later, neighborhood activists led a citywide effort to reject $180 million in federal highway funds, part of which was to have been used to build a freeway across parts of Golden Gate Park. Since the 1960s, three San Francisco freeways have ended in midair, mute testimony to the political prowess of those citizens unwilling to surrender their neighborhoods to concrete on-ramps or to live in the shadow of an elevated roadway.

Another test of strength came when a similar coalition of neighborhood activists, environmentalists, and political liberals blocked a proposed high-rise development adjacent to the Bay Bridge. Efforts to restrict building heights through the initiative process failed in 1971, 1972, and 1983, although voters in 1984 approved an initiative designed to prevent high-rise buildings from shadowing parks. These contests over the future course of urban development inevitably generated the same coalitions: the business community and organized labor (led by the Building Trades) opposed restrictions; neighborhood groups, environmentalists, and political liberals favored limits on development.[10]

While patterns of decision making on urban development in the post–World War II era had been forecast by those who produced the Burnham plan in 1905, the political coalitions of the postwar era proved very different from those of the 1920s. From 1901 through 1932, most issues that drove voter alignments derived from labor relations. The city's politics polarized between business and labor, and those coalitions proved durable so long as business leaders clung to the hope of restoring the open shop in the face of worker commitment to unions. When New Deal legislation quashed open-shop hopes, San Francisco business leaders turned to reinforce those union leaders who defined their purposes narrowly, in terms of bargaining rights and objectives. By the time control of urban development emerged as a major political issue in the 1960s, business and labor had long experience in working together. The labor movement itself changed, as high-rise office buildings (housing nonunion workers) replaced machine shops and light manufacturing and as the introduction of containerized shipping made obsolete most of the city's piers. Machinists' and maritime unions shrank, but the growth of public employee unions kept total union membership from a sharp decline.

CHANGING ETHNIC AND SOCIAL PATTERNS

Just as federal legislation in the 1930s helped to bring an end to the class divisions of earlier years, so the population movements of World War II and after brought new ethnic and social groups into a city that had experienced nearly a half-century of ethnic stability. During the war, black neighborhoods developed in the Western Addition and near the shipyards of Hunter's Point. Following the war, Irish Catholics moved out of the Mission District to suburbs or to new neighborhoods in the Sunset District. Hispanics from Central America and Mexico replaced the Irish as the largest ethnic group in the Mission District. Immigration from Asia resumed in the late 1960s, and Chinatown began to expand into erstwhile Italian areas of North Beach; parts of the Richmond District became a second Chinatown. By the 1970 census, the city had become 14 percent Asian (Chinese, Filipino, Japanese, and Korean, with Vietnamese to be added in the 1970s), 12 percent Hispanic, and 13 percent black. By the early 1970s, some sections of the city had already become "gay ghettos" as the city's reputation for tolerance attracted men from other parts of the nation.[11]

Former lines of political polarity weakened or disappeared, and many new lines of political cleavage appeared, along lines of class, neighborhood, race and ethnicity, and sexual preference. A politics of pluralism emerged from the city's new ethnocultural mix and from the changes in political loyalty deriving from presidential and congressional divisions during the 1930s. Political analysts in the 1960s and 1970s tracked the emergence of identifiable, although sometimes overlapping, blocs of voters: blacks, Chinese, Hispanics, gays, environmentalists, labor supporters, business supporters, liberals, conservatives, and others, many of them organized into political clubs for the purposes of endorsement, fund-raising, and mobilization. Since the late 1960s, running for city office has become an exercise in collecting endorsements from the city's many political organizations, including the Black Leadership Forum, the Mexican-American Political Alliance, the Labor Council's Committee on Political Education, the Chamber of Commerce, the Republican County Central Committee, and a host of Democratic clubs, including neighborhood clubs, the Feminist Democrats, the Chinese-American Democratic Club, and several gay clubs, especially the Alice B. Toklas Lesbian/Gay Democratic Club and the Harvey Milk Gay and Lesbian Democratic Club.[12]

THE POLITICS OF PLURALISM

In 1963, newly arrived ethnic groups (especially blacks) joined with liberals and labor to elect the city's first Democratic mayor since James Phelan.[13] John Shelley, liberal member of Congress and former secretary-treasurer of the Labor Council, served from 1964 to 1968. His successor, Joseph Alioto, also a liberal Democrat, was a lawyer and successful businessman. George Moscone, a liberal Democratic state senator, followed Alioto into the mayor's office in 1976, winning an election that sharply divided the city; unions joined blacks, environmentalists, liberals, and gays to give Moscone a narrow victory over John Barbagelata, an arch-conservative Republican real estate broker. Moscone's assassination in 1978 made Dianne Feinstein mayor; a moderate-to-liberal Democrat, Feinstein won election on her own in 1979 and 1983, drawing much of the support Moscone had garnered and adding support from business interests.[14]

Although politics affecting urban development showed little change from the patterns of 1905, recent mayoral elections reflect coalitional alignments that have made recent charter reform movements seem light-years removed from those of the 1890s or 1920s. Earlier charter revision efforts had been marked by the polarization characteristic of the city's politics more generally during those years, but charter revision efforts in 1968–1969 and 1979–1980 exhibited the full-blown political pluralism that emerged after World War II.

During the closing days of Shelley's administration, the Board of Supervisors created a Citizens' Charter Revision Committee (CCRC) to study and propose revisions in the 1932 charter. Unlike charter revision groups in the 1890s and 1920s, when the business community took the lead in developing charter proposals for consideration by an elected Board of Freeholders, the CCRC was created by the supervisors and the mayor. Each supervisor appointed one member, and incoming mayor Alioto appointed ten. The result was the most politically balanced charter revision group in the city's history: the CCRC contained men and women, representatives of labor, business, and all the city's major ethnic groups. The voters received CCRC's first proposals in 1969 and defeated them by almost a two-to-one margin; although the CCRC package, in good pluralist fashion, seemed to offer something to every major political group in the city, it also had something that every major group found objectionable. With the defeat of the CCRC proposals, the drive for charter reform moved to grassroots levels.[15]

In 1973, a coalition of neighborhood political activists, including veterans of the freeway revolt, used the initiative process to propose changes in the election of supervisors, advocating election from individual districts instead of at large. The measure drew opposition from business, labor, and most city officials and lost by two to one. In the next few years, city employee strikes produced punitive actions by the Board of Supervisors, urged on by the business community. In 1976, when a new effort at district election surfaced, the Labor Council allied itself with neighborhood activists to punish incumbent supervisors for their antilabor measures. The proposition passed by a narrow margin, with voters aligning themselves almost exactly as they had in the Moscone-Barbagelata election the year before. A repeal measure two years later failed, again by a close margin.[16]

In 1978, San Francisco voters elected a Charter Commission to rewrite the 1932 charter. The 1978 Charter Commission showed the pluralism characteristic of the CCRC a decade before; among the commissioners were Asians, blacks, women, a gay man, liberals, conservatives, labor representatives, businessmen, and professionals. The outcome in 1980, when voters passed on the commission's work, was also a replay of 1969. The same year, the voters repealed district elections and returned to the at-large election of supervisors.[17] It was this turn of events that prompted the commission's executive director to condemn the process as "pluralism run amok."

□   □   □

From this brief survey, three elements emerge as central in understanding the post-1932 evolution of San Francisco politics from polarity to pluralism. One is the role of federal legislation and regulation in removing labor relations from the agenda of city politics, except for municipal employee labor relations. A second is the emergence of issues focusing on the desirability of unrestricted growth and development. A third is the arrival of new sociocultural groups carrying noneconomic political objectives. Together, these factors have transformed the nature and process of city politics.

Overlapping Company Representation in San Francisco, 1911-1935

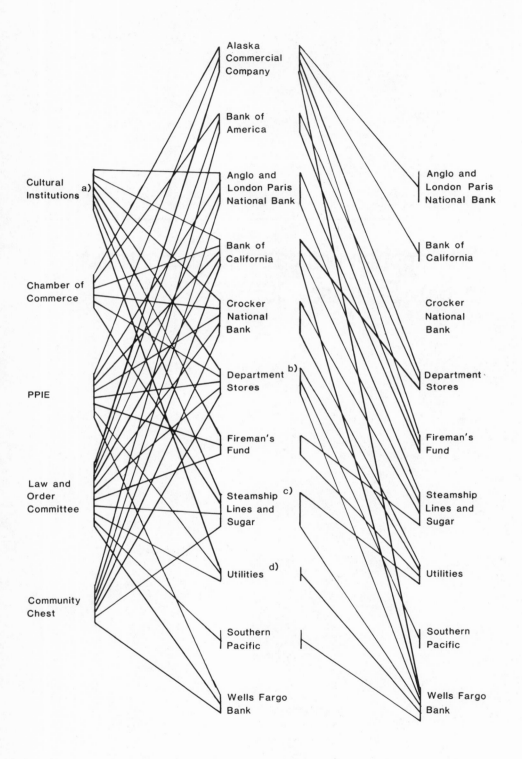

Cultural
Institutions   a)

Chamber of
Commerce

PPIE

Law and
Order
Committee

Community
Chest

Alaska
Commercial
Company

Bank of
America

Anglo and
London Paris
National Bank

Bank of
California

Crocker
National
Bank

Department
Stores   b)

Fireman's
Fund

Steamship   c)
Lines and
Sugar

Utilities   d)

Southern
Pacific

Wells Fargo
Bank

Anglo and
London Paris
National Bank

Bank of
California

Crocker
National
Bank

Department
Stores

Fireman's
Fund

Steamship
Lines and
Sugar

Utilities

Southern
Pacific

Wells Fargo
Bank

KEY TO ILLUSTRATION

a Cultural institutions: Symphony Association, Opera, Museum of Art, Library and Park commissions.

b Department stores: Hale Brothers, Emporium, Grant Company, City of Paris.

c Steamship lines and sugar companies: Matson and Dollar Lines, Hakalau, Paauhau and Hilo Sugar companies, California and Hawaiian Sugar Refining Company.

d Utilities: Pacific Gas and Electric, Pacific Lighting Corporation, San Francisco Gas and Electric.

SOURCES: *National Cyclopedia of American Biography,* vols. 26–29 (New York: James T. White Co., 1938–1941); *Walker's Manual of California Securities and Directory of Directors* (San Francisco: Walker's Manual, Inc., 1915–1935); *Who's Who in California, 1928–1929* (San Francisco: Who's Who Publishing Co., 1929); trustees of San Francisco Museum of Art and Community Chest Directors in box 38, folder 28, John Francis Neylan Papers, Bancroft Library, University of California, Berkeley; San Francisco Chamber of Commerce, *Law and Order in San Francisco: A Beginning* (San Francisco: H. S. Crocker Co., 1916).

Notes

INTRODUCTION

1. For a sample of several approaches to this period, see Robert H. Wiebe, *The Search for Order, 1877–1920* (New York, 1967); Henry F. May, *The End of American Innocence: A Study of the First Years of Our Own Time, 1912–1917* (Chicago, 1964); Samuel P. Hays, *The Response to Industrialism, 1885–1914* (Chicago, 1957); William Appleman Williams, *The Contours of American History* (Chicago, 1966); Morris Janowitz, *The Last Half-Century: Societal Change and Politics in America* (Chicago, 1978).

2. The flourishing debate on these topics can be pursued in the following works: John B. Sharpless and Sam Bass Warner, Jr., "Urban History," *American Behavioral Scientist* 21 (Nov./Dec. 1977):221–244; Theodore Hershberg, "The New Urban History: Toward an Interdisciplinary History of the City," *Journal of Urban History* 5 (Nov. 1978):3–40; Willis D. Hawley, ed., *Theoretical Perspectives on Urban Politics* (Englewood Cliffs, N.J., 1976); G. William Domhoff, *Who Really Rules: New Haven and Community Power Reexamined* (Santa Monica, Ca., 1978); Paul E. Peterson, *City Limits* (Chicago, 1981).

3. See Robert A. Dahl, *Who Governs: Democracy and Power in an American City* (New Haven, 1961).

4. See Floyd Hunter, *Community Power Structure: A Study of Decision Makers* (Garden City, N.Y., 1963), as well as Domhoff, *Who Really Rules,* esp. ch. 4. See also Timothy K. Barnekov and Daniel Rich, "Privatism and Urban Development: An Analysis of the Organized Influence of Local Business Elites," *Urban Affairs Quarterly* 12 (June 1977): 431–460.

5. Domhoff, *Who Really Rules,* p. 13. For Marxist viewpoints, see William K. Tabb and Larry Sawers, eds., *Marxism and the Metropolis: New Perspectives in Urban Political Economy,* 2nd ed. (New York, 1984).

6. David M. Gordon, "Capitalist Development and the History of American Cities," in Tabb and Sawers, eds., *Marxism and the Metropolis,* p. 22.

7. For critiques of such deductive methods of research, by a historian and philosopher, see Edward P. Thompson. *The Poverty of Theory and Other Essays* (New York, 1978); and Richard J. Bernstein, *The Restructuring of Social and Political Theory* (New York, 1976).

8. David C. Hammack, "Problems in the Historical Study of Power in the Cities and Towns of the United States, 1800–1960," *American Historical Review* 83 (April 1978):338; the footnotes in this article constitute an excellent bibliography on the topic. See also Hammack's *Power and Society: Greater New York at the Turn of the Century* (New York, 1982).

9. Hammack, "Problems," pp. 332–333, 337–338. See esp. Samuel P. Hays, "The Changing Political Structure of the City in Industrial America," *Journal of Urban History* 1 (Nov. 1974): 6–38.

10. Hammack, "Problems," pp. 329–332. See esp. Frederic Cople Jaher, *The Urban Establishment: Upper Strata in Boston, New York, Charleston, Chicago, and Los Angeles* (Urbana, Ill., 1982).

11. Hammack, "Problems," pp. 333–337. See, e.g., John D. Buenker, *Urban Liberalism and Progressive Reform* (New York, 1973).

12. Domhoff, *Who Really Rules,* p. 127. The following series of questions for research follow Domhoff's reappraisal of the methodology of community power structure analysis, as well as the suggestions of Kenneth Fox in his review of Hammack's *Power and Society,* in *Journal of Interdisciplinary History* 14 (Winter 1984):711–713.

CHAPTER 1

1. William McKendree Gwin, quoted in Robert V. P. Steele [Lately Thomas], *Between Two Empires: The Life Story of California's First Senator* (Boston, 1969), pp. 376–377.

2. Morris Birkbeck, *Notes on a Journey in America from the Coast of Virginia to the Territory of Illinois,* 3rd ed. (London, 1818), p. 69, quoted in John W. Reps, *The Making of Urban America: A History of City Planning in the United States* (Princeton, 1965), p. 347.

3. Father Font, quoted in Theodore E. Treutlein, *San Francisco Bay: Discovery and Colonization, 1769–1776* (San Francisco, 1968), p. 80.

4. Hubert Howe Bancroft, *History of California,* 7 vols. (San Francisco, 1888), 6:6.

5. Treutlein, *San Francisco Bay,* pp. 9, 46; George Vancouver, *A Voyage of Discovery to the North Pacific Ocean and Round the World,* 6 vols. in 3 (London, 1801), p. 14; for Khvostov's and Rezanov's comments, see Richard A. Pierce, ed., *Rezanov Reconnoiters California, 1806* (San Francisco, 1972), pp. 25, 53; August C. Mahr, *The Visit of the "Rurik" to San Francisco in 1816,* Stanford University Publications in History, Economics, and Political Science, vol. 2 (Stanford, 1932), p. 33.

6. Thomas C. Cochran, "The Business Revolution," *American Historical Review* 79 (Dec. 1974): 1451.

7. Pierce, ed., *Rezanov Reconnoiters California,* pp. 25, 26.

8. Thomas C. Cochran, *Frontiers of Change: Early Industrialism in America* (New York, 1981), pp. 7, 8. This and the following paragraph are very much indebted to Cochran's formulations in his book and in his article cited in note 6 above. The approach here is also influenced by Allan Pred's work, particularly his *Urban Growth and City-Systems in the United States, 1840–1860* (Cambridge, 1980).

9. Cochran, "Business Revolution," p. 1452.

10. Andrew Rolle, Introduction, in Alfred Robinson, *Life in California* (Santa Barbara, 1970), p. vii.

11. Norman A. Graebner, *Empire on the Pacific: A Study in American Continental Expansion* (New York, 1955), p. 51.

12. Henry Price to William D. M. Howard, Jan. 20, 1846, William D. M. Howard Papers, California Historical Society, San Francisco.

13. John Henry Brown, *Reminiscences and Incidents of Early Days of San Francisco, 1845–1850* (Oakland, 1949), pp. 24–25, in John W. Reps, *Cities of the American West: A History of Frontier Urban Planning* (Princeton, 1979), p. 110; Jessie Davies Francis, "An Economic and Social History of Mexican California (1822–1846)," Ph.D. dissertation, University of California, Berkeley, 1936, p. 287; see also Douglas Watson, "An Hour's Walk Through Yerba Buena," *California Historical Society Quarterly* 17 (Dec. 1938):291–302; and Geoffrey P. Mawn, "Framework for Destiny: San Francisco, 1847," *California Historical Quarterly* 51 (Summer 1972):165–178.

14. Richard Henry Dana, *Two Years Before the Mast* (New York, 1936), p. 243.

15. Graebner, *Empire on the Pacific*, pp. 63, 71–72, 99.

16. S. J. Hastings to Thomas Oliver Larkin, Nov. 9, 1845, in G. P. Hammond, ed., *The Larkin Papers*, 10 vols. (Berkeley, 1951–1964), 4:92.

17. Robinson, *Life in California*, p. 157.

18. See Mawn, "Framework for Destiny"; and Bruno Fritzsche, "San Francisco, 1846–1848: The Coming of the Land Speculator," *California Historical Quarterly* 51 (Spring 1972):17–34.

19. William H. Pickens, " 'A Marvel of Nature; the Harbor of Harbors': Public Policy and the Development of the San Francisco Bay, 1846–1926," Ph.D. dissertation, University of California, Davis, 1976, pp. 7–8.

20. Roger Lotchin points out that Bartlett's order merely legalized a change that had occurred three months earlier; see Roger W. Lotchin, *San Francisco, 1846–1856: From Hamlet to City* (New York, 1974), p. 33. See also Pickens, "A Marvel of Nature," pp. 14–16, who argues that the rapid development of the San Francisco waterfront played an important role in Benicia's demise.

21. Samuel C. Upham, *Notes of a Voyage to California Together with Scenes in El Dorado, 1849–1850* (Philadelphia, 1878), pp. 221–222, quoted in John B. McGloin, *San Francisco: The Story of a City* (San Rafael, Ca., 1978), pp. 34–35; Bayard Taylor, *El Dorado; or Adventures in the Path of Empire*, vol. 2 (New York, 1850), p. 55.

22. See Peter R. Decker, *Fortunes and Failures: White-Collar Mobility in Nineteenth-Century San Francisco* (Cambridge, Mass., 1978), pp. 60–86.

23. Ibid.

24. Ibid. See also Lotchin, *San Francisco*, pp. 102–105; and Robert A. Burchell, *The San Francisco Irish, 1848–1880* (Berkeley, 1980), pp. 1–4.

25. "Proceedings of the Chamber of Commerce on Warehousing," Dec. 10, 1861; Memorial from Chamber of Commerce to Congress, Dec. 24, 1861; letters from Chamber of Commerce to the California Congressional delegation and to Milton S. Latham, Dec. 26, 1861, and May 15, 1862. All in folder 5, Milton Slocum Latham Papers, California Historical Society, San Francisco.

26. Lotchin, *San Francisco*, pp. 45–82.

27. Ibid., p. 125; Decker, *Fortunes and Failures*, p. 83.

28. Decker, *Fortunes and Failures*, pp. 87–97, 118; Burchell, *San Francisco Irish*, pp. 52–72. See also Douglas Henry Daniels, *Pioneer Urbanites: A Social and Cultural History of Black San Francisco* (Philadelphia, 1980), pp. 33–34.

29. Taylor, *El Dorado*, p. 62.

30. Statement of defendant, *Charlotte L. Brown v. The Omnibus Railroad Company*, Twelfth District Court, City and County of San Francisco, 1863, manuscript copy, Charlotte L. Brown Papers, California Historical Society, San Francisco. A similar case, in 1867, went on appeal to the California Supreme Court when the company claimed that the jury's award of damages to the plaintiff had been influenced by the "question of race and color which was entirely foreign to the case." See Brief for appellant, *Emma Jane Turner v. North Beach and Mission Railroad Company*, Supreme Court of the State of California, copy in the Wellington Cleveland Burnett Papers,

California Historical Society, San Francisco; Frank Soulé et al., *The Annals of San Francisco* (Palo Alto, 1966), p. 369; Daniels, *Pioneer Urbanites*, p. 35.

31. Daniels, *Pioneer Urbanites*, p. 108.

32. Alexis de Tocqueville, *Democracy in America*, ed. Phillips Bradley, 2 vols. (New York, 1945), 2:114. See also Bradford Luckingham, "Associational Life on the Urban Frontier: San Francisco, 1848–1856," Ph.D. dissertation, University of California, Davis, 1968, pp. 165–166.

33. Daniels, *Pioneer Urbanites*, pp. 108–122.

34. Burchell, *San Francisco Irish*, pp. 88, 96–101.

35. *Alta California*, Dec. 23, 1854, quoted in Bradford Luckingham, "Immigrant Life in Emergent San Francisco," *Journal of the West* 12 (Oct. 1973):605.

36. Ibid., p. 612.

37. William Ingraham Kip, "The Chinese in California," *The Spirit of Missions* 20 (March 1855): 85–90, quoted in Luckingham, "Immigrant Life," p. 602.

38. See Decker, *Fortunes and Failures*, pp. 120–143.

39. See Lotchin, *San Francisco*, pp. 160–163, 230–239, 245–275.

40. Decker, *Fortunes and Failures*, p. 108.

41. George Howard to William Howard, Nov. 2, 1844; William B. Gay to William Howard, Dec. 3, 1844, in William D. M. Howard Papers, California Historical Society, San Francisco.

42. George R. Stewart, *Take Your Bible in One Hand: The Life of William Henry Thomas* (San Francisco, 1939), pp. 30–31; Timothy Dwight Hunt, *Address Delivered Before the New England Society of San Francisco* (San Francisco, 1853), p. 20, quoted in Luckingham, "Immigrant Life," p. 606; Robert B. Wallace to his father, June 16, 1852, Robert B. Wallace Letters, California Historical Society, San Francisco.

43. For a thorough analysis of Broderick and San Francisco politics, see David A. Williams, *David C. Broderick: A Political Portrait* (San Marino, Ca., 1969).

44. Decker, *Fortunes and Failures*, pp. 123–125; Lotchin, *San Francisco*, pp. 192–201. Lotchin points out that the committee's claim to have created peace and tranquility was overstated and that it sometimes applied a double standard; see pp. 200–201.

45. Lotchin, *San Francisco*, p. 225; Burchell, *San Francisco Irish*, p. 129. Robert B. Wallace, aide to William T. Coleman and his second in command during "the revolution" of 1856, was still convinced in 1860 that "a fall back to old ways would be certain death to many of us in San Francisco"; letter from Robert B. Wallace, March 4, 1860 (first page with addressee missing), Robert B. Wallace Letters, California Historical Society, San Francisco.

46. Steven P. Erie, "The Development of Class and Ethnic Politics in San Francisco, 1870–1910: A Critique of the Pluralist Interpretation," Ph.D. dissertation, University of California, Los Angeles, 1975, pp. 110–114; Burchell, *San Francisco Irish*, pp. 131–154.

47. William T. Sherman to John T. Doyle, Jan. 4, 1884, William Tecumseh Sherman Letters, California Historical Society, San Francisco; for a defense of the committee by one of its leading merchant supporters, see the statement (n.d.) by Frederick William Macondray, Jr., in the Frederick William Macondray, Jr., Papers, California Historical Society, San Francisco.

48. Decker, *Fortunes and Failures*, pp. 147–150.

CHAPTER 2

1. Lawrence H. Larsen, *The Urban West at the End of the Frontier* (Lawrence, Kans., 1978), p. 39; U.S. Census Office, Department of the Interior, *Report on the Social Statistics of Cities*, 2 vols. (Washington, D.C., 1887), 2:804–805; James Bryce, *The American Commonwealth*, 2 vols. (New York, 1908), 2:428.

2. Titus Fey Cornise, *The Natural Wealth of California* (San Francisco, 1868), p. 658; Leroy Armstrong and J. O. Denny, *Financial California: An Historical Review of the Beginnings and Progress of Banking in the State* (San Francisco, 1916), p. 29.

3. *Builders of a Great City: San Francisco's Representative Men* (San Francisco, 1891), pp. 57, 82, 58, 86.

4. Robert A. Elgie, "The Development of San Francisco Manufacturing, 1848–1880," master's thesis, University of California, Berkeley, 1966, pp. 25, 28, 30, 49, 52, 124, 127.

5. Neil Larry Shumsky, "Tar Flat and Nob Hill: A Social History of Industrial San Francisco During the 1870s," Ph.D. dissertation, University of California, Berkeley, 1972, pp. 42, 57.

6. Robert J. Trusk, "Sources of Capital of Early California Manufacturers, 1850–1880," Ph.D. dissertation, University of Illinois, Urbana, 1960, p. 172.

7. *Builders of a Great City,* pp. 58, 25, 60, 84.

8. Ibid., p. 58.

9. Fred H. Hackett, ed., *The Industries of San Francisco* (San Francisco, 1884), pp. 141, 79, 91.

10. Ibid., pp. 67, 133.

11. Ibid., p. 53.

12. Ibid., pp. 92, 118, 85, 83, 84, 181.

13. *Langley's San Francisco Directory, 1880–1881* (San Francisco, 1881), pp. 18–19; Hackett, ed., *Industries of San Francisco,* p. 67.

14. Charles A. Fracchia, "The Founding of the Hibernia Savings and Loan Society," unpublished typescript in the authors' possession, pp. 6, 9–11; Armstrong and Denny, *Financial California,* p. 190; *Langley's San Francisco Directory, 1879–1880* (San Francisco, 1880), p. 23.

15. Ira B. Cross, *Financing an Empire: History of Banking in California,* 4 vols. (Chicago, 1927), 1:370, 402–404.

16. David Lavender, *Nothing Seemed Impossible: William Chapman Ralston and Early San Francisco* (Palo Alto, 1975), p. 382; Asbury Harpending, *The Great Diamond Hoax and Other Stirring Incidents in the Life of Asbury Harpending* (San Francisco, 1913), p. 125; Neil C. Wilson, *400 California Street: A Century Plus Five,* 2nd ed. (San Francisco, 1969), p. 49.

17. Armstrong and Denny, *Financial California,* p. 191; *Langley's San Francisco Directory, 1879–1880,* p. 23.

18. Hackett, ed., *Industries of San Francisco,* pp. 161, 174.

19. Ibid., pp. 117, 157, 155, 133, 168, 64.

20. Ibid., pp. 167, 74, 96, 84; see also David Warren Ryder, *A Century of Hardware and Steel* (San Francisco, 1949), pp. 63–69.

21. Hackett, ed., *Industries of San Francisco,* pp. 151, 83.

22. Ibid., pp. 154, 138, 144.

23. Ibid., pp. 188, 173, 125, 106–107, 54, 57.

24. *Langley's San Francisco Directory, 1880–1881,* pp. 21–22.

25. Alfred D. Chandler, Jr., *The Visible Hand: The Managerial Revolution in American Business* (Cambridge, Mass., 1977), pp. 81–144; Stuart Daggett, *Chapters on the History of the Southern Pacific* (New York, 1922), p. 140.

26. John S. Hittell, *The Commerce and Industries of the Pacific Coast* (San Francisco, 1882), pp. 154, 661–662; on the "Big Four" and the "Silver Kings," see two books by Oscar Lewis, *The Big Four: The Story of Huntington, Stanford, Hopkins, and Crocker, and the Building of the Central Pacific* (New York, 1938); and *Silver Kings: The Lives and Times of Mackay, Fair, Flood, and O'Brien, Lords of the Nevada Comstock Lode* (New York, 1947).

27. Albert Shumate, *A Visit to Rincon Hill and South Park* (San Francisco, 1963); Alonzo Phelps, *Contemporary Biography of California's Representative Men,* 2 vols. (San Francisco, 1881–1882), 1:29–31.

28. Hittell, *Commerce and Industries,* p. 138.

29. *Builders of a Great City,* pp. 281–283; Phelps, *Contemporary Biography,* pp. 355–356.

30. *Illustrated Fraternal Directory* (San Francisco, 1889), p. 51.

31. *Builders of a Great City,* pp. 272–273.

32. *Illustrated Fraternal Directory,* p. 28; Phelps, *Contemporary Biography,* pp. 200–201.

33. *Builders of a Great City,* pp. 117–118, 278–288.

34. Ibid., pp. 158–159, 172, 325.

35. Henry George, "What the Railroad Will Bring Us," *Overland Monthly* 1 (Oct. 1868):302–303.

36. Decker, *Fortunes and Failures,* pp. 239, 233.

37. Thomas C. Cochran and William Miller, *The Age of Enterprise: A Social History of Industrial America,* rev. ed. (New York, 1961), p. 153.

38. Charles E. Lindblom, *Politics and Markets: The World's Political-Economic Systems* (New York, 1977), p. 172.

39. Herbert Hoover, quoted in *A Man and His Friends: A Life Story of Milton H. Esberg* (San Francisco, 1953), p. 121.

40. Burton W. Folsom, Jr., has also used this criterion in his study of Pennsylvania business leaders; see his *Urban Capitalists: Entrepreneurs and City Growth in Pennsylvania's Lackawanna and Lehigh Regions, 1800–1920* (Baltimore, 1981), p. 43. The term *San Francisco business leaders* includes the officers and directors of firms with San Francisco headquarters as listed in the following: *Walker's Manual of California Securities and Directory of Directors, 1915* (San Francisco, 1915); *Walker's Manual of Corporate Securities and Directory of Directors, 1925* (San Francisco, 1925); *Walker's Directory of Directors, 1931* (San Francisco, 1931); *Walker's Manual of Pacific Coast Securities, 1935* (San Francisco, 1935). References to these sources will appear as: *Walker's,* followed by the date.

41. *San Francisco News,* Aug. 11, 1930; *San Francisco Chronicle,* Sept. 29, 1937.

42. Leland W. Cutler, *America Is Good to a Country Boy* (Stanford, 1954), p. 126.

43. Judd Kahn, *Imperial San Francisco: Politics and Planning in an American City, 1897–1906* (Lincoln, Nebr., 1979), p. 60; Bailey Millard, *History of the San Francisco Bay Region,* 2 vols. (Chicago, 1924), 2:10–11; *Walker's, 1925,* p. 394.

44. *Who's Who in California, 1928–1929* (San Francisco, 1929), p. 521 (hereafter cited as *Who's Who*); *San Francisco Daily News,* June 7, 1930; Neill Compton Wilson, ed., *Deep Roots: The History of Blake, Moffitt, and Towne, Pioneers in Paper Since 1855* (San Francisco, 1955), p. 87.

45. Aubrey Drury, *John A. Hooper and California's Robust Youth* (San Francisco, 1952), pp. 25–26, 43–44; Lewis F. Byington and Oscar Lewis, eds., *The History of San Francisco,* 3 vols. (Chicago, 1931), 2:44–47; *Who's Who,* p. 426; *Palo Alto Times,* Aug. 6, 1927.

46. *Walker's, 1925,* p. 112; *Who's Who,* p. 422.

47. *Walker's, 1925,* p. 380; Millard, *History of the San Francisco Bay Region,* pp. 404–405; *Who's Who,* p. 51.

48. *San Francisco Examiner,* Jan. 1, 1926; Robert Glass Cleland and Frank B. Putnam, *Isaias W. Hellman and the Farmers and Merchants Bank* (San Marino, Ca., 1965); Martin A. Meyer, *Western Jewry* (San Francisco, 1916), p. 191; *San Francisco Bulletin,* Oct. 12, 1895; Millard, *History of the San Francisco Bay Region,* pp. 47–48; *Who's Who,* p. 502; Lillie Bernheimer Lilienthal, *In Memoriam, Jesse Warren Lilienthal* (San Francisco, 1921); F. Gordon O'Neill, *Ernest Reuben Lilienthal and His Family* (Stanford, 1949), pp. 103–106, 123–139.

49. David Warren Ryder, *Great Citizen: A Biography of William H. Crocker* (San Francisco, 1962), pp. 47–67; O'Neill, *Ernest Reuben Lilienthal*, p. 30.

50. Ryder, *Great Citizen*, p. 71.

51. Ibid., pp. 79–86, 139–144; *Walker's, 1935*, p. 870; *Walker's, 1925*, p. 668.

52. Ryder, *Great Citizen*, pp. 145–146.

53. Ibid., pp. 94–95.

54. Ibid., p. 94.

55. Cutler, *America Is Good to a Country Boy*, p. 106; Ryder, *Great Citizen*, pp. 120–125.

56. Arthur Caylor, in the *News*, July 11, 1944, quoted in *A Man and His Friends*, p. 133; Charles H. Kendrick, quoted in *Memoirs of Charles Kendrick*, ed. David Warren Ryder (San Francisco, 1972), p. xiv.

57. Arthur L. Dean, *Alexander and Baldwin, Ltd.* (Honolulu, 1950), pp. 41–44, 75, 139–140; *Who's Who*, p. 271.

58. *National Cyclopedia of American Biography*, vol. E (New York, 1938), pp. 291–292, and vol. 29 (New York, 1941), p. 339; Meyer, *Western Jewry*, pp. 89–90.

59. O'Neill, *Ernest Reuben Lilienthal*, pp. 31–35; J. B. Levison, *Memories for My Family* (San Francisco, 1933), p. 72.

60. Levison, *Memories for My Family*, pp. 77, 117, 185; *Who's Who*, p. 28.

61. Levison, *Memories for My Family*, p. 78; Monroe A. Bloom, *A Century of Pioneering: A Brief History of the Crocker-Citizens National Bank* (San Francisco, 1970), pp. 5–6; John P. Young, *Journalism in California* (San Francisco, 1915), p. 266; *Who's Who*, pp. 37, 72.

62. San Francisco Chamber of Commerce, *San Francisco: The Financial, Commercial, and Industrial Metropolis of the Pacific Coast* (San Francisco, 1915), p. 22; Cleland and Putnam, *Isaias W. Hellman*, p. 86.

63. Frank Morton Todd, "San Francisco City and County," in *California Blue Book or State Roster, 1911* (Sacramento, 1913), pp. 773, 774; *Chamber of Commerce Journal* (San Francisco) 1 (July 1912):11, quoted in Mel G. Scott, *The San Francisco Bay Area: A Metropolis in Perspective* (Berkeley, 1959), pp. 313, 137.

64. H. Austin Adams, *The Man, John D. Spreckels* (San Diego, 1924), pp. 293, 294, 171, 182–199, 263; *San Francisco: Its Builders, Past and Present*, 2 vols. (Chicago, 1913), 1:15–17.

65. B. M. Rastall, *The San Francisco Program* (San Francisco, 1921), Foreword.

66. Colbert Coldwell and James Bacigalupi, quoted in Roger W. Lotchin, "The Darwinian City: The Politics of Urbanization in San Francisco Between the World Wars," *Pacific Historical Review* 48 (Aug. 1979):360; Lotchin offers a somewhat different interpretation. On Coldwell, Cornwall, and Banker, see Jo Ann L. Levy, *Behind the Western Skyline: Coldwell Banker: The First Seventy-Five Years* (Los Angeles, 1981), p. 28; V. P. Brun, *My Years with Coldwell Banker* (Los Angeles, n.d.), pp. 10A–12; on the Bank of Italy, see Marquis James and Bessie Rowland James, *Biography of a Bank: The Story of the Bank of America* (New York, 1954), chs. 6–13.

67. See Cleland and Putnam, *Isaias W. Hellman*, p. 86.

68. O'Neill, *Ernest Reuben Lilienthal*, pp. 109–113; *Walker's, 1915*, pp. 143–144, 132–133, 74; *Walker's, 1925*, pp. 255–256, 170–171, 311, 340–341; *Walker's, 1935*, pp. 226–227, 224–225, 399–400.

69. *Walker's, 1935*, p. 361.

70. *Walker's, 1925*, p. 414; *Walker's, 1935*, pp. 566–567, 271–272, 984–985.

71. O'Neill, *Ernest Reuben Lilienthal*, pp. 82–87; *Walker's, 1915*, p. 121; *Walker's, 1935*, pp. 735–736.

72. *Walker's, 1915*, pp. 118–119; *Walker's, 1925*, pp. 496–497; *Walker's, 1935*, pp. 753–754, 475–476, 557–558.

73. *Walker's, 1925*, pp. 408–409, 507, 467; *Walker's, 1935*, pp. 306–307.

74. Joseph D. Grant, *Redwoods and Reminiscences: The World Went Very Well Then* (San Francisco, 1973), pp. 108–111.

75. *Walker's, 1925,* pp. 638–639, 625–627, 655–658; *Walker's, 1935,* pp. 1037–1038.

76. Grant, *Redwoods and Reminiscences,* pp. 98–101; *Walker's, 1915,* pp. 61–62; *Walker's, 1925,* pp. 163–164.

77. *Walker's, 1915,* pp. 112–113, 126–127; *Walker's, 1925,* p. 174.

78. *Walker's, 1915,* pp. 136, 271–272, 159–161; *Walker's, 1925,* pp. 316–318, 216–218; *Walker's, 1935,* pp. 245–249.

79. *Walker's, 1915,* pp. 175–176; *Walker's, 1925,* pp. 234–235; *Walker's 1935,* 273–274, 277, 284, 288.

80. *Walker's, 1915,* p. 182; *Walker's, 1935,* pp. 301, 921.

81. *Walker's, 1915,* pp. 295–296, 284–286, 289–291; *Walker's, 1925,* pp. 618–619, 600, 378–379, 605–606, 610–612; *Walker's, 1935,* pp. 1009–1010, 1000–1001, 993–994.

82. *Walker's, 1915,* pp. 59–60, 101–102; *Walker's, 1925,* pp. 381–382, 452–453; *Walker's, 1935,* pp. 485–486, 656–657.

83. *Walker's, 1915,* p. 70; *Walker's, 1925,* pp. 582, 386; *Walker's, 1935,* pp. 492, 404, 828; *Walker's, 1925,* pp. 552–553, 347–348; *Walker's, 1935,* pp. 622–623, 681–682, 687–688, 749.

84. *Walker's, 1915,* pp. 262, 178; *Walker's, 1925,* pp. 570, 509; *Walker's, 1935,* p. 940.

85. Harold L. Zellerbach, "Art, Business, and Public Life in San Francisco," transcript of an interview conducted in 1971–1973 by the Regional Oral History Office, University of California, Berkeley, 1978, pp. 61–62; *Coast Banker* (San Francisco) 4 (April 1910):209; *Walker's, 1915,* pp. 81–82; *Walker's, 1925,* pp. 404, 592; *Walker's, 1935,* pp. 543–544, 586–587, 770–771, 628, 828.

86. *Walker's, 1925,* pp. 505, 428; *Walker's, 1935,* pp. 411–412, 364–365; *Walker's, 1935,* pp. 448, 635, 661, 888.

87. Robert Newton Lynch, "San Francisco Looks at Its World," *San Francisco Business,* May 14, 1938, p. 18; Capen A. Fleming, "Industrial Growth of the Central City," ibid., p. 112; Harrison S. Robinson, "The San Francisco Metropolitan Area," ibid., p. 110. On Frederick W. Dohrmann, Jr., and the Regional Plan Association, see Scott, *San Francisco Bay Area,* pp. 188–201.

88. Grant, *Redwoods and Reminiscences,* p. 116; San Francisco Chamber of Commerce, *The San Francisco–Oakland Metropolitan Area: An Industrial Study,* 1931, in Chamber of Commerce Records, California Historical Society, San Francisco.

89. *Walker's, 1925,* pp. 399–400, 387–388; *Walker's, 1935,* pp. 494, 974, 630–631, 619, 480, 615–616, 526.

90. U.S. Bureau of the Census, Department of Commerce, *County Data Book* (Washington, D.C., 1947), pp. 48–49; San Francisco Chamber of Commerce Research Department, *San Francisco Economic Survey, 1938* (San Francisco, 1938), p. 15.

91. *San Francisco Call and Post,* Dec. 31, 1926; San Francisco Chamber of Commerce Research Department, *San Francisco Economic Survey, 1938* (San Francisco, 1938), p. 20; State of California, Superintendent of Banks, *Annual Report* (Sacramento, 1934), abstract of report (40 percent common stock, 62 percent preferred stock).

92. *Chronicle,* March 7, 1930; letter from D. V. Nicholson to A. P. Giannini, May 25, 1932, Bank of America Archives, San Francisco.

CHAPTER 3

1. Jack London, "South of the Slot," in *Moon-Face and Other Stories* (New York, 1919), p. 34.

2. Table 117, "Total Persons 10 Years of Age and over Engaged in Gainful Occupations and in Each Class of Occupations, Classified by Sex, for Cities Having 50,000 Inhabitants or More: 1890," U.S. Census Office, Department of the Interior, *Eleventh Census of the United States: 1890,* 15 vols. (Washington, D.C., 1892), vol. 1, pt. 2, pp. 628—629.

3. Table 118, "Total Males and Females 10 Years of Age and over Engaged in Selected Occupations, Classified by General Nativity, Color, Age Periods, Conjugal Conditions, Illiteracy, Inability to Speak English, Months Unemployed, and Country of Birth, for Cities Having 50,000 Inhabitants or More: 1890," ibid., pp. 636—639, 702—703, 704—705, 728—729; Table 3, "Total Persons 10 Years of Age and over Engaged in Each Specified Occupation, Classified by Sex, for Cities of 100,000 Inhabitants or More: 1910," U.S. Bureau of the Census, Department of Commerce and Labor, *Thirteenth Census of the United States: 1910,* 11 vols. (Washington, D.C., 1914), 4:200—201; Table 3, "Gainful Workers 10 Years Old and over, by General Divisions of Occupations," U.S. Bureau of the Census, Department of Commerce, *Fifteenth Census of the United States: 1930,* 6 vols. (Washington, D.C., 1932—1933), 4:173.

4. For an argument that San Francisco was in fact a major manufacturing center, see Shumsky, "Tar Flat and Nob Hill," pp. 20—64. Being a "manufacturing city" implies some sort of comparative dimension, however, and a comparative analysis shows clearly that the city's economy was never dominated by manufacturing and that manufacturing in the city never dominated production of any particular item. The city unquestionably *had* manufacturing. It was *not* a manufacturing city in the pattern of Pittsburgh, Lawrence, or Detroit.

5. Table 43, "Total Males and Females 10 Years of Age and over Engaged in Selected Groups of Occupations, Classified by General Nativity, Color, Conjugal Conditions, Months Unemployed, Age Periods, and Parentage, for Cities Having 50,000 Inhabitants or More: 1900," U.S. Census Office, Department of the Interior, *Twelfth Census of the United States: 1900,* 37 vols. (Washington, D.C., 1902—1904), 20:720—724.

6. Table 104, "Population, Dwellings, and Families, for Places Having 2,500 Inhabitants or More: 1900," ibid., vol. 2, pt. 2, p. 640; Table 23, "Population by Sex, General Nativity, and Color, for Places Having 2,500 Inhabitants or More: 1900," ibid., p. 610; Table 5, "Composition and Characteristics of the Population for Wards (or Assembly Districts) of Cities of 50,000 or More," U.S. Bureau of the Census, Department of Commerce and Labor, *Thirteenth Census of the United States: Abstract of the Census with Supplement for California* (Washington, D.C., 1913), p. 616. The relevant assembly districts for the 1900 census are the 28th through the 31st; for 1910, the 28th through the 30th. For a good history of the region, see Alvin Averbach, "San Francisco's South of Market District, 1850—1950: The Emergence of a Skid Row," *California Historical Quarterly* 52 (Fall 1973):197—223; Averbach cites numerous studies of various aspects of the area and the observations of various visitors.

7. Table 118, "Total Males and Females 10 Years of Age and over Engaged in Selected Occupations, Classified by General Nativity, Color, Age Periods, Conjugal Conditions, Illiteracy, Inability to Speak English, Months Unemployed, and Country of Birth, for Cities Having 50,000 Inhabitants or More: 1890," *Eleventh Census of the United States: 1890,* vol. 1, pt. 2, pp. 636—639, 702—703, 704—705, 728—729; Table 3, "Total Persons 10 Years of Age and over Engaged in Each Specified Occupation, Classified by Sex, for Cities of 100,000 Inhabitants or More: 1910," *Thirteenth Census of the United States: 1910,* 4: 200—201; Table 3, "Gainful Workers 10 Years Old and over, by General Divisions of Occupations," *Fifteenth Census of the United States: 1930,* 4:173.

8. U.S. National Archives and Records Service, General Services Administration, *1900 Federal Population Census Schedules,* microfilm, T623, roll 100 [hereafter cited as *1900 Census Schedules*]. See also Jerry P. Schofer, *Urban and Rural Finnish Communities in California: 1860–1960* (San Francisco, 1975), pp. 31–34; Hyman Weintraub, *Andrew Furuseth: Emancipator of the Seamen* (Berkeley, 1959), pp. 5, 6; James Fell, *British Merchant Seamen in San Francisco, 1892–1898* (London, 1899); State of California, Bureau of Labor Statistics, *Investigation into Condition of Men Working on the Waterfront and on Board Pacific Coast Vessels, San Francisco, June 29–July 10, 1887* (Sacramento, 1887); "Boarding Houses" file, Walter Macarthur Manuscript Collection, carton 1, Bancroft Library, University of California, Berkeley; Peter B. Gill and Ottilie Dombroff, "History of the Sailors' Union of the Pacific," typed manuscript, ca. 1942, carton 3, Paul Scharrenberg Manuscript Collection, Bancroft Library, University of California, Berkeley, pp. 20–23; Averbach, "South of Market," p. 202.

9. Table 43, "Total Males and Females 10 Years of Age and over Engaged in Selected Groups of Occupations, Classified by General Nativity, Color, Conjugal Conditions, Months Unemployed, Age Periods, and Parentage, for Cities Having 50,000 Inhabitants or More: 1900," *Twelfth Census of the United States: 1900,* 20:720–724; Paul Scharrenberg, "History of the Sailors' Union of the Pacific," typed manuscript, ca. 1960, carton 3, Scharrenberg Manuscript Collection, Bancroft Library, University of California, Berkeley, p. 4; Gladys C. Hansen, *San Francisco Almanac,* rev. ed. (San Rafael, Ca., 1980), p. 74; Weintraub, *Andrew Furuseth,* p. 8.

10. Averbach, "South of Market", pp. 203–205; testimony of Paul Scharrenberg and John P. McLaughlin, U.S. Commission on Industrial Relations, *Industrial Relations: Final Report and Testimony,* 10 vols. (Washington, D.C., 1916), 5:5041, 5053–5054; Carleton H. Parker, *The Casual Laborer and Other Essays* (New York, 1920), p. 80.

11. Sanborn Insurance maps, 1885, microfilm, California Historical Society, San Francisco; photographic collection, California Historical Society, San Francisco; Kate Douglas Wiggin, *My Garden of Memory: An Autobiography* (Boston, 1923), p. 108; see also Wiggin's description of her kindergarten students, pp. 109–126.

12. The 100 block of Tehama has ceased to exist in the redevelopment of South of Market. All that remains is the entrance to the parking lot of the headquarters of the Marine Firemen's Union. The information on the street's residents comes from *1900 Census Schedules,* roll 100.

13. Ibid., supplemented by reference to the *Crocker-Langley San Francisco Directory, 1900* (San Francisco, 1900).

14. *Crocker-Langley San Francisco Directory, 1900;* Wiggin, *My Garden of Memory,* p. 109; Averbach, "South of Market," pp. 200–201; Michael M. Zarchin, *Glimpses of Jewish Life in San Francisco* (Berkeley, 1952), p. 169; Robert McElroy et al., *"The Retrospect": A Glance at Thirty Years of the History of Howard Street Methodist-Episcopal Church of San Francisco* (San Francisco, 1883).

15. *1900 Census Schedules,* roll 100. For the Palace Hotel, see Oscar Lewis and Carroll D. Hall, *Bonanza Inn: America's First Luxury Hotel* (New York, 1939), esp. pp. 4, 19–29; Guillermo Prieto, *San Francisco in the Seventies: The City as Viewed by a Mexican Political Exile,* trans. and ed. Edwin S. Marby (San Francisco, 1938), p. 8.

16. Table 104, "Population, Dwellings, and Families, for Places Having 2,500 Inhabitants or More: 1900," *Twelfth Census of the United States: 1900,* vol. 2, pt. 2, p. 640; Table 23, "Population by Sex, General Nativity, and Color, for Places Having 2,500 Inhabitants or More: 1900," ibid., p. 610; Table 5, "Composition and Characteristics of the Population for Wards (or Assembly Districts) of Cities of 50,000 or More," *Thirteenth Census of the United States: Abstract of the Census with Supplement for California,* p. 616. The relevant assembly districts for 1900 are 32nd through the 36th, with the 34th and 35th squarely in the heart of the area; for 1910, the relevant districts are 31st through the 36th, with the 35th squarely in the center of the district.

For a good, concise description of the built environment of the Mission District, see Randolph Delehanty, *Walks and Tours in the Golden Gate City: San Francisco* (New York, 1980), pp. 154, 161–167, esp. p. 167. For information on the history of many surviving houses from the late nineteenth century, see, in addition to Delehanty, Judith Lynch Waldhorn and Sally B. Woodbridge, *Victoria's Legacy* (San Francisco, 1978), pp. 41–89, which includes information on hundreds of specific houses as to the date of construction, the contractor, and sometimes the early residents. See also Roger Olmsted and T. H. Watkins, *Here Today: San Francisco's Architectural Heritage* (San Francisco, 1968), pp. 102–111. For the streetcar lines, see "Guide Map of the City of San Francisco" (San Francisco, 1879); and Charles C. Hoag, ed., *Our Society Blue Book: 1902* (San Francisco, 1902), pp. 37–44.

17. The 400 block on Bartlett still retains some sense of what it must have been like at the turn of the century, although the numbers today do not correspond to those in 1900. The houses at 476–478 and 494–496 are Italianate-style duplexes, dating from the 1870s. The house at 492 was probably originally a single-family, Italianate-style house. The building at 446, constructed in the Stick style popular in the 1880s, was probably once a single-family house, and the single-story Italianate cottage at 432, built in 1875, is a splendid example of a working family's home. Around the corner on Twenty-fifth Street between Bartlett and Mission are a row of four Stick-style two-story houses, probably from the 1880s. The information on families comes from *1900 Census Schedules,* roll 103. See Nellie McGraw Hedgpeth, *My Early Days in San Francisco* (San Francisco, 1974), for an account of life on Twenty-first Street between Valencia and Guerrero, from about 1880 to 1889, esp. pp. 12–35.

18. The information on occupations comes from *1900 Census Schedules,* roll 103, supplemented by reference to *Crocker-Langley San Francisco Directory, 1900.*

19. *Crocker-Langley San Francisco Directory, 1900.*

20. Ibid.; Ruth Kelson Rafael, *Continuum—A Selective History of San Francisco Eastern European Jewish Life, 1880–1940,* rev. ed. (Berkeley, 1977), p. 8; Zarchin, *Glimpses of Jewish Life,* p. 169; Fred Massarik, *A Report on the Jewish Population of San Francisco, Marin County, and the Peninsula: 1959* (San Francisco, 1959), pp. 7–8, 11.

21. Delehanty, *Walks and Tours,* p. 162; Julia Cooley Altrocchi, *Spectacular San Franciscans* (New York, 1949), p. 154; Hansen, *San Franciso Almanac,* pp. 41, 232. For pictures of Woodward's Gardens, see T. H. Watkins and Roger R. Olmsted, *Mirror of the Dream: An Illustrated History of San Francisco* (San Francisco, 1976), pp. 112–113. Jerry Flamm, *Good Life in Hard Times: San Francisco's Twenties and Thirties* (San Francisco, 1978), includes a lengthy account of the Seals, pp. 60–71.

22. Delehanty, *Walks and Tours,* p. 132; Frank Norris, *McTeague: A Story of San Francisco,* ed. Donald Pizer (New York, 1977), esp. pp. 106, 263–268; Flamm, *Good Life in Hard Times,* pp. 72–83; Writers' Program of the Work Projects Administration in Northern California, *San Francisco: The Bay and Its Cities* (New York, 1940), p. 285; Harriet Lane Levy, *920 O'Farrell Street* (Garden City, N.Y., 1947), p. 3. For examples of Western Addition houses from the late nineteenth century that have survived "redevelopment," see the area around Alamo Square, the 2000, 2100, 2200, or 2800 blocks on Bush Street, the 1800 block on Laguna, the 700 block on Broderick, the 300 block on Scott, the 800 block on Grove, the 700 block on Webster, the 800 block on Fulton, or the 900 block on Ellis. See Waldhorn and Woodbridge, *Victoria's Legacy,* pp. 97–112.

23. Table 104, "Population, Dwellings, and Families, for Places Having 2,500 Inhabitants or More: 1900," *Twelfth Census of the United States: 1900,* vol. 2, pt. 2, p. 640; Table 23, "Population by Sex, General Nativity, and Color, for Places Having 2,500 Inhabitants or More: 1900," ibid., p. 610; Table 5, "Composition and Characteristics of the Population for Wards (or Assembly Districts) of Cities of 50,000 or

More," *Thirteenth Census of the United States: Abstract of the Census with Supplement for California,* p. 616. The relevant assembly districts for 1900 are 37th, 38th, and 40th; for 1910, the same. The 38th and 40th are squarely in the heart of the Western Addition.

24. Only two houses from the nineteenth century survive on the 1700 block of Bush, those at 1710 and 1712, both Italianate-style structures built in 1875. See Olmsted and Watkins, *Here Today,* p. 254. The information on families comes from *1900 Census Schedules,* roll 105.

25. Zarchin, *Glimpses of Jewish Life,* pp. 59, 61, 70, 72, 114–115, 169, 172; Delehanty, *Walks and Tours,* p. 304; Flamm, *Good Life in Hard Times,* pp. 77–78; Irena Narell, *Our City: The Jews of San Francisco* (San Diego, 1981), pp. 49–50; Massarik, *A Report on the Jewish Population,* pp. 7–8, 11; Rafael, *Continuum,* pp. 1–9, 34; see also Gustav Adolf Danziger, "The Jew in San Francisco: The Last Half-Century," *Overland Monthly* 25 (April 1895):381–410; and K. M. Nesfield, "From a Gentile Standpoint," ibid., pp. 410–420.

26. *1900 Census Schedules,* roll 105, supplemented by *Crocker-Langley San Francisco Directory, 1900;* Levy, *920 O'Farrell,* p. 12. See also Narell, *Our City,* esp. chs. 7–12.

27. *Crocker-Langley San Francisco Directory, 1900.*

28. Shumate, *A Visit to Rincon Hill;* Averbach, "South of Market," pp. 199–200.

29. Delehanty, *Walks and Tours,* pp. 176–178; Olmsted and Watkins, *Here Today,* pp. 66–69; Lewis, *Silver Kings,* pp. 232–233; Ambrose Bierce, *The Ambrose Bierce Satanic Reader,* quoted in John Van der Zee and Boyd Jacobson, *The Imagined City: San Francisco in the Minds of Its Writers* (San Francisco, 1980), p. 23; Altrocchi, *Spectacular San Franciscans,* pp. 173–176, 180; Gertrude Atherton, *My San Francisco: A Wayward Biography* (Indianapolis, 1946), pp. 32–37, esp. pp. 32–33.

30. Altrocchi, *Spectacular San Franciscans,* pp. 170–171; Atherton, *My San Francisco,* pp. 31–32, 37–39; Olmsted and Watkins, *Here Today,* p. 66. Flood's mansion was the only one to survive the fire in 1906; it now houses the city's most prestigious club, the Pacific Union.

31. Delehanty, *Walks and Tours,* pp. 132–148; Olmsted and Watkins, *Here Today,* pp. 14–39; Narell, *Our City,* p. 167; Hoag, ed., *Our Society Blue Book: 1902,* pp. 149–196. Just under a third of the *Blue Book* families were in the Western Addition, about 10 percent were in the Nob Hill area, nearly 10 percent were elsewhere in Downtown, just under 10 percent were in the Mission District, and about 1 percent each were South of Market or in North Beach.

32. For one example of the reaction of white San Franciscans to Chinatown, see Atherton, *My San Francisco,* pp. 53–56, where she recounts a visit to a Chinatown restaurant and theater in the 1880s, complete with encounters with an opium smoker and a group of prostitutes. Ivan Light, "From Vice District to Tourist Attraction: The Moral Career of American Chinatowns, 1880–1940," *Pacific Historical Review* 43 (Aug. 1974):367–394; Stanford M. Lyman, "Conflict and the Web of Group Affiliation in San Francisco's Chinatown, 1850–1910," *Pacific Historical Review* 43 (Nov. 1974):473–499; Victor G. Nee and Brett de Bary Nee, *Longtime Californ': A Documentary Study of an American Chinatown* (Boston, 1974), pp. 65–69, 272–277; William Hoy, *The Chinese Six Companies: A Short General Historical Resume of the Origin, Function, and Importance in the Life of the California Chinese* (San Francisco, 1942).

33. Delehanty, *Walks and Tours,* pp. 197–198; W. F. Rae, *Westward by Rail* (London, 1871), quoted in Oscar Lewis, ed., *This Was San Francisco: Being First-Hand Accounts of the Evolution of One of America's Cities* (New York, 1962), pp. 172–173; Arnold Genthe, *As I Remember* (New York, 1936), quoted in Laverne Mau Dicker, *The Chinese in San Francisco: A Pictorial History* (New York, 1979), p. 16; a map of streets and walkways may be found following p. 214, in San Francisco, Board of Supervisors,

Municipal Reports (San Francisco, 1884–1885). See also Helen Virginia Cather, *The History of San Francisco's Chinatown* (San Francisco, 1974).

34. Wei Bat Liu, quoted in Nee and Nee, *Longtime Californ,'* pp. 64–65.

35. Table 14, "The Chinese Population by Counties: 1890, 1880, 1870," and Table 20, "Population as Native- and Foreign-Born and White and Colored, Classified by Sex," U.S. Census Office, Department of the Interior, *Compendium of the Eleventh Census: 1890,* 3 vols. (Washington, D.C., 1892), 1:516, 668–669; "Supplemental Tables for Indian, Chinese, and Japanese Population," U.S. Bureau of the Census, Department of Commerce, *Fourteenth Census of the United States: 1920,* 11 vols. (Washington, D.C., 1922–1923), 3:128. Each house of prostitution, gambling establishment, and opium den is located and identified as Chinese or white as of 1885; see "Condition of the Chinese Quarter," in San Francisco, *Municipal Reports* (1884–1885), pp. 160–214, esp. the map following p. 214, which locates sixty-six houses of prostitution for Chinese and thirty-eight for whites; Dicker, *Chinese in San Francisco,* pp. 23–24; Mildred Crowl Martin, *Chinatown's Angry Angel: The Story of Donaldina Cameron* (Palo Alto, 1977), pp. 36–211; Flamm, *Good Life in Hard Times,* ch. 6.

36. Table 66, "Occupations: Fifty Cities," U.S. Census Office, Department of the Interior, *Compendium of the Ninth Census* (Washington, D.C., 1872), pp. 618–619; Table 36, "Persons in Selected Occupations in Fifty Principal Cities," U.S. Census Office, Department of the Interior, *Tenth Census of the United States: 1880,* 22 vols. (Washington, D.C., 1883), 1:902; Cather, *The History of . . . Chinatown,* pp. 33–39; Dicker, *Chinese in San Francisco,* pp. 3–6; Alexander Saxton, *The Indispensable Enemy: Labor and the Anti-Chinese Movement in California* (Berkeley, 1971), pp. 57–66. For descriptions of door-to-door peddlers, see Levy, *920 O'Farrell,* pp. 196–198; Hedgpeth, *My Early Days,* p. 17; and Amelia Ransome Neville, *The Fantastic City: Memoirs of the Social and Romantic Life of Old San Francisco* (Boston, 1932). Levy also describes their Chinese laundryman (pp. 198–200), Hedgpeth describes both their laundryman and a door-to-door Chinese ragpicker (p. 18), and Neville tells of Chinese door-to-door peddlers selling silks and brocades, carved ivory and sandalwood, lacquer ware and tea.

37. Table 43, "Total Males and Females 10 Years of Age and over Engaged in Selected Groups of Occupations, Classified by General Nativity, Color, Conjugal Conditions, Months Unemployed, Age Periods, and Parentage, for Cities Having 50,000 Inhabitants or More: 1900," *Twelfth Census of the United States: 1900,* 20:720–724; Elgie, "Development of San Francisco Manufacturing," pp. 89–91.

38. Table 8, "Manufactures in Cities by Specified Industries: 1900," *Twelfth Census,* vol. 8, pt. 2, 52–57; U.S. Census Office, Department of the Interior, *Report on the Statistics of Wages in Manufacturing Industries* (Washington, D.C., 1886), pp. 15, 41, 379; Nee and Nee, *Longtime Californ,'* p. 45.

39. Rae, *Westward by Rail,* quoted in Lewis, *This Was San Francisco,* p. 173; a survey of the *1900 Census Schedules* for various neighborhoods will show the laundries and, for the Western Addition, Nob Hill, and Pacific Heights, the live-in servants; Gim Chang, quoted in Nee and Nee, *Longtime Californ,'* p. 72. For another account of the dangers posed to Chinese by "hoodlums" outside Chinatown, see Samuel Williams, "The City of the Golden Gate," *Scribner's Monthly* 10 (July 1875):276. For a list of manufacturing done in Chinatown, see San Francisco, *Municipal Reports* (1884–1885), pp. 215–219.

40. For the decline in population, see the census sources cited in note 35; for school segregation, see Charles M. Wollenberg, *All Deliberate Speed: Segregation and Exclusion in California Schools: 1855–1975* (Berkeley, 1976), pp. 31–44; Nee and Nee, *Longtime Californ,'* pp. 32–33, 61.

41. The descriptions are by Will Irwin, *The City That Was: A Requiem of Old San Francisco* (New York, 1906), pp. 45–46. See also his description of the bay filled with orange-brown lateen sails, p. 19. Deanna Paoli Gumina, *The Italians of San Francisco, 1850–1930* (New York, 1978), pp. 18, 20–33, esp. p. 25.

42. Table 104, "Population, Dwellings, and Families, for Places Having 2,500 Inhabitants or More: 1900," *Twelfth Census of the United States: 1900*, vol. 2, pt. 2, p. 640; Table 23, "Population by Sex, General Nativity, and Color, for Places Having 2,500 Inhabitants or More: 1900," ibid., p. 610; Table 5, "Composition and Characteristics of the Population for Wards (or Assembly Districts) of Cities of 50,000 or More," *Thirteenth Census of the United States: Abstract of the Census with Supplement for California,* p. 616. For 1900, North Beach was a part of assembly districts 44 and 45, dividing it along Kearny Street and including a good deal of Downtown in the 45th. Much of the 44th was also not Italian. For 1910, the 45th District included all of North Beach and some small surrounding areas. See Dino Cinel, *From Italy to San Francisco: The Immigrant Experience* (Stanford, 1982), esp. chs. 5–7.

43. Table 43, "Total Males and Females 10 Years of Age and over Engaged in Selected Groups of Occupations, Classified by General Nativity, Color, Conjugal Conditions, Months Unemployed, Age Periods, and Parentage, for Cities Having 50,000 Inhabitants or More: 1900," *Twelfth Census of the United States: 1900,* 20: 720–724; Gumina, *Italians of San Francisco,* ch. 4.

44. Gumina, *Italians of San Francisco,* ch. 4, and also pp. 33–37.

45. Julian Dana, *A. P. Giannini: Giant in the West* (New York, 1947); James and James, *Biography of a Bank.*

46. James E. Vance, Jr., *Geography and Urban Evolution in the San Francisco Bay Area* (Berkeley, 1964), pp. 18–24; Herbert Asbury, *The Barbary Coast: An Informal History of the San Francisco Underworld* (Garden City, N.Y., 1933); Helen Hunt Jackson, quoted in Lewis, *This Was San Francisco,* pp. 175–176; David Ward, *Cities and Immigrants* (New York, 1971), pp. 87–102.

47. Table 104, "Population, Dwellings, and Families, for Places Having 2,500 Inhabitants or More: 1900," *Twelfth Census of the United States: 1900*, vol. 2, pt. 2, p. 640; Table 23, "Population by Sex, General Nativity, and Color, for Places Having 2,500 Inhabitants or More: 1900," ibid., p. 610; Table 5, "Composition and Characteristics of the Population for Wards (or Assembly Districts) of Cities of 50,000 or More," *Thirteenth Census of the United States: Abstract of the Census with Supplement for California,* p. 616. The relevant assembly districts for Downtown in 1900 were the 39th, 42nd, 43rd, and 45th. The 45th was nearest the waterfront and included part of North Beach. The 43rd included Chinatown. The 42nd and 39th are best for summarizing the characteristics of other parts of downtown, although the 39th included many residential areas not unlike parts of the Western Addition. For 1910, the relevant districts are the 42nd through the 44th. The 44th was nearest the waterfront and included Chinatown. The 42nd and 43rd were between Mason and Van Ness and Market and Broadway, the heart of the apartment district to the west of the central business district. Williams, "City of the Golden Gate," p. 280; see also his comments on boardinghouse living (p. 277). Twenty of the "prominent hotels" are listed with their permanent guests in Hoag, ed., *Our Society Blue Book: 1902.*

48. Cinel, *From Italy to San Francisco,* pp. 106–116, 124–133; Dana, *A. P. Giannini,* pp. 45–46; Gumina, *Italians of San Francisco,* p. 33

49. Michael Piore, "Notes for a Theory of Labor Market Stratification," in *Labor Market Segmentation,* ed. Richard C. Edwards, Michael Reich, and David M. Gordon (Lexington, Mass., 1975), esp. pp. 126–128, 144–146. See also Michael Piore, "Jobs and Training," in *The State and the Poor,* ed. Samuel Beer and Richard Barringer (Cambridge, Mass., 1970); Michael Piore, "On-the-Job Training in a Dual Labor Market," in *Public Private Manpower Policies,* ed. Arnold Weber et al. (Madison, Wis.,

1969); Barry Bluestone, "Lower-Income Workers and Marginal Industries," in *Poverty in America,* ed. Louis Ferman et al. (Ann Arbor, 1968).

50. Williams, "City of the Golden Gate," p. 280.

51. Piore notes:

> The lower-class subculture is a derivative of the working-class pattern in which people fail to make a transition into a routine life-style pattern as adults; . . . the transition is associated with family formation and with the availability of stable jobs not only to the individual but also to enough other members of his or her peer groups so that the groups' norms change in such a way as to support the changes in the individual life-style. ("Notes for a Theory," pp. 146, 128)

52. Averbach, "South of Market," pp. 203–204; Scott, *San Francisco Bay Area,* p. 112; Gumina, *Italians of San Francisco,* pp. 23, 33; Flamm, *Good Life in Hard Times,* p. 72; Zarchin, *Glimpses of Jewish Life,* p. 169; Rafael, *Continuum,* pp. 1–8; Delehanty, *Walks and Tours,* p. 154.

53. Frederick M. Wirt, *Power in the City: Decision Making in San Francisco* (Berkeley, 1974), pp. 30–38; Delehanty, *Walks and Tours,* pp. 48–50; Hansen, *San Francisco Almanac,* pp. 203–204.

CHAPTER 4

1. Lucile Eaves, *A History of California Labor Legislation with an Introductory Sketch of the San Francisco Labor Movement,* University of California Publications in Economics, vol. 2 (Berkeley, 1910), pp. 1–81, esp. p. 6; Ira B. Cross, *A History of the Labor Movement in California* (Berkeley, 1935), pp. 10–28, esp. pp. 14–16; Carl C. Plehn, "Labor in California," *Yale Review* 4 (1895–1896):409–425.

2. John P. Young, *San Francisco: A History of the Pacific Coast Metropolis,* 2 vols. (San Francisco, 1912), 2:667–669; U.S. Census Office, Department of the Interior, *Report on the Social Statistics of Cities* (Washington, D.C., 1886), pt. 2, pp. 813–815; Table 3, "Manufactures in 165 Principle Cities," U.S. Census Office, Department of the Interior, *Report on Manufacturing Industries in the United States at the Eleventh Census: 1890* (Washington, D.C., 1895), pt. 2, pp. 530–539.

3. Cross, *A History of the Labor Movement in California,* pp. 166–209.

4. Ibid., pp. 130–150; Frank Roney, *Frank Roney: Irish Rebel and California Labor Leader: An Autobiography,* ed. Ira B. Cross (Berkeley, 1931), pp. 347–364; Saxton, in *Indispensable Enemy,* argues that "the anti-Chinese impulse overshadowed and permeated every action of the Trades Assembly and its locals" (p. 171).

5. Cross, *A History of the Labor Movement in California,* pp. 151–155.

6. Ibid.; Roney, *Frank Roney,* pp. 325–326; Bernard K. Johnpoll, "Burnette G. Haskell: Firebrand or Fraud?" paper delivered at the Fifth Annual Southwest Labor Studies conference, California State University, Dominguez Hills, April 21, 1979.

7. Cross, *A History of the Labor Movement in California,* pp. 166–197; Roney, *Frank Roney,* pp. 435–524.

8. Cross, *A History of the Labor Movement in California,* pp. 215–216, 333, 335; Robert Verner Ohlson, "History of the San Francisco Labor Council, 1892–1939," master's thesis, University of California, Berkeley, 1941, pp. 3–7. Cross and Ohlson agree that both previous councils were dissolved and a new organization formed in 1892, with a new constitution and bylaws. Macarthur, in 1904, referred to the federation as having been "reorganized" into the Labor Council; Walter Macarthur, "The San Francisco Labor Council," *San Francisco Labor Clarion,* Nov. 11, 1904, pp. 11–15, esp. p. 13. An anonymous account of the history of the Labor Council, published in 1908, includes the following: "The Labor Council of the metropolis of the Pacific Coast was organized in December, 1892, not as an entirely new body, but

practically as a re-organization of the Council of Federated Trades"; ibid., Sept. 4, 1908, p. 2. A similar account appears in ibid., Sept. 2, 1910, p. 2. See also Walter Macarthur to Ira B. Cross, March 13, 1935, filed with "Miscellaneous Papers," carton 1, Walter Macarthur Manuscript Collection, Bancroft Library, University of California, Berkeley.

9. Cross, *A History of the Labor Movement in California*, pp. 209–213, esp. p. 210; Robert E. L. Knight, *Industrial Relations in the San Francisco Bay Area, 1900–1918* (Berkeley, 1960), pp. 28–34.

10. Michael Kazin, "Barons of Labor: The San Francisco Building Trades, 1896–1922," Ph.D. dissertation, Stanford University, 1983, pp. 72–124, soon to be published by University of Illinois Press. See also Ohlson, "History of the San Francisco Labor Council," p. 4; Cross, *A History of the Labor Movement in California*, pp. 217–239; Knight, *Industrial Relations*, pp. 26–95; "List of Trade Unions," *Labor Clarion*, June 17, 1904, p. 14. In some part, the burst of organization in 1901 resulted from the activities of the first AFL organizer to spend any considerable amount of time in the city—Jefferson D. Pierce, who arrived early in 1901 and stayed throughout the year.

11. Frederick L. Ryan, *Industrial Relations in the San Francisco Building Trades* (Norman, Okl., 1935), esp. pp. 25–60; Olaf A. Tveitmoe, "Building Trades Council," *Labor Clarion*, Nov. 11, 1904, pp. 20–21; testimony of Grant Fee and of Patrick H. McCarthy, in U.S. Commission on Industrial Relations, *Final Report and Testimony*, 6:5171–5218, esp. pp. 5172–5173, 5175–5176, 5193, 5211–5215. The best treatment of the Building Trades Council is Kazin's "Barons of Labor."

12. Kazin, "Barons of Labor," esp. chs. 3, 5, 7, 9; Ryan, *Industrial Relations*, pp. 33–35; Cross, *A History of the Labor Movement in California*, pp. 336–337; John Alan Lawrence, "Behind the Palaces: The Working Class and the Labor Movement in San Francisco, 1877–1901," Ph.D. dissertation, University of California, Berkeley, 1979, pp. 353–361.

13. Kazin, "Barons of Labor," esp. pp. 162–175; Tveitmoe, "Building Trades Council," p. 21; Ryan, *Industrial Relations*, pp. 58–59, 79–88, 110–115, 120; U.S. Commission on Industrial Relations, *Final Report and Testimony*, 6:5172, 5312–5315.

14. Cross, *A History of the Labor Movement in California*, pp. 32–33, 143, 166–167, 226–228, 248–249, 256; Ryan, *Industrial Relations*, pp. 21, 45, 57, 51–53; Knight, *Industrial Relations*, pp. 21, 28, 35–36, 58–61, 69, 114; Matthew Josephson, *Union House, Union Bar: The History of the Hotel and Restaurant Employees and Bartenders International Union, AFL-CIO* (New York, 1956), p. 48; "The Iron Trades Council," *Labor Clarion*, Sept. 4, 1908, p. 4; "The Iron Trades Council of San Francisco," ibid., Sept. 2, 1910, p. 26; "Iron Trades Council" file, San Francisco Labor Council Manuscript Collection, Bancroft Library, University of California, Berkeley; David F. Selvin, "History of the San Francisco Typographical Union," master's thesis, University of California, Berkeley, 1935; "Allied Printing Trades Council" file, Labor Council Manuscript Collection; Robert M. Robinson, "San Francisco Teamsters at the Turn of the Century," *California Historical Society Quarterly* 35 (1956):59–69, 144–153, esp. pp. 59–61; "The Brotherhood of Teamsters," *Labor Clarion*, Sept. 4, 1908, pp. 14–15; "Teamsters' Joint Council," ibid., March 1, 1912, p. 6; Donald Garnel, *The Rise of Teamster Power in the West* (Berkeley, 1972), pp. 49–51.

15. Cross, *A History of the Labor Movement in California*, pp. 20–21; "The California Letters of Edward Hotchkiss," *Quarterly of the California Historical Society* 10 (1933):99.

16. There are four full-scale treatments of either the Sailors' Union of the Pacific (SUP) or Andrew Furuseth, its longtime leader. See Paul S. Taylor, *The Sailors' Union of the Pacific* (New York, 1923); Weintraub, *Andrew Furuseth;* Gill and Dombroff, "History of the Sailors' Union," and Scharrenberg, "History of the Sailors' Union

of the Pacific." Another history of the SUP is in preparation by Stephen Schwartz. Other important material is to be found in the Paul Scharrenberg Manuscript Collection and in that of Walter Macarthur, both at the Bancroft Library. The *Coast Seamen's Journal,* available at the Bancroft Library, is an important chronicle of the union's development. See also Scharrenberg's testimony before the U.S. Commission on Industrial Relations, *Final Report and Testimony,* 5:5043. Information on the SUP and other sea-faring unions is also to be found in Robert Coleman Francis, "A History of Labor on the San Francisco Waterfront," Ph.D. dissertation, University of California, Berkeley, 1934; and in Cross, *A History of the Labor Movement in California,* pp. 132–133, 168–169. For a brief description of the "shape-up," see Lawrence M. Kahn, "Unions and Internal Labor Markets: The Case of the San Francisco Longshoremen," *Labor History* 21 (Summer 1980):372–373.

17. Weintraub, *Furuseth;* Scharrenberg and Macarthur manuscript collections, Bancroft Library.

18. For longshoremen's organizations, see Francis, "A History of Labor on the San Francisco Waterfront," esp. pp. 16, 32–33, 58, 65–66, 85–88, 133–134, 144–148, 181–182. For the various councils, see ibid., pp. 65–66, 131–132, 140, 149–150; and George Charles Jensen, "The City Front Federation of San Francisco: A Study in Labor Organization," master's thesis, University of California, Berkeley, 1912, esp. pp. 17–22, 29–62; Gill and Dombroff, "History of the Sailors' Union," pp. 313–314, 338–369; Cross, *A History of the Labor Movement in California,* pp. 183, 198, 203, 207, 339; Knight, *Industrial Relations,* pp. 28, 61, 173, 272; John Kean, "City Front Federation," *Labor Clarion,* Nov. 11, 1904, p. 22; John Kean, "The City Front Federation," ibid., Jan. 19, 1906, pp. 1–3, 10; "Riggers and Stevedores," ibid., July 2, 1920, p. 10; "City Front Federation of the Port of San Francisco" file, San Francisco Labor Council Manuscript Collection, Bancroft Library, University of California, Berkeley.

19. The strike of 1901 has been described many times. Knight, *Industrial Relations,* pp. 58–95, esp. pp. 60–67; Cross, *A History of the Labor Movement in California,* pp. 239–249; Robinson, "San Francisco Teamsters," pp. 64–66; Thomas Walker Page, "The San Francisco Labor Movement in 1901," *Political Science Quarterly* 17 (1902):664–688, esp. pp. 668–669; Ed R. Rosenberg, "The San Francisco Strikes of 1901," *American Federationist* 9 (Jan. 1902):15–18; Jules Tygiel, "Workingmen in San Francisco, 1880–1901," Ph.D. dissertation, University of California, Los Angeles, 1977, ch. 6.

20. Cross, *A History of the Labor Movement in California,* p. 242; Knight, *Industrial Relations,* pp. 67–77; Page, "San Francisco Labor Movement in 1901," pp. 676–678; Robinson, "San Francisco Teamsters," pp. 66–68, 145–148.

21. Knight, *Industrial Relations,* pp. 77–84; Robinson, "San Francisco Teamsters," p. 150; Bernard Cornelius Cronin, *Father Yorke and the Labor Movement in San Francisco, 1900–1910* (Washington, D.C., 1943), pp. 48–70; esp. pp. 65–66. For the analysis of the labor leaders, see Walter Macarthur, "San Francisco—A Climax in Civics," typed manuscript, 1906, Macarthur Manuscript Collection, Bancroft Library, University of California, Berkeley, carton 1, in which Macarthur writes:

> In only one particular did the situation of 1900 differ from that of 1890, namely, in the knowledge of the events that had transpired between these dates. That knowledge led to suspicion and distrust concerning the attitude of the employers . . . the defensive features of the movement, as conducted by the older men, were based upon a justifiable presumption of the opponents' object. This difference in the particulars of the situation in 1900, as compared with that of 1890, is important as an explanation of much that transpired. (pp. 7–8)

22. Knight, *Industrial Relations,* pp. 78–80, 82–83; Robinson, "San Francisco Teamsters," pp. 45–150.

23. Knight, *Industrial Relations*, pp. 84 – 86; Cronin, *Father Yorke*, pp. 55 – 85, esp. p. 63; Page, "San Francisco Labor Movement in 1901," pp. 679, 685 – 687; Robinson, "San Francisco Teamsters," pp. 150 – 152; Joseph S. Brusher, S. J., *Consecrated Thunderbolt: Father Yorke of San Francisco* (Hawthorne, N.J., 1973), ch. 5.

24. Page, "San Francisco Labor Movement in 1901," pp. 686 – 688; Macarthur, "Climax in Civics," p. 13; Paul Scharrenberg, "Reminiscences," transcript of an interview in 1954 for the Bancroft Library Oral History Project, Bancroft Library, University of California, Berkeley, p. 53; Ray Stannard Baker, "A Corner in Labor: What Is Happening in San Francisco Where Unionism Holds Undisputed Sway," *McClure's* 22 (Feb. 1904) 366 – 378.

25. Knight, *Industrial Relations*, pp. 96 – 138, 150; "List of Trade Unions," *Labor Clarion*, June 17, 1904, p. 14.

26. Knight, *Industrial Relations*, pp. 140 – 143; for George's career in Colorado, see George C. Suggs, *Colorado's War on Militant Unionism: James H. Peabody and the Western Federation of Miners* (Detroit, 1972).

27. Knight, *Industrial Relations*, pp. 131, 136, 139 – 166, 290 – 291; "Citizens' Alliance" file, carton 6, Labor Council Manuscript Collection, Bancroft Library; "A Few of the Things Done by the Citizens' Alliance of San Francisco" (San Francisco, n.d.), a pamphlet in the Bancroft Library, University of California, Berkeley; the constitution and bylaws of the Citizens' Alliance, Bancroft Library, University of California, Berkeley; Herbert George to George C. Pardee, Oct. 25, 1904, George C. Pardee Manuscript Collection, Bancroft Library, University of California, Berkeley; letter to members, Dec. 9, 1907, box 37, James Duval Phelan Papers, Bancroft Library, University of California, Berkeley; "Citizens' Alliance Promise and Performance," *Labor Clarion*, Aug. 19, 1904, pp. 3, 8; "Citizens' Alliance Annual Report," ibid., Feb. 26, 1909, p. 8; "A 'Liberal' Citizens' Alliance," ibid., March 31, 1911, p. 3.

28. Knight, *Industrial Relations*, p. 29; Cross, *A History of the Labor Movement in California*, p. 214; Cronin, *Father Yorke*, p. 50; letter to members, Dec. 9, 1907, box 37, Phelan Papers, Bancroft Library; Pierre Beringer to "Dear Sir," Dec. 11, 1911, "Citizens' Alliance" file, carton 10, Labor Council Manuscript Collection, Bancroft Library.

29. *Labor Clarion*, Aug. 7, 1908, p. 3; Andrew Gallagher testimony, U.S. Commission on Industrial Relations, *Final Report and Testimony*, 6:5448 – 5449.

30. Michael Kazin, "Personal Management and Labor in the Early 1920s: The Case of San Francisco," seminar paper, Stanford University, 1977, p. 12; John O'Connell testimony, U.S. Commission on Industrial Relations, *Final Report and Testimony*, 6:5281 – 5282.

31. Kahn, *Imperial San Francisco*, chs. 4, 7, 8.

32. Kazin, "Barons of Labor," pp. 274 – 275; Knight, *Industrial Relations*, pp. 175 – 179.

33. Knight, *Industrial Relations*, pp. 167 – 298; "Organized Labor Unites to Finance the Strikes," *Labor Clarion*, June 14, 1907, p. 1.

34. For census data, see Table 8, "Total Males and Females 10 Years of Age and over Engaged in Selected Occupations, Classified by Age Periods and Color and Race, Nativity, and Parentage, for Cities of 100,000 Inhabitants or More: 1910," U.S. Bureau of the Census, Department of Commerce and Labor, *Thirteenth Census of the United States: 1910*, 11 vols. (Washington, D.C., 1914), 4:600 – 601; for the culinary union membership figures, see "Hotel and Restaurant Employees" file, Labor Council Manuscript Collection, Bancroft Library, which includes data on monthly per capita dues from Sept. 1909 through April 1910.

35. For the extent of unionization among office workers, see Lillian R. Matthews, *Women in Trade Unions in San Francisco*, University of California Publications in Economics, vol. 3 (Berkeley, 1913), p. 73, and also pp. 53 – 64, 84 – 86. For public employees'

unions, see *Labor Clarion,* July 4, 1919, p. 2; for teachers, see Harriet Talan, "San Francisco Federation of Teachers, 1919–1949," master's thesis, San Francisco State University, 1982, pp. 9–16. For general information on the extent of unionization among women in San Francisco, see Matthews, *Women in Trade Unions;* Jessica Peixotto, "Women of California as Trade Unionists," *Publications of the Association of Collegiate Alumnae* 3 (Dec. 1908):40–49; and Harriet Talan, "The Female Labor Force in San Francisco at the Turn of the Century: Some Features of Its Impulse Toward Trade Unionism," independent study paper, San Francisco State University, 1978. For blacks, see Table 8, cited above, and also Knight, *Industrial Relations,* pp. 79, 88, 144, 213. For one of the best-known racial restrictions by a national union, that of the machinists, see Mark Perlman, *The Machinists: A New Study in American Trade Unionism* (Cambridge, Mass., 1961), pp. 16–17, 277–280. For Asian workers, see Table 8 cited above; Cross, *A History of the Labor Movement in California,* pp. 130–142, 147, 169–174; Saxton, *Indispensable Enemy,* pp. 73–75, 213–218, 245–253; Matthews, *Women in Trade Unions,* pp. 34–36, 95–100; Eaves, *A History of California Labor Legislation,* chs. 3–8, 18; Lucile Eaves, "Labor Day in San Francisco and How Attained," *Labor Clarion,* Sept. 2, 1910, p. 6. The culinary workers did not take their defeat on the issue of organizing Asian workers as final, and in 1916 they announced their intention to organize Japanese culinary workers; see *Labor Clarion,* Aug. 18, 1916, p. 10.

36. *Chamber of Commerce Journal,* Dec. 1911, esp. pp. 1, 5; *Coast Banker,* March 1911, p. 200. See also *Chamber of Commerce Journal,* Feb. 1912, p. 12; ibid., Nov. 1912, p. 1.

37. Knight, *Industrial Relations,* pp. 249–250, 290–298, 329.

38. *San Francisco Chamber of Commerce Activities,* June 22, 1916, p. 1; ibid., July 13, 1916, pp. 1, 3–5; San Francisco Chamber of Commerce, *Law and Order in San Francisco: A Beginning* (San Francisco, 1916), pp. 1–19; Knight, *Industrial Relations,* pp. 300–307.

39. Chamber of Commerce, *Law and Order,* pp. 1–19; Knight, *Industrial Relations,* pp. 300–307.

40. Knight, *Industrial Relations,* pp. 309–336, 346–350; Chamber of Commerce, *Law and Order,* pp. 20–37; *Chamber of Commerce Activities,* Sept. 7, 1916, pp. 1–3; Curt Gentry, *Frame-Up: The Incredible Case of Tom Mooney and Warren Billings* (New York, 1967).

41. Knight, *Industrial Relations,* pp. 332–347, 351–357; *Chamber of Commerce Activities,* March 15, 1917, p. 53; ibid., May 17, 1917, p. 101; ibid., May 24, 1917, p. 104; ibid., June 7, 1917, p. 1; ibid., July 19, 1917, p. 158; ibid., Aug. 2, 1917, p. 171; ibid., Aug. 30, 1917, pp. 200–201; ibid., Sept. 27, 1917, p. 231; ibid., May 30, 1918, p. 162; ibid., July 18, 1918, p. 225.

42. Ryan, *Industrial Relations,* p. 137; Ohlson, "History of the San Francisco Labor Council," pp. 100–101; Francis, "History of Labor on the San Francisco Waterfront," pp. 147–148, 181–182; Paul Scharrenberg, "The San Francisco Longshore," typed manuscript, 1920, Scharrenberg Manuscript Collection, Bancroft Library, University of California, Berkeley; "The Waterfront," *Labor Clarion,* Dec. 3, 1920, p. 8; ibid., July 2, 1920, p. 10.

43. Ohlson, "History of the San Francisco Labor Council," pp. 99–100.

44. Kazin, "Barons of Labor," ch. 11; Ryan, *Industrial Relations,* pp. 137–166; Cross, *A History of the Labor Movement in California,* pp. 251–252.

45. The information on financial contributions is from a binder in the Labor Council Manuscripts Collection, Bancroft Library, "Industrial Association" file, carton 10. The binder, not identified by title, contains fifty pages of names of companies and individuals with sums of money after each name. The dollar amounts listed for some appear in an anonymous mimeographed report on the disputes between the

Industrial Association and the Iron Molders; ibid. In 1925, the Labor Council wrote letters to all the banks cited on the list, asking if the sum indicated was correct. Several banks waffled or denied in their replies. Another letter went to the full list of contributors. Rudolph Spreckels, an opponent of the Industrial Association from its origin, replied: "I have made inquiry and find that under its former management the Merchants National Bank did contribute $1000.00 to the support of the Industrial Association of San Francisco." The general tone of the responses, however, was not to acknowledge a specific dollar amount nor to acknowledge memberships at all; some of the responses, however, did not deny either. A. E. Sbarboro, president of the Italian-American Bank, replied: "We are always ready to contribute to anything which in our opinion will contribute to the development and general good of our community," and F. L. Lipman, president of Wells Fargo Bank, replied: "Our consistent policy is strongly to favor the prosperity of our State and City and that of all our citizens." The "Hawaiian interests" are separated from the others in the list and included, in addition to C&H Sugar, Alexander and Baldwin ($10,000), American Factors ($10,000), Hawaiian Commercial and Sugar Company ($10,000), Matson Navigation ($10,000), and Welch and Company ($10,000). The list also includes the "Industrial Finance Committee" of thirteen, including Frank B. Anderson, chairman of the Bank of California; William H. Crocker of Crocker Bank; Herbert Fleishhacker of the Anglo and London Paris National Bank; F. L. Lipman of Wells Fargo Bank; William Roth of Matson Navigation; Paul Shoup of the Southern Pacific Railroad; B. F. Schlesinger of the Emporium, the city's largest department store; and James Tyson of the Charles Nelson Company, a lumber and shipping concern. See also Ryan, *Industrial Relations*, pp. 167–175; *American Plan* (San Francisco), Oct. 1923, p. 8; Katherine Scott, "The Industrial Association," seminar paper, San Francisco State University, 1979, pp. 20–24.

46. Some files of the Industrial Association are apparently in the possession of the San Francisco Employers' Council, but efforts to secure access to them have been to no avail; most of its files were destroyed. A list of all directors is thus far incomplete, missing some of the early years. For directors and other officers, see *American Plan*, Jan. 1923, p. 6; ibid., Oct. 1923, p. 8; ibid., Jan. 1924, pp. 7–8; ibid., Jan. 1925, p. 7; and in virtually every issue beginning in 1925. We estimate that we found about 90 percent of all directors and officers.

47. For examples of the activities of leading figures, see the information on Atholl McBean in *National Cyclopedia of American Biography* 55 (1974):72–73; *Who's Who in America* 18 (1934–1935):1587; or that on Wallace Alexander, in *Who's Who in America* 16 (1930–1931):164; ibid. 18 (1934–1935):163; *Who's Who in Commerce and Industry: 1936* (Chicago, 1936), p. 12; or that on Colbert Coldwell in *National Cyclopedia of American Biography* 53 (1971):624. See also *Who's Who in America* 16 (1930–1931):1249, 1303, 2394; ibid. 18 (1934–1935):1326, 2134; *Who's Who in Commerce and Industry: 1936*, pp. 356, 543, 602, 852, 1049; *National Cyclopedia of American Biography* 27 (1939):368; ibid. 37 (1951):494–495; ibid. 43 (1961):584; ibid. 48 (1965):614–615; ibid. 49 (1966):80; *American Plan*, July 1924, p. 1.

48. *American Plan*, July 1922, pp. 2–4; ibid., Oct. 1923, pp. 6–8; ibid., Sept. 1926, p. 1; ibid., Dec. 1926, pp. 1–3; ibid., Jan./Feb. 1927, p. 3; ibid., Jan./Feb. 1929, pp. 1–3; ibid., Dec. 1931, p. 6; Industrial Association of San Francisco, *San Francisco: A City That Achieved Freedom* (San Francisco, 1931); Ryan, *Industrial Relations*, pp. 173–175.

49. *American Plan*, July 1922, pp. 2–4; ibid., Oct. 1923, pp. 6–7; ibid., Sept. 1926, p. 1; ibid., Dec. 1926, pp. 1–3; ibid., Jan./Feb. 1927, p. 3; ibid., Jan./Feb. 1929, pp. 1–3; ibid., Dec. 1931, p. 6; Industrial Association of San Francisco, *A City That Achieved Freedom*.

50. Ryan, *Industrial Relations,* pp. 173–175; Industrial Association of San Francisco, *A City That Achieved Freedom; American Plan,* Dec. 1931, p. 3; ibid., Oct. 1923, p. 2.

51. "Industrial Association" file, carton 10, Labor Council Manuscript Collection, Bancroft Library.

52. *American Plan Progress,* Oct. 25, 1926; *American Plan,* Jan./Feb. 1927, pp. 1–3; Eric Levy, "The 1926 San Francisco Carpenters' Strike," *New Labor Review* 6 (1984): 12–26, esp. 15.

53. Ibid.; Ryan, *Industrial Relations,* pp. 191–193; Ryan dates the end of the strike in December, but the agreement was not signed until January.

54. *American Plan,* June/July 1928, pp. 1–3; ibid., Nov. 1925, pp. 1–3; Jan./Feb. 1927, pp. 1–3; *American Plan Progress* (San Francisco), Oct. 25, 1926; copy of letter from Industrial Association Executive Finance Committee, Sept. 20, 1930, "Industrial Association" file, carton 10, Labor Council Manuscript Collection, Bancroft Library.

55. "Industrial Association" file, carton 10, Labor Council Manuscript Collection, Bancroft Library: open letter to Albert Boynton, Dec. 11, 1924; "To the Merchants of San Francisco," June 1, 1926; open letter to the public, April 9, 1926; "To the Contributors of the Industrial Association," Oct. 31, 1925; materials and affidavits on the molders' strike. One informant, aligned with the employers' side rather than the unions, characterized the Industrial Association as "a rough bunch."

56. "Affiliated Unions and Delegates," carton 23, Labor Council Manuscript Collection, Bancroft Library; *American Plan,* Oct. 1922, p. 2.

57. Industrial Association of San Francisco, *A City That Achieved Freedom.*

58. The general strike of 1934 resulted from a similar use of police power.

CHAPTER 5

1. Our use of the term *moral order* is indebted to Paul Boyer's fine synthesis in *Urban Masses and Moral Order in America, 1820–1920* (Cambridge, Mass., 1978). We have followed his lead by focusing on "individuals and groups who sought through consciously planned and organized (but voluntarist and extralegal) effort to influence the range of social behavior usually considered outside the purview of criminal law, yet not entirely private and personal" (p. viii). The quotation at the head of the chapter is by Sarah Ingersoll Cooper, as quoted in Carol Roland, "The California Kindergarten Movement: A Study in Class and Social Feminism," Ph.D. dissertation, University of California, Riverside, 1980, p. 56. David A. Wells, *Recent Economic Changes and Their Effect on Production and Distribution of Wealth and the Well-Being of Society* (New York, 1889), p. 324; Henry George, *Progress and Poverty* (New York, 1929), p. 8.

2. Wells, *Recent Economic Changes,* p. 466.

3. For a comprehensive study of public school reform in relation to economic and social change, see David B. Tyack, *The One Best System: A History of American Urban Education* (Cambridge, Mass., 1974).

4. William H. Maxwell, "City School Systems," *Journal of Proceedings and Addresses* (National Education Association) (1890):447–450; Frank Rollins, *School Administration in Municipal Government* (New York, 1902), p. 16.

5. This complex set of issues has only recently received serious attention. For a general statement, see Marvin Lazerson, "Understanding American Catholic Educational History," *History of Education Quarterly* 17 (Fall 1977):297–317. For San Francisco, see Victor Lee Shradar, "Ethnic Politics, Religion, and the Public Schools of San Francisco, 1849–1933," Ph.D. dissertation, Stanford University, 1974; Victor

L. Shradar, "Ethnicity, Religion, and Class: Progressive School Reform in San Francisco," *History of Education Quarterly* 20 (Winter 1980):385–401; Victor Low, "The Chinese in the San Francisco Public School System," Ph.D. dissertation, University of San Francisco, 1981.

6. William Warren Ferrier, *Ninety Years of Education in California* (Berkeley, 1937), p. 11. *Bancroft Scraps,* Bancroft Library, University of California, Berkeley (newspaper clipping that quotes the Quarterly Report of the Superintendent of Common Schools, 1852).

7. Shradar, "Ethnic Politics," pp. 28–29.

8. *Bulletin,* Aug. 17, 1874, quoted in Miriam Mead Hawley, "Schools for Social Order: Public Education as an Aspect of San Francisco's Urbanization and Industrialization Processes," master's thesis, California State University, San Francisco, 1971, p. 59.

9. Cross, *A History of the Labor Movement in California,* p. 217.

10. Shradar, "Ethnic Politics," p. 27.

11. Ibid., pp. 33, 38, 53–54.

12. John Pelton, quoted in ibid., p. 29.

13. Hawley, "Schools for Social Order," p. 54–55.

14. *Examiner,* March 8 and March 18, 1878; April 10, 1878.

15. Tyack, *One Best System,* p. 71.

16. Lee S. Dolson, "The Administration of the San Francisco Public Schools, 1847–1947," Ph.D. dissertation, University of California, Berkeley, 1964, pp. 177, 180. San Francisco, Board of Education, *Annual Report of the Superintendent of Public Schools* (1878).

17. Roland, "California Kindergarten Movement," pp. 1, 42, 91, 121.

18. Ibid., pp. 93–94.

19. Ibid., pp. 62, 96.

20. Ibid., p. 13.

21. Ibid., pp. 13–14, 96–97.

22. Ibid., pp. 56, 53.

23. Ibid., p. 56.

24. Liston F. Sabraw, "Mayor James Rolph, Jr., and the End of the Barbary Coast," master's thesis, San Francisco State College, 1960, pp. 21–22, 25–26, 119. J. C. Westenberg to chief of police, April 6, 1912, enclosed in J. C. Westenberg to James Rolph, Jr., in the James Rolph, Jr., Papers, California Historical Society, San Francisco. See also Neil Larry Shumsky, "Vice Responds to Reform, San Francisco, 1910–1914," *Journal of Urban History* 7 (Nov. 1980):31–47.

25. Clayton Herrington to James Rolph, Jr., May 19, 1912, Rolph Papers, California Historical Society.

26. Unmailed letter of James Rolph, Jr., to J. C. Westenberg, Aug. 9, 1913, Rolph Papers, California Historical Society.

27. William D. Cole to James Rolph, Jr., Sept. 6, 1918, Rolph Papers, California Historical Society.

28. The complete text of the report appeared in the *Examiner,* March 17, 1937. See also Merritt Barnes, " 'Fountainhead of Corruption'—Peter P. McDonough, Boss of San Francisco's Underworld," *California History* 58 (Summer 1979):142–153.

29. *Examiner,* March 17, 1937, pp. 13A, 19.

30. Martha P. Falconer, "Report of the Committee on Social Hygiene," *Social Hygiene* (National Conference of Charities and Correction) 1 (Sept. 1915):524, quoted in Boyer, *Urban Masses and Moral Order,* p. 219.

31. Boyer, *Urban Masses and Moral Order,* pp. 214, 215.

32. Kahn, *Imperial San Francisco,* p. 62. See also Joan Elaine Draper, "The San Francisco Civic Center: Architecture, Planning, and Politics," Ph.D. dissertation, University of California, Berkeley, 1979.

33. Kahn, *Imperial San Francisco,* pp. 81–87.

34. Ibid., p. 101.

35. Ibid., p. 216.

36. Helen Lefkowitz Horowitz, *Culture and the City: Cultural Philanthropy in Chicago from the 1880s to 1917* (Lexington, Ky., 1976), p. x. See also Steven J. Diner, *A City and Its Universities: Public Policy in Chicago, 1892–1919* (Chapel Hill, 1980).

37. See Douglas Sloan, "Cultural Uplift and Social Reform in Nineteenth-Century Urban America," *History of Education Quarterly* 19 (Fall 1979):361–372.

38. For detailed information on the impact of racial exclusion on San Francisco cultural history, see Daniels, *Pioneer Urbanites;* Albert S. Broussard, "The New Racial Frontier; San Francisco's Black Community, 1900–1940," Ph.D. dissertation, Duke University, 1977; Low, "Chinese in the San Francisco Public School System"; Lyman, "Conflict and the Web of Group Affiliation"; Light, "From Vice District to Tourist Attraction"; Joan B. Tranuer, "The Chinese as Medical Scapegoats in San Francisco, 1870–1905," *California History* 57 (Spring 1978):70–87; Lillian Lum, "Attempts to Relocate Chinatown, 1880–1906," undergraduate essay, San Francisco State University, 1975; Melody C. Doss, "Effects of the Depression of 1893 on San Francisco's Chinatown," graduate essay, San Francisco State University, 1975; Robert Schneider, "The Chinese and Their Education in San Francisco of the Nineteenth Century," graduate essay, San Francisco State University, 1975; George Anthony Peffer, "Forbidden Families," master's thesis, San Francisco State University, 1981; James L. Boyer, "Anti-Chinese Agitation in California, 1851–1904," master's thesis, San Francisco State College, 1969; James Boswell Herndon, "The Japanese School Incident: An Anecdote for Racial Hostility," master's thesis, San Francisco State College, 1967.

39. Young, *San Francisco,* 2:727–728; San Francisco, Park Commission, *The M. H. de Young Memorial Museum* (1921), p. 12.

40. *Chronicle,* Oct. 3, 21, 24, 26, 29, 1924; ibid., Nov. 2, 4, 6, 1924.

41. All data on election returns are from the San Francisco Registrar of Voters records.

42. John Francis Neylan, vice-president and counsel for the Hearst publications, took a jaundiced view of the transaction:

> First, Spreckels and De Young each deeded their gifts to the Board of Park Commissioners in trust. The gift to the trustees was absolute, and divested the Spreckels and De Youngs of any interest in these places except of a reversionary interest in the event of failure to comply with the terms. The City has complied with the terms.
>
> Second; After having alienated their property, Mrs. Spreckels—I imagine for social purposes—wanted to appoint a board in perpetuity and take over the direction of the Memorial and of the surrounding lands. De Young personally told me personally [*sic*] what a terrible outrage the proposed Spreckels initiative was. He was going to fight it in the Chronicle. By the initiative Mrs. Spreckels wanted to deed the property to another board of trustees. Of course, she had nothing to deed.
>
> The Spreckels crowd and the De Young crowd got together and suggested to Mike that he do the same in relation to the museum. This evidently put a new picture on the Spreckels ordinance, and he had an identical ordinance submitted covering his museum, and he deeded to a board of trustees something he no longer owned, and incidentally plastered on San Francisco a minimum maintenance appropriation of forty thousand dollars a year.
>
> The result is that both Spreckels and De Young have messed up two beautiful gifts. The whole city is laughing about the matter. (John Francis Neylan to William Randolph

Hearst, Nov. 25, 1924, John Francis Neylan Papers, Bancroft Library, University of California, Berkeley)

43. See the publication of the San Francisco Bureau of Governmental Research, *City* 6 (Oct. 1926):78; ibid. 7 (May 31, 1927):119–120; ibid. 8 (Oct. 25, 1928):130–131.

44. Moses Lasky, "History of the San Francisco Museum of Art and Analysis of Its Relations to the City and County of San Francisco," typescript, 1961, 1963, San Francisco History Collection, San Francisco Public Library; "History of the War Memorial" by Charles Kendrick and other documents are attached to Lasky's report.

45. See Kendrick, "History of the War Memorial," in Lasky, "History of the San Francisco Museum of Art," pp. 4–11.

46. Preston Devine, "The Adoption of the 1932 Charter of San Francisco," master's thesis, University of California, Berkeley, 1933, p. 62.

47. Information about the Federation of Arts comes from letters and notes of discussions, as well as minutes of meetings, in the San Francisco Art Institute Archives. The following letters are esp. pertinent: E. Spencer Macky to William L. Gerstle, April 29, 1931; E. Spencer Macky to John V. Van Pelt, April 27, 1931; minutes of meeting of Feb. 5, 1931; "Suggested Composition of Art Commission," n.d.

48. Letter from Organizing Committee, San Francisco Federation of Arts, to Commonwealth Club of California, Attention: Mr. Stuart R. Ward, assistant executive secretary, April 27, 1931, in San Francisco Art Institute Archives.

49. The two quotations are from Organizing Committee, San Francisco Federation of Art, to San Francisco Art Association, April 27, 1931; E. Spencer Macky to William L. Gerstle, April 29, 1931, San Francisco Art Institute Archives.

50. A copy of the original charter sections are in the files of the San Francisco Art Commission.

CHAPTER 6

1. Bryce, *American Commonwealth*, 2:425, 428, 430–431; Christopher A. Buckley, "The Reminiscences of Christopher A. Buckley," *Bulletin*, Jan. 24, 1919, p. 13.

2. Bryce, *American Commonwealth*, 2:143; William A. Bullough, *The Blind Boss and His City: Christopher Augustine Buckley and Nineteenth-Century San Francisco* (Berkeley, 1979), pp. 58–60; Erik Falk Petersen, "The Struggle for the Australian Ballot in California," *California Historical Quarterly* 51 (Fall 1972): 227–243.

3. Bullough, *Blind Boss*, pp. 58–59, 77, 89–91, 154, 195–197; Neil Larry Shumsky, "Tar Flat and Nob Hill: A Social History of Industrial San Francisco During the 1870s," Ph.D. dissertation, University of California, Berkeley, 1972, ch. 6; Jon M. Kingsdale, "The 'Poor Man's Club': Social Functions of the Urban Working-Class Saloon," *American Quarterly* 25 (Oct. 1973):472–489.

4. Bullough, *Blind Boss*, pp. 58–60, 87–89; Bancroft, *History of California*, 7:315–317; Bryce, *American Commonwealth*, 2:85–89; Walton Bean, *Boss Ruef's San Francisco: The Story of the Union Labor Party, Big Business, and the Graft Prosecution* (Berkeley, 1952), pp. 2–4.

5. George W. Plunkitt, *Plunkitt of Tammany Hall*, ed. William L. Riordon (New York, 1948), p. 4; Bullough, *Blind Boss*, pp. 58–60; Henry George, "The Kearney Agitation in California," *Popular Science Monthly* 17 (Aug. 1880):438–439; Petersen, "Struggle for the Australian Ballot," pp. 228–229. Bullough and Petersen both use "piece club"; George used "price club."

6. San Francisco, Board of Supervisors, *Municipal Reports* (1872–1873), pp. 558–559; ibid. (1874–1875), pp. 768–775; ibid. (1875–1876), pp. 750–751; ibid. (1876–1877), pp. 1042–1043; ibid. (1878–1879), pp. 523–526, 758–807.

7. Bryce, *American Commonwealth*, 2:425.

8. Daggett, *Southern Pacific,* pp. 26–36, 55; George T. Clark, *Leland Stanford: War Governor of California, Railroad Builder, and Founder of Stanford University* (Stanford, 1931), chs. 6, 7; Norman E. Tutorow, *Leland Stanford: Man of Many Careers* (Menlo Park, Ca., 1971), chs. 3, 4, esp. pp. 74–77; Cerinda W. Evans, *Collis Potter Huntington,* 2 vols. (Newport News, Va., 1954), esp. chs. 16, 17, 27.

9. Daggett, *Southern Pacific,* pp. 31–40; Tutorow, *Leland Stanford,* pp. 76–77; Clark, *Leland Stanford,* pp. 196–203; Lewis, *Big Four,* pp. 355–359.

10. Daggett, *Southern Pacific,* pp. 85–102; Lewis, *Big Four,* pp. 361–362; Tutorow, *Leland Stanford,* pp. 83–84, 102–104; Clark, *Leland Stanford,* pp. 230, 313–326; Ward McAfee, *California's Railroad Era: 1850–1911* (San Marino, Ca., 1973), ch. 7; Lavender, *Nothing Seemed Impossible,* pp. 348–352; Evans, *Collis Potter Huntington,* ch. 30.

11. Daggett, *Southern Pacific,* ch. 12, esp. pp. 211, 216–217, 219; Lewis, *Big Four,* p. 314; Evans, *Collis Potter Huntington,* ch. 43, esp. p. 354; Clark, *Leland Stanford,* pp. 71, 432–436; Tutorow, *Leland Stanford,* pp. 24–35.

12. Fremont Older and Cora Older, *George Hearst: California Pioneer* (Los Angeles, 1966), p. 195; Robert E. Stewart, Jr., and Mary Frances Stewart, *Adolph Sutro: A Biography* (Berkeley, 1962), 5–13, esp. pp. 52, 77, 115, 126–127, 140–141; Lavender, *Nothing Seemed Impossible,* pp. 232, 267, 366–367; Lewis, *Silver Kings,* pp. 166–169, 171, 173.

13. Ernest Gruening, *The State of Alaska* (New York, 1968), pp. 66–70, 72, 85, 252; Samuel P. Johnston, ed., *Alaska Commercial Company: 1868–1940* (n.p., 1941?), esp. pp. 6–8, 25, 27, 35, 37; Lavender, *Nothing Seemed Impossible,* p. 225.

14. Young, *San Francisco,* 2:312; Bancroft, *History of California,* 6:768–772, 7:251–252; John S. Hittell, *A History of the City of San Francisco and Incidentally of the State of California* (San Francisco, 1878), pp. 357, 360–362, 365.

15. Lavender, *Nothing Seemed Impossible,* pp. 242–250, 361; James H. Wilkins, ed., *The Great Diamond Hoax and Other Stirring Incidents in the Life of Asbury Harpending* (San Francisco, 1913), pp. 111–127, 146–157, esp. pp. 152–153; Julian Dana, *The Man Who Built San Francisco: A Study of Ralston's Journey with Banners* (New York, 1937), pp. 236–241; George D. Lyman, *Ralston's Ring: California Plunders the Comstock Lode* (New York, 1937), p. 121.

16. Lavender, *Nothing Seemed Impossible,* pp. 370–372; Hittell, *A History of the City of San Francisco,* pp. 405–406; Lyman, *Ralston's Ring,* pp. 272–274, 304–305.

17. Lavender, *Nothing Seemed Impossible,* pp. 376–377, 382–383; Lyman, *Ralston's Ring,* pp. 275, 285–288, 320; Hittell, *A History of the City of San Francisco,* pp. 421–424; Charles A. Lévy, "Working-Class Life in San Francisco: An Examination of Social and Economic Dislocation Caused by the Depression of 1877–1879," seminar paper, San Francisco State University, 1977, pp. 6–7; Shumsky, "Tar Flat and Nob Hill," ch. 3, esp. p. 126; Cross, *A History of the Labor Movement in California,* pp. 88–90; Saxton, *Indispensable Enemy,* pp. 113–114; Michael Kazin, "Prelude to Kearneyism: The July Days in San Francisco, 1877," *New Labor Review* 3 (1980):5–47.

18. Eaves, *A History of California Labor Legislation,* chs. 3–5, esp. pp. 136–138, 142–145, 148–149; Mary Roberts Coolidge, *Chinese Immigration* (New York, 1909), chs. 4, 5; Wollenberg, *All Deliberate Speed,* pp. 30–34. See also Stuart Creighton Miller, *The Unwelcome Immigrant: The American Image of the Chinese, 1785–1882* (Berkeley, 1969), esp. ch. 7; and Trauner, "Chinese as Medical Scapegoats."

19. Kazin, "July Days"; Robert V. Bruce, *1877: Year of Violence* (Indianapolis, 1959), ch. 8 and passim; James A. B. Scherer, *"The Lion of the Vigilantes": William T. Coleman and the Life of Old San Francisco* (Indianapolis, 1939), pp. 267–278; Saxton, *Indispensable Enemy,* pp. 113–115; Cross, *A History of the Labor Movement in California,* pp. 88–93; George, "Kearney Agitation," pp. 437–438.

20. Among the numerous accounts of the Workingmen's party of California (WPC) are J. C. Stedman and R. A. Leonard, *The Workingmen's Party of California: An Epitome of Its Rise and Progress* (San Francisco, 1878); George, "Kearney Agitation," esp. pp. 440–441; Bryce, *American Commonwealth*, 2:425–448; Winfield J. Davis, *History of Political Conventions in California, 1849–1892* (Sacramento, 1893), pp. 365–421; Roney, *Frank Roney*, pp. 268–308; Ralph Kauer, "The Workingmen's Party in California," *Pacific Historical Review* 13 (Sept. 1944):278–291; Shumsky, "Tar Flat and Nob Hill," chs. 6, 7; Neil L. Shumsky, "San Francisco's Workingmen Respond to the Modern City," *California Historical Quarterly* 55 (Spring 1976):46–57; Cross, *A History of the Labor Movement in California*, ch. 7; Saxton, *Indispensable Enemy*, chs. 6, 7; Doyce B. Nunis, Jr., "The Demagogue and the Demographer: Correspondence of Denis Kearney and Lord Bryce," *Pacific Historical Review* 36 (Aug. 1967): 269–288, esp. pp. 278–279.

21. Carl Brent Swisher, *Motivation and Political Technique in the California Constitutional Convention, 1878–1879* (Claremont, Ca., 1930), chs. 2–8, esp. ch. 2; Kauer, "Workingmen's Party," pp. 282–286; George, "Kearney Agitation," pp. 445–446; Bryce, *American Commonwealth*, 2:436–439; Bancroft, *History of California*, 7:370–406; Eaves, *A History of California Labor Legislation*, pp. 150–160, 216; Davis, *History of Political Conventions*, pp. 381–385; Dudley T. Moorhead, "Sectionalism and the California Constitution of 1879," *Pacific Historical Review* 12 (Sept. 1943):287–293; Young, *Journalism in California*, ch. 12; A. Russell Buchanan, *David S. Terry of California: Dueling Judge* (San Marino, Ca., 1956), ch. 11.

22. Irving McKee, "The Shooting of Charles de Young," *Pacific Historical Review* 16 (Aug. 1947):271–284, esp. pp. 280–281; Kauer, "Workingmen's Party," pp. 287–288; George, "Kearney Agitation," p. 447; Bancroft, *History of California*, 7:412, 420.

23. Bryce, *American Commonwealth*, 2:433–435; George, "Kearney Agitation," pp. 442, 444; Buckley, "Reminiscences," *Bulletin*, Dec. 25, 1918, p. 9; Alexander Callow, Jr., "San Francisco's Blind Boss," *Pacific Historical Review* 25 (Aug. 1956):264.

24. Lévy has calculated the rank-order coefficient of correlation between these two measures of the party's strength at +0.965; "Working-Class Life in San Francisco," pp. 22, 23; part of this analysis is based on Lévy's paper.

25. Kauer, "Workingmen's Party," p. 289, George, "Kearney Agitation," p. 449; Bryce, *American Commonwealth*, 2:430–431, 443–445; Cross, *A History of the Labor Movement in California*, pp. 125–128, 130.

26. Bryce, *American Commonwealth*, 2:441, 445.

27. Bullough, *Blind Boss*, ch. 1.

28. Ibid., passim; for Maguire and the sale of the theater, see Lotchin, *San Francisco: 1846–1856*, pp. 219, 223.

29. Terrence Joseph McDonald, "Urban Development, Political Power, and Municipal Expenditure in San Francisco, 1860–1910: A Quantitative Investigation of Historical Theory," Ph.D. dissertation, Stanford University, 1979, pp. 141–161; Lotchin, *San Francisco: 1846–1856*, ch. 9; Burchell, *San Francisco Irish*, pp. 117–118, 129–154; Bullough, *Blind Boss*, pp. 65–66, 82, 92, 136, 162–163, 178–180, 205, 220–221, 239–241.

30. Bullough, *Blind Boss*, pp. 64, 93–95, 165, 208–209; Callow, "San Francisco's Blind Boss," pp. 263, 267.

31. Bullough, *Blind Boss*, pp. 93, 118–119, 136, 176–179, 214–216, 220–221; Robert W. Righter, "Washington Bartlett: Mayor of San Francisco, 1883–1887," *Journal of the West* 3 (Jan. 1964):102–114, esp. pp. 105, 109; H. Brett Melendy, "California's Washington Bartletts," *Pacific Historical Review* 31 (May 1962):139–142.

32. Bullough, *Blind Boss*, pp. 137–147; Buckley, "Reminiscences," *Bulletin*, Jan.

28, 1919, p. 8.

33. Martin Kelly, "Martin Kelly's Story," *Bulletin*, Sept. 7, 1917, p. 8; Bullough, *Blind Boss*, pp. 137–147.

34. Bullough, *Blind Boss*, pp. 146–148, 264–265, note 33 on p. 299, note 47 on p. 300. Others give the figure of $900,000 for Buckley's worth in 1890; see R. Hal Williams, *The Democratic Party and California Politics: 1880–1896* (Stanford, 1973), p.150.

35. Bullough, *Blind Boss*, pp. 147–150; for a full discussion of expenditure patterns, see McDonald, "Urban Development," ch. 4.

36. Buckley, "Reminiscences," *Bulletin*, Jan. 13, 1919, p. 14; Bullough, *Blind Boss*, pp. 77, 154, 172, 202, 217, 221, 223; Williams, *Democratic Party*, pp. 149–150; Curtis E. Grassman, "Prologue to California Reform: "The Democratic Impulse, 1886–1898," *Pacific Historical Review* 42 (Nov. 1973):518–536.

37. Kelly, "Story," *Bulletin*, Oct. 3, 1917, p. 8; Bullough, *Blind Boss*, pp. 227, 237; William A. Bullough, "Hannibal Versus the Blind Boss: The 'Junta,' Chris Buckley, and Democratic Reform Politics in San Francisco," *Pacific Historical Review* 46 (May 1977):198–199; Callow, "San Francisco's Blind Boss," pp. 277–278.

38. Bullough, "Hannibal," pp. 193–194, 197; Bullough, *Blind Boss*, pp. 240–241.

39. Election data for the period 1888–1896 is fragmentary and often incomplete. The official tabulations burned in the fire of 1906. The *Municipal Reports*, the source for data by district or ward for both earlier and later times, did not break returns down during this period. The newspapers sometimes printed summaries by assembly districts, but usually only for early returns. Sources for this analysis, and those which follow: *Examiner*, Nov. 6, 1890, p. 1 (summary of 201 of the 310 precincts for the 1890 election); *Bulletin*, Nov. 10, 1892, p. 2 (summary based on 30 percent of the ballots for the 1892 election); *Examiner*, Nov. 9, 1894, p. 3 (results of an exit poll, based on ten voters per precinct; the results for the two leading candidates are within ten percentage points of the official returns; those for the other two candidates are within two percentage points); *Examiner*, Nov. 4, 1896, p. 11 (another exit poll, conducted in the same fashion; the winning candidate is within one percentage point in his official tally). For the official tally citywide, see the *Municipal Reports* for the various years.

40. For election data, see sources listed in note 39 for 1892, 1894, and 1896; San Francisco *Call*, Nov. 10, 1892, p. 8.

41. Petersen, "Struggle for the Australian Ballot," pp. 232–239; Stewart and Stewart, *Adolph Sutro*, p. 202–204; Bullough, "Hannibal," p. 195.

42. Buckley, "Reminiscences," *Bulletin*, Jan. 28, 1919, p. 8; Bullough, *Blind Boss*, pp. 122, 129–130; see also Robert K. Merton, *Social Theory and Social Structure*, rev. ed. (New York, 1968), pp. 129–132.

43. Kelly, "Story," *Bulletin*, Sept. 19, 1917, p. 8; Bullough, *Blind Boss*, p. 116.

44. Older and Older, *George Hearst*, pp. 177–180.

45. Jacob Adler, *Claus Spreckels: The Sugar King in Hawaii* (Honolulu, 1966), pp. 36–41, 52–68; Arthur B. Darling, ed., *The Public Papers of Francis G. Newlands*, 2 vols. (Boston, 1932), 1:2–4.

46. J. Glocker to "Dear Sir," Sept. 1, 1877, San Francisco Early Documents Scrapbook, California Historical Society, San Francisco; Abraham Ruef, "The Road I Traveled: An Autobiographic Account of My Career from the University to Prison, with an Intimate Recital of the Corrupt Alliance Between Big Business and Politics in San Francisco," *Bulletin*, June 8, 1912, p. 1; Callow, "San Francisco's Blind Boss," p. 277; Kelly, "Story," *Bulletin*, Sept. 7, 1917, p. 8; Bullough, *Blind Boss*, p. 141; Daggett, *Southern Pacific*, p. 211.

47. George, "Kearney Agitation," pp. 452–453.

CHAPTER 7

1. Quotations at the head of the chapter are from the *Monitor,* Nov. 7, 1896 (Yorke) and the *Examiner,* Aug. 25, 1911 (Rolph). For New York City, see Martin Shefter, "The Emergence of the Political Machine: An Alternative View," in *Theoretical Perspectives on Urban Politics,* ed. Willis Hawley et al. (Englewood Cliffs, N.J., 1976), pp. 14–44.

2. Terrence McDonald has made a comprehensive statistical study of municipal government expenditure for the 1860–1910 period and concludes that during "the reform mayoralties of the 1890s, expenditure increased more annually than during the era of machine domination . . . the 'machines' were more fiscally conservative and the reformers more expansionary." He argues that the

> case of San Francisco suggests that although the reformers campaigned for economy and against the extravagance of the machine, in fact the machine had been too penurious. What was at stake, was not just how government should be structured, but what it should do, not just politics, but policy, and in the new political economy the power of politics was to be used to expand public expenditure and indebtedness in order to encourage local economic development. (McDonald, "Urban Development," pp. 188–189, 204–205)

3. *Monthly Review* (San Francisco), Sept. 1896; *Evening Post,* Aug. 21, 1894; see also Young, *San Francisco,* 2:713.

4. *Chronicle,* Oct. 16, 19, 1894, Nov. 17, 1894.

5. Ibid., Nov. 17, 1894. Self-made millionaire Adolph Sutro, elected on the Populist ticket and mayor from Jan. 1895 to Jan. 1897, similarly supported a municipal government modeled on business methods as well as popular accountability. See *Chronicle,* Jan. 13, 1895, and his speech as he left the mayor's office in the *Chronicle,* Jan. 5, 1897.

6. *Chronicle,* Dec. 29, 1894, Jan. 12, 1895.

7. *Chronicle,* Jan. 11, 19, 1895.

8. For the Civic Federation, see the *Chronicle* and the *San Francisco Call,* Jan. 13–Feb. 26, 1895; *Chronicle,* Jan. 13, 27, 1895.

9. *Chronicle,* Jan. 20, 1895.

10. *Chronicle,* Jan. 19, 20, 1895.

11. *Voice of Labor* (San Francisco), Feb. 2, 1895, March 2, 1895; *Call,* March 13, 19, 1895; *Chronicle,* June 25, 1895, July 17, 1895; Gustav Gutsch, *A Comparison of the Consolidation Act with the New Charter* (San Francisco, 1896), quoted in McDonald, "Urban Development," p. 203.

12. *Call,* Feb. 17, 1896; *Monitor* (San Francisco), June 27, 1896; *Voice of Labor,* May 2, 1896. Yorke had earlier criticized alleged charges by the American Protective Association (APA) that "60 percent of the teachers in San Francisco are Roman Catholics" as a "groundless untruth"; see *Monitor,* Jan. 11, 1896. On the details of Yorke's battle against the APA, see Brusher's biography, *Consecrated Thunderbolt,* ch. 2.

13. James P. Walsh, *Ethnic Militancy: An Irish Catholic Prototype* (San Francisco, 1972), pp. 15–19, tables on pp. 16–17; see also James P. Walsh, "Abe Ruef Was No Boss: Machine Politics, Reform, and San Francisco," *California Historical Quarterly* 51 (Spring 1972):13–14.

14. San Francisco Merchants' Association, Minutes of the board of directors, July 9, 1896, California Historical Society, San Francisco, hereafter cited as M.A. Minutes; *Monitor,* July 25, 1896.

15. *Voice of Labor,* Aug. 8, 15, 1896.

16. M.A. Minutes, Aug. 6, 1896; Frank McCoppin, *Address on the New Charter,* pamphlet dated Aug. 11, 1896, p. 11, Bancroft Library, University of California, Berkeley; the statement had appeared in *Voice of Labor,* March 2, 1895.

17. *Chronicle,* Aug. 13, 20, 1896; M.A. Minutes, Aug. 20, 1896.

18. The *Chronicle* began its muckraking campaign on Sept. 13, 1896, with head-lines announcing "Disease Lurks in the Corridors" of city hall. See also stories on Sept. 14, 15, 16, 1896. The pamphlet, prepared by J. Richard Freud, was entitled *New Charter Catechism, Plain Questions and Honest Answers* (San Francisco, 1896), copy in California Historical Society, San Francisco. Freud urged voters to "Take up the *Chronicle* and see the pictures" in speeches in favor of the charter; see *Chronicle,* Sept. 16, 1896.

19. *Chronicle,* Sept. 20, 25, 1896; *Call* and *Examiner,* Sept. 25, 1896. Albert Lyser, principal of the John Swett School, made the claim about divisions among teachers in an interview with a journalist (the name of the newspaper and the date have been clipped) in vol. 1 of the Phelan Scrapbooks, Phelan Papers, Bancroft Library.

20. For the day-to-day details see the following: *Chronicle,* Sept. 19, 22, 29, 1896, Oct. 2, 1896; *Monitor,* Oct. 3, 1896; *Call,* Oct. 8, 1896; *Post,* Oct. 10, 1896; *Chronicle,* Oct. 28, 29, 1896; *Nation,* Oct. 24, 1896; *Examiner,* Oct. 28, 1896; *Chronicle,* Oct. 31, 1896.

21. *Chronicle,* Oct. 23, 1896. See also *Monitor* and *Star* (San Francisco), Oct. 3, 1896, and *Socialist,* n.d., in vol. 1, Phelan Scrapbooks, Bancroft Library.

22. San Francisco Labor Council, *The New Charter: Why It Should Be Defeated* (San Francisco, 1896), pp. 3, 5, 6, 11, copy in California Historical Society, San Francisco.

23. Yorke's recommendations appeared in *Monitor,* Nov. 7, 1896.

24. *Chronicle,* Nov. 14, 1896; see also M.A. Minutes, Nov. 5, 1896.

25. *Chronicle,* Dec. 9, 1896, Jan. 5, 1897; *Bulletin,* Jan. 6, 1897. For details on the school controversies, see *Chronicle,* Feb. 1, 1897, March 14, 1897, April 23, 30, 1897, May 13, 1897, June 14, 1897, July 24, 1897.

26. M.A. Minutes, Jan. 7, 21, 1897, Feb. 8, 25, 1897; *Examiner,* Feb. 24, 1897; *Monthly Review,* Jan.–March 1897; *Chronicle,* Jan. 22, 1897.

27. *Voice of Labor,* Aug. 7, 1897; see also the Aug. 14 and Sept. 4 issues. In keeping with the Merchants' Association strategy of making the charter campaign more representative, Phelan appointed both Walter Macarthur and Patrick McCarthy to the Committee of 100. At the same time, the committee remained very much an upper- and middle-class group because only five were blue-collar workers besides the two labor union officials. Occupations of 104 of the 115 members of the com-mittee can be traced in city directories. Forty owned or managed business firms; another thirty-one were independent professionals; fourteen were salaried profes-sionals; nine worked in white-collar jobs. There were two state and one federal government employees. A list of the committee appeared in the *Chronicle,* Aug. 3, 1897.

28. *Chronicle,* Aug. 18, 1897.

29. *Chronicle,* Sept. 10, 1897. Richard Freud, secretary to the Merchants' Asso-ciation and the Committee of 100, later stated that the original committee reports had all been destroyed because, he wrote, "they differed frequently so much from their form after final adoption by the Committee"; letter from Richard Freud to J. C. Rowell (librarian of the University of California), dated March 13, 1899, bound with pamphlets on San Francisco charters, vol. 1, Bancroft Library, University of California, Berkeley.

30. *Wave* (San Francisco), Oct. 16, 1897; see also *Call,* Oct. 21, 1897; *Chronicle,* Oct. 27, 1897; *Coast Seamen's Journal* (San Francisco), Nov. 17, 1897.

31. *Voice of Labor,* Sept. 25, 1897; *Wave,* Oct. 16, 1897; *Call and Post,* Oct. 21, 1897.

32. *Chronicle,* Sept. 29, 1897; *Monthly Review,* Nov. 1897; *Chronicle,* Nov. 25, 1897.

33. The details can be followed in *Examiner,* Oct. 21, 25, 1897; *Call,* Oct. 22, 23, 1897; *Chronicle,* Oct. 27, 28, 31, 1897, Nov. 3, 8–12, 18, 1897; *Wave,* Nov. 20, 1897; *Chronicle,* Nov. 28, 1897, Dec. 3, 1897; *Town Talk,* Dec. 13, 1897; *Post,* Dec. 16, 1897.

34. *Chronicle,* Dec. 18, 1897; a table listing the delegates by assembly district appeared in the article.

35. This and the later discussions of class, ethnicity, and voting rest upon data compiled from the following sources: *California Blue Book, 1899* (Sacramento, 1899), maps of assembly districts; San Francisco, *Municipal Reports* (1897–1898, 1900–1901), pp. 375, 374; U.S. Census Office, Department of the Interior, *Twelfth Census of the United States: 1900,* 37 vols. (Washington, D.C., 1902), 1:738–739, 868, 876–877, 884–885, 892–893, 900–901, 904–905; 2:702, 754, Bulletin 66, p. 8; Averbach, "South of Market," pp. 202–203, and note 38 on p. 220. See also Alexander Saxton, "San Francisco Labor and the Populist and Progressive Insurgencies," *Pacific Historical Review* 34 (Nov. 1965):421–438; and Michael P. Rogin and John L. Shover, *Political Change in California: Critical Elections and Social Movements, 1890–1966* (Westport, Conn., 1970), ch. 1. *Old stock* is used to describe native-born persons with native-born parents whereas *ethnic* refers to foreign-born persons and natives with at least one foreign parent.

36. *Monitor,* Dec. 25, 1897.

37. *Chronicle,* Dec. 28, 29, 1897; *Coast Seamen's Journal,* March 2, 1898. See also sources in note 35.

38. *Chronicle,* Dec. 31, 1897, Feb. 18, 1898, March 2, 3, 22, 1898.

39. *Chronicle,* March 26, 1898.

40. *Chronicle,* April 25, 1898; *Voice of Labor,* May 14, 21, 1898. See also *Coast Seamen's Journal,* March 2, 1898; *Star,* May 14, 1898; and letter to the *Chronicle,* May 21, 1898.

41. *Monitor,* May 21, 1898; *Examiner,* May 25, 1898.

42. *Coast Seamen's Journal,* May 25, 1898.

43. Sources in note 35; and Cross, *A History of the Labor Movement in California,* pp. 330, 336–337.

44. *Monthly Review,* May 1898; *Chronicle,* April 25, 1898; *Chronicle,* May 6, 1898; *Examiner,* May 21, 1898; see *Chronicle* during April 1898 for the details on Augustus Widber.

45. *Coast Seamen's Journal,* June 1, 1898; *Report* (San Francisco), May 27, 1898. Terrence McDonald calculated the mean voter turnout ("participation rate") in "Urban Development," p. 164.

46. Ibid., and *Report,* May 27, 1898.

47. Wiebe, *Search for Order,* pp. 111–132. Note that whereas the Irish ethnics outnumbered the old-stock residents by about one-fourth, they owned more than twice the number of homes. See *Twelfth Census of the United States: 1900,* vol. 2, pt. 2, Table 115, p. 754.

48. The charter has traditionally been known as "the Phelan Charter."

49. *Coast Seamen's Journal,* May 25, 1898; *Monthly Review,* June 1898.

50. *Monitor,* May 21, 1898.

51. Martin J. Schiesl, *The Politics of Efficiency: Municipal Administration and Reform in America: 1880–1920* (Berkeley, 1977), p. 47.

52. Phelan pointed this out in his inaugural address; see *Chronicle,* Jan. 5, 1897.

53. Phelan, quoted in Kahn, *Imperial San Francisco,* pp. 62, 66.

54. *Merchants' Association Review* (Jan. 1899):2.

55. McDonald, "Urban Development," pp. 197, 198, 203, Table 4.12.

56. Ibid., p. 204; Kahn, *Imperial San Francisco,* p. 69.

57. Quoted in Jules Tygiel, "The Union Labor Party of San Francisco: A Reappraisal," typescript, 1979, pp. 6–7. See also Jules Tygiel, " 'Where Unionism Holds Undisputed Sway': A Reappraisal of San Francisco's Union Labor Party," *California History* 62 (Fall 1983):196–215, Tables 1 and 2.

58. Tygiel, "Union Labor Party," p. 201; Bean, *Boss Ruef's San Francisco,* pp. 12–17; Franklin Hichborn, *"The System" as Uncovered by the San Francisco Graft Prosecution* (San Francisco, 1915), p. 12.

59. Bean, *Boss Ruef's San Francisco,* pp. 9–10.

60. Tygiel, "Union Labor Party," p. 11; Bean, *Boss Ruef's San Francisco,* p. 20.

61. Quoted in Tygiel, "Union Labor Party," pp. 13–14, 15–16.

62. Ibid., pp. 16–18, esp. p. 18. Table 9 describes the ways in which the city's assembly districts remained more or less polarized over the Union Labor party between 1901 and 1911. With only three exceptions in four of the six elections, the party's mayoral candidates consistently received higher percentages of the vote than the citywide figures in the nine districts (28–36) where working-class voters predominated. By contrast, eight of the nine middle- and upper-class districts gave the party substantially less than the citywide percentage in two of the six elections, and seven of the nine did so in four of the six elections.

63. Bean, *Boss Ruef's San Francisco,* p. 27.

64. Ibid., pp. 40–54, 61, 75–77; Knight, *Industrial Relations,* pp. 120–121.

65. For details, see Bean, *Boss Ruef's San Francisco,* pp. 153–267. See also Walsh, "Abe Ruef Was No Boss," pp. 3–16.

66. Walsh, "Abe Ruef Was No Boss," p. 12.

67. Ibid.

68. Richard L. McCormick, "The Discovery That Business Corrupts Politics: A Reappraisal of the Origins of Progressivism," *American Historical Review* 86 (April 1981):272–273.

69. On the national scene, see Robert H. Wiebe, *Businessmen and Reform: A Study of the Progressive Movement* (Chicago, 1968), p. 68.

70. *Coast Banker,* Nov. 1908, p. 5; ibid., Oct. 1908, p. 5.

71. Ibid., April 1909, p. 153.

72. Ibid., March 1911, p. 158.

73. Ibid., April 1909, p. 154.

74. Ibid.

75. Ibid.

76. *Coast Banker,* special issue for the American Bankers' Association meeting in Los Angeles, Oct. 3–7, 1910, p. 132.

77. San Francisco Merchants' Association, *Seventeenth Annual Review: A Year of Civic Work* (San Francisco, 1911), p. 13; Richard Hume Werking, "Bureaucrats, Businessmen, and Foreign Trade: The Origins of the United States Chamber of Commerce," *Business History Review* 52 (Autumn 1978):322–341.

78. *Chamber of Commerce Journal,* Dec. 1911, p. 1. For the activities of the Merchants' Association, see the monthly issues of its *Review* during 1910 and 1911, especially the article "Year's Work of Merchants' Association Covers a Wide Field of City Betterment," July 1911, pp. 5–6. As in 1896–1898, the association joined forces with the neighborhood improvement associations.

79. Young, *San Francisco,* 2:919–926; Carole Hicke, "The 1911 Campaign of James Rolph, Jr., Mayor of All the People," master's thesis, San Francisco State University, 1978, pp. 11–12.

80. Hicke, "1911 Campaign," p. 21.

81. Ibid., pp. 12–13.

82. Ibid., p. 20.

83. Ibid., pp. 15–16.
84. Rolph, quoted in ibid., pp. 22, 24.
85. *Chronicle,* Aug. 13, 1911.
86. Hicke, "1911 Campaign," pp. 23–24.
87. *Examiner,* Aug. 25, 1911. For the Hays argument, see Samuel P. Hays, "Political Parties and the Community-Society Continuum," in *The American Party Systems: Stages of Political Development,* ed. William N. Chambers and Walter D. Burnham (New York, 1967), pp. 152–181.
88. Rolph, quoted in Hicke, "1911 Campaign," pp. 25, 27.
89. Ibid., pp. 28, 31.
90. Ibid., pp. 41, 54, 59.
91. Connelly, quoted in ibid., p. 58.
92. Ibid., pp. 65–66.
93. Ibid., pp. 67, 69.
94. Ibid., pp. 75–76. See also Table 3, note 45, in Tygiel, "Union Labor Party," where Tygiel points out: "Since class and ethnic origins overlapped so greatly . . . it is difficult to distinguish between the two and they were probably mutually reinforcing factors."
95. *Coast Banker,* Oct. 1911, p. 251.

CHAPTER 8

1. The quotation at the head of the chapter is from Rolph's letter to the Public Ownership Association, April 15, 1913, Rolph Papers, California Historical Society; see also Morley Segal, "James Rolph, Jr., and the Municipal Railway, A Study in Political Leadership," master's thesis, San Francisco State College, 1959, p. 89; William M. Hines, "Our American Mayors: James Rolph, Jr., of San Francisco," *National Municipal Review* 18 (March 1929):163–167, esp. p. 163; see also Moses Rischin, "Sunny Jim Rolph: The First 'Mayor of All the People,' " *California Historical Quarterly* 53 (Summer 1974):165–172; David Wooster Taylor, *The Life of James Rolph, Jr.* (San Francisco, 1934); and Sabraw, "Mayor James Rolph," ch. 4.
2. Bruce Allen Hardy, "Civil Service in San Francisco: The Rationalization of Municipal Employment, 1881–1910," master's thesis, San Francisco State College, 1967, esp. chs. 1, 2; Franklin Hichborn, *Story of the Session of the California Legislature of 1909* (San Francisco, 1909), chs. 8–11; Franklin Hichborn, *Story of the Session of the California Legislature of 1911* (San Francisco, 1911), chs. 5–7, 10, 27; Franklin Hichborn, *Story of the Session of the California Legislature of 1913* (San Francisco, 1913), ch. 28.
3. H. Brett Melendy, "California's Cross-Filing Nightmare: The 1918 Gubernatorial Election," *Pacific Historical Review* 33 (1964):324; Duncan Aikman, "California's Sun God," *Nation* 132 (Jan. 14, 1931):37; Rischin, "Sunny Jim Rolph," p. 169; Taylor, *Life of James Rolph,* pp. 15–20, 44, 68–69, 76–78, 95–96.
4. E. R. Zion, "San Francisco's Bureau of Efficiency," *Chamber of Commerce Journal,* Sept. 1912, p. 13; Schiesl, *Politics of Efficiency,* ch. 6, esp. pp. 111–112; J. Rogers Hollingsworth, "Perspectives on Industrializing Societies," in *Emerging Theoretical Models in Social and Political History,* ed. Allen G. Bogue (Beverly Hills, 1973), pp. 109–110.
5. Scott, *San Francisco Bay Area,* pp. 162–167; Lawrence Kinnaird, *History of the Greater San Francisco Bay Region,* 3 vols. (New York, 1966), 2:214; Kahn, *Imperial San Francisco,* chs. 4, 5, 8, and Conclusion; see also ch. 7 above.
6. Frank Morton Todd, *The Story of the Exposition: Being the Official History of the International Celebration Held at San Francisco in 1915 to Commemorate the Discovery of*

the Pacific Ocean and the Construction of the Panama Canal, 5 vols. (New York, 1921), 1:34–37, 50–54, 71–98, 312, esp. pp. 54, 88.

7. Ibid.

8. Ibid., 1:101–118, 126–128, 325–330.

9. Kahn, *Imperial San Francisco,* ch. 8; Bean, *Boss Ruef's San Francisco,* chs. 21–23; Knight, *Industrial Relations,* pp. 237–241, 292, 305–307, 386.

10. Todd, *Story of the Exposition,* 1:287, 2:262–273, esp. p. 265; see also Gray Brechin, "Sailing to Byzantium: The Architecture of the Panama Pacific International Exposition," *California History* 62 (Summer 1983):106–121.

11. Todd, *Story of the Exposition,* 1:134–139, 166–167, 202–207, 290–296, 347–353, 2:31–35, 5:132.

12. Ibid., 1:65–66, 124.

13. Taylor, *Life of James Rolph,* 55; Frances A. Groff, "The Exposition Mayor," *Sunset* 28 (Jan. 1912):68–70; Herman A. Goldbeck, "The Political Career of James Rolph, Jr.: A Preliminary Study," master's thesis, University of California, Berkeley, 1936, pp. 37–38.

14. Draper, "San Francisco Civic Center," pp. 62–70, 77, 89–92, 102–104; Kahn, *Imperial San Francisco,* pp. 90–91, 100–101, 159–162; Hansen, *San Francisco Almanac,* p. 45; Goldbeck, "Political Career of James Rolph," p. 8; Daniel H. Burnham, *Report on a Plan for San Francisco* (San Francisco, 1905); Daniel H. Burnham, *Plan of Proposed Street Changes in the Burned District* (San Francisco, 1906).

15. Rolph's inaugural speech, Jan. 8, 1912, in *Chronicle,* Jan. 9, 1912, p. 2; Draper, "San Francisco Civic Center," p. 114.

16. Draper, "San Francisco Civic Center," pp. 116–124.

17. Ibid., pp. 54, 168–169.

18. Todd, *Story of the Exposition,* 2:242–246, 5:1–6, 100–121; Rischin, "Sunny Jim Rolph," p. 171; Draper, "San Francisco Civic Center," pp. 121–122, 155–156.

19. Draper, "San Francisco Civic Center," pp. 205–207, 215–222, 225–228; B. J. S. Cahill, "The New City Hall, San Francisco," *Architect and Engineer* 46 (Aug. 1916):39. The opera house site is still vacant, save for a parking lot and a "temporary" building put up during World War II as a hospitality center for soldiers and sailors, currently housing city offices.

20. San Francisco Charter, adopted Jan. 26, 1899 (in effect Jan. 8, 1900), Article 12.

21. Charles A. Smallwood, *The White Front Cars of San Francisco,* rev. ed. (Glendale, Ca., 1978), pp. 39, 45–46, 241–243.

22. Segal, "Rolph and the Municipal Railway," pp. 33, 38–42; Bean, *Boss Ruef's San Francisco,* pp. 108–118, esp. pp. 117, 211–218; Knight, *Industrial Relations,* pp. 186–189, 193–197; Goldbeck, "Political Career of James Rolph," pp. 22–30; Byington and Lewis, eds., *History of San Francisco,* 1:482–484; Anthony Perles, *The People's Railway: The History of the Municipal Railway of San Francisco* (Glendale, Ca., 1981), pp. 13–16.

23. Segal, "Rolph and the Municipal Railway," pp. 43–44; Perles, *People's Railway,* p. 19.

24. In fairness to McCarthy, the slow pace of construction during his administration resulted in part from a court challenge by Patrick Calhoun to the creation of the Municipal Railway and in part from a refusal by many banks to subscribe to the bond issue because it was intended to create a municipally owned utility. See Kazin, "Barons of Labor," pp. 406–408.

25. Segal, "Rolph and the Municipal Railway," pp. 53–54, 57–59, 61–63, 65, 67–68; Perles, *People's Railway,* pp. 19–29.

26. Rolph to Public Ownership Association, April 15, 1913, Rolph Papers, California Historical Society; Segal, "Rolph and the Municipal Railway," pp. 72–74,

77–78, 80–91, 102–107; Smallwood, *White Front Cars,* pp. 48–49; Perles, *People's Railway,* pp. 29–46.

27. Kendrick A. Clements, "Politics and the Park: San Francisco's Fight for Hetch Hetchy, 1908–1913," *Pacific Historical Review* 48 (1979): 187–188; Ray W. Taylor, *Hetch Hetchy: The Story of San Francisco's Struggle to Provide a Water Supply for Her Future Needs* (San Francisco, 1927), pp. 36–38, 45–49.

28. Kendrick A. Clements, "Engineers and Conservationists in the Progressive Era," *California History* 58 (1979–1980): 286–300, esp. p. 300; Elmo R. Richardson, "The Struggle for the Valley: California's Hetch Hetchy Controversy, 1905–1913," *California Historical Society Quarterly* 38 (Sept. 1959): 249–258; Holway R. Jones, *John Muir and the Sierra Club: The Battle for Yosemite* (San Francisco, 1965), pp. 86–151; Spring Valley Water Company, *The Future Water Supply of San Francisco* (San Francisco, 1912).

29. Bean, *Boss Ruef's San Francisco,* pp. 141–142; Taylor, *Hetch Hetchy,* pp. 99–102; see also Ted Wurm, *Hetch Hetchy and Its Dam Railroad* (Berkeley, 1973).

30. 63rd Congress, 1st Session, H.R. 7207, Sec. 6, quoted in Taylor, *Hetch Hetchy,* p. 195; Taylor, *Hetch Hetchy,* pp. 121–127; Byington and Lewis, eds., *History of San Francisco,* 2:153–155; Clements, "Politics and the Park," pp. 206–212; Richardson, "Struggle for the Valley," pp. 254–256; Jones, *John Muir,* pp. 153–167; Goldbeck, "Political Career of James Rolph," pp. 30–31.

31. Taylor, *Hetch Hetchy,* pp. 145–146, 176–178; Wurm, *Hetch Hetchy,* pp. 41–124, 179–228; Todd, *Story of the Exposition,* 2:125–127; Goldbeck, "Political Career of James Rolph," pp. 32–33.

32. Segal, "Rolph and the Municipal Railway," p. 56; Sabraw, "Rolph and the Barbary Coast," pp. 69–70, 73; marginal comments by Rolph on a letter from F. J. Koster, Aug. 23, 1916, Rolph Papers, California Historical Society; Goldbeck, "Political Career of James Rolph," pp. 7, 51–53; Taylor, *Life of James Rolph,* pp. 57–58; *Chronicle,* Jan. 9, 1912, p. 2.

33. Chester Rowell to Theodore Roosevelt, Dec. 1, 1917, quoted in Richard H. Frost, *The Mooney Case* (Stanford, 1968), p. 233; Todd, *Story of the Exposition,* 3:80–81, 95–97.

34. Knight, *Industrial Relations,* pp. 299–307; see also ch. 4, above.

35. Frost, *Mooney Case,* pp. 63–64, 80–85; *Organized Labor* (San Francisco), July 22, 1916, quoted in Frost, *Mooney Case,* p. 81; Gentry, *Frame-Up,* pp. 79–81.

36. Frost, *Mooney Case,* pp. 1–3, 11–18, 19–25, 39, 72–79, 85–87; Gentry, *Frame-Up,* pp. 11–23, 33–114, 441–477.

37. Frost, *Mooney Case,* pp. 118–258; Gentry, *Frame-Up,* pp. 115–227; Zechariah Chafee, Jr., et al., *The Mooney-Billings Report Suppressed by the Wickersham Commission* (New York, 1932), pp. 242–243.

38. Frost, *Mooney Case,* pp. 144–150, 153–155, 231; Gentry, *Frame-Up,* pp. 25–26, 142, 173, 205–215, 224, 233.

39. Frost, *Mooney Case,* p. 232, 233, 262–267, 273–276; Gentry, *Frame-Up,* pp. 229–236; Carl A. Silvio, "A Social Analysis of the Special Recall Election of San Francisco District Attorney Charles M. Fickert, 18 December 1917," student paper, Dean's prize competition, San Francisco State University, 1978.

40. Frost, *Mooney Case,* pp. 295–299, 311–313, 318–319, 483–488; Gentry, *Frame-Up,* pp. 240–243, 251, 260–262, 422–423, 430–431, 439.

41. Knight, *Industrial Relations,* pp. 313–322; Steven C. Levi, "The Battle for the Eight-Hour Day in San Francisco," *California History* 57 (Winter 1978–1979):349–352; "Rolph Answers Koster," *Labor Clarion,* Aug. 31, 1917, pp. 54–55.

42. Assistant secretary to the mayor to A. H. Duke, Jan. 15, 1916, and assistant secretary to the mayor to S. Asano, Jan. 15, 1916, Rolph Papers, California Historical Society; Taylor, *Life of James Rolph,* pp. 9–10, 20–23, 79–82; Sabraw, "Rolph and

the Barbary Coast," pp. 54, 74–75; Roger W. Lotchin, "John Francis Neylan: San Francisco Irish Progressive," in *The San Francisco Irish: 1850–1976*, ed. James P. Walsh (San Francisco, 1978), p. 99; H. Brett Melendy and Benjamin F. Gilbert, *The Governors of California: Peter H. Burnett to Edmund G. Brown* (Georgetown, Ca., 1965), pp. 363–364; John Francis Neylan to William Randolph Hearst, Jan. 18, 1924, Neylan Papers, Bancroft Library.

43. Hines, "Our American Mayors," p. 164.

44. Andrew Gallagher, quoted in Sabraw, "Rolph and the Barbary Coast," p. 55.

45. Perles, *People's Railway*, pp. 63–70, 81, 91, 96–97; Rolph quoted in McGloin, *San Francisco*, pp. 179–181.

46. San Francisco Board of Supervisors, *Journal of Proceedings* (n.s.) 13 (1918): 3–5; Perles, *People's Railway*, pp. 64, 99.

47. Perles, *People's Railway*, pp. 118–119, 121–122; John Francis Neylan to William Randolph Hearst, May 22, 1925, Neylan Papers, Bancroft Library; Marigold Cole, "The 1927 San Francisco Election," seminar paper, San Francisco State University, 1979, p. 7; Goldbeck, "Political Career of James Rolph," pp. 76–77, 113–114, 131–132.

48. Wurm, *Hetch Hetchy*, pp. 63, 67, 191, 193, 222; San Francisco, City Engineer, *The Hetch Hetchy Water Supply and Power Project of San Francisco* (San Francisco, 1931).

49. San Francisco, Board of Supervisors, *Journal of Proceedings* (n.s.) 18 (1923):148, 689, 744–746, 758–760, 839–842, 983–995, 1015–1019, 1029–1030, 1037–1040, 1091–1093, 1123–1125, 1174–1175, 1301–1305, 1360, 1370–1371; ibid. (n.s.) 19 (1924):51; Goldbeck, "Political Career of James Rolph," pp. 77–83; Lotchin, "John Francis Neylan," pp. 96–99; *City* 3 (June 1923):42–44; ibid. 3 (July 1923):51–54; ibid. 3 (Aug. 1923):58–59; ibid. 3 (Sept. 1923):66–76; ibid. 3 (Dec. 1923):107–108; ibid. 4 (March 1924):36–47.

50. San Francisco, Board of Supervisors, *Journal of Proceedings* (n.s.) 19 (1924):2, 18–19, 36–37, 50–56, 147, 161; Goldbeck, "Political Career of James Rolph," pp. 93–97; Lotchin, "John Francis Neylan," pp. 99–100; John Francis Neylan to William Randolph Hearst, June 13, 1924, Neylan Papers, Bancroft Library; *City* 4 (Jan. 1924): 2–4; ibid. 4 (Feb. 1924):10–12; ibid. 4 (March 1924):19–59; ibid. 4 (June 1924):82–84, 90–92; ibid. 4 (July 1924):94–95.

51. Goldbeck, "Political Career of James Rolph," pp. 97–125, esp. pp. 93–110; Lotchin, "John Francis Neylan," pp. 100–104.

52. Franck Roberts Havenner, "Reminiscences," transcript of interview conducted in 1953 for the Bancroft Library Oral History Project, Bancroft Library, University of California, Berkeley, pp. 69–72; *City* 5 (June 1925):62–68; ibid. 5 (Aug. 1925):78–81; ibid. 5 (Sept. 1925):92–95; ibid. 5 (Dec. 1925:118–121; ibid. 6 (July 1926):50–52; ibid. 6 (Sept. 1926):63; ibid. 7 (Feb. 1927):22–23; ibid. 7 (Oct. 1927):171–173; ibid. 10 (Aug. 1930):46–71.

53. Goldbeck, "Political Career of James Rolph," pp. 32–33, 71–74, 127–129; Taylor, *Hetch Hetchy*, 177–183; Wurm, *Hetch Hetchy*, pp. 222, 229; *San Francisco Municipal Record* 4 (March 1930):64; *Examiner*, April 9, 1928; *News*, Oct. 15, 1929 (clippings), Bank of America Archives.

54. Harry S. Peters, "The Life Story of Tom Finn," *Chronicle*, Jan. 9, 1938, p. 16; ibid., Jan. 10, 1938, p. 9; ibid., Jan. 11, 1938, p. 14; ibid., Jan. 12, 1938, p. 14; ibid., Jan. 13, 1938, p. 28; ibid., Jan. 14, 1938, p. 14; Scharrenberg, "Reminiscences," pp. 97–98; Barnes, " 'Fountainhead of Corruption,' " pp. 142–153; *Chronicle*, Aug. 6, 1920, p. 4.

55. Peters, "Life Story of Tom Finn," *Chronicle*, Jan. 14, 1938, p. 14; Havenner, "Reminiscences," pp. 67–69; Barnes, " 'Fountainhead of Corruption,' " pp. 148, 152; *News*, March 16, 1937, pp. 1–2, 13A–14, esp. p. 13A; Goldbeck, "Political Career of James Rolph," pp. 115–125.

56. Havenner, "Reminiscences," pp. 67–69; Taylor, *Life of James Rolph,* pp. 44–45; Sabraw, "Rolph and the Barbary Coast," pp. 63–64; Lotchin, "John Francis Neylan," p. 90. By 1930, 82 percent of the city's registered voters were Republicans; see the records in the San Francisco Registrar of Voters office.

57. Scharrenberg, "Reminiscences," pp. 54–55, 83; Lotchin, "John Francis Neylan," pp. 91–92; *Truth,* Oct. 28, 1927 (clipping), Bank of America Archives; Dana, *A. P. Giannini,* pp. 144–146.

58. All voting data are from the office of the Registrar of Voters. Linear regression and correlation for pairs of elections indicate very close relationships. Many of the coefficients are more significant than 0.9 (or −0.9), and nearly all are more significant than 0.7 (or −0.7). Regression coefficients show similar patterns of significance, with the slope often near 1.0.

59. Barnes, " 'Fountainhead of Corruption,' " p. 148.

60. Devine, "Adoption of the 1932 Charter," p. 6; Bureau of Municipal Research, New York, *Report on a Survey of the Government of the City and County of San Francisco* . . . (San Francisco, 1916); *City* 3 (Nov. 1923):99–100; San Francisco Chamber of Commerce, minutes of the board of directors, Sept. 19, 1916, California Historical Society, San Francisco. The directors and officers of the Bureau for Governmental Research are listed in the *City.*

61. *City* 3 (Oct. 1923):87–89; ibid. 3 (June 1923):44–45; ibid. 3 (Nov. 1923): 94–95; ibid. 4 (Sept. 1924):110–112; ibid. 7 (March 1927):46–116; ibid. 8 (Oct. 1928):129–130.

62. Ibid. 3 (Oct. 1923):87; Bureau of Municipal Research, New York, *Report on a Survey,* pp. 45, 55–56.

63. Devine, "Adoption of the 1932 Charter," pp. 9–15.

64. *City* 8 (March 1928):45, 49, 52, 56–57, 68–69, 73, 77–78; ibid. 8 (Oct. 1928):110, 114–118, 129–131; ibid. 9 (Jan. 1929):2–4.

65. Devine, "Adoption of the 1932 Charter," pp. 22–26, 31; *Examiner,* June 9, 1930, pp. 15, 26; ibid., June 24, 1930, p. 1.

66. Devine, "Adoption of the 1932 Charter," pp. 27–31; Frost, *Mooney Case,* p. 276; "Union Labor Party–Miscellaneous–1929" file, San Francisco Labor Council Manuscript Collection, Bancroft Library.

67. Devine, "Adoption of the 1932 Charter," pp. 80–88.

68. Voting data are from the San Francisco Registrar of Voters.

69. Devine, "Adoption of the 1932 Charter," pp. 51–52, 59–61; San Francisco Charter, adopted March 26, 1931, in effect Jan. 8, 1932, sections 69–73.

70. San Francisco Charter, in effect, Jan. 8, 1932, sections 9–11, 22; Devine, "Adoption of the 1932 Charter," pp. 49–50, 53–54.

71. *City* 8 (March 1928):43, 49–50; ibid. 11 (March 1931):8–9, 11; Wurm, *Hetch Hetchy,* pp. 225–226; San Francisco Charter, in effect, Jan. 8, 1932, sections 35–51.

72. Cole, "1927 San Francisco Election"; Scharrenberg, "Reminiscences," pp. 36–37; Goldbeck, "Political Career of James Rolph," p. 118; Ryan, *Industrial Relations,* pp. 185–186.

73. Wirt, *Power in the City,* pp. 11–12.

74. Marylou Almada, "The Appointment of Angelo J. Rossi as Mayor (San Francisco, 1930)," seminar paper, San Francisco State University, 1979.

CHAPTER 9

1. Max Weber, "Class, Status, Party," in *From Max Weber: Essays in Sociology,* ed. and trans. H. H. Gerth and C. Wright Mills (New York, 1946), p. 180; see also Hammack, *Power and Society,* p. 5.

2. Carl V. Harris, *Political Power in Birmingham, 1871–1921* (Knoxville, Tenn., 1977); Hammack, *Power and Society.*

3. McDonald, "Urban Development."

4. Hunter, *Community Power Structure;* Dahl, *Who Governs.*

5. Hammack, *Power and Society,* esp. pp. 303–326.

6. Lotchin, "The Darwinian City"; Roger W. Lotchin, "The Metropolitan-Military Complex in Comparative Perspective: San Francisco, Los Angeles, and San Diego, 1919–1941," in *The Urban West,* ed. Gerald D. Nash, pp. 19–30 (Manhattan, Kans., 1979); Roger W. Lotchin, "The City and the Sword in Metropolitan California, 1919–1941," *Urbanism Past and Present* 7 (Summer/Fall 1982):1–16.

7. See parts of ch. 2, above; and William Issel, "Business in California, 1890–1940," paper presented at the American Historical Association annual meeting, San Francisco, Dec. 29, 1983.

8. Knight, *Industrial Relations,* pp. 226–235 and passim.

9. Lucile Eaves, "Labor Day in San Francisco and How Attained," *Labor Clarion,* Sept. 2, 1910, p. 6; see also Saxton, *Indispensable Enemy.*

10. William F. Heintz, *San Francisco's Mayors: 1850–1880* (Woodside, Ca., 1975), pp. 42–89. The mayors were Ephraim W. Burr (1856–1859), People's party, merchant and financier; Henry F. Teschemaker (1859–1863), People's party, merchant; Henry P. Coon (1863–1867), People's party, physician, druggist, lawyer, judge, and landowner; Thomas H. Selby (1869–1871), Republican and Taxpayers' parties, merchant and manufacturer; William Alvord (1871–1873), Taxpayers' and Republican parties, importer and manufacturer; James Otis (1873–1875), several parties, importer.

11. U.S. Census Office, Department of the Interior, *Report on the Social Statistics of Cities,* pt. 2, *The Southern and the Western States* (Washington, D.C., 1887), pp. 805–811.

12. McDonald, "Urban Development."

13. Kahn, *Imperial San Francisco,* pp. 210–216.

POSTSCRIPT

1. Frederick M. Wirt, "The Politics of Hyperpluralism," in *Culture and Civility in San Francisco,* ed. Howard S. Becker (New Brunswick, N.J., 1971); Wirt, *Power in the City*, p. 350.

2. Kevin Starr, *Americans and the California Dream: 1850–1915* (New York, 1973); *Examiner,* Aug. 21, 1980; Carol Kroot, "San Francisco: 'Pluralism Run Amok,' " *San Francisco Progress,* Aug. 15, 1980.

3. David F. Selvin, *A Place in the Sun: A History of California Labor* (San Francisco, 1981), p. 42; Selvin cites a former union official for his account of workers walking the halls.

4. Data on voting registration from the San Francisco Registrar of Voters office records.

5. David F. Selvin, *Sky Full of Storm: A Brief History of California Labor,* rev. ed. (San Francisco, 1975), p. 52.

6. Havenner, "Reminiscences."

7. Dick Meister, "Labor Power," *San Francisco Bay Guardian* (Dec. 23, 1970): 2, 3, 25.

8. Chester Hartman, *Yerba Buena: Land Grab and Community Resistance in San Francisco* (San Francisco, 1974); and Chester Hartman, *The Transformation of San Francisco* (Totowa, N.J., 1984).

9. J. Allen Whitt, *Urban Elites and Mass Transportation: The Dialectics of Power* (Princeton, 1982), esp. ch. 2.

10. Wirt, *Power in the City,* pp. 197−213; Bruce G. Brugmann et al., *The Ultimate Highrise: San Francisco's Mad Rush Toward the Sky* (San Francisco, 1971); John H. Mollenkopf, *The Contested City* (Princeton, 1983), esp. chs. 4, 5.

11. Meriel Burtle et al., *The District Handbook: A Coro Foundation Guide to San Francisco's Supervisorial Districts* (San Francisco, 1979), esp. p. 14.

12. See Wirt, *Power in the City,* p. 90; and Manuel Castells and Karen Murphy, "Cultural Identity and Urban Structure: The Spatial Organization of San Francisco's Gay Community," in *Urban Policy Under Capitalism,* ed. Norman I. Fainstein and Susan S. Fainstein (Beverly Hills, 1982), pp. 237−259.

13. Some might claim Edward Taylor (1907−1909) as a Democrat, but he was elected primarily as a nonpartisan.

14. San Francisco Registrar of Voters voting data; see also Wirt, *Power in the City,* p. 175; Burtle, *District Handbook,* p. 27.

15. For a succinct summary of the Citizens' Charter Revision Committee, see Wirt, *Power in the City,* pp. 142−154.

16. Robert W. Cherny, "San Francisco's Return to District Elections: The Role of the Labor Council," paper presented at the Fifth Annual Southwest Labor Studies conference, California State College, Dominguez Hills, 1979.

17. "Charter Commissioners—Biographical Notes," mimeographed, Charter Commission, 1979.

Bibliography

MANUSCRIPT COLLECTIONS AND ARCHIVES

Bank of America Archives. San Francisco, California.
Charlotte L. Brown Papers. California Historical Society, San Francisco.
Wellington Cleveland Burnett Papers. California Historical Society, San Francisco.
William David Merry Howard Papers. California Historical Society, San Francisco.
Hiram Johnson Papers. Bancroft Library. University of California, Berkeley.
Milton Slocum Latham Papers. California Historical Society, San Francisco.
Walter Macarthur Manuscript Collection. Bancroft Library. University of California, Berkeley.
Frederick William Macondray, Jr., Papers. California Historical Society, San Francisco.
John Francis Neylan Papers. Bancroft Library. University of California, Berkeley.
George C. Pardee Manuscript Collection. Bancroft Library. University of California, Berkeley.
James Duval Phelan Papers. Bancroft Library. University of California, Berkeley.
James Rolph, Jr., Papers. California Historical Society, San Francisco.
Sanborn Insurance maps of San Francisco. California Historical Society, San Francisco.
San Francisco Art Commission files. San Francisco.
San Francisco Art Institute Archives. San Francisco.
San Francisco Chamber of Commerce records. California Historical Society, San Francisco.
San Francisco Charters. Pamphlets. Bancroft Library. University of California, Berkeley.
San Francisco Early Documents Scrapbook. California Historical Society, San Francisco.
San Francisco election records. Registrar of Voters, City and County of San Francisco.
San Francisco Labor Council Manuscript Collection. Bancroft Library. University of California, Berkeley.
San Francisco Merchants' Association. Minutes of the board of directors. California Historical Society, San Francisco.
Paul Scharrenberg Manuscript Collection. Bancroft Library. University of California, Berkeley.
William Tecumseh Sherman Letters. California Historical Society, San Francisco.

Adolph Sutro Papers. California Historical Society, San Francisco.
Edward R. Taylor Papers. California Historical Society, San Francisco.
Robert B. Wallace Letters. California Historical Society, San Francisco.
Wells Fargo Bank Archives. San Francisco.
Western Jewish History Center. Judah L. Magnes Museum, Berkeley.

NEWSPAPERS AND PERIODICALS

Palo Alto Times.
San Francisco. *American Plan.*
San Francisco. *American Plan Progress.*
San Francisco Bulletin.
San Francisco Call.
San Francisco Call and Post.
San Francisco Chamber of Commerce Activities.
San Francisco. *Chamber of Commerce Journal.*
San Francisco *Chronicle.*
San Francisco. *The City.*
San Francisco. *Coast Banker.*
San Francisco. *Coast Seamen's Journal.*
San Francisco Daily News.
San Francisco Examiner.
San Francisco Labor Clarion.
San Francisco. *The Monitor.*
San Francisco. *The Monthly Review.*
San Francisco Municipal Record.
San Francisco News.
San Francisco. *Organized Labor.*
San Francisco Post.
San Francisco. *The Socialist.*
San Francisco. *The Voice of Labor.*
San Francisco. *The Wave.*

GOVERNMENT PUBLICATIONS

San Francisco. Board of Education. *Annual Report of the Superintendent of Public Schools.* San Francisco, 1878.

San Francisco. Board of Supervisors. *Journal of Proceedings,* new series. San Francisco, 1918–1930.

San Francisco. Board of Supervisors. *Municipal Reports.* San Francisco, 1871–1901.

San Francisco. Charter of the City and County of San Francisco. Adopted Jan. 26, 1899; in effect Jan. 8, 1900.

San Francisco. Charter of the City and County of San Francisco. Adopted March 26, 1931; in effect Jan. 8, 1932.

San Francisco. City Engineer. *The Hetch Hetchy Water Supply and Power Project of San Francisco.* San Francisco, 1931.

San Francisco. Park Commission. *The M. H. de Young Museum.* San Francisco, 1921.

San Francisco. *Report on the Improvement and Development of the Transportation Facilities of San Francisco.* San Francisco, 1913.

State of California. Bureau of Labor Statistics. *Investigation into Condition of Men Working on the Waterfront and on Board Pacific Coast Vessels, San Francisco, June 29–July 10, 1887.* Sacramento, 1887.

State of California. Railroad Commission. *Report and Recommendation in the Matter of the Valuation of the Spring Valley Water Company's Properties.* Sacramento, 1920.

State of California. Superintendent of Banks. *Annual Report.* Sacramento, 1934.

U.S. Bureau of the Census. Department of Commerce. *Fifteenth Census of the United States: 1930.* 6 vols. Washington, D.C.: U.S. Government Printing Office, 1932–1933.

———. *Fourteenth Census of the United States: 1920.* 11 vols. Washington, D.C.: U.S. Government Printing Office, 1922–1923.

U.S. Bureau of the Census. Department of Commerce and Labor. *Thirteenth Census of the United States: 1910.* 11 vols. Washington, D.C.: U.S. Government Printing Office, 1914.

U.S. Census Office. Department of the Interior. *Eleventh Census of the United States: 1890.* 15 vols., compendium. Washington, D.C.: U.S. Government Printing Office, 1892.

————. *Ninth Census of the United States: 1870*. 3 vols., compendium. Washington, D.C.: U.S. Government Printing Office, 1872.

————. *Report on the Social Statistics of Cities*. 2 vols. Washington, D.C., 1886.

————. *Report on the Statistics of Wages in Manufacturing Industries*. Washington, D.C., 1886.

————. *Tenth Census of the United States: 1880*. 22 vols., compendium. Washington, D.C.: U.S. Government Printing Office, 1883.

————. *Twelfth Census of the United States: 1900*. 37 vols. Washington, D.C.: U.S. Government Printing Office, 1902–1904.

U.S. Commission on Industrial Relations. *Industrial Relations: Final Report and Testimony*. 10 vols. Washington, D.C., 1916.

U.S. National Archives and Records Service. General Services Administration. *1900 Federal Population Census Schedules*. Washington, D.C.: National Archives and Records Service. Microfilm, T623.

DIRECTORIES AND GUIDEBOOKS

Hackett, Fred H., ed. *The Industries of San Francisco: Her Rank, Resources, Advantages, Trade, Commerce, and Manufactures*. San Francisco: Payot & Co., 1884.

Hoag, Charles C., ed. *Our Society Blue Book: 1902*. San Francisco: Charles C. Hoag, 1902.

Illustrated Fraternal Directory. San Francisco: Bancroft Co., 1889.

Langley's San Francisco Directory, 1880–1881. San Francisco: Francis, Valentine, & Co., 1881.

National Cyclopedia of American Biography. Vols. 26–55. New York: James T. White Co., 1938–1974.

San Francisco Chamber of Commerce. *San Francisco: The Financial, Commercial, and Industrial Metropolis of the Pacific Coast*. San Francisco: H. S. Crocker Co., 1915.

San Francisco city directories. 1879–1930. Various titles and publishers.

Walker's Manual of California Securities and Directory of Directors. San Francisco: Walker's Manual, Inc., 1915–1935.

Who's Who in America. Vols. 16, 18. Chicago: A. N. Marquis & Co., 1930–1931, 1934–1935.

Who's Who in California, 1928–1929. San Francisco: Who's Who Publishing Co., 1929.

Who's Who in Commerce and Industry: 1936. Chicago: A. N. Marquis & Co., 1936.

BOOKS AND ARTICLES

A Man and His Friends: A Life Story of Milton H. Esberg. San Francisco: Recorder-Sunset Press, 1953.

Adams, H. Austin. *The Man, John D. Spreckels*. San Diego: Frye & Smith, 1924.

Adler, Jacob. *Claus Spreckels: The Sugar King in Hawaii*. Honolulu: University of Hawaii Press, 1966.

Aikman, Duncan. "California's Sun God," *Nation* 132 (Jan. 14, 1931):35–37.

Altrocchi, Julia Cooley. *Spectacular San Franciscans*. New York: E. P. Dutton, 1949.

Armstrong, Leroy, and J. O. Denny. *Financial California: An Historical Review of the Beginnings and Progress of Banking in the State*. San Francisco: Coast Banker Publishing Co., 1916.

Asbury, Herbert. *The Barbary Coast: An Informal History of the San Francisco Underworld*. Garden City, N.Y.: Garden City Publishing Co., 1933.

Atherton, Gertrude. *My San Francisco: A Wayward Biography*. Indianapolis: Bobbs-Merrill Co., 1946.

Averbach, Alvin. "San Francisco's South of Market District, 1850–1950: The Emergence of a Skid Row." *California Historical Quarterly* 52 (Fall 1973):197–223.

Baker, Ray Stannard. "A Corner in Labor: What Is Happening in San Francisco Where Unionism Holds Undisputed Sway." *McClure's* 22 (Feb. 1904):366–378.

Bancroft, Hubert Howe. *History of California*. 7 vols. San Francisco: San Francisco History Co., 1884–1890.

Barnekov, Timothy K., and Daniel Rich. "Privatism and Urban Development: An Analysis of the Organized Influence of Local Business Elites." *Urban Affairs Quarterly* 12 (June 1977):431–460.

Barnes, Merritt. " 'Fountainhead of Corruption'—Peter P. McDonough, Boss of San Francisco's Underworld." *California History* 58 (Summer 1979):142–153.

Bean, Walton. *Boss Ruef's San Francisco: The Story of the Union Labor Party, Big Business, and the Graft Prosecution*. Berkeley: University of California Press, 1952.

Bernstein, Richard J. *The Restructuring of Social and Political Theory*. New York: Harcourt Brace Jovanovich, 1976.

Birmingham, Stephen. *California Rich*. New York: Simon & Schuster, 1980.

Bloom, Monroe A. *A Century of Pioneering: A Brief History of the Crocker-Citizens National Bank*. San Francisco, 1970.

Bluestone, Barry. "Lower-Income Workers and Marginal Industries." In *Poverty in America*. Edited by Louis Ferman et al. Ann Arbor: University of Michigan Press, 1968.

Boyer, Paul. *Urban Masses and Moral Order in America, 1820–1920*. Cambridge, Mass.: Harvard University Press, 1978.

Brechin, Gray. "Sailing to Byzantium: The Architecture of the Panama Pacific International Exposition." *California History* 62 (Summer 1983):106–121.

Bruce, Robert V. *1877: Year of Violence*. Indianapolis: Bobbs-Merrill Co., 1959.

Brugmann, Bruce G., et al. *The Ultimate Highrise: San Francisco's Mad Rush Toward the Sky*. San Francisco: San Francisco Bay Guardian Books, 1971.

Brun, V. P. *My Years with Coldwell Banker*. Los Angeles: Privately printed, n.d.

Brusher, Joseph S., S. J. *Consecrated Thunderbolt: Father Yorke of San Francisco*. Hawthorne, N.J.: Joseph F. Wagner, 1973.

Bryce, James. *The American Commonwealth*. 2 vols. 3rd ed., rev. New York: Macmillan Co., 1908.

Buchanan, A. Russell. *David S. Terry of California: Dueling Judge*. San Marino, Ca.: Huntington Library, 1956.

Buckley, Christopher A. "The Reminiscences of Christopher A. Buckley." *San Francisco Bulletin*, Aug. 31, 1918–Feb. 5, 1919.

Builders of a Great City: San Francisco's Representative Men. San Francisco: Journal of Commerce, 1891.

Bullough, William A. "The Steam Beer Handicap: Chris Buckley and the San Francisco Municipal Election of 1896." *California Historical Quarterly* 54 (Fall 1975):245–262.

———. "Hannibal Versus the Blind Boss: The 'Junta,' Chris Buckley, and Democratic Reform Politics in San Francisco." *Pacific Historical Review* 46 (May 1977):181–206.

———. *The Blind Boss and His City: Christopher Augustine Buckley and Nineteenth-Century San Francisco*. Berkeley: University of California Press, 1979.

Burchell, Robert A. *The San Francisco Irish, 1848–1880*. Berkeley: University of California Press, 1980.

Bureau of Municipal Research, New York. *Report on a Survey of the Government of the City and County of San Francisco Prepared by the San Francisco Real Estate Board*. San Francisco: Rincon Publishing Co., 1916.

Burnham, Daniel H. *Report on a Plan for San Francisco*. San Francisco: City of San Francisco, 1905.

Burtle, Meriel, et al. *The District Handbook: A Coro Foundation Guide to San Francisco's Supervisorial Districts.* San Francisco: Coro Foundation, 1979.

Byington, Lewis F., and Oscar Lewis, eds. *The History of San Francisco.* 3 vols. Chicago: S. J. Clarke Publishing Co., 1931.

Cahill, B. J. S. "The New City Hall, San Francisco." *Architect and Engineer* 46 (Aug. 1916):38–77.

Callow, Alexander, Jr. "San Francisco's Blind Boss." *Pacific Historical Review* 25 (Aug. 1956):261–280.

Castells, Manuel, and Karen Murphy. "Cultural Identity and Urban Structure: The Spatial Organization of San Francisco's Gay Community." In *Urban Policy Under Capitalism.* Edited by Norman I. Fainstein and Susan S. Fainstein, pp. 237–259. Beverly Hills: Sage Publications, 1982.

Cather, Helen Virginia. *The History of San Francisco's Chinatown.* San Francisco: R & E Research Associates, 1974.

Chaffee, Zachariah, Jr., et al. *Draft of Mooney-Billings Report Submitted to the National Commission on Law Observance and Enforcement by the Section on Lawless Enforcement of the Law.* Published as *The Mooney-Billings Report Suppressed by the Wickersham Commission.* New York: Gotham House, 1932.

Chandler, Alfred D., Jr. *The Visible Hand: The Managerial Revolution in American Business.* Cambridge, Mass.: Belknap Press of Harvard University Press, 1977.

Choy, Philip P. "Golden Mountain of Lead: The Chinese Experience in California." *California Historical Quarterly* 50 (Sept. 1971):267–276.

Cinel, Dino. *From Italy to San Francisco: The Immigrant Experience.* Stanford: Stanford University Press, 1982.

Clark, George T. *Leland Stanford: War Governor of California, Railroad Builder, and Founder of Stanford University.* Stanford: Stanford University Press, 1931.

Cleland, Robert Glass, and Frank B. Putnam. *Isaias W. Hellman and the Farmers and Merchants Bank.* San Marino, Ca.: Huntington Library, 1965.

Clements, Kendrick A. "Politics and the Park: San Francisco's Fight for Hetch Hetchy, 1908–1913." *Pacific Historical Review* 48 (1979):183–215.

———. "Engineers and Conservationists in the Progressive Era." *California History* 58 (1979–1980):282–303.

Cochran, Thomas C. "The Business Revolution." *American Historical Review* 79 (Dec. 1974):1449–1466.

———. *Frontiers of Change: Early Industrialism in America.* New York: Oxford University Press, 1981.

Cochran, Thomas C., and William Miller. *The Age of Enterprise: A Social History of Industrial America.* Rev. ed. New York: Harper & Row, 1961.

Coolidge, Mary Roberts. *Chinese Immigration.* New York: Henry Holt & Co., 1909.

Cornise, Titus Fey. *The Natural Wealth of California.* San Francisco: H. H. Bancroft, 1868.

Cronin, Bernard Cornelius. *Father Yorke and the Labor Movement in San Francisco, 1900–1910.* Washington, D.C.: Catholic University of America Press, 1943.

Cross, Ira Brown. *Financing an Empire: History of Banking in California.* 4 vols. Chicago: S. J. Clarke Publishing Co., 1927.

———. *A History of the Labor Movement in California.* Berkeley: University of California Press, 1935.

Cutler, Leland W. *America Is Good to a Country Boy.* Stanford: Stanford University Press, 1954.

Daggett, Stuart. *Chapters on the History of the Southern Pacific.* New York: Ronald Press Co., 1922.

Dahl, Robert A. *Who Governs: Democracy and Power in an American City.* New Haven:

Yale University Press, 1961.

Dana, Julian. *The Man Who Built San Francisco: A Study of Ralston's Journey with Banners.* New York: Macmillan Co., 1937.

———. *A. P. Giannini: Giant in the West.* New York: Prentice-Hall, 1947.

Dana, Richard Henry. *Two Years Before the Mast.* New York: Modern Library, 1936.

Daniels, Douglas Henry. *Pioneer Urbanites: A Social and Cultural History of Black San Francisco.* Philadelphia: Temple University Press, 1980.

Danziger, Gustav Adolf. "The Jew in San Francisco: The Last Half-Century." *Overland Monthly* 25 (April 1895):381–410.

Darling, Arthur B., ed. *The Public Papers of Francis G. Newlands.* 2 vols. Boston: Houghton Mifflin Co., 1932.

Davis, Winfield J. *History of Political Conventions in California, 1849–1892.* Publications of the California State Library, no. 1. Sacramento: California State Library, 1893.

Dean, Arthur L. *Alexander & Baldwin, Ltd.* Honolulu: Alexander & Baldwin, 1950.

Decker, Peter R. *Fortunes and Failures: White-Collar Mobility in Nineteenth-Century San Francisco.* Cambridge, Mass.: Harvard University Press, 1978.

Delehanty, Randolph. *Walks and Tours in the Golden Gate City: San Francisco.* New York: Dial Press, 1980.

Dicker, Laverne Mau. *The Chinese in San Francisco: A Pictorial History.* New York: Dover Publications, 1979.

Dillon, Richard H. *The Hatchet Men: The Story of the Tong Wars in San Francisco's Chinatown.* New York: Coward-McCann, 1962.

Diner, Steven J. *A City and Its Universities: Public Policy in Chicago, 1892–1919.* Chapel Hill: University of North Carolina Press, 1980.

Dobie, Edith. *The Political Career of Stephen Mallory White: A Study of Party Activities Under the Convention System.* Stanford University Publications, History, Economics, and Political Science, vol. 2. Stanford: Stanford University Press, 1927.

Domhoff, G. William. *Who Really Rules: New Haven and Community Power Reexamined.* Santa Monica, Ca.: Goodyear Publishing Co., 1978.

Drinnon, Richard. "The *Blast:* An Introduction and Appraisal." *Labor History* 11 (1970):82–88.

Drury, Aubrey. *John A. Hooper and California's Robust Youth.* San Francisco: Arthur W. Hooper, 1952.

Eaves, Lucile. *A History of California Labor Legislation with an Introductory Sketch of the San Francisco Labor Movement.* University of California Publications in Economics, vol. 2. Berkeley: University of California Press, 1910.

Eliel, Paul. *The Waterfront and General Strikes, San Francisco, 1934.* San Francisco: Hooper Printing Co., 1934.

Evans, Cerinda W. *Collis Potter Huntington.* 2 vols. Newport News, Va.: Mariners' Museum, 1954.

Farwell, Willard B. *The Chinese at Home and Abroad: Together with the Report of the Special Committee of the Board of Supervisors of San Francisco on the Conditions of the Chinese Quarter of That City.* San Francisco: A. L. Bancroft & Co., 1885.

Fell, James. *British Merchant Seamen in San Francisco, 1892–1898.* London: E. Arnold, 1899.

Ferrier, William Warren. *Ninety Years of Education in California.* Berkeley: Sather Gate Book Shop, 1937.

Flamm, Jerry. *Good Life in Hard Times: San Francisco's Twenties and Thirties.* San Francisco: Chronicle Books, 1978.

Fleming, Capen A. "Industrial Growth of the Central City." *San Francisco Business,* May 14, 1930, p. 112.

Folsom, Burton W., Jr. *Urban Capitalists: Entrepreneurs and City Growth in Pennsylvania's Lackawanna and Lehigh Regions, 1880–1920*. Baltimore: Johns Hopkins University Press, 1981.

Freeman, John R. *A Report on the Proposed Use of a Portion of the Hetch Hetchy, Eleanor, and Cherry Valleys*. San Francisco: Rincon Publishing Co., 1912.

Freud, J. Richard. *New Charter Catechism, Plain Questions and Honest Answers*. San Francisco: Charter Association, 1896.

Fritzsche, Bruno. "San Francisco, 1846–1848: The Coming of the Land Speculator." *California Historical Quarterly* 51 (Spring 1972):17–34.

Frost, Richard H. *The Mooney Case*. Stanford: Stanford University Press, 1968.

Garnel, Donald. *The Rise of Teamster Power in the West*. Berkeley: University of California Press, 1972.

Gentry, Curt. *Frame-Up: The Incredible Case of Tom Mooney and Warren Billings*. New York: W. W. Norton & Co., Inc., 1967.

George, Henry. "What the Railroad Will Bring Us." *Overland Monthly* 1 (Oct. 1868):297–310.

———. "The Kearney Agitation in California." *Popular Science Monthly* 17 (Aug. 1880):433–453.

———. *Progress and Poverty*. New York: Modern Library, 1929.

Gordon, David M. "Capitalist Development and the History of American Cities." In *Marxism and the Metropolis*. 2nd ed. Edited by William K. Tabb and Larry Sawers, pp. 21–53. New York: Oxford University Press, 1984.

Gordon, David M., Richard Edwards, and Michael Reich. *Segmented Work, Divided Workers: The Historical Transformation of Labor in the United States*. New York: Cambridge University Press, 1982.

Grady, Henry F., and Robert M. Carr. *The Port of San Francisco: A Study in Traffic Competition, 1921–1933*. Berkeley: University of California Press, 1934.

Graebner, Norman A. *Empire on the Pacific: A Study in American Continental Expansion*. New York: Ronald Press Co., 1955.

Grant, Joseph D. *Redwoods and Reminiscences: The World Went Very Well Then*. San Francisco: Save the Redwoods League & the Menninger Foundation, 1973.

Grassman, Curtis E. "Prologue to California Reform: The Democratic Impulse, 1886–1898." *Pacific Historical Review* 42 (Nov. 1973):518–536.

Greb, G. Allen. "Opening a New Frontier: San Francisco, Los Angeles, and the Panama Canal, 1900–1914." *Pacific Historical Review* 47 (Aug. 1978):405–424.

Groff, Frances A. "The Exposition Mayor." *Sunset: The Pacific Monthly* 28 (Jan. 1912):68–70.

Gruening, Ernest. *The State of Alaska*. New York: Random House, 1968.

Gumina, Deanna Paoli. *The Italians of San Francisco, 1850–1930*. New York: Center for Migration Studies, 1978.

Hammack, David C. "Problems in the Historical Study of Power in the Cities and Towns of the United States, 1800–1960." *American Historical Review* 83 (April 1978):323–349.

———. *Power and Society: Greater New York at the Turn of the Century*. New York: Basic Books, 1982.

Hammond, G. P., ed. *The Larkin Papers*. 10 vols. Berkeley: University of California Press, 1951–1964.

Hansen, Gladys C. *San Francisco Almanac*. Rev. ed. San Rafael, Ca.: Presidio Press, 1980.

Hansen, Gladys C., and William F. Heintz, comp. *The Chinese in California: A Brief Bibliographic History*. Portland, Ore.: Richard Abel & Co., 1970.

Harpending, Asbury. *The Great Diamond Hoax and Other Stirring Incidents in the Life of Asbury Harpending.* Edited by James H. Wilkins. San Francisco: James H. Barry Co., 1913.

Hartman, Chester. *Yerba Buena: Land Grab and Community Resistance in San Francisco.* San Francisco: Glide Publications, 1974.

———. *The Transformation of San Francisco.* Totowa, N.J.: Rowman & Allenheld, 1984.

Hays, Samuel P. *The Response to Industrialism, 1885–1914.* Chicago: University of Chicago Press, 1957.

———. "Political Parties and the Community-Society Continuum." In *The American Party Systems: Stages of Political Development.* Edited by William N. Chambers and Walter D. Burnham, pp. 152–181. New York: Oxford University Press, 1967.

Hedgpeth, Nellie McGraw. *My Early Days in San Francisco.* San Francisco: Victorian Alliance, 1974.

Heintz, William F. *San Francisco's Mayors: 1850–1880.* Woodside, Ca.: Gilbert Richards Publications, 1975.

Hershberg, Theodore. "The New Urban History: Toward an Interdisciplinary History of the City." *Journal of Urban History* 5 (Nov. 1978):3–40.

Hichborn, Franklin. *"The System" as Uncovered by the San Francisco Graft Prosecution.* San Francisco: James H. Barry, 1915.

Hines, William M. "Our American Mayors: James Rolph, Jr., of San Francisco." *National Municipal Review* 18 (March 1929):163–167.

Hittell, John S. *A History of the City of San Francisco and Incidentally of the State of California.* San Francisco: A. L. Bancroft & Co., 1878.

———. *The Commerce and Industries of the Pacific Coast.* San Francisco: A. L. Bancroft & Co., 1882.

Hollingsworth, J. Rogers. "Perspectives on Industrializing Societies." In *Emerging Theoretical Models in Social and Political History.* Edited by Allen G. Bogue, pp. 97–121. Beverly Hills: Sage Publications, 1973.

Hopkins, Ernest Jerome. *What Happened in the Mooney Case.* New York: Brewer, Warren, & Putnam, 1932.

Horowitz, Helen Lefkowitz. *Culture and the City: Cultural Philanthropy in Chicago from the 1880s to 1917.* Lexington: University Press of Kentucky, 1976.

Hotchkiss, Edward. "The California Letters of Edward Hotchkiss." *Quarterly of the California Historical Society* 10 (1933):99.

Hoy, William. *The Chinese Six Companies: A Short Historical Resume of the Origin, Function, and Importance in the Life of the California Chinese.* San Francisco: Chinese Consolidated Benevolent Association, 1942.

Hunt, Henry T. *The Case of Thomas J. Mooney and Warren K. Billings: Abstract and Analysis of Record Before Governor Young of California.* New York: C. G. Burgoyne, 1929.

Hunter, Floyd. *Community Power Structure: A Study of Decision Makers.* Garden City, N.Y.: Anchor Books, 1963.

Industrial Association of San Francisco. *San Francisco: A City That Achieved Freedom.* San Francisco, 1931.

Irwin, Will. *The City That Was: A Requiem of Old San Francisco.* New York: B. W. Heubsch, 1906.

James, Marquis, and Bessie Rowland James. *Biography of a Bank: The Story of the Bank of America.* New York: Harper & Brothers, 1954.

Janowitz, Morris. *The Last Half-Century: Societal Change and Politics in America.* Chicago: University of Chicago Press, 1978.

Johnston, Samuel P., ed. *Alaska Commercial Company: 1868–1940.* N.p.: Edwin E. Wachter, Printer, 1941.

Jones, Holway R. *John Muir and the Sierra Club: The Battle for Yosemite*. San Francisco: Sierra Club, 1965.

Josephson, Matthew. *Union House, Union Bar: The History of the Hotel and Restaurant Employees and Bartenders International Union, AFL-CIO.* New York: Random House, 1956.

Kahn, Judd. *Imperial San Francisco: Politics and Planning in an American City, 1897–1906*. Lincoln: University of Nebraska Press, 1979.

Kahn, Lawrence M. "Unions and Internal Labor Markets: The Case of the San Francisco Longshoremen." *Labor History* 21 (Summer 1980):369–391.

Kauer, Ralph. "The Workingmen's Party of California." *Pacific Historical Review* 13 (Sept. 1944):278–291.

Kazin, Michael. "Prelude to Kearneyism: The July Days in San Francisco, 1877." *New Labor Review* 3 (1980):5–47.

Kelly, Martin. "Martin Kelly's Story." *San Francisco Bulletin*, Sept. 1–Nov. 26, 1917.

Kessler, Sidney H. "Mayor Jimmie Rolph—An Institution." *Sunset* 60 (June 1928):16–18, 54.

Kingsdale, Jon M. "The 'Poor Man's Club': Social Functions of the Urban Working-Class Saloon." *American Quarterly* 25 (Oct. 1973): 472–489.

Kinnaird, Lawrence. *History of the Greater San Francisco Bay Region*. 3 vols. New York: Lewis Historical Publishing Co., 1966.

Kleppner, Paul. *The Cross of Culture: A Social Analysis of Midwestern Politics, 1850–1922*. New York: Free Press, 1970.

Knight, Robert Edward Lee. *Industrial Relations in the San Francisco Bay Area, 1900–1918*. Berkeley: University of California Press, 1960.

Kroninger, Robert H. *Sarah and the Senator*. Berkeley: Howell-North, 1964.

Larrowe, Charles P. *Harry Bridges: The Rise and Fall of Radical Labor in the United States*. New York: Lawrence Hill & Co., 1972.

Larsen, Lawrence H. *The Urban West at the End of the Frontier*. Lawrence: Regents Press of Kansas, 1978.

Lavender, David. *Nothing Seemed Impossible: William Chapman Ralston and Early San Francisco*. Western Biography Series. Palo Alto: American West Publishing Co., 1975.

Lazerson, Marvin. "Understanding American Catholic Educational History." *History of Education Quarterly* 17 (Fall 1977):297–317.

Levi, Steven C. "The Battle for the Eight-Hour Day in San Francisco." *California History* 57 (Winter 1978–1979):342–353.

Levy, Eric. "The 1926 San Francisco Carpenters' Strike." *New Labor Review* 6 (1984):12–26.

Levy, Harriet Lane. *920 O'Farrell Street*. Garden City, N.Y.: Doubleday & Co., 1947.

Levy, Jo Ann L. *Behind the Western Skyline: Coldwell Banker: The First Seventy-Five Years*. Los Angeles: Coldwell Banker, 1981.

Lewis, Oscar. *The Big Four: The Story of Huntington, Stanford, Hopkins, and Crocker, and of the Building of the Central Pacific*. New York: Alfred A. Knopf, 1938.

———. *Silver Kings: The Lives and Times of Mackay, Fair, Flood, and O'Brien, Lords of the Nevada Comstock Lode*. New York: Alfred A. Knopf, 1947.

———. *This Was San Francisco: Being First-Hand Accounts of the Evolution of One of America's Cities*. New York: David McKay Co., Inc., 1962.

Lewis, Oscar, and Carroll D. Hall. *Bonanza Inn: America's First Luxury Hotel*. New York: Alfred A. Knopf, 1939.

Light, Ivan. "From Vice District to Tourist Attraction: The Moral Career of American Chinatowns, 1880–1940." *Pacific Historical Review* 43 (Aug. 1974):367–394.

Lilienthal, Lillie Bernheimer. *In Memoriam, Jesse Warren Lilienthal*. San Francisco:

John Henry Nash, 1921.

Lindblom, Charles E. *Politics and Markets: The World's Political-Economic Systems.* New York: Basic Books, 1977.

Lotchin, Roger W. *San Francisco, 1846–1856: From Hamlet to City.* New York: Oxford University Press, 1974.

———. "John Francis Neylan: San Francisco Irish Progressive." In *San Francisco Irish: 1850–1976.* Edited by James P. Walsh, pp. 87–110. San Francisco: Irish Literary & Historical Society, 1978.

———. "The Darwinian City: The Politics of Urbanization in San Francisco Between the World Wars." *Pacific Historical Review* 48 (Aug. 1979):357–381.

———. "The Metropolitan-Military Complex in Comparative Perspective: San Francisco, Los Angeles, and San Diego, 1919–1941." In *The Urban West.* Edited by Gerald D. Nash, pp. 19–30. Manhattan, Kans.: Sunflower University Press, 1979.

———. "The City and the Sword in Metropolitan California, 1919–1941." *Urbanism Past and Present* 7 (Summer/Fall 1982):1–16.

Luckingham, Bradford. "Immigrant Life in Emergent San Francisco." *Journal of the West* 12 (Oct. 1973):600–617.

Lyman, George D. *Ralston's Ring: California Plunders the Comstock Lode.* New York: Charles Scribner's Sons, 1937.

Lyman, Stanford M. "Conflict and the Web of Group Affiliation in San Francisco's Chinatown, 1850–1910." *Pacific Historical Review* 43 (Nov. 1974):473–499.

Lynch, Robert Newton. "San Francisco Looks at Its World." *San Francisco Business,* May 14, 1930, p. 18.

McAfee, Ward. *California's Railroad Era: 1850–1911.* San Marino, Ca.: Golden West Books, 1973.

Macarthur, Walter. "The San Francisco Labor Council." *Labor Clarion,* Nov. 11, 1904, pp. 11–15.

McCormick, Richard L. "The Discovery That Business Corrupts Politics: A Reappraisal of the Origins of Progressivism." *American Historical Review* 86 (April 1981):247–274.

McElroy, Robert, et al. *"The Retrospect": A Glance at Thirty Years of the History of the Howard Street Methodist-Episcopal Church of San Francisco.* San Francisco: A. Buswell & Co., Printers, 1883.

McGloin, John Bernard. *San Francisco: The Story of a City.* San Rafael, Ca.: Presidio Press, 1978.

McKee, Irving. "The Shooting of Charles de Young." *Pacific Historical Review* 16 (Aug. 1947):271–284.

Martin, Mildred Crowl. *Chinatown's Angry Angel: The Story of Donaldina Cameron.* Palo Alto: Pacific Books, 1977.

Massarik, Fred. *A Report on the Jewish Population of San Francisco, Marin County, and the Peninsula: 1959.* San Francisco: Jewish Welfare Federation, 1959.

Matthews, Lillian R. *Women in Trade Unions in San Francisco.* University of California Publications in Economics, vol. 3. Berkeley: University of California Press, 1913.

Mawn, Geoffrey P. "Framework for Destiny: San Francisco, 1847." *California Historical Quarterly* 51 (Summer 1972):165–178.

Maxwell, William H. "City School Systems." *Journal of Proceedings and Addresses* (National Education Association) (1890):447–450.

May, Henry F. *The End of American Innocence: A Study of the First Years of Our Own Time, 1912–1917.* Chicago: Quadrangle Books, 1964.

Meister, Dick. "Labor Power." *San Francisco Bay Guardian,* Dec. 23, 1970, pp. 2, 3, 25.

Melendy, H. Brett. "California's Washington Bartletts." *Pacific Historical Review* 31 (May 1962):139–142.

————. "California's Cross-Filing Nightmare: The 1918 Gubernatorial Election." *Pacific Historical Review* 33 (1964):317–330.

Melendy, H. Brett, and Benjamin F. Gilbert. *The Governors of California: Peter H. Burnett to Edmund G. Brown.* Georgetown, Ca.: Talisman Press, 1965.

Merton, Robert K. *Social Theory and Social Structure.* Rev. ed. New York: Free Press, 1968.

Meyer, Martin A. *Western Jewry.* San Francisco: Emanu-El, 1916.

Millard, Bailey. *History of the San Francisco Bay Region.* 2 vols. Chicago: American Historical Society, 1924.

Miller, Stuart Creighton. *The Unwelcome Immigrant: The American Image of the Chinese, 1785–1882.* Berkeley: University of California Press, 1969.

Mollenkopf, John H. *The Contested City.* Princeton: Princeton University Press, 1983.

Mooney-Billings Report Suppressed by the Wickersham Commission. New York: Gotham House, 1932.

Moorhead, Dudley T. "Sectionalism and the California Constitution of 1879." *Pacific Historical Review* 12 (Sept. 1943):287–294.

Narell, Irena. *Our City: The Jews of San Francisco.* San Diego: Howell-North Publishers, 1981.

Nash, Gerald D. "The Influence of Labor on State Policy, 1860–1920." *California Historical Society Quarterly* 42 (Sept. 1963):241–257.

Nee, Victor G., and Brett de Bary Nee. *Longtime Californ': A Documentary Study of an American Chinatown.* Boston: Houghton Mifflin Co., 1974.

Nesfield, K. M. "From a Gentile Standpoint." *Overland Monthly* 25 (April 1895): 410–420.

Neville, Amelia Ransome. *The Fantastic City: Memoirs of the Social and Romantic Life of Old San Francisco.* Boston: Houghton Mifflin Co., 1932.

Norris, Frank. *McTeague: A Story of San Francisco.* Edited by Donald Pizer. New York: W. W. Norton & Co., 1977.

Nunis, Doyce B., Jr. "The Demagogue and the Demographer: Correspondence of Denis Kearney and Lord Bryce." *Pacific Historical Review* 36 (Aug. 1967):269–288.

Older, Cora. *San Francisco: Magic City.* New York: Longmans, Green, & Co., 1961.

Older, Fremont. *My Own Story.* Oakland: Post-Enquirer Publishing Co., 1925.

Older, Fremont, and Cora Older. *George Hearst: California Pioneer.* Los Angeles: Westernlore, 1966.

Olmsted, Roger, and T. H. Watkins. *Here Today: San Francisco's Architectural Heritage.* San Francisco: Chronicle Books, 1968.

O'Neill, F. Gordon. *Ernest Reuben Lilienthal and His Family.* Stanford: Stanford University Press, 1949.

O'Shaughnessy, Michael M. *The Hetch Hetchy Water Supply and Power Project of San Francisco.* San Francisco: n.p., 1931.

————. "A History of the Spring Valley Acquisition." *San Francisco Municipal Record* 4 (March 1930):62–64.

Page, Thomas Walker. "The San Francisco Labor Movement in 1901." *Political Science Quarterly* 17 (1902):664–688.

Parker, Carleton H. *The Casual Laborer and Other Essays.* New York: Harcourt, Brace & Howe, 1920.

Peixotto, Jessica. "Women of California as Trade Unionists." *Publications of the Association of Collegiate Alumnae* 3 (Dec. 1908):40–49.

Perles, Anthony. *The People's Railway: The History of the Municipal Railway of San Francisco.* Glendale, Ca.: Interurban Press, 1981.

Perlman, Mark. *The Machinists: A New Study in American Trade Unionism.* Cambridge, Mass.: Harvard University Press, 1961.

Peters, Harry S. "The Life Story of Tom Finn" (title varies). *San Francisco Chronicle,*

Jan. 9, 1938, p. 16; Jan. 10, 1938, p. 9; Jan. 11, 1938, p. 14; Jan. 12, 1938, p. 14; Jan. 13, 1938, p. 28; Jan. 14, 1938, p. 14.

Petersen, Erik Falk. "The End of an Era: California's Gubernatorial Election of 1894." *Pacific Historical Review* 38 (May 1969):141–156.

————. "The Struggle for the Australian Ballot in California." *California Historical Quarterly* 51 (Fall 1972):227–243.

Phelps, Alonzo. *Contemporary Biography of California's Representative Men.* 2 vols. San Francisco: A. L. Bancroft & Co., 1881–1882.

Pierce, Richard A., ed. *Rezanov Reconnoiters California, 1806.* San Francisco: Book Club of San Francisco, 1972.

Piore, Michael. "On-the-Job Training in the Dual Labor Market." In *Public-Private Manpower Policies.* Edited by Arnold Weber et al., pp. 101–132. Madison, Wisc.: Industrial Relations Research Association, 1969.

————. "Notes for a Theory of Labor Market Stratification." In *Labor Market Segmentation.* Edited by Richard C. Edwards, Michael Reich, and David M. Gordon, pp. 125–150. Lexington, Mass.: D. C. Heath & Co., 1975.

Plehn, Carl C. "Labor in California." *Yale Review* 4 (1895–1896):409–425.

Plunkitt, George W. *Plunkitt of Tammany Hall.* Edited by William L. Riordan. New York: Alfred A. Knopf, 1948.

Posner, Russell M. "The Lord and the Drayman: James Bryce vs. Denis Kearney." *California Historical Quarterly* 50 (Sept. 1971):277–284.

Pred, Allan. *Urban Growth and City-Systems in the United States, 1840–1860.* Cambridge, Mass.: Harvard University Press, 1980.

Prieto, Guillermo. *San Francisco in the Seventies: The City as Viewed by a Mexican Political Exile.* Translated and edited by Edwin S. Marby. San Francisco: John Henry Nash, 1938.

Putnam, Jackson. "The Persistence of Progressivism in the 1920s: The Case of California." *Pacific Historical Review* 35 (1966):395–411.

Rafael, Ruth Kelson. *Continuum—A Selective History of San Francisco Eastern European Jewish Life, 1880–1940.* Rev. ed. Berkeley: Judah L. Magnes Museum, 1977.

Reps, John W. *The Making of Urban America: A History of City Planning in the United States.* Princeton: Princeton University Press, 1965.

————. *Cities of the American West: A History of Frontier Urban Planning.* Princeton: Princeton University Press, 1979.

Richardson, Elmo R. "The Struggle for the Valley: California's Hetch Hetchy Controversy, 1905–1913." *California Historical Society Quarterly* 38 (Sept. 1959):249–258.

Righter, Robert W. "Washington Bartlett: Mayor of San Francisco, 1883–1887." *Journal of the West* 3 (Jan. 1964):102–137.

Riordan, John. "Garret McEnerney and the Pursuit of Success." In *The San Francisco Irish: 1850–1976.* Edited by James P. Walsh, pp. 73–84. San Francisco: Irish Literary & Historical Society, 1978.

Rischin, Moses. "Sunny Jim Rolph: The First 'Mayor of All the People.' " *California Historical Quarterly* 53 (Summer 1974):165–172.

Robinson, Alfred. *Life in California.* Santa Barbara: Peregrine Publishers, 1970.

Robinson, Harrison S. "The San Francisco Metropolitan Area." *San Francisco Business,* May 14, 1930, p. 110.

Robinson, Robert M. "San Francisco Teamsters at the Turn of the Century." *California Historical Society Quarterly* 35 (1956):56–69, 144–153.

Rogin, Michael P., and John L. Shover. *Political Change in California: Critical Elections and Social Movements, 1890–1966.* Westport, Conn.: Greenwood Press, 1970.

Rollins, Frank. *School Administration in Municipal Government.* New York: Columbia University Press, 1902.

Roney, Frank. *Frank Roney: Irish Rebel and California Labor Leader: An Autobiography.* Edited by Ira B. Cross. Berkeley: University of California Press, 1931.

Rosenberg, Ed R. "The San Francisco Strikes of 1901." *American Federationist* 9 (Jan. 1902):15–18.

Ruef, Abraham. "The Road I Traveled." *San Francisco Bulletin,* April 6–Sept. 5, 1912.

Ryan, Frederick L. *Industrial Relations in the San Francisco Building Trades.* Norman: University of Oklahoma Press, 1935.

Ryan, Paul William [Mike Quin]. *The Big Strike.* Olema, Ca.: Olema Publishing Co., 1949.

Ryder, David Warren. *A Century of Hardware and Steel.* San Francisco: Historical Publications, 1949.

———. *Great Citizen: A Biography of William H. Crocker.* San Francisco: Historical Publications, 1962.

San Francisco: Its Builders, Past and Present. 2 vols. Chicago: S. J. Clarke Publishing Co., 1913.

San Francisco Chamber of Commerce. *Law and Order in San Francisco: A Beginning.* San Francisco: H. S. Crocker Co., 1916.

———. *The San Francisco–Oakland Metropolitan Area: An Industrial Study.* San Francisco, 1931.

San Francisco Chamber of Commerce Research Department. *San Francisco Economic Survey, 1938.* San Francisco, 1938.

San Francisco Citizens' Alliance. *A Few of the Things Done by the Citizens' Alliance of San Francisco.* San Francisco, n.d.

San Francisco Labor Council. *The New Charter: Why It Should Be Defeated.* San Francisco, 1896.

San Francisco Merchants' Association. *Seventeenth Annual Review: A Year of Civic Work.* San Francisco, 1911.

Saxton, Alexander. "San Francisco Labor and the Populist and Progressive Insurgencies." *Pacific Historical Review* 34 (Nov. 1965):421–438.

———. *The Indispensable Enemy: Labor and the Anti-Chinese Movement in California.* Berkeley: University of California Press, 1971.

Scherer, James A. B. *"The Lion of the Vigilantes": William T. Coleman and the Life of Old San Francisco.* Indianapolis: Bobbs-Merrill Co., 1939.

Schiesl, Martin J. *The Politics of Efficiency: Municipal Administration and Reform in America, 1800–1920.* Berkeley: University of California Press, 1977.

Schneider, Norman, et al. *San Francisco Arts Policy: A Background Paper.* San Francisco: Art Commission, 1980.

Schofer, Jerry P. *Urban and Rural Finnish Communities in California: 1860–1960.* San Francisco: R & E Research Associates, 1975.

Scott, Mel G. *The San Francisco Bay Area: A Metropolis in Perspective.* Berkeley: University of California Press, 1959.

Segal, Morley. "James Rolph, Jr., and the Early Days of the San Francisco Municipal Railway." *California Historical Society Quarterly* 43 (March 1964):3–18.

Selvin, David F. *Sky Full of Storm: A Brief History of California Labor.* Rev. ed. San Francisco: California Historical Society, 1975.

———. *A Place in the Sun: A History of California Labor.* San Francisco: Boyd & Fraser Publishing Co., 1981.

Sharpless, John B., and Sam Bass Warner, Jr. "Urban History." *American Behavioral Scientist* 21 (Nov./Dec. 1977):221–244.

Shefter, Martin. "The Emergence of the Political Machine: An Alternative View." In *Theoretical Perspectives on Urban Politics.* Edited by Willis Hawley et al., pp. 14–44. Englewood Cliffs, N.J.: Prentice-Hall, 1976.

Shradar, Victor L. "Ethnicity, Religion, and Class: Progressive School Reform in San Francisco." *History of Education Quarterly* 20 (Winter 1980):385–401.

Shumate, Albert. *A Visit to Rincon Hill and South Park.* San Francisco: Tamalpais Press, 1963.

Shumsky, Neil Larry. "San Francisco's Workingmen Respond to the Modern City." *California Historical Quarterly* 55 (Spring 1976):46–57.

———. "Vice Responds to Reform, San Francisco, 1910–1914." *Journal of Urban History* 7 (Nov. 1980):31–47.

Shumsky, Neil Larry, and Larry M. Springer. "San Francisco's Zone of Prostitution, 1880–1934." *Journal of Historical Geography* 7 (1981):71–89.

Sloan, Douglas. "Cultural Uplift and Social Reform in Nineteenth-Century Urban America." *History of Education Quarterly* 19 (Fall 1979):361–372.

Smallwood, Charles A. *The White Front Cars of San Francisco.* Rev. ed. Glendale, Ca.: Interurbans, 1978.

Soulé, Frank, James H. Gihon, and James Nisbet. *The Annals of San Francisco.* Palo Alto: Lewis Osborne, 1966.

Spoehr, Luther W. "Sambo and the Heathen Chinee: Californians' Racial Stereotypes in the Late 1870s." *Pacific Historical Review* 42 (May 1973):185–204.

Spring Valley Water Company. *The Future Water Supply of San Francisco.* San Francisco: Rincon Publishing Co., 1912.

Starr, Lando. *Blue Book of San Franciscans in Public Life.* San Francisco: McLaughlin Publishing Co., 1941.

Steadman, J. C., and Leonard, R. A. *The Workingmen's Party of California: An Epitome of Its Rise and Progress.* San Francisco: n.p., 1878.

Steele, Robert V. P. [Lately Thomas]. *Between Two Empires: The Life Story of California's First Senator.* Boston: Houghton Mifflin Co., 1969.

Stewart, Robert E., Jr., and Mary Frances Stewart. *Adolph Sutro: A Biography.* Berkeley: Howell-North, 1962.

Swisher, Carl Brent. *Motivation and Political Technique in the California Constitutional Convention, 1878–1879.* Claremont, Ca.: Pomona College, 1930.

Tabb, William K., and Larry Sawers, eds. *Marxism and the Metropolis: New Perspectives in Urban Political Economy.* 2nd ed. New York: Oxford University Press, 1984.

Taft, Philip. *Labor Politics American Style: The California State Federation of Labor.* Cambridge, Mass.: Harvard University Press, 1968.

Taylor, Bayard. *El Dorado; or Adventures in the Path of Empire.* Vol. 2. New York: George P. Putnam, 1850.

Taylor, David Wooster. *The Life of James Rolph, Jr.* San Francisco: Recorder Printing & Publishing Co., 1934.

Taylor, Paul S. *The Sailors' Union of the Pacific.* New York: Ronald Press Co., 1923.

Taylor, Ray W. *Hetch Hetchy: The Story of San Francisco's Struggle to Provide a Water Supply for Her Future Needs.* San Francisco: Ricardo J. Orozco, Publisher, 1927.

Thompson, Edward Palmer. *The Poverty of Theory and Other Essays.* New York: Monthly Review Press, 1978.

Todd, Frank Morton. "San Francisco City and County." In *California Blue Book or State Roster, 1911.* Compiled by Frank C. Jordan, p. 770–784. Sacramento: Superintendent of State Printing, 1913.

———. *The Story of the Exposition: Being the Official History of the International Celebration Held at San Francisco in 1915 to Commemorate the Discovery of the Pacific Ocean and the Construction of the Panama Canal.* 5 vols. New York: G. P. Putnam's Sons, Knickerbocker Press, 1921.

Trauner, Joan B. "The Chinese as Medical Scapegoats in San Francisco, 1870–1905." *California History* 57 (Spring 1978):70–87.

Treutlein, Theodore E. *San Francisco Bay: Discovery and Colonization, 1769–1776.* San Francisco: California Historical Society, 1968.

Tutorow, Norman E. *Leland Stanford: Man of Many Careers.* Menlo Park, Ca.: Pacific Coast Publishers, 1971.

Tveitmoe, Olaf A. "Building Trades Council." *Labor Clarion,* Nov. 11, 1904, pp. 20–21.

Tyack, David B. *The One Best System: A History of American Urban Education.* Cambridge, Mass.: Harvard University Press, 1974.

Tygiel, Jules. " 'Where Unionism Holds Undisputed Sway': A Reappraisal of San Francisco's Union Labor Party." *California History* 62 (Fall 1983):196–215.

Vance, James E., Jr. *Geography and Urban Evolution in the San Francisco Bay Area.* Berkeley: Institute of Governmental Studies, 1964.

Vancouver, George. *A Voyage of Discovery to the North Pacific Ocean and Round the World.* Vol. 3. London: J. Stockdale, 1801.

Van der Zee, John, and Boyd Jacobson. *The Imagined City: San Francisco in the Minds of Its Writers.* San Francisco: California Living Books, 1980.

Waldhorn, Judith Lynch, and Sally B. Woodbridge. *Victoria's Legacy.* San Francisco: 101 Publications, 1978.

Walsh, James P. "Abe Ruef Was No Boss: Machine Politics, Reform, and San Francisco." *California Historical Quarterly* 51 (Spring 1972):3–16.

———. *Ethnic Militancy: An Irish Catholic Prototype.* San Francisco: R & E Research Associates, 1972.

———. "Machine Politics, Reform, and San Francisco." In *The San Francisco Irish: 1850–1976.* Edited by James P. Walsh, pp. 59–72. San Francisco: Irish Literary & Historical Society, 1978.

———. "Peter C. Yorke: San Francisco's Irishman Reconsidered." In *The San Francisco Irish: 1850–1976.* Edited by James P. Walsh, pp. 43–57. San Francisco: Irish Literary & Historical Society, 1978.

———, ed. *The San Francisco Irish: 1850–1976.* San Francisco: Irish Literary & Historical Society, 1978.

Walters, Donald E. "The Feud Between California Populist T. V. Cator and Democrats James Maguire and James Barry." *Pacific Historical Review* 27 (Aug. 1958): 281–298.

Ward, David. *Cities and Immigrants.* New York: Oxford University Press, 1971.

Watkins, T. H., and Roger R. Olmsted. *Mirror of the Dream: An Illustrated History of San Francisco.* San Francisco: Scrimshaw Press, 1976.

Watson, Douglas. "An Hour's Walk Through Yerba Buena." *California Historical Society Quarterly* 17 (Dec. 1938):291–302.

Weintraub, Hyman. *Andrew Furuseth: Emancipator of the Seamen.* Berkeley: University of California Press, 1959.

Wells, David A. *Recent Economic Changes and Their Effect on Production and Distribution of Wealth and the Well-Being of Society.* New York: D. Appleton, 1889.

Werking, Richard Hume. "Bureaucrats, Businessmen, and Foreign Trade: The Origins of the United States Chamber of Commerce." *Business History Review* 52 (Autumn 1978):322–341.

Whitt, J. Allen. *Urban Elites and Mass Transportation: The Dialectics of Power.* Princeton: Princeton University Press, 1982.

Wiebe, Robert H. *The Search for Order, 1877–1920.* New York: Hill & Wang, 1967.

———. *Businessmen and Reform: A Study of the Progressive Movement.* Chicago: Quadrangle Books, 1968.

Wiggin, Kate Douglas. *My Garden of Memory: An Autobiography.* Boston: Houghton Mifflin Co., 1923.

Wilkins, James H., ed. *The Great Diamond Hoax and Other Stirring Incidents in the Life of Asbury Harpending*. San Francisco: James H. Barry Co., 1913.

Williams, David A. *David C. Broderick: A Political Portrait*. San Marino, Ca.: Huntington Library, 1969.

Williams, R. Hal. *The Democratic Party and California Politics: 1880–1896*. Stanford: Stanford University Press, 1973.

Williams, Samuel. "The City of the Golden Gate." *Scribner's Monthly* 10 (July 1875): 266–285.

Williams, William Appleman. *The Contours of American History*. Chicago: Quadrangle Books, 1966.

Wilson, Neil C. *400 California Street: A Century Plus Five*. 2nd ed. San Francisco: Bank of California, 1969.

Wilson, Neill Compton, ed. *Deep Roots: The History of Blake, Moffitt, and Towne, Pioneers in Paper Since 1855*. San Francisco: Privately printed, 1955.

Wirt, Frederick M. "The Politics of Hyperpluralism." In *Culture and Civility in San Francisco*. Edited by Howard S. Becker. New Brunswick, N.J.: Transaction Books, 1971.

———. *Power in the City: Decision Making in San Francisco*. Berkeley: University of California Press, 1974.

Wolfe, W. C., ed. *Men of California*. San Francisco: Western Press Reporter, 1925.

Wollenberg, Charles M. *All Deliberate Speed: Segregation and Exclusion in California Schools, 1855–1975*. Berkeley: University of California Press, 1976.

"Workingmen's Party of California." *California Historical Quarterly* 55 (Spring 1976):58–73.

Writers' Program of the Works Projects Administration in Northern California. *San Francisco: The Bay and Its Cities*. New York: Hastings House, 1940.

Wurm, Ted. *Hetch Hetchy and Its Dam Railroad*. Berkeley: Howell-North, 1973.

Young, John P. *San Francisco: A History of the Pacific Coast Metropolis*. 2 vols. San Francisco: S. J. Clarke Publishing Co., 1912.

———. *Journalism in California*. San Francisco: Chronicle Publishing Co., 1915.

Zarchin, Michael M. *Glimpses of Jewish Life in San Francisco*. Berkeley: Willis E. Berg, 1952.

UNPUBLISHED WORKS

Almada, Marylou. "The Appointment of Angelo J. Rossi as Mayor (San Francisco, 1930)." Seminar paper, San Francisco State University, 1979.

Barnhart, Jacqueline Baker. "Working Women: Prostitution in San Francisco from the Gold Rush to 1900." Ph.D. dissertation, University of California, Santa Cruz, 1976.

Boyer, James L. "Anti-Chinese Agitation in California, 1851–1904." Master's thesis, San Francisco State College, 1969.

Broussard, Albert S. "The New Racial Frontier: San Francisco's Black Community, 1900–1940." Ph.D. dissertation, Duke University, 1977.

Cinel, Dino. "Conservative Adventurers: Italian Migrants in Italy and San Francisco." Ph.D. dissertation, Stanford University, 1979.

Cole, Marigold. "The 1927 San Francisco Election: Test Case for the Nature of Power in Cities." Seminar paper, San Francisco State University, 1979.

Devine, Preston. "The Adoption of the 1932 Charter of San Francisco." Master's thesis, University of California, Berkeley, 1933.

Dolson, Lee S. "The Administration of the San Francisco Public Schools, 1847–1947." Ph.D. dissertation, University of California, Berkeley, 1964.

Doss, Melody C. "Effects of the Depression of 1893 on San Francisco's Chinatown." Graduate essay, San Francisco State University, 1975.

Draper, Joan Elaine. "The San Francisco Civic Center: Architecture, Planning, and Politics." Ph.D. dissertation, University of California, Berkeley, 1979.

Elgie, Robert Andrew. "The Development of San Francisco Manufacturing, 1848–1880: An Analysis of Regional Locational Factors and Urban Spatial Structure." Master's thesis, University of California, Berkeley, 1966.

Erie, Steven P. "The Development of Class and Ethnic Politics in San Francisco, 1870–1910: A Critique of the Pluralist Interpretation." Ph.D. dissertation, University of California, Los Angeles, 1975.

Fracchia, Charles A. "The Founding of the Hibernia Savings and Loan Society." Unpublished typescript in the authors' possession.

Francis, Jessie Davies. "An Economic and Social History of Mexican California (1822–1846)." Ph.D. dissertation, University of California, Berkeley, 1936.

Francis, Robert Coleman. "A History of Labor on the San Francisco Waterfront." Ph.D. dissertation, University of California, Berkeley, 1934.

Gill, Peter B., and Ottilie Dombroff. "History of the Sailors' Union of the Pacific." Typed manuscript, ca. 1942. Carton 3, Paul Scharrenberg Manuscript Collection. Bancroft Library, University of California, Berkeley.

Goldbeck, Herman G. "The Political Career of James Rolph, Jr.: A Preliminary Study." Master's thesis, University of California, Berkeley, 1936.

Hardy, Bruce Allen. "Civil Service in San Francisco: The Rationalization of Municipal Employment, 1881–1910." Master's thesis, San Francisco State College, 1967.

Havenner, Franck Robert. "Reminiscences." Transcript of an interview conducted in 1953 for the Bancroft Library Oral History Project. Bancroft Library, University of California, Berkeley.

Hawley, Miriam Mead. "Schools for Social Order: Public Education as an Aspect of San Francisco's Urbanization and Industrial Processes." Master's thesis, California State University, San Francisco, 1971.

Hennings, Robert Edward. "James D. Phelan and the Wilson Progressives of California." Ph.D. dissertation, University of California, Berkeley, 1961.

Herndon, James Boswell. "The Japanese School Incident: An Anecdote for Racial Hostility." Master's thesis, San Francisco State College, 1967.

Hicke, Carole. "The 1911 Campaign of James Rolph Jr., Mayor of All the People." Master's thesis, San Francisco State University, 1978.

Jensen, George Charles. "The City Front Federation of San Francisco: A Study in Labor Organization." Master's thesis, University of California, Berkeley, 1912.

Johnpoll, Bernard K. "Burnette G. Haskell: Firebrand or Fraud?" Paper delivered at the Fifth Annual Southwest Labor Studies Conference, California State University, Dominguez Hills, April 21, 1979.

Kazin, Michael. "Personnel Management and Labor in the Early 1920s: The Case of San Francisco." Seminar paper, Stanford University, 1977.

———. "The Ideology of Union Power: The San Francisco Building Trades Council, 1896–1916." Paper delivered at the Sixth Annual Southwest Labor Studies Conference, San Francisco State University, 1980.

———. "Barons of Labor: The San Francisco Building Trades, 1896–1922." Ph.D. dissertation, Stanford University, 1983.

Lasky, Moses. "History of the San Francisco Museum of Art and Analysis of Its Relations to the City and County of San Francisco." Typescript, San Francisco History Collection, San Francisco Public Library, 1961, 1963.

Lawrence, John Alan. "Behind the Palaces: The Working Class and the Labor Movement in San Francisco, 1877–1901." Ph.D. dissertation, University of California, Berkeley, 1979.

Lévy, Charles A. "Working-Class Life in San Francisco: An Examination of Social and Economic Dislocation Caused by the Depression of 1877–1879." Seminar paper, San Francisco State University, 1977.

Low, Victor. "The Chinese in the San Francisco Public School System: An Historical Study of One Minority Group's Response to Education." Ph.D. dissertation, University of San Francisco, 1981.

Luckingham, Bradford. "Associational Life on the Urban Frontier: San Francisco, 1848–1856." Ph.D. dissertation, University of California, Davis, 1968.

Lum, Lillian. "Attempts to Relocate Chinatown, 1880–1906." Undergraduate essay, San Francisco State University, 1975.

Macarthur, Walter. "San Francisco—A Climax in Civics." Typed manuscript, 1906. Carton 1, Walter Macarthur Manuscript Collection. Bancroft Library, University of California, Berkeley.

McDermott, Bill. "Residential Development and the Growth of Municipal Transportation: 1912–1923." Seminar paper, San Francisco State College, 1973.

McDonald, Terrence Joseph. "Urban Development, Political Power, and Municipal Expenditure in San Francisco, 1860–1910: A Quantitative Investigation of Historical Theory." Ph.D. dissertation, Stanford University, 1979.

Ohlson, Robert Verner. "History of the San Francisco Labor Council, 1892–1939." Master's thesis, University of California, Berkeley, 1941.

Parker, Barbara M. "The Fourth Party System and the Decline in Turnout in San Francisco, 1890–1928." Seminar paper, San Francisco State University, 1975.

Peffer, George Anthony. "Forbidden Families." Master's thesis, San Francisco State University, 1981.

Pickens, William H. " 'A Marvel of Nature; the Harbor of Harbors': Public Policy and the Development of the San Francisco Bay, 1846–1926." Ph.D. dissertation, University of California, Davis, 1976.

Roland, Carol. "The California Kindergarten Movement: A Study in Class and Social Feminism." Ph.D. dissertation, University of California, Riverside, 1980.

Sabraw, Liston F. "Mayor James Rolph, Jr., and the End of the Barbary Coast." Master's thesis, San Francisco State College, 1960.

Scharrenberg, Paul. "The San Francisco Longshore." Typed manuscript, 1920. Paul Scharrenberg Manuscript Collection. Bancroft Library, University of California, Berkeley.

———. "Reminiscences." Transcript of an interview conducted in 1954 for the Bancroft Library Oral History Project. Bancroft Library, University of California, Berkeley.

———. "History of the Sailors' Union of the Pacific." Typed manuscript, ca. 1960. Carton 3, Paul Scharrenberg Manuscript Collection. Bancroft Library, University of California, Berkeley.

Schneider, Robert. "The Chinese and Their Education in San Francisco of the Nineteenth Century." Graduate essay, San Francisco State University, 1975.

Scott, Katherine. "The Industrial Association." Seminar paper, San Francisco State University, 1979.

Segal, Morely. "James Rolph, Jr., and the Municipal Railway, a Study in Political Leadership." Master's thesis, San Francisco State College, 1959.

Selvin, David F. "History of the San Francisco Typographical Union." Master's thesis, University of California, Berkeley, 1935.

Shradar, Victor Lee. "Ethnic Politics, Religion, and the Public Schools of San Francisco, 1849–1933." Ph.D. dissertation, Stanford University, 1974.

Shumsky, Neil Larry. "Tar Flat and Nob Hill: A Social History of Industrial San Francisco During the 1870s." Ph.D. dissertation, University of California, Berkeley, 1972.

Silvio, Carl A. "A Social Analysis of the Special Recall Election of San Francisco District Attorney Charles M. Fickert, 18 December 1917." Student paper, Dean's prize competition, San Francisco State University, 1978.

Talan, Harriet. "The Female Labor Force in San Francisco at the Turn of the Century: Some Features of Its Impulse Toward Trade Unionism." Independent study paper, San Francisco State University, 1978.

————. "San Francisco Federation of Teachers, 1919–1949." Master's thesis, San Francisco State University, 1982.

Trusk, Robert J. "Sources of Capital of Early California Manufacturers, 1850–1880." Ph.D. dissertation, University of Illinois, Urbana, 1960.

Tygiel, Jules. "Workingmen in San Francisco, 1880–1901." Ph.D. dissertation, University of California, Los Angeles, 1977.

————. "The Union Labor Party of San Francisco: A Reappraisal." Typescript in authors' possession, 1979.

Yee, Bill. "San Francisco, Al Smith and Presidential Election of 1928." Seminar paper, San Francisco State University, 1979.

Zellerbach, Harold L. "Art, Business, and Public Life in San Francisco." Transcript of an interview conducted in 1971–1973 by the Regional Oral History Office, University of California, Berkeley, 1978.

Index

Designer: Lisa Mirski
Compositor: Graphic Typesetting Service
Text: 10/12 Baskerville
Display: Barnum
Printer: Hamilton Printing
Binder: Hamilton Printing